A Critical Companion to Christopher Nolan

CRITICAL COMPANIONS TO CONTEMPORARY DIRECTORS

Series Editors: Adam Barkman and Antonio Sanna

Critical Companions to Contemporary Directors covers many directors who have not been studied previously in academic publications and whose works nonetheless are highly renowned nowadays. The intent of the series is to offer interesting and illuminating interpretations of the various directors' films that will be accessible to both scholars of the academic community and critically minded fans of the directors' works. Each volume combines discussions of a director's oeuvre from a broad range of disciplines and methodologies, thus offering the reader a variegated and compelling picture of the directors' works. In this sense, the volumes will be of interest (and will be instructive) for students and scholars engaged in subjects as different as film studies, literature, philosophy, popular culture studies, religion and others. We welcome proposals for both monographs and edited collections that offer interdisciplinary analyses, focusing on the complete oeuvre of one contemporary director per volume.

Titles in the Series

A Critical Companion to Robert Zemeckis
    Edited by Adam Barkman and Antonio Sanna
A Critical Companion to Stanley Kubrick
    Edited by Elsa Colombani
A Critical Companion to Terrence Malick
    Edited by Joshua Sikora
A Critical Companion to Steven Spielberg
    Edited by Adam Barkman and Antonio Sanna
A Critical Companion to Sofia Coppola
    Edited by Naaman K. Wood and Christopher Booth
A Critical Companion to Terry Gilliam
    Edited by Sabine Planka, Philip van der Merwe, and Ian Bekker
A Critical Companion to Christopher Nolan
    Edited by Claire Parkinson and Isabelle Labrouillère

A Critical Companion to Christopher Nolan

Edited by

Claire Parkinson and Isabelle Labrouillère

LEXINGTON BOOKS
Lanham • Boulder • New York • London

Published by Lexington Books
An imprint of The Rowman & Littlefield Publishing Group, Inc.
4501 Forbes Boulevard, Suite 200, Lanham, Maryland 20706
www.rowman.com

86-90 Paul Street, London EC2A 4NE

Copyright © 2023 by The Rowman & Littlefield Publishing Group, Inc.

All rights reserved. No part of this book may be reproduced in any form or by any electronic or mechanical means, including information storage and retrieval systems, without written permission from the publisher, except by a reviewer who may quote passages in a review.

British Library Cataloguing in Publication Information Available

Library of Congress Cataloging-in-Publication Data

Names: Parkinson, Claire, editor. | Labrouillère, Isabelle, editor.
Title: A critical companion to Christopher Nolan / edited by Claire Parkinson and Isabelle Labrouillère.
Description: Lanham : Lexington Books, [2023] | Series: Critical companions to contemporary directors | Includes bibliographical references and index.
Identifiers: LCCN 2022043049 (print) | LCCN 2022043050 (ebook) | ISBN 9781793652515 (cloth) | ISBN 9781793652522 (ebook)
Subjects: LCSH: Nolan, Christopher, 1970---Criticism and interpretation. | LCGFT: Film criticism.
Classification: LCC PN1998.3.N65 C75 2023 (print) | LCC PN1998.3.N65 (ebook) | DDC 791.4302/33092--dc23/eng/20220922
LC record available at https://lccn.loc.gov/2022043049
LC ebook record available at https://lccn.loc.gov/202204305

∞™ The paper used in this publication meets the minimum requirements of American National Standard for Information Sciences—Permanence of Paper for Printed Library Materials, ANSI/NISO Z39.48-1992.

*Claire: For Dex and Nobby who taught me so much
and Frankie who was gone too soon.
Isabelle: For my beloved ones.*

Contents

Introduction   1
Claire Parkinson and Isabelle Labrouillère

SECTION 1: NARRATIVE AND TIME   13

Chapter 1: Precursor to the Puzzle: Narrational Strategies in *Following*   15
Warren Buckland

Chapter 2: "We All Need Mirrors to Remind Ourselves Who We Are": Anamorphosis and the Singularity of Mirror Motifs in Christopher Nolan's *Memento* (2000)   31
Isabelle Labrouillère

Chapter 3: *The Prestige*, From Text to Screen: Transformation, Manipulation, Reflexivity   47
Gilles Menegaldo

Chapter 4: The Trauma Chronotope in Nolan's *Dunkirk* and *Inception*: Time, Space, and Trauma   63
Fran Pheasant-Kelly

Chapter 5: Back From the Future: *Tenet* and the Politics of Nachträglichkeit   79
Todd McGowan

SECTION 2: COLLABORATIONS AND RELATIONSHIPS   95

Chapter 6: "There's a Point Where We Just Let the Music Take Over Everything": The Collaboration of Christopher Nolan and Hans Zimmer   97
Bernadette Pace

Chapter 7: A "Virtual Carte Blanche": Christopher Nolan, Warner
  Bros., and Authorial Power in Contemporary Hollywood　　115
  Kimberly A. Owczarski

Chapter 8: Transnational Filmmaker, Fanboy-Auteur: Screening
  Nolan's *Inception* in China　　133
  Lara Herring

Chapter 9: Fractured Men and Cockney Boy: Michael Caine as Star
  Persona in the Films of Christopher Nolan　　149
  Stella Hockenhull

Chapter 10: Christopher Nolan and the Quays: Curation, Fandom,
  and the Filmmaker　　163
  Claire Parkinson

SECTION 3: POLITICS, IDEOLOGY, AND GENRE　　179

Chapter 11: Situating Christopher Nolan's Ideological Use of
  Technology: Between Romanticism and Posthumanism　　181
  Ben Lamb

Chapter 12: Dark Vision, Global Impact: Christopher Nolan, Box
  Office Hit Patterns, and *Interstellar*　　197
  Peter Krämer

Chapter 13: Mementos of the Afternoon: Christopher Nolan's
  Ambiguous Debt to Maya Deren　　213
  Will Brooker

Chapter 14: "Some Men Just Want to Watch the World Burn": The
  Politics of Christopher Nolan's *Dark Knight* Trilogy　　229
  Gregory Frame

Chapter 15: The Experimental Short Films of Christopher Nolan　　245
  Stuart Joy

Chapter 16: Catwoman in All but Name: Gender and Adaptation in
  Christopher Nolan's Selina Kyle　　261
  Miriam Kent

Index　　279

About the Editors　　285

Introduction

Claire Parkinson and Isabelle Labrouillère

Christopher Nolan is considered one of the preeminent filmmakers of the twenty-first century. Born in 1970 to an American mother and British father, Christopher Nolan spent the early years of his life living between Chicago and London. Nolan would return to Chicago as an adult to film *Batman Begins* (2005), using the city as the Gotham backdrop to the movie which revived the ailing Batman franchise for Warner Bros. and cemented Nolan's status as, what one British journalist referred to as, "the most meteorically successful film-maker this country ever produced" (Pulver 2005). Not without his critics, Nolan has built a reputation as a writer and director of blockbuster puzzle movies with complex, multi-layered storytelling that have garnered him plaudits such as "the thinking man's blockbuster master" and "one of the most celebrated directors working in Hollywood" whose "ascent has been near vertical" (Film Forum 2015; Sharf 2021; Shone 2020, 18). The narrative of this ascent tends to focus on Nolan's first two feature films *Following* (1998) and *Memento* (2000) and what has been referred to as "a perfect outsider journey into Hollywood filmmaking" that makes "transforming into one of the world's foremost A-list directors look simple" (Rotten Tomatoes 2022). In this oversimplified version of Nolan's story, the filmmaker directs a self-funded film in Britain (*Following* 1998) before moving to America to make his second feature (*Memento* 2000)—a film that captures the attention of the studios and catapults him straight into his first studio directorial role on *Insomnia* (2002), working with high-profile actors Robin Williams and Al Pacino. Although there is no doubt that Nolan's success measured in box office receipts has been impressive and the move from indie director to big budget studio filmmaker is remarkable, beginning the story of Nolan's career from the point where he makes *Following* misses some important details about his filmmaking background and ignores entirely the part played by his short films. Before his career took off in America, Nolan's start in filmmaking was quite modest, beginning as a university student making films with his friends then, after graduating, working as a commercial videographer during the week and shooting his own film on weekends.

Nolan started making films on Super 8mm when he was a child. In 1989, while studying English Literature at University College London (UCL), Nolan made *Tarentella* with his childhood friend Roko Belic. Shot on Super 8 film using his father's camera, the nightmarish four-minute short about a young man who dreams of spiders eventually aired the following year on Chicago-based WTTW, a Public Broadcasting Service (PBS) member station, in an episode of the long-running independent series *Image Union*, titled "Halloween Fright." Nolan did not study film at university but with Emma Thomas (his future wife) did join the UCL Film Society. With proceeds from screening second-run films, the film society funded short films through a bidding process whereby the members would write a script and a committee decided which would be funded. After graduating in 1993, Nolan found work as a camera operator and director, making corporate videos and earning enough to help fund his next two short films, *Larceny* (1996) and *Doodlebug* (1997). *Larceny*, a film that, at time of writing, remains publicly unavailable, cost a mere $245, was shot over a single weekend on 16mm, and screened only once at the 1996 Cambridge Film Festival. The following year, Nolan directed *Doodlebug* (1997), but what followed was a failed attempt in the mid-1990s to make a feature titled *Larry Mahoney* and a "stack of rejection letters" (Nolan quoted in Pulver 2005). Indeed, Nolan would explain later in his career that he owed nothing to the British film industry which he regarded as "a very clubby kind of place. . . . In England there's a great suspicion of the new. . . . Never had any support whatsoever from the British Film industry, other than Working Title. . . . They let me use their photocopier" (Nolan quoted in Pulver 2005).

Nolan's feature film career began with the self-funded 1998 release *Following*. Based on his experience of making *Larceny* with such a small budget, Nolan calculated that he would be able to make a feature film for $2,500. This relied on borrowing the equipment and paying only for film stock and processing. The crew for the film—a group of friends who had worked together before—would end up changing depending on who was available. Nolan was able to shoot the film over fourteen weekends while he continued to work as a commercial videographer, using his salary to fund the film. *Following* would be his first feature, shot on 16mm and running for only sixty-nine minutes.

With funding from New Wave Pictures, *Following* was transferred to a 35mm print and screened at a series of film festivals where it received good reviews and a small number of awards. Distributed by Zeitgeist Films in the United States, Nolan's debut feature grossed only $43,000, but the film gave the director visibility, and he was able to find support to fund and distribute his breakout indie hit *Memento* (2000). In stark contrast to his experience in the UK, Nolan found Hollywood to be open to new talent and ideas. Initially unable to find distribution due to concerns that *Memento* would be too complicated for audiences, the independent production company Newmarket decided to distribute the film, the company's first such venture. *Memento* was a breakout success attracting critical acclaim and a fanbase who was invested in debating various interpretations of the film. It was *Memento* which proved to be the "calling card" that propelled Nolan from the independent sector into studio filmmaking where he would helm *Insomnia* (2002), marking the start of a long-standing association between the director and Warner Bros.

Early on in Nolan's career, his first feature films and even his short films pointed toward the working practices, collaborations, thematic concerns, and film style that would later become recognized as the characteristics which established the director as an auteur. Nolan's preoccupation with nonlinear storytelling, crosscutting between timelines, the distinctive color palette, preferences for film over digital video, and practical effects over CGI were all in evidence early on. Nolan also developed important working relationships with producer (and Nolan's wife) Emma Thomas, composer David Julyan, cinematographer Wally Pfister, and writer (and brother) Jonathan Nolan. The director would later become well known for his frequent collaborations with Hoyte van Hoytema, composer Hans Zimmer, production designer Nathan Crowley, and actors Michael Caine, Christian Bale, and Tom Hardy.

After *Insomnia* (2002), Nolan directed the first film in the Dark Knight trilogy, *Batman Begins* (2005), followed by *The Prestige* (2006), an adaptation of the 1995 novel by Christopher Priest. Released in between *The Dark Knight* (2008) and *The Dark Knight Rises* (2012), *Inception* (2010) initially began life as a treatment for a horror film but later became a heist movie and was, at that time, the second Nolan feature film to be based on an original story idea from the director. After concluding the Dark Knight trilogy, Nolan co-wrote, with his brother Jonathan, the 2014 science fiction film *Interstellar* (2014). *Interstellar* was nominated for five Academy Awards, winning in the Best Visual Effects category. A departure from commercial feature films, in 2015, Nolan produced, shot, and edited an eight-minute documentary about the Quay Brothers, screened as part of a theatrical tour of the Quays' films which was also curated by Nolan. Changing genres once again, Nolan wrote and directed the 2017 war film *Dunkirk*, the first film for which the director received a Best Director Academy Award nomination. In 2020 and after multiple delays, the spy thriller *Tenet* was released amid speculation that a Nolan film could save cinemas from the financial ruin that had been wrought by the global Covid pandemic. However, after Warner Bros.'s decision to give *Tenet* a hybrid release, making the film available in theaters and on HBO Max,

Nolan and Warner Bros. parted ways, citing Nolan's anger over *Tenet* going straight to a streaming service as the reason for the split after a nineteen-year relationship.

Nolan's body of work has attracted widespread attention and intense debate from critics, fans, and academics alike. This volume contributes to the scholarly debates on Nolan and includes original essays that examine all his publicly available films including, for the first time in an academic collection, his short films. It is structured into three sections that deal broadly with: narrative and time; collaborations and relationships; and, ideology, politics, and genre. The authors of the sixteen chapters include established Nolan scholars as well as academics with expertise in approaches and perspectives germane to the study of Nolan's body of work. To these ends, the chapters employ intersectional, feminist, political, ideological, narrative, economic, aesthetic, genre, and auteur analysis in addition to perspectives from star theory, short film theory, performance studies, fan studies, adaptation studies, musicology, and media industry studies.

In the first section of the book, the authors are broadly concerned with Nolan's manipulation of time and his construction of complex narratives, and across these chapters we find recurring themes of trauma and ambiguity. The chapters are organized according to the chronology of the films discussed—*Following*, *Memento*, *The Prestige*, *Dunkirk*, *Inception*, and *Tenet*—to provide a development arc across Nolan's career. Warren Buckland's chapter opens the section with his comprehensive analysis of the ways in which Nolan's first feature film *Following* combines classical storytelling conventions—and what is regarded as reliable storytelling—with narrational strategies found in puzzle and mind-game films. Buckland highlights the similarities between *Following* and David Lynch's *Lost Highway* (1997) and argues that Nolan's use of this hybrid form of storytelling identifies *Following* as a precursor to the puzzle film form of filmmaking that would later define his next feature *Memento*. Through close narratological analysis of each scene in *Following*, Buckland examines in detail *how* Nolan achieves narrational ambiguity and revises the primacy effect, resulting in a story with no definitive ending.

In her chapter on *Memento*, Isabelle Labrouillère also considers the puzzle aspect of the film by considering Nolan's singular and original use of mirrors. The mirror, Labrouillère argues, is first used in the film less as a token of the world's duality and duplicity—as in the classic film noir—and more as an unexpected vector of cohesion. The mirror's interventions in the film are indeed based initially on a referential indexation of the world on which the film's enigma is based. In fact, Nolan's *Memento* rests upon a paradox: while deploying the motifs of the double on all the movie's thematic, structural, and symbolic levels, the film pretends to promote a linear progression of the investigation based on a logic of transparency first symbolized by the use of the mirror. But as the film progresses, the mirror and its variations intervene in complex visual devices inviting us to finally renounce its apparent legibility in order to better embrace the complexity of Nolan's universe. The mirror, then taking on an anamorphic structure, invites us to readjust our gaze, thus turning into the figure par excellence of what Labrouillere, resorting to the theory of quantum physics, calls Nolan's multiverse.

The narrative structure of *The Prestige*, Nolan's fifth feature and one that marked his return to working with independent producer and distributor Newmarket, is examined by Gilles Menegaldo through the lens of adaptation studies. Through an exploration of the main changes made by the filmmaker to the literary source Menegaldo draws attention to the narrative devices of the film and shows how, while paying tribute to the precursor text, Nolan draws parallels between cinema and magic. *The Prestige* (1995)—the novel—was written by Christopher Priest and adapted by Christopher Nolan and Jonathan Nolan for the screen. The film and novel share themes of obsession, revenge, trauma, and significantly "the double"—a recurring motif in Nolan's work—but the film dispenses with the frame narrative used in the book and changes many plot elements. Menegaldo's chapter examines the Nolan brothers' additions, deletions, and expansions to the narrative, explaining how they were important to its dramatization. The manipulation of time—a characteristic of many Christopher Nolan movies—is examined to explain that, unlike the novel, the film offers few time markers and in doing so is able to blur the timelines.

Fran Pheasant-Kelly continues with the discussion of time in Nolan's films, focusing on two of his later films *Dunkirk* and *Inception*. Arguing that there is a relationship between time, space, and trauma in Nolan's films, Pheasant-Kelly develops Mikhail Bakhtin's concept of the "chronotope"—the fusion of spatial and temporal indicators in literary sources—to examine the connection in Nolan's films. Drawing on the visual strategies of *Dunkirk* and *Inception* which, Pheasant-Kelly proposes, use time and space to implicate trauma, the chapter argues that the temporal and spatial perspectives of the films which are fundamental to Nolan's style also comprise a "trauma chronotope." While time and trauma have been discussed elsewhere within Nolan scholarship, Pheasant-Kelly's use of the concept of the "trauma chronotope" represents a new intervention in these debates.

The first section of this book closes with Todd McGowan's analysis of *Tenet*. This chapter explores how the future can alter the past, reading it through the Freudian concept of *Nachträglichkeit* (or retroactivity), a perspective which provides the viewer with a direction for orienting their political thinking. McGowan points out that in the 2014 film *Interstellar*, Nolan's preoccupation with times shifts as he starts to contemplate how future events can alter the past, and that this can offer a new way of thinking about political activity in ways that are suggested by Hegel and Freud. Hegel, McGowan explains, proposes that while immersed in events it is difficult to recognize their significance. Instead, it is only through the interpretation of past events in the present that their significance becomes apparent. Freud names this process *Nachträglichkeit*—when an occurrence in the past is transformed retroactively into trauma. McGowan shows not only that an earlier memory or event thus becomes activated as trauma in the future but also that the future can change the past. McGowan applies this framework to his analysis of *Tenet* and proposes that by illustrating how *Nachträglichkeit* works, Nolan provides us with a way to reconsider our political thinking as less focused on the future, instead looking to the past.

Nolan's various collaborations and partnerships are explored in the second section of the book. In these chapters we find a focus on Nolan the auteur, a concept which is placed within a variety of intellectual frameworks. Across his career, Nolan has become well known for collaborating with the same institutions and individuals, the longest-running relationship of which has been with the producer Emma Thomas. This section opens with a chapter that provides a bridge from the analysis of narrative in section 1 to the interrogation of Nolan's collaborations that feature throughout section 2. To these ends, Bernadette Pace's chapter explores the director's collaboration with composer Hans Zimmer and draws on audiovisual analysis to explore the patterns of music-narrative interrelation in *Inception*, *Interstellar*, and *Dunkirk*, paying particular attention to the way music builds a sense of narrative continuity and unity in fragmented universes. Pace argues that the music in these films helps audiences navigate their way through the complex narratives. The chapter presents a history of Nolan and Zimmer's collaboration and an account of their working practices, pointing out how their working methods align with and differ from traditional practices in studio filmmaking. In the film analysis, Pace examines how, in *Inception*, Zimmer's score and particularly the infamous "braaam" sound act to guide the viewer through the multilayered narrative and orient the characters in the film through the use of sonic cues. The use of music to build tension and the ways in which Nolan and Zimmer use recurring motifs is explored through analysis of *Interstellar*, where Pace argues that the film's soundscape and the manipulations of tension are used to locate the audience within the film's narrative. The use of the Shepard tone in the score for *Dunkirk* is similarly explored in relation to the building of tension and manipulations of time, a theme which figures strongly throughout this collection.

Most of the films discussed in the second section emerge from Nolan's relationship with Warner Bros. which came to an abrupt end in 2021 following the studio's decision to release *Tenet* on the HBO Max streaming service.

Kimberly A. Owczarski investigates Nolan's unique relationship with Warner Bros., from *Insomnia* to *Tenet*, and shows how this partnership demonstrates the power of the director's authorship in the contemporary filmmaking environment. This chapter gives a comprehensive account of the relationship between the director and the studio, exploring the often-cited autonomy that Nolan is purported to have, arguing that his collaboration with the studio is unreplicated in the American film industry. In this chapter Owczarski unpicks the narrative of Nolan's ascent from indie filmmaker to studio blockbuster director, exploring how he cultivated specific relationships with Warner Bros. executives which proved fruitful when good timing gave Nolan the opportunity to pitch his vision for *Batman Begins*. The chapter traces through Nolan's relationship with Warner Bros. to its unexpected ending following *Tenet's* release and speculates about the short- and long-term future of the director's relationship with Universal.

Lara Herring's chapter shifts the focus to Nolan's status as a transnational filmmaker set within the context of the complex relationship between Hollywood and China. Her chapter demonstrates how Nolan's films, and *Inception* in particular, received despite many obstacles—such as censorship and the quota system—a very positive reaction from Chinese audiences, notably thanks to its popularity among fanboys. Herring argues that Hollywood's focus on the economic potential presented by international markets has led to the application of transnational film techniques in films such as *Inception*. China's multiplex boom in the 2010s saw increased cinema attendance, and with changes to the quota of films that could be released there, China offered a vital new market that the studios were keen to exploit. Nolan's films had the benefit of a market that was less hostile to American films than in previous decades, and Herring examines how Nolan's film have features consistent with transnational film that can, in part, account for their success in China. The chapter also discusses Nolan's appeal to Chinese audiences which, Herring argues, can be understood by recourse to the concept of the "fanboy-auteur."

Stella Hockenhull's chapter also discusses Nolan's auteur status as the context for his collaboration with the actor Michael Caine and the eight films—The Dark Knight trilogy, *The Prestige*, *Inception*, *Interstellar*, *Dunkirk*, and *Tenet*—in which the actor has appeared. Starting with the argument that stars can undermine the auteur because they have their own style of performance and expressive techniques, Hockenhull considers what Caine's distinctive performance traits bring to Nolan's films. The chapter provides an account of Caine's career, and through a combination of auteur theory, star theory, and performance studies, Hockenhull explores the extratextual meanings of Caine's performance starting with Alfred in *Batman Begins*, a role he reprises in *The Dark Knight* and *The Dark Knight Rises*. Arguing that Caine's characters in the Batman trilogy and in *The Prestige*, where he plays John Cutter, the *ingenieur*, possess similar traits, the chapter proposes that these performance traits can also be identified in Caine's later roles in Nolan's films. As a result, Caine's persona has changed over the course of his career but shows certain consistencies during the time he has worked with Nolan where the actor has played characters who are steering figures for the troubled men in Nolan's films. As Hockenhull concludes, Caine has developed new distinguishing characteristics: No longer the star "on the margins of society," Caine's persona has been replaced in Nolan's films by a kindly, shrewd British gentleman.

The concept of the auteur is once again explored by Claire Parkinson in chapter 10 which considers Nolan's auteur status in relation to his collaboration with the Quay Brothers and the short documentary *Quay*. This chapter argues that, like all of Nolan's short films, *Quay* has been overlooked in academic scholarship. It went relatively unnoticed by much of Nolan's fanbase and, unusually, received little interest from the press. Parkinson examines this previously unconsidered film and the context of its making. Drawing on the concepts of the indie auteur and the fanboy auteur, chapter 10 explores Nolan's collaboration with the Quays and particularly his curation of their work, arguing that they can be read as expressions of the director's fan behavior that also borrow meanings from his identity as an "indie auteur." Nolan has stated that the Quay Brothers have been an influence on his own filmmaking since having discovered their work by accident during his teenage years. The chapter concludes with an analysis of the short documentary *Quay* to argue that it has a place within Nolan's oeuvre, sharing many themes and characteristics that have been identified in the director's feature-length films.

The third section of the book explores Nolan's films in relation to politics, ideology, and genre. Ben Lamb's chapter opens the final section of the book with an essay that proposes that Nolan's films exhibit an ideological formula that has become increasingly influenced by neo-romantic affect. Lamb's chapter surveys the representations of technology in Nolan's post-2010 films—*Interstellar*, *Inception*, and *Tenet*—to explore the balance between the endorsement of posthumanism and a newfound romantic sensibility. Lamb proposes a new framework through which to study the ideological development of Nolan's films and argues that as Nolan develops his authorial signature, his relationship with technology changes. The chapter concludes by applying the neo-romantic framework to an analysis of the changing significance of bullets in Nolan's films.

Peter Krämer's essay situates Nolan's hit movies within general trends at the global box office, considering the scarcity of films based on original scripts in recent annual charts. The chapter argues that Nolan's box office success can be understood as part of wider trends that have favored science fiction films and cinematic visions of global destruction. Krämer explains however that while other filmmakers can lay claim to having multiple global hits, Nolan stands out for co-writing the scripts for six major hit movies between 2008 and 2020. Moreover, four of the six were original screenplays, something which Krämer points out is unprecedented in recent decades. With a particular focus on *Interstellar* the chapter argues that the film presents an uncritical celebration of the institutional deployment of science and technology. As this chapter makes apparent, the importance placed on the scientific accuracy of *Interstellar* resulted in the film being taken seriously as a contribution to public debates about global crises. This intervention in public debates, Krämer speculates, combined with the emotional focus on the father-daughter relationship and complex storytelling, may account for the film's box office success.

Will Brooker's chapter returns to Nolan's breakout film *Memento* to offer an original reading of the film which focuses on the influence of noir on Nolan and draws out the similarities and differences between *Memento* and *Meshes of the Afternoon* (1943) by Maya Deren. Brooker identifies matching motifs in the two films—the use of black-and-white film stock, the debt to noir, their shared focus on dreamlike states, multiples, use of objects—a key, a blade, and a telephone—and the question of who is chasing whom. Establishing that we can locate traces of Maya Deren's 1943 film in *Memento*, Brooker offers a new reading of Leonard's (Guy Pearce) identity crisis which the chapter argues wrestles between masculine norms and feminine objectification. There has been widespread speculation among fans and critics about whether or not Leonard's wife, Catherine Shelby (Jorja Fox), actually died. Brooker's reading of the film takes this question further and asks if Leonard's wife even existed at all and, if not, what might that suggest about his identity crisis. Brooker's analysis concludes with a "twist" that is fitting for a discussion of this archetypal puzzle film.

Gregory Frame's chapter explores the politics of Nolan's Batman trilogy in light of the release of the 2019 film *Joker* directed by Todd Phillips. Placing Nolan's Dark Knight films within the context of neoliberalism, Frame argues that *The Dark Knight* and *The Dark Knight Rises* exemplify "capitalist realism," a position which proposes that the current system is, despite its problems, the only option and that alternatives and change will result in disastrous consequences. The chapter reassesses critiques of Nolan's Dark Knight films which initially read them as reflecting the political upheaval of the time, particularly in relation to the "war on terror" and the Occupy movement. Frame however explores the notion that Nolan's films are not necessarily critical of the neoliberal order but in fact reinforce it and the tenets of capitalist realism. Arguing that, with the benefit of hindsight and when contrasted with *Joker*,

Bruce Wayne/Batman should be regarded as the defender of the neoliberal status quo, this chapter concludes that "Nolan's vision of the caped crusader is no longer the hero we deserve, or need."

Stuart Joy addresses the often-overlooked short films of Christopher Nolan. Joy points out that while lack of access to *Tarantella* and *Larceny* may have prevented academic engagement with his short films, the availability but relative lack of scholarly interest in *Doodlebug* leads to a conclusion that there has been a general disregard for these films. This chapter addresses this oversight, providing a detailed analysis of both *Tarantella* and *Doodlebug*, which Joy argues reveal that Nolan's preoccupation with time owes a significant debt to the structural and stylistic properties of the short film form. Joy draws on Tom Gunning's "cinema of attractions" to propose that Nolan's short films should not be overlooked as they are significant to the development of the filmmaker's artistic identity. To these ends, Joy explores how Nolan's engagement with modernist art techniques in feature films can be traced to his experimentation in the short film *Tarantella*. Nolan then continues to develop the formal and thematic foundations in *Doodlebug*, themes that Joy argues would go on to shape Nolan's subsequent films.

Miriam Kent closes the book with a return to *The Dark Knight Rises* and a focus on the character of Catwoman through the lenses of representation, adaptation, and authorship. Kent points out that Nolan's realist aesthetics have attracted critiques of the ideological stances of his films and that his adaptation of existing texts complicates traditional auteurist definitions. For this reason, the chapter focuses on how Nolan's authorial vision and adaptation of an existing property intersect with gender representation in *The Dark Knight Rises*. This chapter provides an account of the relationship between different iterations of Catwoman that have appeared on screen and in comics and adopts an intersectional feminist approach to examine how Nolan's realist aesthetics inscribed hegemonic models of femininity. The chapter argues that *The Dark Knight Rises* presents a postfeminist fantasy and disarticulation of feminism that arises from the film's claims to realism. Using McRobbie's work, Kent shows that Nolan's use of postfeminist masquerade as a means of self-recreation eventually becomes a way for the disempowered to assimilate to the status quo.

A Critical Companion to Christopher Nolan sheds new light on much-discussed films as well as on works that have been little or not at all explored. It offers new analyses and thinking that provide an overview of the current research on the subject. At the time of writing, Christopher Nolan has parted company with Warner Bros. to work with Universal on *Oppenheimer*, an ambitious project co-produced by Syncopy Inc. and Atlas Entertainment and shot, at least in part, on IMAX 65mm. Based on the life of J. Robert Oppenheimer, the theoretical physicist credited as the "father of the atomic bomb," the film will be a first for Nolan who has not made a biographical drama. Whether or not it is a biopic is yet to be seen. As ever, there is secrecy around the details of the film. While a new Nolan project is always shrouded in mystery, after two decades working with Warner Bros. *Oppenheimer* marks a new phase in Nolan's career. This volume covers the previous phases of that career: Nolan's early short films, his indie films, and his time working with Warner Bros. As some authors in this volume have done, we might speculate about what is to come next in this director's career, but we have no doubt Christopher Nolan's films will continue to engage audiences and scholarly interest for some time to come.

REFERENCES

Film Forum. 2015. "Conversation with Chris Nolan/Stephen & Timothy Quay/Michael Atkinson." Recorded August 19, 2015, at 7pm. filmforum.org/film/quay-brothers-on-35mm-film.

Pulver, Andrew. 2005. "He's not a god—he's human." *The Guardian*. June 15, 2005. www.theguardian.com/film/2005/jun/15/features.features11.

Rotten Tomatoes. 2022. "All Christopher Nolan movies ranked by Tomatometer." *Rotten Tomatoes*. Accessed June 1, 2022. editorial.rottentomatoes.com/guide/all-christopher-nolan-movies-ranked-by-tomatometer/.

Sharf, Zack. 2021. "Christopher Nolan's favourite movies: 35 films the director wants you to see." *IndieWire*. January 27, 2021. www.indiewire.com/gallery/christopher-nolan-favorite-movies/.

Shone, Tom. 2020. *The Nolan Variations*. London: Faber and Faber.

SECTION 1
NARRATIVE AND TIME

Chapter 1

Precursor to the Puzzle
Narrational Strategies in Following

Warren Buckland

In *Lost Highway* (David Lynch, 1997), a series of events changes the life of the film's main character Fred Madison (Bill Pullman): he befriends the "Mystery Man" (Robert Blake) and is later charged with murdering his wife, Renee (Patricia Arquette), apparently under the Mystery Man's influence. In jail Fred imagines himself to be someone with a different appearance and name (Pete), who becomes involved with a blonde femme fatale called Alice who sets him up into stealing from (and inadvertently killing) Andy (Michael Massee), her lover. In *Following* (Christopher Nolan, 1998), a series of events changes the life of the main character called in the credits the "Young Man" (Jeremy Theobold): he befriends a burglar called Cobb (Alex Haw), and at the end of the film he is about to be charged with the murder of the character called in the credits the "Blonde" (Lucy Russell), a murder that Cobb apparently committed. The young man follows people, steals from them, including the blonde woman, and changes his appearance to look more like Cobb. He befriends the blonde woman, who persuades him to break into a nightclub owned by her former boyfriend. When the police interview the young man about the blonde woman's death, he presumes that Cobb must have killed her.

The parallels between *Lost Highway* and *Following* are evident: the Mystery Man is like Cobb, a false helper who implicates the main protagonist (Fred Madison, the young man) in murder; the main protagonists change their appearance; and the blonde woman in *Following* performs similar functions to Renee (the murder victim) and Alice (the femme fatale) in *Lost Highway*. But, more importantly, there are parallels in the way both films are narrated: *nonchronologically* (both display a dense symbolic network of forms that transcend linear storytelling) and from the *restricted perspective* of an *unreliable* and *unstable protagonist* (Fred Madison, the young man). From the protagonist's limited perspective (the perspective shared with film spectators), the Mystery Man and Cobb are actual characters. However, both films present clues that cast doubt on the existence of the Mystery Man and Cobb. In *Following*, the police reinterpret the same events from a different perspective (primarily, one in which Cobb plays no role), which undermines the young man's version of events, transforms his comprehension of reality, and changes his narrative role (from hero-victim to potential villain). The same applies to the role of the police in *Lost Highway*: they take the Mystery Man out of the equation, thereby placing Fred at the center of their investigations (whose identity, comprehension of reality, and narrative role similarly change). *Fight Club* (1999), another film in which the protagonist befriends an imaginary character, goes one step further by staging a scenario in which the imaginary friend is eventually exposed as nonexistent.

Lost Highway is the quintessential "puzzle film," which I have previously defined in narratological terms as films that embrace nonlinearity, time loops, and fragmented spatio-temporal reality, films that blur the boundaries between different levels of reality, that are riddled with gaps, deception, labyrinthine structures, ambiguity, coincidences, and that are populated with characters who are schizophrenic, lose their memory, are unreliable narrators, or are dead (Buckland 2009, 6). Thomas Elsaesser developed the parallel concept of the "mind-game film," which he defined more broadly from multiple perspectives: not only narratology, but also psychology, history, politics, and ontology. In the mind-game film, Elsaesser informs us that: (1) the protagonist participates in unusual events, whose structure does not follow a cause–effect logic/linear progression; (2) a deluded protagonist cannot distinguish between fantasy and reality (and this experience is shared with the spectator); (3) the protagonist also has a friend who turns out to be imaginary; (4) the protagonist questions his/her own identity and existence; (5) the narrative undergoes a dramatic plot twist (2009, 17–18).[1] These five elements are prevalent not only in *Lost Highway* but also in *Following* (although to a lesser degree). Other films such as *Fight Club* are also structured along the same lines, with its emphasis on a deluded protagonist unable to distinguish between fantasy and reality, befriending someone who turns out to be imaginary. I combine Elsaesser's narratological account of the mind-game film with my definition of the puzzle film to bring into sharp relief the specificity of the narration in *Following*.

The success of films such as *Lost Highway, Fight Club*, and *Following* is determined by the effectiveness of their narration. Narration reorganizes narrative actions and events and controls spectators' access to those events by filtering them through characters and narrators. In nonchronological storytelling (a key trait of puzzle and mind-game films), the sequence of events as presented in the film is not the sequence in which they happen. Spectators attempt to reconstruct the chronology of events from the narration's nonchronological presentation. However, they do not merely try to line up causes and effects by putting scenes back into chronological order, for they also perceive the nonchronological sequencing of events, which affects their comprehension and alters the meaning or significance of those events.

Characters and narrators are fundamental narratological agents. The character, existing within the storyworld, performs and motivates the story's actions, whereas the narrator (or, more technically, a "heterodiegetic narrator" [Genette 1980, 245]) is an omniscient and omnipresent agent outside the storyworld who ultimately controls what happens within it. Focalizers are characters whose experiences are conveyed to spectators and who provide spectators access to the storyworld. Characters can also be narrators—or, at least, a hybrid character-narrator (what Gérard Genette calls the "homodiegetic narrator"), who controls the storytelling but who is also embedded in the storyworld (and, if characters narrate their own story, they are "autodiegetic narrators" [Genette 1980, 245]). All stories entail the presence of an external heterodiegetic narrator, whose presence is constant but usually concealed or covert. Nonetheless, the cinematic heterodiegetic narrator is indirectly revealed in the very act of arranging and presenting images on screen—for example, in the way shots are framed and edited, in the way the camera moves, and in the use of optical effects (fades, dissolves). The heterodiegetic narrator also employs techniques such as restricted narration, which filters the storyworld through the consciousness of one character.

The focalizer and the autodiegetic character-narrator dominate *Following* (and are embodied in the same character, the young man), although like all stories the heterodiegetic narrator is always silently present in the background and occasionally comes to the fore. The following analysis centres on what the film's focalizer and character-narrator knows and does not know, what he decides to tell, and in what order. However, as with many puzzle and mind-game films, the character-narrator in *Following* is destabilized; in particular, whether the young man is a reliable or unreliable character-narrator is key to understanding how the film generates its twist ending.

Following combines a series of classical storytelling devices (such as a character-centred cause-effect narrative and a voiceover, both of which frame the action and drive the narrative forward, and *anagnorisis*, the protagonists' sudden recognition of their true situation) with narrational strategies common to puzzle and mind-game films (nonchronological ordering of cause and effect, conspicuous gaps, ambiguity, unreliable narrators, an unstable, deluded protagonist possibly suffering from amnesia, an imaginary character, a dramatic plot twist). The resulting combination creates a hybrid form of storytelling that defines *Following* as a precursor to the puzzle film, a form of filmmaking Nolan fully realized in his next film, *Memento* (2000).

ANACHRONY: REORDERING THE SEQUENCE OF EVENTS

In textbox 1 I reconstruct the linear chronology of *Following*'s narrative by dividing it into 30 scenes (labelled 0 to 29) with some split into subsections (labelled a, b, c, etc.). A change in scene is marked by a change in space and/ or time.[2] The following comments chart the film narration's reorganization of scenes, which is visually represented in figure 1.1.

(0) The credit sequence depicts a series of closeup shots of anonymous hands in latex gloves handling a box of personal objects and photographs. Although similar closeups reappear later in the film (such as scene 10), these images in the credit sequence are detached and abstracted from the rest of the film due to the way they are filmed: in an undefined space and detached from a body. Thierry Kuntzel's analysis of *The Most Dangerous Game* (Schoedsack and Pichel, 1932) is relevant for understanding how these shots function: "the credits and opening sequence [are] considered as endowed with

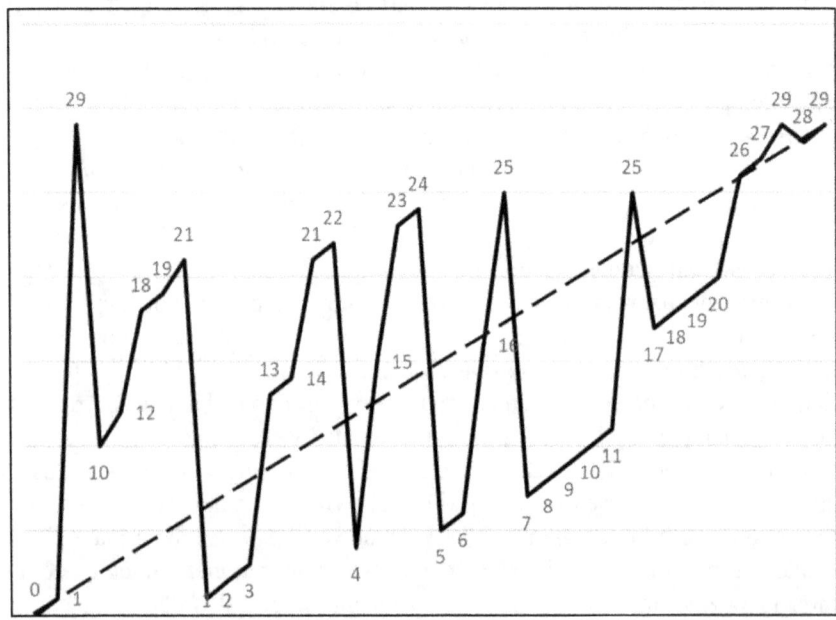

Figure 1.1. Progression of the Narration in Following (Black Line: the narration's scene by scene progression. Dotted Line: the narrative's linear unfolding). Created by Warren Buckland.

TEXTBOX 1.1. CHRONOLOGY OF NARRATIVE EVENTS IN *FOLLOWING*

0. Credit sequence.
1. The young man follows Cobb.
2. Cobb confronts the young man in a café.
3. The young man and Cobb carry out their first burglary but are interrupted by the owner returning.
4. The young man and Cobb carry out a second burglary (the young man's own apartment).
5. The young man and Cobb carry out a third burglary (the blonde woman's apartment).
6. The young man and Cobb go to a hideout.
7. The young man and Cobb go to a restaurant; the young man signs a stolen credit card.
8. The young man types a story (about Cobb).
9. The young man changes his appearance.
10. The young man sorts through the blonde woman's box of possessions.
11. (a) The young man phones Cobb about the blonde woman's stolen possessions. (b) The scene stays with Cobb to reveal that he lives with the blonde woman. Both discuss how they are setting up the young man.
12. The young man watches the blonde woman as she leaves her apartment.
13. The young man meets the blonde woman in a nightclub.
14. The young man and the blonde woman go to his apartment.
15. The young man meets the blonde woman in her apartment; they talk again about the burglary.
16. The young man meets the blonde woman in a café; she tells him about her former boyfriend killing a man in her apartment; they argue, and she storms out of the café.
17. The young man meets the blonde woman in her apartment; he apologises apologizes and makes plans to help her by stealing compromising photographs of her from the nightclub safe.
18. (a) The young man meets Cobb on a rooftop; he says he is seeing the blonde woman and tells Cobb about his plan to break into the nightclub; Cobb beats him up and (b) stuffs a latex glove in his mouth.
19. The young man types a story.
20. Cobb and the blonde woman talk about why they are setting up the young man – –to to frame him as a possible suspect in a burglary where Cobb found an old woman murdered and was interviewed by police.
21. The young man watches the nightclub and the club's owner (the blonde woman's former boyfriend).
22. The young man phones Cobb for advice about breaking into the club.
23. The young man watches the club.
24. The young man prepares to break into the club.
25. The young man steals photographs and money from the club; he injures a security guard with a hammer.
26. The young man returns to his apartment; he looks at photographs of the blonde woman (which are not compromising).
27. The young man goes to the blonde woman and confronts her; she tells him that Cobb is setting him up. The young man threatens her, then threatens to go to the police.
28. Cobb kills the blonde woman with the young man's hammer.
29. (a) The young man goes to the police and tells his story. (b) The police tell him they have no open cases of an old woman murdered in an apartment and that they do not know who Cobb is. The police confront the young man about the murder of the blonde woman.

a certain structural autonomy (the sequence) and as a privileged link in the chain that constitutes the film: a segment where the entire film may be read, *differently*" (1980, 7). In Schoedsack and Pichel's classical Hollywood film as well as in the non-classical *Following*, the opening credits form a sequence of images separate from the remainder of the film that present the film in condensed form, as a constellation of its elements. In *Following*, the credit sequence sets up an enigma (Whose box is this? Who is handling the objects wearing gloves?). A plot is formed and developed in this credit sequence, but as we shall see, it is not completely resolved at the end of the film. The enigma is sustained by David Julyan's soundtrack, consisting of a rapid and agitated electronic pulse, which is heard during the credits and which reappears throughout the film during moments of tension.

After the credit sequence, a new scene begins (scene 1), comprising brief shots of the young man following Cobb, interrupted by other shots of the young man writing. On the soundtrack we hear a voiceover (presumably the young man's) describing his activity of following people. The heterodiegetic narrator intervenes soon afterwards by shifting the action forward to the end of the narrative (29a), where we see the young man talking to the police. This dramatic shift in chronology is justified because it anchors the voiceover in a body: it shows where and when the voice is located, and it also identifies the narratee, the character in the narrative (the policeman) who is listening to the young man. The heterodiegetic narrator then shifts the narration back to scene (10) where the young man sorts through the box of possessions, which rhymes with the credit sequence (although he is not wearing gloves). On the voiceover the young man talks about not following women, which creates a counterpoint to the image track showing him with the blonde woman's possessions and watching her as she leaves her apartment (12). Additional brief shots show the young man with a latex glove stuffed in his mouth (18b), followed by a shot of him writing (19) and following the night club owner (the blonde woman's former boyfriend) (21). The narrator then returns the narration to (1) where the young man continues to follow Cobb. The voiceover accompanying these fragments functions as concentrated exposition that frames and codifies the film's actions and events as a flashback. And by briefly showing the character-narrator in (29) talking to the police in "the present" (the narrating situation) before moving into the past, the voiceover takes on a "classical" storytelling purpose to the extent that it confers on the narration a strong forward momentum, for it is driven to work its way toward the narrating situation. The nonlinear ordering of scenes is not disruptive at this stage because it is motivated by the young man's voiceover, as he selects specific moments to emphasize to the police and decides their ordering. And the moments he selects are thematically linked: after his initial focus on Cobb, all involve his obsession with the blonde woman.

Following's voiceover imitates the way voiceovers are used in many *films noir*. Sarah Kozloff notes that "a large number of *noirs* use voice-over precisely to stress the narrative's subjective source" (1988, 63). In other words, the voiceover foregrounds a character's act of narration, although its main purpose is to explain how the character's current state of affairs came to pass. The stories of these character-narrators, in Kozloff's words,

> are almost always confessions and often these confessions revolve around problems of seeing and perceiving—they have been too trusting or too suspicious—they have misjudged themselves and the lay of the land. These narrators' stories climax in their recognition of their mistakes and their new ability to tell us what really happened. (1988, 63)

All we know in the film's opening minutes is that the young man is making a statement-confession, one in which his activity of following strangers has led to a serious incident that he initially misunderstood. In making the statement, he appears to possess full knowledge of the events and is able to say what really happened—although that belief is undermined in the film's final moments, in which the heterodiegetic narrator introduces (via another character, the policeman) a discrepancy between what the young man (the homodiegetic narrator) knows and what apparently happened.

The remainder of the film is narrated from scene (29), although the voiceover is no longer heard. But the opening scene makes spectators aware that the selection of shots and scenes is narrated from the limited perspective of a character-narrator within the storyworld and that this character-narrator may not know everything (unlike an omniscient heterodiegetic narrator). Furthermore, that he narrates his statement-confession by focusing on his obsession with the blonde woman does not bode well for him in the film's final revelation in the closing scene. Like the credit sequence, this opening also conforms to what Kuntzel calls a constellation of elements condensed into one sequence: it builds upon the credit sequence by setting up the woman as enigma, but also identifies the young man as a writer and as the voyeur handling her box of possessions (he no longer wears the latex gloves, but a brief shot intercut from sequence [18b] shows that he has one stuffed in his mouth). We know he is telling the story, but the shot of him typing (19) may suggest that he is also writing the story that we are watching.

After the condensed credit and opening scenes, the narrative begins with the young man and Cobb joining forces: Cobb realizes he is being followed and confronts the young man in a café (2), and both decide to carry out a burglary but are interrupted by the owner returning (3). Cobb tells the young man about the boxes of personal items one always finds. Rather than continue the chronological retelling of the relationship between the two men, the heterodiegetic narrator shifts the narration forward to scene (13), of the young man, now smartly dressed, meeting the blonde woman in a nightclub and (14) going to his apartment (she tells him she was "burgled yesterday"). She picks up a wooden mannequin that is broken. In the next scene, this storyline continues chronologically but jumps forward to (21), the young man (now beaten up) watching the nightclub and (22) phoning Cobb for advice about breaking into the club (to help out the blonde woman), a job that does not interest Cobb. The narrator then returns to the progression of the young man–Cobb friendship as they (4) carry out a second burglary—of the young man's own apartment, which he chose in order to try and impress Cobb. But Cobb is not impressed and breaks a wooden mannequin. This scene repeats with minor differences the blonde woman's visit to the apartment (14). The spectator knows Cobb visited the young man's apartment before the blonde woman because Cobb breaks the mannequin and the blonde woman picks it up and notes that it is broken, a cause-effect sequence in which the effect is presented before the cause. But, more importantly, the heterodiegetic narrator's repetition of this scene, the visual rhyme and the (reversed) cause-effect logic linking them, implies that Cobb and the blonde woman are somehow related.

The next scene jumps forward again to the young man–blonde woman storyline (15) as they meet in her apartment and talk again about her burglary. This storyline continues but moves forward to (23), the young man (now beaten up) watching the nightclub, followed by (24), his preparations to break into the club—he picks up a hammer and puts on latex gloves. Here the film's narration becomes more complex, for it introduces multiple discontinuities: within the flashback framing device the narration alternates between two storylines ("young man–Cobb" vs. "young man–blonde woman"). And within the "young man–blonde woman" storyline the narration is noticeably out of sequence, for effects are experienced before their cause—the burglary of the blonde woman's apartment is mentioned twice before it is committed; the young man's appearance suddenly changes without explanation; and, after (18), his face is bruised even though spectators have yet to see how he was injured.

After the young man prepares to steal from the club, the heterodiegetic narrator shifts the narrative to scene (5) where the young man and Cobb burgle the blonde woman's apartment (echoing the young man's later visit, shown moments earlier [15]), before sorting through her possessions (6). The next scene jumps forward to the young man–blonde woman storyline as they meet in a café (16). She tells him about her former boyfriend (the nightclub owner) killing a man in her apartment with a hammer (shown in a flashback); they argue, and she storms out.

The spectator's perception of the two nonchronological storylines continues to generate implicit meanings: the narration presents in close proximity a series of events that are far apart in terms of narrative time and that are presented out of sequence. But their juxtaposition creates a cognitive aftereffect which links them in the minds of spectators: we see the young man make preparations to break into the club (23); he picks up a hammer and put on latex gloves (24); but then he and Cobb are shown entering the blonde woman's apartment and sorting through her possessions (5–6), immediately followed by the scene in the café (16) where the blonde woman talks about how her former boyfriend murdered a man in her apartment with a hammer. In terms of the heterodiegetic narrator's sequencing of nonchronological events, it looks like the young man is putting on gloves and trying out his hammer just before he enters the blonde woman's apartment, which was the scene of a crime committed with a hammer (and is the location where she is later murdered with the young man's hammer).

This storyline jumps from the café (16) to a second key scene (25) of the young man stealing money and photographs of the blonde woman from the club's safe. In the middle of the burglary, the narrator intervenes by returning the narration to the young man–Cobb relationship. Three scenes are presented that go back in time: they eat in a restaurant, and the young man signs a stolen credit card with the card owner's name, before both leave quickly (7); back home he begins typing (8); and (9) he changes his appearance (giving the cause to an effect we have seen already). In other words, as he writes (perhaps about Cobb), he takes on a new appearance and a new name. The sequencing of these events again creates perceptual links between the two storylines: the young man meets the blonde woman in a café/meets Cobb in a restaurant; the two men leave the restaurant quickly/the blonde woman storms out of the café; the young man uses a stolen credit card/steals money from the club's safe; the young man steals photographs from the blonde woman's apartment/steals other photographs of her from the safe. This nonchronological series of events establishes a network of internal relations within the film, which generate symbolic echoes that transcend the linear unfolding of narrative events.

The narration progresses to (10), the young man sorting through the blonde woman's stolen possessions, including the box seen in the credit sequence. He then phones Cobb about the possessions (11a). After their conversation ends, the scene stays with Cobb to reveal that he is living with the blonde woman. Both discuss how they are setting up the young man (11b). Up to this point in the film, the narration has been restricted, for the spectator has been bound tightly to the consciousness of the protagonist. But in (11b) the narration shifts away from the young man to become omniscient over him, for it reveals to the spectator that the two characters in the separate storylines (Cobb and the blonde woman) not only know each other but that they are setting up the young man. Although they do not yet reveal what he is being set up for, the heterodiegetic narrator provides a clue by finally cutting back to (25), completion of the burglary of the night club, where the young man injures a security guard with a hammer. Once the burglary is complete, the narration remains with the young man–blonde woman storyline—it goes back in time to (17) to the young man apologizing to the blonde woman (about [16] their argument in the café) and making plans to help her by stealing compromising photographs of her from the nightclub safe (again the effect is presented first—the burglary of the nightclub—before the cause and its planning). From this moment onward (with one exception, the murder of the blonde woman), the narration presents the actions and events in chronological order. The young man meets Cobb on a rooftop (18a); he says he is seeing the blonde woman and tells Cobb about his plan to steal from the nightclub; Cobb beats him up and (18b) stuffs a latex glove into his mouth (giving two causes to effects we have already seen). The young man (now beaten up) begins typing (19). Cobb and the blonde woman talk about why they are setting up the young man—to frame him as a possible suspect in a burglary where Cobb found an old woman murdered and was interviewed by police (20). This is the second shift to omniscient narration. The young man returns to his apartment (26) after committing the burglary at the nightclub; he looks at the photographs of the blonde woman (which are not compromising) and, in a moment of *anagnorisis*, recognizes what the film's spectators already know, that he has been set up. When he confronts the blonde woman in (27), she tells him why he has been set up. He threatens her with his hammer but then warns he will go to the police. In (29a) the narration returns to the narrating situation where the young man is indeed talking to the police. However, he is not the only character to reveal information. The policeman introduces a dramatic plot twist by telling him they have no open cases of an old woman murdered with a hammer and that they do not know who Cobb is (29b). The significance of the second piece of omniscient information presented by Cobb in scene (20)—the young man is being set up for the murder of a woman carried out with a hammer—appears to be false. The police instead confront the young man with the murder of the blonde woman, shown in flashback ([28] Cobb kills the blonde woman with the young man's hammer). Cobb's story about the murder of the old woman suddenly takes on a different meaning—when he told the story in (20), it was not so much false as proleptic, for it links the young man to a future murder. In a second moment of *anagnorisis* (this time experienced simultaneously with the film's spectators), the young man realizes he has been set up for the murder of the blonde woman. The film ends on a shot of Cobb as he suddenly disappears into a crowd.

Figure 1.1 represents the unfolding narration scene by scene. If the heterodiegetic narrator retold the narrative chronologically and linearly (as reconstructed in textbox 1), it would follow the dotted black line. Instead, figure 1.1 shows the narration unfolding by jumping from scene 1 to scene

29 and then back to scene 10 before progressing to 12 and then jumping to 18, 19, and 21. Scenes that appear below the dotted line go back in time (at least in relation to the hypothetical temporal norm represented by the dotted line); and scenes above the line jump forward in time. After scene 1, the narration jumps to the final scene (29), visually represented by the huge spike in the graph above the dotted line. By jumping to scene 10 the narration is still above the line, which means it is still ahead of the hypothetical norm: in other words, scene 10 takes the slot in the narrative where scene 3 would have occurred if the narrative were told in a purely sequential-linear manner. The narration falls below the dotted line when it jumps from scene 21 (the young man, beaten up, watches the nightclub—a scene repeated on two other occasions) to scene 1 (the young man watches Cobb—a scene repeated from earlier). The graph shows that the young man–Cobb relation is dominant below the dotted line (1 to 9, 11), while fragments of the young man–blonde woman relation are dominant above the line (12 to 17). Scenes 10 and 11 mark the transition from Cobb to the blonde woman. In (10), the young man sorts through the blonde woman's box of possessions, and in (11) he phones Cobb about those possessions. It is at this moment that the scene stays with Cobb to reveal that he is living with the blonde woman. In scene (12), the young man follows and introduces himself to the blonde woman. Cobb does not return to the narrative until scene (18).

The graph also visualizes the preparation for and burglary of the club (21, 22, 24) and the burglary itself (25), which again are clearly visible above the dotted line. In sum, the solid black line in figure 1.1 gives an approximation of the way the heterodiegetic narrator intervenes to manipulate the resequencing of narrative events.

THE HETERODIEGETIC NARRATOR'S INTERVENTION

On two occasions the heterodiegetic narrator intervenes to shift the narration from restricted to omniscient by presenting the spectator with more information than the young man knows (scenes 11 and 20). On both occasions Cobb and the blonde woman talk about setting up the young man, information that functions as exposition. But in the second omniscient scene the information is false, for Cobb was not interviewed by the police. However, if the film is presented from the young man's perspective, how can he narrate these scenes? This, of course, is a common issue with flashbacks: they always exceed the character-narrator's experience, for the heterodiegetic narrator intervenes to convey additional information directly to spectators.

Does the heterodiegetic narrator also intervene directly in (27), where the young man confronts the blonde woman about setting him up, and in

(28), the blonde woman's murder? In (27), the young man acts aggressively toward her with his hammer before leaving suddenly. However, he leaves without the blonde woman or the spectator realizing: he walks out while the camera is focused on the blonde woman's back. The shot of her back appears to be from the young man's perspective, focalized around his awareness or optical experience. The camera disengages from him for these few moments without signifying its disengagement, which is unusual in a film where the camera remains closely tied to the main protagonist. As he disengages, the heterodiegetic narrator (always in the background) silently comes to the foreground to "claim" the shot. The blonde woman's murder is shown through a flashback as the policeman interviews the young man (28). In the flashback Cobb carries out the murder with the young man's hammer, and says he is keeping the money stolen from the safe—even though it was the young man who stole the money. The discrepancies in scenes (27) and (28) therefore pile up: the young man threatens the blonde woman with a hammer before suddenly leaving the scene; Cobb kills her with the same hammer; Cobb says he is keeping the money from the safe, even though it was the young man who took the money; the police do not believe that the young man is being set up for the murder of an old woman because they do not have any such unsolved murders; and the police have not interviewed anyone called Cobb. One way to address these discrepancies is to ask: Who is narrating the flashback of the blonde woman's murder? The young man is shocked to discover that she has been murdered (this flashback does not conform to the rest of the film, which largely represents his experiences); and, because the police do not believe that Cobb exists, why would he appear in the policeman's flashback? The flashback could be the young man's internal visual reconstruction of the murder as the police describe it to him. Another possibility is that it could be the young man's repressed memory of committing the murder, a memory in which he represents himself as Cobb (just as Fred Madison thinks of himself as Pete when he kills Alice's boyfriend Andy, or as the Edward Norton character in *Fight Club* thinks of himself as Tyler Durden). Finally, it could be the heterodiegetic narrator's flashback—in other words, the narrator by-passes characters by conveying information directly to spectators.

Following does not end in a classical manner by resolving ambiguities and tying up the narrative threads; instead, it does the opposite. It ends like a puzzle or mind-game film by highlighting unresolved ambiguities and by bringing into question the young man's character traits—is he unstable, schizophrenic, or suffering from memory loss? How reliable are his flashbacks? And why are his flashbacks presented in such a nonchronological zigzagging pattern (as illustrated in figure 1.1)? The film's narration (especially its nonchronological ordering) not only challenges character traits and character narration, but it also challenges and brings into question the spectator's cognitive thinking that is grounded in and limited to linear cause–effect logic, a reductive logic that searches for singular, fixed, permanent meanings.

REVISING THE PRIMACY EFFECT

The progress of the action from (1) to (9) represents the young man's developing relationship with Cobb. However, this relationship is interrupted with multiple actions that take place later: specifically, the young man developing a relationship with the blonde woman and preparing to break into the night club (for her benefit). A clear logic motivates the selection of scenes: a series of actions depicting the young man developing a relationship with Cobb is interrupted with a series of actions that show him developing a relationship with the blonde woman. After (9), the same pattern emerges but inverted: (10) to (17) represent the developing relationship between the young man and the blonde woman, a storyline that is, however, interrupted with the young man carrying out burglaries with Cobb.

Any jarring effects introduced via the narration's alternation between the two storylines and the forward jumps in time in the second storyline are diminished by the young man appearing in both storylines as a character. Although the narration presents sufficient information for the construction of a single coherent (internally consistent) storyworld, the film's final scene introduces ambiguity and doubt. That is, rather than the final scene tying up and resolving all the storylines, it unravels what initially appeared to be the young man's consistently narrated coherent and unambiguous story. The final scene challenges the primacy effect (the tendency to accept the initial interpretation of events) in that the policeman radically recontextualizes the same events in order to reposition the young man as the murderer. Twist endings successfully challenge and revise the primacy effect, and this is precisely what the final moments of *Following* achieve: the policeman undoes the young man's specific configuration of narrative events and reconfigures them into a new pattern, one that eliminates the character of Cobb but incorporates the event the young man left out—the murder of the blonde woman. It is through this reconfiguration that the policeman renders the young man's narration unreliable, which simultaneously creates the second moment of *anagnorisis* as well as the film's all-important twist ending.

However, *Following* does not definitively dismiss the initial interpretation of events; instead, it throws into doubt the fixed single meaning created by the primacy effect. The result for the young man and for film spectators is not resolution but ambiguity, confusion, and uncertainty. The young man is confused because he voluntarily went to the police to explain how he had been set up, but by doing so he implicated himself in the murder of the blonde woman, whose death did not feature in his version of events. (He is therefore an unintentionally misguided—rather than deliberately deceptive—unreliable narrator.) By creating a new interpretation of the young man's account of events, the policeman creates an alternative storyworld that throws into doubt the feasibility of the events the young man has just narrated to the police and to the film's spectators. By the end of the film, two versions of events exist with no definitive account of which one is true. The film simply ends with a slow motion shot of Cobb suddenly disappearing into a crowd. This shot in itself is ambiguous: is it a continuation of scene (1), of the young man following Cobb (some of which is shot in a crowd in slow motion), or is it authored by the heterodiegetic narrator who reinforces the policeman's aim to raise doubts and to bring into question Cobb's existence? If we look closely at this final shot, we see the "ultimate" embodiment of the heterodiegetic narrator on screen: the director, Christopher Nolan, appears briefly screen left, looking at Cobb, to engineer Cobb's sudden disappearance and to sow doubt in the spectator's mind, prepping spectators for the puzzlement of his next film, *Memento*.

NOTES

1. Elsaesser lists a sixth element—the loss of a child—but this is not relevant to *Following*.
2. I reconstructed the film's narrative before seeing Nolan's chronological re-edit of the film (on the Criterion DVD). Nolan's re-edit begins 17 minutes in, after the first attempted burglary (where the two men are interrupted by the owner returning home). This means the displaced shots and scenes in the opening moments remain out of sequence, including scene 12 (the young man watching the blonde woman leave her apartment).

REFERENCES

Buckland, Warren, ed. 2009. *Puzzle Films: Complex Storytelling in Contemporary Cinema*. Oxford: Wiley-Blackwell.
Elsaesser, Thomas. 2009. "The Mind-Game Film." In *Puzzle Films: Complex Storytelling in Contemporary Cinema*, edited by Warren Buckland, 13–41. Oxford: Wiley-Blackwell.
Genette, Gérard. 1980. *Narrative Discourse: An Essay in Method*. Translated by Jane E. Lewin. Ithaca, NY: Cornell University Press.

Kozloff, Sarah. 1988. *Invisible Storytellers: Voice-Over Narration in American Fiction Film*. Berkeley: University of California Press.

Kuntzel, Thierry. 1980. "The Film Work 2." *Camera Obscura*, no. 5: 6–69.

Chapter 2

"We All Need Mirrors to Remind Ourselves Who We Are"

Anamorphosis and the Singularity of Mirror Motifs in Christopher Nolan's Memento *(2000)*

Isabelle Labrouillère

Many *Memento* exegetes have noted the importance of the mirror in Christopher Nolan's film due to its recurrence at the diegetic, narrative, structural, and symbolic levels. The image of the mirror is regularly invoked by critics to account for its importance in apprehending the work: Elvis Mitchell, for example, describes Memento as an "intense, through the looking-glass *noir*" (quoted in Mottram 2002, 25). In a more literal way, Diran Lyons notices that the mirror triggers "the initial tragedy that drives the story" (2006, 129) while other authors have analyzed the founding role of the mirror in the construction of Leonard Shelby's (Guy Pearce) identity on the psychoanalytical level. When Leonard's head struck from behind collides with the bathroom mirror during his wife's attack, the shattered object literalizes the schism of an individual whose identity is now split by his memory loss. On the diegetic level we can also note the omnipresence of this object, which makes it a real motif within the work: for instance it is through the mirror that the character manages to give unity to the fragmented conception he has not only of his body—just like any individual—but also of his mind.

On the structural level, the metaphor of the mirror can also account for the repetitive effects which permeate the structure of the fiction. For example, the black-and-white sequences and the color sequences that weave a system of echoes in the film are each 22 in number. Within the black-and-white segment,

Sammy Jankis's (Stephen Tobolowsky) story functions as an embedded narrative, which, according to Mieke Bal, can be seen as "a mirror-text [which] serves as directions for us: the embedded story contains a suggestion on how the text should be read" (2009, 63). The mirror is then understood less as a "smooth or polished surface that forms images by reflection" than in a larger sense as a duplication principle "to reproduce or show (an exact likeness) as a mirror would" (Merriam-Webster).[1] The architecture of the movie is also reminiscent of a fractal composition wherein the elements of repetition and duplication appear as irregular fragments on various scales. In fact, the recurrence of the same objects and shapes neutralizes to a certain extent the baroque profusion of the signs the spectator must interpret. Thus, in the backward narrative, each sequence picks up exactly where the previous one ends. Besides, some of these sequences are shown twice in the movie, much like certain shots and objects reflected in patterns, like so many diffracted reflections.[2] From one sequence to the next, for example, we find many examples of signs functioning as motifs like the Polaroids or Leonard's tattoos which the camera lingers on many times, particularly on the "Remember Sammy Jankis" phrase written on his left hand.

Even when the scenes or the sequences are not duplicated, the idea of repetition is present in the background. Leonard is thus caught in the flow of identically repeated actions, whether consciously or not. If he has come up with a routine consisting of writing everything down to avoid forgetting, he is doomed to reproduce the same actions. In the sequence at the refinery, where he burns his wife's possessions, his voice-over says: "Probably tried this before. Probably burned truckloads of your stuff." This process of repetition is at times suggested by the film: during his confrontation with Dodd (Callum Keith Rennie) at the motel, Leonard shows a combativeness which can lead us to believe that the situation has happened before. In the same vein, at the end of the movie, Teddy's (Joe Pantoliano) monologue and the arbitrary way in which Leonard chooses his next victim lead us to believe that he is trapped in a never-ending downward spiral.

Even Leonard's words are contaminated by this principle of repetition: as Teddy reminds us, he keeps telling Sammy's story to whomever crosses his path, talking about his amnesia ("I have this condition") and alluding to his wife's memory. Leonard is, par excellence, the character who symbolizes repetition and duplication in the film not only because he has turned it into a system, but also because, like a chameleon, he continuously borrows others' identities.[3] Leonard proceeds by imitation, and by putting his persona forward, the film emphasizes his capacity to reproduce rather than embody. For example, the fact that Natalie (Carrie-Anne Moss) accuses him of reciting a speech when he invokes his wife's remembrance shows that he is repeating a text, much like a bad actor stuck in the same disembodied refrain. By widening the gap between the image—the reflection the characters give of themselves—and what they truly are, *Memento* raises metafilmic questions about acting, and our capacity to play a role likely to dupe others in the staging of everyday life.[4]

Indeed, in a more obvious and traditional way, the metaphor of the mirror in *Memento* encapsulates different aspects of the double in the film around the questions related to the duality of reality and the characters' duplicity. The deception of Burt (Mark Boone Junior), the motel receptionist, is thus revealed by means of duplication: Leonard accidentally discovers that he charged him for two rooms instead of one. As for Teddy—the audience never knows when is lying or not—his duplicity is *in fine* not unlike a diffraction principle: he has an assumed identity and says he is acting under cover. Finally, as pointed out by Claire Molloy (2010, 75), it is by echoing and recontextualizing sequence 17—in which Natalie pretends she has been beaten up by Dodd—through sequence 18—where she spurs Leonard to punch her in the face—that we understand the origins of the marks they both have on their faces and Natalie's dishonesty.

The mirror is also used more literally in the movie: in a classic way, meeting the reflection then brings to light the characters' duality. The mirror is then used less in its capacity to duplicate the real than to split it by insisting on variation rather than identical repetition.[5] For example, when Natalie attempts to calm down Leonard, whom she has manipulated to get rid of Dodd, she guides him to a mirror. Like an artist arranging the compositional elements of a painting, Natalie orchestrates a scenography around the mirror by undressing Leonard and placing herself successively behind and then in front of him. The character is in keeping with the tradition of the femme fatale, the archetype of the classic film noir: "The mirrored reflection of the *femme fatale* in *films noirs* acts as a metaphor for duplicity or narcissism, about which Place comments: 'They are visually split thus not to be trusted'" (Molloy 2010, 91).

However, within the framework of this chapter it is less Nolan's conventional use of the mirror that is of interest than the way in which *Memento* revisits this *topos* of classic cinema. I indeed intend to show the filmmaker's paradoxical use of the mirror. The director appropriates the *singularity* of the mirror, not only in terms of its original use in the fiction, but because he makes it an unexpected vector of cohesion, and univocal understanding of the world.

Indeed, the presence of the mirror in the film is first used not so much to bring out a latent subtext—like revealing the duplicity of a character—but, on the contrary, as a way of apprehending reality to promote an illusory univocity to a disoriented spectator. Indeed, Nolan's *Memento* rests upon a paradox: while deploying the motifs of the double on all the movie's thematic, structural, and symbolic levels, the film pretends to promote a linear progression of the investigation based on an aesthetic and a logic of transparency.[6] I will thus demonstrate how the mirror actually intervenes in complex visual devices inviting us to eventually renounce its apparent legibility to better embrace the complexity of Nolan's universe. *Memento* indeed unfolds according to an anamorphic or fanlike structure where each motif is developed and reshaped as the movie progresses and proposes new perspectives.

As a matter of fact, the mirror invites us to a two-step reading which echoes the metafilmic processes proper to the construction and manipulation of seeing. I will thus show that the intervention of the mirror within the filmic device incites us to carry out the readjustment of what we see and understand, in a two-step process akin to the construction of the anamorphic glance (Collins 1992, 73).[7] It is indeed through this eccentric gaze that Nolan invites us to leave the frontality of the traditional fiction (which claims to convey a totalizing, immutable perception of the world) so as to embrace the polyphony of his universe. This is why I will finally show in this chapter how *Memento*, by inviting us to leave the familiar shores of a reality abiding by Newtonian physics, twists the linearity of the classic fiction in undulating movements, so as to bring to light the heterogeneous, random, and contradictory character of the fiction.

Memento, while claiming affiliation with the traditional film noir, inserts itself into a movement of disruption and generic renewal akin to what we call "narrative puzzles." This movement is described by Jason Mittel as follows: "Cinema has . . . seen the emergence of a popular cycle of 'puzzle films' that require the audience to learn the particular rules of a film to comprehend its narrative . . . [the films resorting to] a game aesthetic, inviting the audiences to play along with the creators to crack the interpretive codes to make sense of their complex narrative strategies" (2006, 37–38).

The idea of puzzle pieces to be reconstructed and rearranged is all the more alluring as it echoes the indexical mechanics of Leonard's investigation, and the lacuna functioning of his memory, in the image of the broken mirror at the origin of the story. It indeed seems tempting to extend the metaphor and see, in the scattered shards of glass, the symbol not only of the memory fragmentation that Leonard tries to fill, but also of the clues intended to solve his investigation. In this sense, the cracking of the mirror would act as a mise-en-abyme of the puzzle imagery constituted by Leonard's investigation and the film itself.

However, if a jigsaw puzzle, in line with Merriam-Webster's definition, "consist[s] of small irregularly cut pieces that are to *be fitted together to form a picture*,"[8] *Memento* does not belong to this category. The puzzle is a finite object whose incompleteness is only temporary: *in fine*, the various pieces are destined to form a unified and coherent whole, each fragment joining perfectly with the others to create a totality. This conception of the fragment corresponds to what Daniel Arasse calls a "detail *particolare*," that is, "a small part of a figure, an object, or an ensemble" (1996, 11). In contrast, what Arasse refers to as the *dettaglio* is a detail which, "as the intimate bearer of the artist's private, innermost intents . . . may assume a 'dislocating' as opposed to a harmonizing function" (Athanassoglou-Kallmyer 2013, 649).

This could be but an anecdotal remark if it did not bring to light the two functions of the sign emblematic of the film's discursive strategy. Indeed, in *Memento*, the mirror's function is not simply to occasionally shed light on the characters' duplicity through the duplication of reality as is usually the case in fiction. In a more singular way, the mirror intervenes within the film's mechanics, where it first acts as the cornerstone of the manipulation device, and then of the mechanism of revelation set up by the narrative. At the start, the movie deploys different strategies intended to give the illusion of a linear progression in a plot likely to be elucidated. This is why *before* being a metaphor for the world's variability, the mirror is paradoxically presented as a cohesive space, a place where coherence can be restored.

Every time Leonard wakes up, his reflection allows him to reassign a stable identity to a body and mind only perceived in an incomplete way. Each time he looks in the mirror, he verifies his identity not because he does not know who he is, but because any subsequent event to his wife's alleged murder escapes him. The way the fiction makes reality (Lenny in front of the mirror) coincides with its representation (the reflection facing him) turns the mirror into an anchor point that stabilizes—in the spectators' eyes even more than Lenny's—the character's identity, both thanks to the repetition of this ritual and the reassertion of the character's conformity with what we know or think we know about him. He is always dressed in the same way, and if he is surprised to discover his tattooed body, it is never the object of a change revealed through the mirror.

Indeed, if, every time he meets his reflection, the character reconnects with an apprehension of his body which he has forgotten in the meantime, the spectators, for their part, do not discover any clues likely to help them progress in the resolution of the enigma or make it deviate in an unexpected way. In the same way, at no point is Leonard's reflection the vector of revelations about the character that would be made in and through the mirror. The reflection of the body never reveals new information likely to lead the investigation on a new track and create a split between reality and its duplication by the image. If the mirror generates an anagnorisis, it is not through its reflection but through the way its presence is staged: as mentioned above, the staging orchestrated around the mirror by Natalie—whose reflected body is not the focus of (our) attention in front of the mirror—points to her own duplicity retroactively in light of the manipulation she demonstrates in sequence 18.

It could be argued, however, that one of the mirror's occurrences orchestrates a revelation: the one allowing us to decipher the inscription on Leonard's torso: "JOHN G. RAPED AND MURDERED MY WIFE." This expression, which can only be read in the mirror and which in this sense revives the revelations in the mirror that classic cinema is so fond of, functions like a chiasmus in the way its deciphering is structured in the film. A chiasmus is a stylistic figure in which words, grammatical constructions, or concepts are repeated in reverse order. Working on the mirror model BA/AB, a chiasmus repeats elements to create an opposition effect, or a cause-and-effect relationship producing a redoubling. The mirror is thus the chiastic structure par excellence since it duplicates and produces a reversed image of the object or body it reflects. In the present case, the chiastic device is made more complex as the first phrasal segment (the tattooed text in reverse order) is only grasped through the process of duplication. If the chiasmus uses repetition to create parallels or antitheses, in *Memento*, the formal disruption of the sentence provoked by its reflection, and the surprise that ensues, is counterbalanced by the cohesiveness produced on the level of meaning.

Indeed, the phrase which appears in the mirror is integrated in the informational fabric composed by the clues—tattoos, Polaroids, notes, etc.—available to the viewer at that moment. In fact, not only does the tattoo on the torso clarify the meaning of the various writings on his body, but it also promotes a univocal reading that dispels the doubt introduced by the other texts. Whereas the tattoo on his thigh reads: "FACT 3: FIRST NAME JOHN OR JAMES," the centrality of the phrase on the torso and its precision ("JOHN G." instead of "JOHN OR JAMES") give us the feeling that it clarifies and specifies the one on the thigh and thus was written afterward, therefore superseding any other. In this respect, the information thus revealed is more akin to the *particolare* than the *dettaglio*. The way it functions here is indeed the antipodes of another tattoo, the one that Leonard, in a shot revealed at the end of the movie, displays while lying next to his wife: "I'VE DONE IT." If there is a discrepancy between the image and its repetition, it is done less in the mirror than through this second image perceived by the viewer as competing with the other fragments of the puzzle that he is trying to piece together.

This is why one can legitimately wonder about the importance of the tattoo's discovery through this optical process. Although it is true that this tattoo—which is fundamental for Leonard since it encapsulates, in a way, all the others—has the advantage of being legible in the mirror, it is never the one he discovers first, contrary to those engraved on his hands, arms, or thighs. The latter are indeed more easily accessible as they are written "from the bottom up," which makes them immediately readable upon waking up.[9]

We can then think that it is the use of the mirror as an anamorphosis—this optical illusion which perturbs the visible to provoke the manipulative games

Nolan is so fond of—which is at play here. According to its definition, an anamorphosis is a "distorted projection or drawing which appears normal when viewed from a particular point or with a suitable mirror or lens."[10] Like the mirror, the anamorphosis consists in decomposing the gaze according to a *two-time* structure. At first, the illegible phrase running across Leonard's torso is reminiscent of the blurred contour of the object intended for anamorphosis ("a distorted projection"). In a second viewing, however, thanks to the perspective change offered by the mirror, the stain becomes recognizable and transforms itself into a meaningful object (it "appears normal when viewed from a particular point or with a suitable mirror").

The originality of the mirror here comes from the fact that it rests on a binary principle, not only because it produces a doubling of objects *in the physical space*, but because it imposes, like an anamorphosis, a reading in two steps. However, unlike the system that the film will subsequently deploy—in which each scene, each attitude, each object of importance, is likely to be reassessed—here, the two stages of reading promote successive and mutually exclusive versions of reality.

Indeed, by making us go from information disorder to its elucidation, the mirror lets us access the truth of the referent. Indeed, by bringing to light the optical principle at the origin of the tattoo, the mirror allows us to go back to the strategy used to design the tattoo and thus find its lost origin. The diegetic universe progresses along the idea that to know is to know by the cause, according to an Aristotelian conception of the world. In fact, the image resorts here to a type of inferential reasoning, the abduction, which Umberto Eco, taking up Pierce's theory, associates to the first stage of the criminal investigation (1994, 158). When faced with a surprising fact, the abduction consists in making one hypothesis susceptible to explain it and to put it to the test because it is always possible to find the "Rule" which either already exists somewhere, exists elsewhere, or must be invented (1994, 159).

By restoring meaning through the transformation of the object into a sign, representation is thus portrayed in the film as a vector of knowledge. In *Memento*, the mirror contributes to the elucidation of the cryptic signs of reality, since access to the truth allows us—thanks to the framing provided by the duplicated image—to invalidate the erroneous hypotheses the sentence might have been subject to. The spectator is then tempted to infer that any representation is prone not only to go back to its source, but also to reconstruct the meaning of a past event. The mirror is here at the service of a splitting of the real, intended to maintain the lure of a representation that would likely be grasped (that is to say both seen and understood) in its entirety *from the moment it is considered from the right angle*. In this respect, sequence 18, by giving us access to the origin of Leonard's and Natalie's wounds, functions like an anamorphic composition.

Indeed, the confrontation between Leonard and Natalie unfolds in two steps. In the first step, Leonard mistakenly attributes the blows on Natalie's face to Dodd, Jimmy's former partner. If the clues Leonard gleans from texts or images are indeed the trace of a "*ça-a-été*" (Barthes 1980, 120), they are nonetheless signs to decipher and contextualize. In the absence of contextualization Leonard cannot go back to the origin of the marks according to the Serendipian technique (Catellin 2014). Indeed, abduction alone is not enough to reach the truth. This method, which consists in seeking causes or explanatory hypotheses, is uncertain by nature. As Sylvie Catellin reminds us,[11] "One cannot affirm with certainty that an explanation constitutes the real cause of an observation, as the uncertainty can relate to the plausibility of the explanation or the validity of the knowledge allowing the explanation" (2004, 180). Yet, the sidestep taken by the recontextualization of the scene allows us, like an anamorphosis, to reconsider the initially uninterpretable or misinterpreted signs. By revealing the genesis of the signs presented in the frame, the sequence offers a resolution both univocal and definite. If this explanation is not of a symbolic nature, as in the case of the classical anamorphosis, it nonetheless ensures that the effects are traced back to their cause as in the mirror anamorphosis used by Nolan.

However, in these two examples, the image functions as a decoy within the story's trap: by elucidating the riddle of the tattoo through the mirror, the movie entertains the idea that the world makes sense, and that this sense can be restored through the representations that emanate from it. Indeed, if the mirror here duplicates reality, it is not to maintain competing versions of it since the initial duplication is only temporary and is intended to allow access to an ultimate truth. As a matter of fact, at first, the fictional device intends to "polarise the piece in a differential fashion" (Rykner 2008, 183), by allowing a unique resolution to emerge from the confrontation of hypotheses. Contrary to the more traditional uses of the mirror in fiction, the reflection is not at the service of the splitting of reality through the revelation of a previously hidden aspect. It is used to promote its redoubling, in the sense that what we discover through it reinforces a totalizing vision of the world.

Then, however, the film revisits this singular use of the mirror. It becomes the agent, not so much of the duality of the world and the duplicity of individuals, but of the variability of reality. The mirror thus functions literally as a prism in the optical sense of the term, that is to say an optical element used "for dispersing light into a spectrum or for reflecting and deviating light."[12] (Collins Dictionary).

It is through the use of another mirror device revisiting the anamorphic structure that the singularity of Nolan's universe is *in fine* brought to light. This revelation occurs at the 85th minute when Leonard evokes what looks like the last episode in the life of Sammy Jankis, now institutionalized in a psychiatric facility. The visual strategy which is set up within a single shot is cut into three distinct segments. First, we see Sammy, in a close-up, sitting in a chair in the middle of the psychiatric hospital ward. Then, Sammy's body is briefly hidden by the silhouette of an individual standing between the camera and the character: the frame is then obstructed by the intrusion of the character whose body is blurred by the movement. Finally, once the individual exits the frame, the perceptive spectator notices that, for a second, Leonard has replaced Sammy. As if by sleight of hand, Leonard's body appears and disappears in a quasi-subliminal image that can go unnoticed. In this triptych, Nolan seems to break down the anamorphic structure. As in the previous example, the "[a]namorphic projection seeks to deny the usual conventions of looking in which an observer views an image frontally from a limited range of viewing angles" (Collins 1992, 73). Thus, the figure first present in the frame disappears and is replaced by a stain—the blurred silhouette—reminiscent of the etymology of the word (*ana-morphe*, "which has no form"). This may remind us of the famous "cuttlebone shape" in Holbein's *Ambassadors* (1533), a blurred, oblong stain that transforms into a skull when viewers change their position in front of the canvas.

In the sequence, the lateral movement of the body from left to right reproduces the dynamics of the classical anamorphosis before giving way to a new image with visible and legible contours.[13] As in the previous instance, the reuse of an optical process unfolding in two steps (before and after the insertion of the stain in the frame) introduces a dialogism in an image initially presented as devoid of narrative stake and mystery. The spectral image of the body moving along seems to contaminate Leonard's body, which in turn becomes spectral.

However, this optical construction presents a certain number of differences compared to a classic anamorphosis. Firstly, it is not the stain itself that, under the observer's eccentric perspective, takes shape and meaning. The stain only initiates the transition that accompanies the replacement of Sammy's body by Leonard's. Furthermore, when faced with the cinematographic image, the spectator is unable to operate the decentering of the gaze due to their change of position, which would allow them to go from the "illusion" to its "denial" (Bonitzer 1985, 35). More so than the observer of the pictorial anamorphosis who actively participates in the resolution of the optical illusion and the construction of the gaze, *Memento*'s spectators seem themselves forced into the revelation.

In fact, Nolan revisits the anamorphic structure to readdress not only his traditional meanings, but also the significance attributed to it in the first occurrence analyzed. Contrary to what we saw through the use of the mirror, the gap created by the duplication of the image exposes the deception of the perceptive continuity of the world advocated by Leonard's investigation.

Traditionally, the anamorphosis is used to transform the observer's point of view on reality. This change of perspective is obtained by the movement of the observer, which involves the erasing of one image in favor of another. The appearance of this second image (the skull in Holbein's *The Ambassadors*, for example) acts as an ironic comment on the previous image. It thus functions as a caption, a label aimed at orienting our reading of the artwork. However, in *Memento*, the different stages of the representation are given to the viewer by the filmic device, and the film is not so much about looking at reality from a different angle as revealing its multiple facets. Indeed, neither our position nor our point of view of the object have been changed, and the angle from which the enunciation represents it stays the same. Sammy's body, framed in a close shot, is replaced by Leonard's, at the same angle and placed in the same spot.

If classic anamorphosis is part of a hermeneutic approach destined to provide us with an interpretive grid of the world without questioning its existence, Nolan's revisitation intervenes on reality itself and gives us no clear explanation. Are we to believe that Sammy does not exist and is a figment of Leonard's imagination? Must we think that the latter has merged his own story with Sammy's? Or that Leonard accidentally killed his wife by giving her an overdose of insulin and was institutionalized?

This is why, more so than in *The Ambassadors*, the anamorphic tilt as used in the film produces an insurrection of the visible characteristic of the *dettaglio*. Indeed, if the pictorial anamorphosis supposes the physical cooperation of the spectator in front of the canvas, it imposes a ready-made interpretive framework. Many scholars have indeed commented on the metaphoric, symbolic, and even psychoanalytic significance of the optical process. In contrast, the image in *Memento* refuses to elucidate the riddle posed by the conjectural space of the fiction: the filmic anamorphosis does not subject the object revealed by the optical device to a prescribed reading grid. Here, the optical illusion disturbs our apprehension of reality instead of stabilizing it, and Nolan undermines the bases of classical representation by refusing to resort to the allegorical stratagem of the anamorphosis[14] which, through the use of symbolic resolution, transforms the detail-*particolare* into a *dettaglio*. On the contrary, Nolan's anamorphosis, which maintains together incompatible interpretations of reality, becomes the metaphor and the metonymy of a fiction that does not let us decide between different versions of reality. This perception of the film would explain that it is now impossible to offer a unique solution to the riddle posed by the movie. As Christopher Nolan points out, "I believe the answers are all in the film, but the terms of the storytelling deliberately prevents people from finding them. If you watch the film and abandon your conventional desire for absolute truth . . . then you can find all the answers you're looking for" (Mottram 2002, 26).

It is in this sense that we can understand the numerous comments proposed by Christopher Nolan about the movie. By presenting, in the DVD supplements, three different solutions to the enigma posed by the film, the director offers a reading grid in the form of propositions and variables that we can choose at random, by selecting one track or another. This presentation in the form of choice suggests that these versions are competing and, in this sense, incompatible, and that spectators can choose the one that suits them best.

However, none of these propositions is satisfactory on its own, because, as the filmmaker reminds us in the above quote, the narrative, through the multiplication of conflicting informational relays—characters with divergent storylines, repetition of the same event at various angles, comparison, in the same shot, of incompatible manifestations of reality put on the same plane—prevents the spectator from choosing an interpretation which would allow them to discard the other propositions. In this sense, these different manifestations of reality are not to be understood in an exclusive mode (one version supposing the eviction of the others) but in an integrative way (not one or the other but both and even more). Since no point of view in the film is coherent from beginning to end (there is no "absolute truth"), we can thus assume that not only do the characters lie to others and themselves, but that reality itself is resistant to any attempt to grasp the truth. In this sense, *Memento* would associate the ambiguity of reality which concerns the interpretation of facts and not the facts themselves, with its ambivalence understood as that which comprises two values, two components, opposed or not. To grasp the scope of this paradigmatic shift which would make these alternate versions of the world less a question of perspective than of the essence of reality, it thus seems interesting to turn to quantum physics, whose principles Nolan has famously resorted to in such movies as *Interstellar* (2014) and *Tenet* (2020).[15]

To do so, I will make a detour through Arnaud Rykner's article, "L'univers quantique de Marguerite Duras et la critique des dispositifs." The author opposes Duras with the traditional realist writer, "this observer and this measuring instrument who depicts a *given state of reality*" (2007, 182). By doing so, the latter can only give an account of the objects and beings of the world by fixing them "in a posture which denies all movement" (2007, 182). In *Memento*, as suggested by the recurrent use of the Polaroid camera throughout the investigation, the will to capture a snapshot of reality unmediated by re/presentation is the fantasy that Leonard (and the viewer with him) nourishes. Indeed, how can we not think of the character in *Memento* when Rykner quotes David Deutsch in *The Fabric of Reality*: "We realists take the view that reality is out there: objective, physical and independent of what we think about it. But we never experience that reality directly" (2007, 121).[16] This quotation clearly reminds us of Leonard's words at the end of the movie. If he asserts that "The world doesn't disappear when you close your eyes," then reality exists through the eye of the observer who only perceives a fragment, a given state of the real. Indeed, the movie has demonstrated the subjectivity of each character's perception of reality and its irreducible incompatibility with the other perspectives provided by the film. In fact, much like Duras's novels, Nolan's filmography has very early on denied the evidence of reality, its provable character, and its immutability (Rykner 2007, 182). Rather than multiplying interpretations aspiring to univocally resolve the plot, which, by definition, is impossible, it seems more relevant to gather these various readings under the same structural principle: that of the *multiverse*. If we are to believe Arnaud Rykner, by giving life and shape to what science has named the multiverse, Duras's writing has echoed the quantum revolution[17] for which "the basis of reality is not a large accumulation of matter, but rather a consciousness" (Schäfer, quoted in Rykner 2007, 183). Within the multiverse, the invariants proper to classical realistic fiction give way to the instability symptomatic of a world characterized by the possible and the virtual.

Thus, while classic fiction wants the protagonist to be the herald of a truth likely to be reconstituted as in a puzzle, the collection of clues can only freeze a given state of the world which is unfit to transmit the latent movement of reality. In *Memento*, each repetition of an event is likely to make it change status from the *particolare*—supporting a classical realistic conception of the world—to the *dettaglio*, which disturbs the unity of the representation and brings out its versatility. The protagonists thus evolve in a labile, elusive universe whose complexity they can only grasp in a partial and biased way. The paradox *Memento* feeds on is thus to project a character whose *modus operandi* is typical of classical realism and a Newtonian understanding of the world, into a fictional universe obeying the revolutionary laws of quantum science. The character, now detached from a fixed and labelable identity, seems to move in a universe proceeding by the superposition of characters, events, places, and times, even if they are contradictory.

Indeed, in *Memento*, the Newtonian universe that gives reality the fixity of a photographic snapshot gives way to a quantum universe in the manner of the Polaroid, which in the inaugural sequence, passes in the blink of an eye from the precision of fixed forms to the latent movement of reality. What was previously presented as the truth then becomes only a possibility among others, and if the spectator is free to believe Teddy or Leonard: in a representation "having no link to a measurable and certifiable truth . . . lying is not a transformation of reality but another one of its states" (Rykner 2007, 191). The world here becomes a place of possibilities, of continuous hypotheses and suppositions since reality is not fixed, and the observer can only apprehend it in a fragmented way.

To put it in a nutshell, in *Memento*, the narrative stratagem not only diffracts but also amplifies, in the manner of a magnifying glass, the mutability of reality seen through the prism of the quantum revolution. Reality can only be grasped the moment it is actualized by an observer-narrator who only conveys one possible version of it. It is thus prone to being constantly altered and modified. However, when Marguerite Duras, in her filmic adaptation of *The Lorry* (1977), juxtaposes the actual movie (that the spectator watches) and the possible movie that audience members construct in their individual minds, she does not create a hierarchy between what belongs to the real perceived as objective reality and its conditional possibility. In contrast with the Durassian reader who accepts as a prerequisite the coexistence of modalities that both contradict and reinforce each other (Rykner 2007, 188), Nolan's spectators, whose expectation is modeled on the classic mystery story, cannot help but try to reconstruct a univocal, coherent universe which they regard as more fulfilling than a so-called chaotic, insignificant multiverse. Used to the Newtonian logic of the classical narrative, lured by the deceptive stability of a reality meant to be reconstitutable by abduction, the spectator misunderstands the value of this informational disorder. Indeed, the latter is not a means to access the truth, but an end in itself, and Nolan's comments on the movie do not say otherwise.

In this sense, the scholars who, twenty years after the movie's release, continue to feed theories in their essays, blogs, or academic articles, not only follow in the wake of the piece, but contribute, in their very diversity, to explore all the possible worlds suggested by the director. Far from desiccating the film through a reductive interpretive grid and assigning a unique place to reality by vectorizing its path and destination, each rereading of *Memento* makes the singular polyphony of the work resound.

NOTES

1. www.merriam-webster.com/thesaurus/mirror. Accessed December 2, 2020.

2. When shooting on the brownfield, Christopher Nolan and Dody Dorn, the movie's editor, decided to keep the same shots to avoid a separation between the original sequence and its reprise at different moments in the film. Mottram, *The Making of Memento*, 81.

3. Nolan's fiction is a game of hide-and-seek which has its source in the genetic history of the work itself: behind Christopher Nolan, the director, hides Jonathan, his brother, the author of the story at the origin of the movie.

4. The iterative principle shaping Leonard's life and the filmic structure allow the spectators to find their way through the meanders of the narrative while putting in place a system of repetition and variation on which their manipulation rests.

5. As put by Nolan, "There are direct repetitions and then there are echoes, if you like or indirect repetitions. It's an outward spiral, a widening gyre." Mottram, *The Making of* Memento, 36.

6. For a detailed analysis, see Isabelle Labrouillère (2022, 132–53).

7. As reminded by the author, an anamorphosis is "1. a drawing presenting a distorted image [that] appears in natural form under certain conditions, as when viewed at a raking angle or reflected from a curved mirror. 2. The method of producing such a drawing." Collins, "Anamorphosis and the Eccentric Observer," 73.

8. www.merriam-webster.com/dictionary/jigsaw%20puzzle. Last accessed July 22, 2021. Italics mine.

9. We may indeed imagine that the tattoo is reversed because Leonard drew it himself. So, he had to look into the mirror to write it in the first place and now has to look in the mirror to make sense of it.

10. www.lexico.com/definition/anamorphosis. Accessed July 30, 2021.

11. All the translations from the French are by the author.

12. www.collinsdictionary.com/dictionary/english/prism. Accessed August 11, 2021.

13. "To view an anamorphic image is to attempt to transform an oblique or non-uniform focal plane into a coherent, two-dimensional image"; Collins, "Anamorphosis and the Eccentric Observer," 74.

14. "The anamorphic image," Bonitzer reminds us, "is opposed to the image of simple perspective like the spirit to the flesh, the idea to the appearance, the mental thing to the sensitive thing." Bonitzer, *Peinture et cinéma*, 58.

15. Nolan called upon the astrophysicist Kip Thorne to conceive the universe in *Interstellar*.

16. Rykner cites Deutsch in French. Our quotation comes from the book in its original version.

17. The author cites Daniel Parrochia in Météores: Essai sur le ciel et la cité in a quote which could be translated as follows: "Quantum physics so challenged the traditional image of the world . . . that it immediately gave rise to multiple interpretations from which it gradually became inseparable"; Rykner, *L'univers quantique*, 181.

REFERENCES

Arasse, Daniel. 1996. *Le détail. Pour une histoire rapprochée de la peinture*. Paris: Flammarion.

Athanassoglou-Kallmyer, Nina. 2013. "Review of Le détail. Pour une histoire rapprochée de la peinture, by Daniel Arasse," 649–651. *Art Bulletin* 95, no. 4 (December).

Bal, Mieke. 2009. *Narratology: Introduction to a Theory of Narrative*. 3rd ed. Toronto: University of Toronto Press.

Barthes, Roland. 1980. *La chambre claire. Note sur la photographie*. Paris: Editions de l'Etoile, Gallimard, Le Seuil.

Bonitzer, Pascal. 1985. *Peinture et cinéma. Décadrages*. Paris: Cahiers du cinéma/Editions de l'Etoile.
Catellin, Sylvie. 2004. "L'abduction: une pratique de la découverte scientifique et littéraire." CNRS Éditions | *Hermès, La Revue* 2, no. 39: 179–85.
Catellin, Sylvie. 2014. *Sérendipité. Du conte au concept*. Paris: Seuil.
Collins, Daniel L. 1992. "Anamorphosis and the Eccentric Observer: Inverted Perspective and Construction of the Gaze," 73–82. *Leonardo* 25, no.1. Accessed August 2021. www.jstor.org/stable/1575625?seq=1#metadata_info_tab_contents.
Deutsch, David. 1997. *The Fabric of Reality*. London: Penguin Books.
Eco, Umberto. 1994. *The Limits of Interpretation*. Bloomington: Indiana University Press.
Labrouillère, Isabelle. 2022. "L'écriture de la peau dans Memento (Christopher Nolan, 2000): du mutisme du corps tatoué à son devenir image." In *Imaginaires cinématographiques de la peau*, ed. Diane Bracco, 132–153. Amsterdam/New York: Brill Rodopi.
Lyons, Diran. 2006. "Vengeance, the Powers of the False and the Time-Image in Christopher Nolan's *Memento*. A note on ressentiment at the beginning of the new millennium." *Angelaki: Journal of the Theoretical Humanities* 2, no. 1 (April): 127–135.
Mittel, Jason. 2006. "Narrative Complexity in Contemporary American Television." *The Velvet Light Trap* 58 (January) 29–40. Accessed April 14, 2021. juliaeckel.de/seminare/docs/mittell%20narrative%20complexity.pdf.
Molloy, Claire. 2010. *Memento. American Indies.* Edinburgh: Edinburgh University Press.
Mottram, James. 2002. *The Making of* Memento. London: Faber and Faber.
Nolan, Christopher. 2001. Memento *& Following*. London: Faber and Faber.
Rykner, Arnaud. 2008. "L'univers quantique de Marguerite Duras et la critique des dispositifs." In *Marguerite Duras et la pensée contemporaine*, ed. Eva Ahlstedt and Catherine Bouthors-Paillart, 181–193. Göteborg: Göteborg Universitet.

Chapter 3

The Prestige, From Text to Screen
Transformation, Manipulation, Reflexivity

Gilles Menegaldo

The Prestige (1995) a neo-Victorian novel by Christopher Priest, was adapted by Christopher Nolan in 2006. The novel tells the story of a long-standing feud between Alfred Borden and Rupert Angier, two stage magicians in the late nineteenth century and its tragic consequences for the protagonists and their descendants. Priest uses a complex narrative structure, based on the diaries of the two rivals, with a consistent use of flashbacks and the interweaving of a frame narrative. The novel deals with obsession, paranoia, spectacular magic tricks, and secrecy, also foregrounding the role of science with the part played by the controversial Nikola Tesla, inventor of alternative current, a rival of Thomas Edison. Hence, the link is established with science-fiction and steampunk aesthetics at the turn of the century.

Nolan's adaptation dispenses with the frame narrative and changes many elements of the plot while keeping the main themes of the novel (the double, trauma, obsession, revenge, sacrifice) and the same paranoid mood. The film uses a strategy of suspense and secrecy and disseminates significant signs, both verbal and visual, which help the spectator unravel some enigmas, but these signs are overlooked on first seeing the film. Nolan manages to convey the mood of the period and the fascination exercised by these magic tricks, pointing to the potential dangers involved, but also offering a reflection upon the modes of manipulation of the spectator.

This chapter will examine first some transformations (deletion, addition, expansion, etc.) carried out by Nolan. Then, it will focus on narrative devices and enunciation strategies. The nonlinear script implies a retrospective reading, and alternative versions of some scenes convey new meanings. Lastly, I will delineate formal features—lighting, sound, editing—by means of which the director both reveals and conceals key information and blurs the frontiers between explainable tricks and true "magic." Nolan manages to pay tribute to the novel, focusing on the relationship between magic and science and establishing a parallel between magic and cinema, highlighting the powers of the cinematic art.

Unlike the movie, the novel starts in contemporary England. The narrator, Andrew Westley, states early on: "I have had the feeling that *someone else* is sharing my life" (Priest 2011, 4). It is the search for a twin that sets off the action. The main narrative arc is set at the turn of the century when scientific knowledge enters the story with Nikola Tesla, a genius inventor. Through this frame, the narratives of two rival stage magicians are disclosed. Each has a seemingly impossible magic trick at the heart of his stage act, and their diaries are in part an account of their careers, but also of their obsessive quests and of the dire consequences of their strife on their private lives.

ADAPTATION PROCESS

The novel got good reviews and the World Fantasy Award in 1996, but it was only in 2000, after various failed attempts, that Newmarket hired Christopher Nolan, with Priest's agreement. It took six years to carry out the project. Meanwhile Nolan had become a famous director with *Insomnia* (2002) and *Batman Begins* (2005). The project grew into a big budget film with Warner Bros. and featured big stars. Priest had no part in the script written by Christopher Nolan and his brother. The magic illusion purports to be spectacular, but it also involves a manipulation of the audience, using tricks that are supposed to go unnoticed. Hence a parallel may be drawn between magic art and cinema, both taking place in front of audiences, both using devices to seduce their spectators. Nolan's film provides a show (stage entertainment) within the show.

In the novel the frame narrative features a descendant of Alfred Borden who receives a diary written by a rival magician, suggesting that the conflict between the two magicians has endured throughout a whole century. It is a counterpoint to the main narrative made of two contradictory diaries corresponding to each magician's point of view. The film script dispenses with this frame, focusing on the conflict that takes place at the turn of the twentieth century. This meant changing the end (Priest 2008, 58). Some theatrical episodes are erased, such as the séance when Angier and his assistant pretend to establish a dialogue with the deceased. Borden intrudes upon them, exposing the cheating and wounding Angier's pregnant wife, who miscarries. This is the starting point of a feud, with mutual sabotaging of magic acts, some added by Nolan such as the "bullet catch" episode where Borden (Christian Bale) loses two fingers through the agency of Angier (Hugh Jackman). This invented scene conveys a sense of the cruelty of the attending crowd and highlights the physical cost of the magic act.

Nolan's additions help dramatize the narrative. Borden's trial is added as well as the Newgate prison scenes and his execution by hanging, which parallels his wife Sarah's (Rebecca Hall) suicidal hanging. This implies new settings and sets of characters (prison guards, judges, lawyers). Another addition is the water-tank escape attraction which leads to the drowning of Julia (Piper Perabo), Angier's wife. The scene introduces the protagonists at an early stage of their career, when they are friends, working as assistants to older illusionists. It foregrounds the water tank which plays an important part, as the instrument of Julia's death and later as part of Angier's illusion. This is one of numerous parallels established by Nolan. In the first occurrence, Julia manages to untie the knots and get out of the tank, bowing to an enthralled public. The second scene goes wrong because Julia is unable to slip out of the type of knot devised by Borden who later expresses his unease at the funeral, unable to speak while a grieving Angier angrily asks him what knot he tied. The two rivals are filmed frontally in shot reverse-shot so as to express their breaking apart.

A FRAGMENTED OPENING SEQUENCE

The opening sequence is a good illustration of Nolan's adaptive choices. In the novel, the incipit is brief and casual: "It began on a train heading North through England although I was soon to discover that the story had really begun more than a hundred years earlier" (Priest 2011, 3). The invented opening scene of the film is more complex, offering a striking example of Nolan's approach, combining addition, condensation, and displacement in time. It starts on an uncanny shot of a forest clearing full of scattered top hats. The camera slowly glides over the hats from right to left while an anonymous male voice-over utters seemingly directly at the spectator: "Are you watching closely?" The screen fades to black. We later learn that the setting was a Colorado forest where the inventor Nikola Tesla built his laboratory. Angier came there to ask Tesla to build a machine for him because he wrongly thinks that Borden has such a machine for his trick, "The Transported Man." We do not realize immediately that all the hats are identical. Nolan introduces two motifs: the double and magic, the top hat being a standard prop. We realize later that the "prestige" is a way of defining the hats, as leftovers of the duplication process. The scene was part of Tesla's experimentation with the machine. Angier, walking randomly in the woods, falls upon a clearing full of similar hats. Two black cats are present, the consequence of another phase in the experiment. At the end of the film this shot of the hats is repeated, but we now know its meaning.

The voice-over, we later learn, is that of Alfred Borden. A privileged link is established between him and the spectator. As the scene is out of context, questions may be raised: What were we watching? Where do these hats come from and what do they represent? Why should we watch them closely?

We shift abruptly to a new setting by means of a pan shot, again from right to left, on a series of cages containing identical canaries. We hear a new voice-over, with a strange cockney accent, this time associated with a face, that of Harry Cutter (Michael Caine), a designer of magic artefacts. Cutter explains for us the three acts of a magic illusion: the Pledge, the Turn, the Prestige. The Pledge "shows something ordinary, a deck of cards, a bird, a man." In the Turn, "the magician takes the ordinary something and makes it do something extraordinary." The Prestige, the hardest part, brings back the object that has disappeared, a bird, a man. Each act is illustrated by crosscutting between shots of the simple trick performed in front of a little enthralled girl and shots of the Scala theatre where the audience watches with the same fascination a magic show illuminated by spectacular electric flashes, among them a bearded man (a disguised Borden), a glove hiding his left hand, who later sneaks beneath the stage, pretending to be part of the act. While the bird as well as the magician (Angier) seem to vanish in the Turn (we see the magician fall through a trap door), only the bird is brought back, not the man. From the outset, the film emphasizes failure and drama. Under the stage, things go wrong as we see, along with Borden's horrified look, the performer trapped in an enormous water tank. While the camera closes up on the drowning man, pounding on the glass, there is another shift. We hear Cutter's voice, not addressing us as we thought, but testifying at a trial where Borden is being accused of Angier's murder. Asked to reveal the secret of Borden's trick, he refuses to comply at first, but eventually accepts to disclose the secret to the judge in private.

Within a few minutes, we are confronted with various narrative levels, implying a manipulation of the time frame. The hats in the forest are a by-product of Tesla's experiment in Colorado. What happens in the theater is part of Angier's show, the "New Transported Man," which makes use of Tesla's machine. Borden's statement, "Are you watching closely?" is not related to the image of the hats, but rather addressed to the film viewers, involving them in a way the novel never attempts. However, Borden uses the same sentence, addressed to three different persons on three different occasions. Cutter's trick is performed in front of a little girl, but his discourse on the three acts is addressed to the child, to the court that judges Borden, and indirectly to the spectator. The canary scene, seemingly introductory, is the closing sequence, taking place after Borden's execution. Angier's drowning leads to a trial that takes place weeks before. Already present in the novel, where he is introduced belatedly in Angier's diary, Cutter becomes a prominent character in the film, with an ethical stand.

TIME MANIPULATION IN THE FILM

Nolan is well known for his handling of time, particularly in *Memento* (2000), *Inception* (2010), *Dunkirk* (2017), and *Tenet* (2020). *The Prestige* refuses linearity and chronology and, contrary to the novel where most entries are dated, offers few precise markers of time. Only three dates are given, March 1897, February 1899, and 1901, three landmarks. The film develops along these timelines which progress in a parallel way. The first one is 1897 when Borden, Angier, and Cutter work for Milton (Ricky Jay), an old school magician. During one of Milton's shows, the water escape, the trick goes wrong, leading to Julia's death. The second timeline, 1899, corresponds with Angier's trip to Colorado—induced by Borden's diary. The last timeline, 1901, corresponds to Angier's death by drowning, leading to Borden's trial and execution, followed by the other Borden twin (Angier's true identity) shooting Lord Caldlow.

These timelines are blurred because of Nolan's nonlinear narration. The mutual readings of their diaries by both magicians enable Nolan to move backward and forward in time, without informing the spectator. Thus, the narrative relies on a system of embedding. Early on, Borden, waiting for his trial, is given Angier's diary by Owens, his solicitor, acting on behalf of Lord Caldlow. The camera closes up on his reading while Angier's voice-over utters the following words: "a cipher, an enigma, a search for answers." We shift from a closeup of Borden reading to a long shot of a train progressing through mountains. The camera zooms in, then cuts to a close shot of a hand writing, leading to a first extended flashback staging Angier's trip to Colorado. We see him writing in his diary about Borden while we also hear his voice commenting: "Even if Colorado is the end of my journey, it will take much longer to unravel the rest of Borden's secret." The camera frames in full screen a page covered with a cryptic assemblage of letters, in meaningless combinations. Angier flips nervously through the pages: "Even if this cypher in his notebook is simple, unlocked by a single word, it will take months to translate his writings and know his mind."

After vainly attempting to see Tesla, Angier continues reading Borden's diary in candlelight. Angier evokes April 3, 1897, the oldest timeline. His voice mentioning a show at the Orpheum theater gives way to Borden's voice-over: "We were two promising young men at the start of a brilliant career, two young men devoted to an illusion, two young men who never intended to hurt anyone." On these words, the camera pans quickly to the two protagonists, both young and full of energy, sitting in the audience, clapping (Angier does not limp, and Borden's hands are intact). Angier and Borden act as accomplices to Milton, an older magician performing a water tank escape with Angier's wife. This flashback covers Julia's tragic death on stage. Borden disregards Cutter's warning about the knot, with the complicity of Julia signified by a quick exchange of looks. Cutter, realizing something has gone wrong, erupts on the stage, draws the curtain, and tries to save Julia by frantically hammering the glass. When the water flows out, Julia has already died by suffocation. Angier, bent over her body, attempts to revive her and expresses his grief, filmed in closeup. The camera then cuts to Borden, silent, awestruck.

We revert to Angier's writing in his notebook, looking at a portrait of Julia. The following shot reveals that Borden is still reading Angier's diary in his cell. The camera glides from the open page to Borden's smiling face, uttering: "The bloody fool!" Then we move back to the older timeline when Borden meets Sarah, his future wife, for the first time, while he is assisting the great Virgil performing a bird trick. The multiplicity of voices and points of view and the embedded structure enable to shift perspectives, to create a system of echoes and mirror effects, challenging our understanding of the events and raising questions about the true identity of the protagonists.

During the bullet catch scene, Angier interferes with Borden's trick and wounds him severely. The sequence is filtered through Angier's reading of Borden's diary. Borden's voice-over contains clues to the enigma that the spectator, as well as Angier, overlooks. When stating "One half of me swearing blind that I tied a simple knot, the other half convinced that I tied a Langford double. I can never know for sure," he alludes to a divided self, but not to the existence of twins. Hence Angier's puzzled, angry reaction: "How can he not know? He must know what he did!"

Throughout the film, we move along these timelines, going back to Borden reading Angier's diary or Angier reading Borden's. Almost all the events are narrated through the prism of either diary, without any possibility of confirmation, hence a sense of unreliability, highlighted by the suggestion that these "authentic" diaries might have been faked, as Borden contends from his prison cell. David Bordwell writes: "The embedded diaries and blended voice-overs create a tense conversation between the rivals across time and space" (Bordwell 2013, 302).

There are other examples of jumps in the past, by means of mental images, often related to traumatic events such as when Angier, grieving over the loss of Julia, plunges his head in a water basin, as if he tried to experience her agony. The scene is intercut with flashback images of Julia's panicking in the tank, to the sound of gurgling water. Borden remembers happy moments with Sarah, conveyed by flash images. The ultimate revelation is given by means of an objective flashback triggered by the remaining Borden twin's disclosure of his secret to the dying Angier, whom he has just shot in revenge for his brother's hanging.

DOUBLE, SACRIFICE, AND ILLUSION

There are many instances of doubling from the outset. In the original script, two black cats slink their way through the hats in the opening shot, but this was cut in the final film, and the cats only appear later. The two magicians are reflections of one another, both being ambitious, curious, manipulative, and revengeful. They are strongly contrasted. Borden is a proletarian version of the magician, manual and pragmatic, with a cockney accent. It is hinted he might have stayed at a poorhouse as a child. Angier is an aristocrat in disguise, faking an American accent. He has two names, Robert Angier and Lord Caldlow, whose identity is revealed belatedly. He calls himself "The Great Danton," an ironical stage name as Danton was a revolutionary, while Borden calls himself "The Professor." Borden uses his skills while Angier relies on Tesla's machinery. Both magicians are assisted by an *ingénieur*, and they both have a female companion. However, Cutter, Angier's *ingénieur*, is in full view, playing an important part while Borden's is discreet, which adds to the mystery.

We discover late[1] in the film that Borden had a twin brother, Bernard Fallon, his *ingénieur*. The existence of a hidden twin is asserted by Cutter, but his explanation is rejected by Angier as too simple, too obvious. Angier imagines a more sophisticated trick which leads him to a compulsive search for his rival's secret, hence his trip to Colorado. Fallon is often close to Borden, almost always silent, confined at the edge of the frame or off screen, except in the opening scene where he is seen at the trial, waving at Borden. We do not pay much attention to him though he shares everything with Borden, including his private life. Borden shares his wife with Fallon as well as a mistress, Olivia Wenscombe (Scarlett Johansson), as each twin shifts his identity every day, being in turn Borden or Fallon as we discover in the scene with a dying Angier, staged as a montage of past images we have never seen before, illustrating Borden's words: "We were both Fallon. And we were both Borden." We first see Fallon in close shot, almost facing the camera for the first time, then taking off his glasses and his wig. Cut to the two brothers in the same frame, shifting identities, performing on stage, playing the part in turn. We then see one twin cutting off his brother's fingers, with a chisel and hammer, while the victim swigs from a gin bottle and stifles a scream of pain. This reminds the audience of Borden's words: "Simple maybe, but not easy." One image explains one previously seen. As she renews the bandaging of Borden's maimed hand, Sarah wonders why the wound is still bleeding, as if it were fresh. On watching the film again, we can see differences[2] in the behavior of both twins. One is more determined, aggressive, obsessed with revenge, the other quieter, subdued, and inclined to forgive and abandon the feud.

Angier, beyond his dual identity and his stage name, also proves to be multiplied as the Tesla machine, which was supposed only to teleport him, generates clones of himself that he has to get rid of by drowning them: "By depicting the drowned body of one of Angier's doubles in the final shot, Nolan reveals the human cost that creating illusions entails" (McGowan 2012, 110). As the dying Angier confesses in a hoarse whisper: "It took courage to climb in the machine every night not knowing if I'd be the man in the box or the prestige."

In the end, we may wonder who the true Angier is as the magician must get rid of a duplicate every night. The original Angier is sacrificed because he cannot coexist with his proliferating doubles. The last shot of the film tracks along a range of water tanks, but we are only allowed a medium shot glimpse of one of Angier's clones, standing upright with closed eyes,[3] while Cutter's voice utters, "You want to be fooled."

Duality is lastly present through the rivalry between Tesla and Edison. Tesla plays an important part in the book and the film, but the latter gives examples of this rivalry. Tesla's show at the Royal Albert Hall attended by Borden and Angier is interrupted by Edison's men, claiming the show is dangerous. This is denounced by Alley, Tesla's assistant, claiming that this is part of "Edison's campaign against Tesla's superior alternative current." One emissary of Edison shouts that the machine will blow up, triggering a movement of panic among the crowd. During his stay in Colorado, Angier is informed of the presence of two agents spying upon Tesla's experiments. These agents are seen by Angier as they leave the premises of Tesla's laboratory, which they have just destroyed by fire. However, the hotel manager does not disclose the existence of the machine that Tesla built for Angier. Thus duality is explicit, but the confirmation of the existence of the Borden twins is concealed until the end.

GOTHIC TROPES: NOVEL AND FILM

The double motif is a gothic trope, but in the film gothic is underplayed in comparison with the novel. Priest inscribes his work in the gothic tradition. First, he uses the device of embedding in the form of diaries, often found in gothic works like Bram Stoker's *Dracula* (1897). Mary Shelley's *Frankenstein* (1818) is a subtext in both novel and film. Priest highlights the ghost motif in the various narrative arcs. In the Victorian plot, stress is laid on what appears to be supernatural occurrences that later find a rational explanation. At the end of his diary, Borden refers to a nightly visitation by a spectral, yet flesh-and-blood being who tries to stab him with a long-bladed knife. He recognizes Angier, but as an uncanny repulsive creature. He describes an almost weightless, semi-transparent body, exhaling a foul rancid breath, "the rank smell of the grave," speaking in a harsh and horrid whisper. The lexis abounds with terms such as "ghost," "haunting," and "spectre": "He was the phantasm of ultimate terror: the spectre in death of my worst enemy in life" (Priest 2011, 117). This apparently supernatural event is explained when it is narrated in Angier's diary. Angier confirms the aggression (not a dream), but also accounts for his physical appearance in a rational way: "I must have been a wild and dreadful sight. I had been unable to shave or cut my hair for more than two months and my face was gaunt" (Priest 2011, 334). Angier's diary provides another kind of gothic horror, the monstrous transformation of the body, an aspect absent from the film. Because of Borden switching off the Tesla machine, the cloning process was not completed, resulting in the semi ghostliness of the prestige double. Both Angier's avatars, the original and the duplicates, are affected physically. The original Angier is still alive but weakened, while his prestige double is frozen in a half-dead, half-alive condition: "I took on the appearance of spectre. I could be seen but also seen through.... I was to most people a hideous vision of the ghostly underworld" (Priest 2011, 329).

This predicament of both entities coexisting has consequences for the descendant who discovers that Angier is still alive, reunited with his prestige, almost immortal. The gothic mood is highlighted in the description closing the novel, reminiscent of the end of *Frankenstein*: "He stepped out on to the flat ground, hunching his shoulders in the blizzard, then moved to the right, between the trees, down the hill, and out of our sight" (Priest 2011, 360).

The film gets rid of some of the gothic paraphernalia, the trope of monstrous metamorphosis, and erases the references to the diseased body and the macabre, only keeping the motif of Borden's mutilated hand. It expands the double motif but dispenses with the co-existing of the two living Angier entities, retaining the Faustian pact present in the book in Borden's diary. In the film, this pact is dual. It first concerns Borden and his twin brother, who hide their true identities in order to preserve a family secret (gothic trope). It is then illustrated by the contract passed between Angier and Tesla whose spectacular appearance under crackling blue lightning bolts gives him a supernatural, almost diabolical character. As Baillon (2012, 318) notes, there are also parallels with *Dracula*: the central European accent, Angier's arrival similar to that of Jonathan Harker coming to an unknown country, the way he is dropped by the coach driver who does not want to go further. Tesla, like Dracula, is an image of the trickster. His machine evokes, because of electricity, all the scientific apparatus found in gothic cinema, from Rotwang's laboratory in Fritz Lang's *Metropolis* (1927) to James Whale's *Frankenstein* (1931) and beyond. Indeed the "Tesla coil" is often used to characterize the mad scientist's laboratory.[4]

Nolan wishes to tone down the gothic/horrific aspects of the novel. This is why he dispenses with the ghost motif and also with the various bodily transformations. The ultimate revelation is however a gothic variation on the Frankenstein myth. We discover by means of a long shot that Angier has created a double by killing himself repeatedly. He is his own creature contrary to Frankenstein, who created another being. Having duplicated himself with the help of the Tesla machine, he must every night drown his "prestige" who cannot be left alive. We may wonder who the remaining Angier shot by Borden is. It cannot be the original Angier who was drowned during the first performance. So it can only be a clone who keeps the memory of the past event and then knows that he will be drowned next time to enable his prestige to appear at the balcony in front of a mesmerized audience. This murderous cycle is gothic, reminiscent of such cinematic images as the row of beautiful dead women encased in glass sarcophagi in Edgar Ulmer's *The Black Cat* (1934).

STRATEGIES OF REVELATION AND CONCEALMENT IN THE FILM

The spectator is given contradictory statements concerning the true secret of Borden's "Transported Man." While Cutter asserts that the only explanation for Borden's trick is his use of a double, Angier denies it vehemently. Angier's conviction is reinforced by Olivia, who believes only one man is involved: "It *is* the same man. He wears padded gloves to hide his damaged fingers, but if you look closely, you can tell." She later declares her admiration to Borden who is able to perform his illusion with one valid hand.

However, Nolan uses various devices in order to hint at the existence of twin brothers. Clues are disseminated both in the images and the dialogues. We first see Borden and Fallon close to one another, especially during the prison scenes when they are filmed in shot reverse-shot, like mirrored images. An early clue is when Sarah's young nephew expresses his sadness despite the reappearance of the canary displayed by the magician. When Borden tries to reassure him by showing him the living bird in his cage, he exclaims: "But where is his brother?" to which Borden comments: "He is a sharp lad." The boy's acumen is confirmed when we see Borden address the bird: "You're the lucky one tonight," revealing a hidden compartment in the table with the flattened cage and the dead bird inside. A little later, Borden produces a two-headed coin he shows the boy, asking him: "Are you watching closely?" an echo of the opening sequence. The boy looks intensely, watching him flip the coin on both sides while Borden advises him in a serious tone, "Never show anyone. The secret impresses no one. The trick you use it for is everything." All these signs can be understood as a metaphor of the Borden twins' secret and of their predicament.

Another important scene follows, implying concealment and sacrifice, that features the Chinese magician Chung-Ling-Soo (Chao Li Chi). During his show attended by both Angier and Borden, the magician produces a large fishbowl to appear on a table he covered with a shawl in front of him, out of nowhere. While Angier is impressed and claps, he looks at Borden who shows no excitement, merely smiling. Outside they watch the seemingly frail magician hobble to a carriage, helped by two assistants. In fact, Borden has understood that Chung pretends to be weak and disabled in all circumstances in order to hide his actual physical strength: "Total devotion to his art, total self-sacrifice." When we watch the film again, we realize this is a way of alluding to the Borden twins' own devotion to their art, each living a half-life.

Sarah's puzzlement is another clue. She becomes suspicious and ill at ease, reproaching her husband with being at times distant and unloving or on the contrary expressing authentic feelings. When one of the Borden twins expresses his love, she reacts calmly: "Not today. Some days it is not true. Today you don't mean it. Maybe today you are more in love with magic than with me. It's all right. I like to be able to tell the difference. It makes the days it is true mean something." This uncertainty becomes more and more unbearable, causing mental suffering to Sarah who takes to drinking and eventually commits suicide by hanging herself. In that scene, Sarah is associated with the encaged canaries that are present in the room. We shift from a shot on the canaries to a subjective close shot on a coiled rope. The scene crosscuts between images of Sarah looking up at the ceiling, taking the rope, and flash images of Borden dressed up as the "Professor," performing his trick. As Sarah hangs herself, we hear a sharp metallic click that disturbs the birds. The camera stays for a while on Sarah's hanging corpse, adumbrating Borden's execution. The bird motif associates both characters, a metaphor of their sacrifice, a price to pay for public success.

This strategy of concealing important clues while disseminating minor signs or symptoms, both verbal and visual, conveys a sense of trouble and puzzlement, leading the spectator to wrong interpretations regarding Borden's seemingly erratic behavior in particular. This is reinforced by a rhetoric of repetition which keeps up suspense and gradually leads to revelation.

EDITING TECHNIQUES

Some scenes are cut before they end and then are repeated, this time complete, altering the understanding we had of the situation. The scene of Angier's drowning in the glass tank is cut short when Borden enters below stage. We may think that he did nothing to save Angier and is thus guilty of his death, which accounts for his trial and condemnation, with Cutter's testimony. The same scene is repeated, but it is prolonged by Borden's horrified look and subsequent attempts to save Angier from drowning by breaking the glass. It becomes clear that Borden was framed by Angier and that we also were fooled at first, like Cutter was.

Olivia's visit to Borden, following the scene between Angier and Olivia when he asks[5] her to spy upon Borden, is also repeated. In the first staging, while we shift abruptly from Tesla's laboratory to Borden's workshop, the scene is cut just after Borden asks Olivia if she is being truthful to him. A reverse shot closes up on Olivia's silent face. So we do not know her true motivations. When the scene is repeated, through Angier's reading of Borden's diary, it is prolonged, disclosing Olivia's true motivations as she answers Borden's query, the camera closing on her face: "The truth is that I loved him, I stood by him, and he sent me to you as he would send a stagehand to pick up his shirts. I hate him for that." Through Olivia's revelation, confirmed by Borden's diary, we learn that she was true to Borden, enabling him to ruin Angier's act and exhibit his "double" on stage tied, gagged, and hanging from a rope. The first test of the teleportation machine is staged twice. In the first scene, a cut prevents us from seeing Angier shooting his clone. In the second, we are given the full scene that appears as cold-blooded murder, degrading even more Angier's image. This fast-edited sequence relies on shot reverse-shot, alternating the two protagonists. While the clone first appears ominously in the frame filmed from the back or as a shadow on the edge of the frame, he then is seen as a helpless victim, facing the camera as he is shot dead by the original Angier, his back now to the camera, thus inverting the initial positions. These gradual revelations account for Cutter's changing sides and also for the spectator's wavering in terms of identification, siding more and more with Borden.

CINEMA AS MAGIC, MAGIC AS CINEMA

Nolan stresses the link between magician and film director, and implicitly the metafilmic dimension of his film: "*The Prestige* is about film making; it is also intended to suggest how the film itself is spooling its narrative out to the audience. We want people really to be aware of the effect the film is having on them as it is unfolding before their eyes" (DVD bonus interview). The director usually refuses to display overt references to the cinematic process. In *Batman Begins* Bruce Wayne's parents, instead of watching *The Mark of Zorro* (1940), attend an opera, *Mefistofele*. In *The Prestige*, there are few references, one of them being the pan shot on the alignment of bird cages which evokes the unrolling of a film. Borden's trick, moving an object through time and space instantaneously, is an equivalent of the film editing process where a straight cut enables a shift in space or time. *The Prestige* exploits this, cutting between embedded memories and narratives. As Olson states: "The necessity of bridging the gaps between discontinuous frames, shots and scenes is represented in *The Prestige* by Borden's red ball and Angier's silk hat, which the magicians use in their 'Transported Man' illusions to imply continuity between the Borden twins and between Angier and his double" (Olson 2015, 53). Thus, the film demonstrates the power of the cinematic medium without jeopardizing the immersive process that Nolan stages in all his films.

By reproducing in the film structure the three stages of the magic trick, the pledge, the turn, and the prestige, Nolan establishes a parallel between the illusionist and the film director. As Ann Heilmann remarks: "Nolan can be compared to a conjuror: like the audience of a stage magician, we know from the start that it is all an act, but judge the quality of the performance by its ability to deceive and mystify us" (Heilmann 2009, 18–19).

At another level, Nolan asserts his passionate love of celluloid. Most effects are mechanical and made in camera. There is also an attempt at realism. Though London is reconstituted in downtown Los Angeles, Nolan discarded studio shooting and strove to find authentic locations that could be used to figure out a turn-of-the-century London. Four old proscenium theaters were rearranged to stand in for London West End venues: the Los Angeles theater (used for the opening scene), the Tower Theatre (the *Pantages* where Borden performs), the Palace, and the Belasco (the deserted theater where Angier performs his "New Transported Man" illusion to Ackerman). One specific set was built, the space below stage with the steam-powered hydraulics machinery that makes the illusions work (Shone 2020, 206).

Nolan wanted to keep the lighting simple, natural light whenever possible. His cinematographer, Wally Pfister, used anamorphic lenses and a handheld camera which breaks the conventional approach to period films and gives a documentary-like style to some scenes: "Chris wanted to give actors total freedom of movement. That meant the camera was on my shoulder the whole picture, which allowed us to handle the entire execution in a very organic way: the actors were free to move around however they wanted, and I followed" (Holben 2006, 69).

Borden and Angier represent different images of the magician. Borden stands for the creative artist devoted to his public, the craftsman who masters all the techniques and takes risks but lacks showmanship. Angier is less skillful, but he is a born showman who knows how to dress up a trick and make it breathtaking and spectacular, as is shown in the film by Ackerman's reaction when he discovers Angier (his "prestige") right behind him: "Pardon me, but it has been a long time since I have seen real magic." At the same time, Angier's trick is dependent on technology, and as Cutter states: "It is pure science." Angier's "New Transported Man" illusion also runs the risk of becoming repetitive and losing its magic "aura."

Through the staging of a deadly rivalry, Nolan explores filmmaking in Hollywood, the dangers of success, the hubris and darker impulses of obsessive artists. The two illusionists stand for two images of the filmmaker and filmmaking. Borden may represent the independent filmmaker who uses few tricks, while Angier and the Tesla apparatus would stand for the big filming machine that makes a lavish use of spectacular effects and CGI. With *The Prestige*, Nolan tries to bridge the gap between two models: a cinema of continuity, transparency, and immersion and a cinema of discontinuity, opaqueness, and reflexivity.

Even if our sympathy gradually shifts from Angier's mourning over his wife's death to Borden expressing dedication to his art as magician as well as love for his daughter, the best definition of magic and cinema is provided by the former in his dying words: "The audience knows the truth. . . . But if you can fool them, even for a second, you need to make them wonder. Then you got to see something very special, extraordinary. You really don't know? [Borden stares silently at Angier]. It was the look on their faces." Cutter's last words are addressed to the spectator who has just finished viewing the film and is invited to watch it again, more "closely."

NOTES

1. The existence of the twins is disclosed early in the novel.
2. In the novel, there are slight differences in writing style and an ambiguous use of the word "I."
3. Awaiting revival like Dracula? Or rather "a waste product of the artistic process" (McGowan 2012, 110).

4. Kenneth Strickfaden, who conceived Frankenstein's laboratory in Whale's films, was influenced by Tesla's instruments.
5. In the novel Julia offers to work for Borden in order to find his secret.

REFERENCES

Baillon, Jean-François. 2012. "Itérabilité et hantise dans le cinéma contemporain: le retour impensable." In *Persistances gothiques dans la littérature et les arts*, edited by Lauric Guillaud and Gilles Menegaldo, 310–326. Paris: Bragelonne.
Bordwell, David, and Thompson, Kristin. 2013. *Film Art, An Introduction*. New York: McGraw-Hill.
Heilmann, Ann. 2009–2010. "Doing it with Mirrors: Neo-Victorian Metatextual Magic in *Affinity*, *The Prestige* and *The Illusionist*." *Neo-Victorian Studies* 2, no. 2: 18–42.
Holben, Jay. 2006. "Lords of Illusion." *American Cinematographer* 87, no. 11 (November): 64–75.
McGowan, Todd. 2012. *The Fictional Christopher Nolan*. Austin: University of Texas Press.
Olson, Jonathan. 2015. "Nolan's Immersive Allegories of Filmmaking in *Inception* and *The Prestige*." In *The Cinema of Christopher Nolan*, ed. Jacqueline Furby and Stuart Joy, 44–61. London: Wallflower Press.
Priest, Christopher. 2008. *The Magic, the Story of a Film*. Grimgrin Studio, Hastings: UK.
Priest, Christopher. 2011. *The Prestige*. London: Gollancz.
Shone, Tom. 2020. *The Nolan Variations: The Movies, Marvels and Mysteries of Christopher Nolan*. New York: Alfred A. Knopf.

Chapter 4

The Trauma Chronotope in Nolan's *Dunkirk* and *Inception*

Time, Space, and Trauma

Fran Pheasant-Kelly

Christopher Nolan's films are known for their consistent narrative and visual themes, particularly trauma and subjective memory, which are commonly connected to distortions of time and space and often produce narrative complexity. As a result, they are frequently described as examples of "puzzle" or "mind-game" films. Thomas Elsaesser makes this connection explicit, stating that "mind-game films tend to revolve around mentally or psychologically unstable characters, whose aberrations fall into three major types, paranoia, schizophrenia, and amnesia . . . the pathologies are often connected to a personal past, mostly a traumatic incident that keeps returning or insists on manifesting itself in the present" (2009, 24–25). He also identifies a temporal element in such films whereby there is an "insistence on temporality as a separate dimension of consciousness and identity" (2009, 21). However, while Elsaesser implies a multi-spatial aspect in mind-puzzle films through reference to "forking narratives" (2009, 21), his discussion does not consider more specific spatial details as they connect time and trauma. Moreover, if several other studies (to be discussed shortly) identify the temporal, spatial, and traumatic qualities of Nolan's films, to date, these have yet to be linked together.

In relation to Nolan's films, I argue that irrespective of narrative complexity, trauma is inevitably interwoven with space and time, generating what is termed here a "trauma chronotope." The chronotope, as Mikhail Bakhtin (1981) postulated it, refers to a connection between space and time in literary sources, whereby spatial and temporal indicators are fused into one carefully thought-out, concrete whole. Time, as it were, thickens, takes on flesh, becomes artistically visible; likewise, space becomes charged and responsive to the movements of time, plot and history. The intersection of axes and fusion of indicators characterizes the artistic chronotope. (1981, 84)

Following Bakhtin's (1981) concept, this essay suggests an equivalent visual connection between space and time in Nolan's films that inevitably implicates trauma. Coincidentally, such a connection is identical in *Dunkirk* and *Inception* (2010). In each film, three separate narrative spaces, united through a singular traumatic scenario, unfold with different temporalities. One might explain this relationship through trauma cinema's spatial and temporal aspects, typically, the flashback, although there are several other symptoms of real trauma that evidence such a correlation.

While Nolan's narrative spaces are usually either constricted and claustrophobic or otherwise, expansive and disorientating, drowning or near-drowning experiences are a common feature, and are evident in both films considered here. *Inception* is characteristic of Nolan's preoccupation with space whereby not only are its diegetic spaces multiplied, but its narrative structure involves several plots unfolding simultaneously and is complicated by traumatic flashbacks and intrusive memories, the underpinning trauma connecting them being the suicide of the protagonist's wife. In addition, physical coordination and architecture within the various spaces do not follow the usual rules of verisimilitude. These plots involve multiple dream layers (dreams within dreams), enabling its protagonists to operate in different settings simultaneously. Each dream narrative advances in causal fashion but at different rates, so that time progressively slows down through the dream layers.

Generally, *Dunkirk* (2017) follows a more usual linear pattern but is likewise complicated by its tracing of multiple protagonists, their synchronicity regularly signaled through parallels in their physical surroundings. For example, a scene of a downed pilot sinking in the sea is crosscut with soldiers drowning in a submerged ship, their respective mise-en-scène and framing conveying identical feelings of claustrophobia. Other times, vast expanses of ocean, sky, and beach are rendered disorienting through subjective camera that assumes a pilot's negotiation of the air while under attack, and the perspectives of drowning soldiers in upturned torpedoed ships. Time in such scenarios is, like *Inception*, distorted and quantified in terms of survival rather than chronicity. Focusing on these two films, this chapter utilizes trauma theory and Bakhtin's discussion of the chronotope to propose that temporal and spatial perspectives are not merely fundamental to Nolan's style but are integrally affiliated with trauma, thus comprising a trauma chronotope.

TRAUMA, TIME, AND SPACE IN CINEMA

While there is significant scholarship concerning trauma, time, and space in film, there is little consideration of these interconnecting aspects in terms of Nolan's productions. Nonetheless, there are multiple references to trauma in his work, illustrated, for example, by Stuart Joy's (2020) examination of his canon, as well as academic studies of specific Nolan films (McGowan, 2011; Pheasant-Kelly, 2015; Russo, 2014; Stratton, 2019). Here, Joy considers the chronological aspects of his films in terms of trauma but does not explicitly define the connections between space, time, and trauma. Crucially, however, he notes that "through the operation of [Freud's concept of] *Nachträglichkeit*, time becomes visible" (2020, 41),[1] this factor of visibility particularly correlating with Bakhtin's notion of the chronotope. Todd McGowan too focuses on the intersections of time and trauma but extends this across a range of directors' work to consider what he terms "atemporal cinema" (2011), referring to *Memento* (2002) as an example. At the same time, he suggests that cinema is inherently disposed to a temporal consciousness and points out that "changing a film's running time . . . effectively changes a film, whereas the performance time of a dance or play inevitably varies, at least by a few seconds" (McGowan, 2011, 5). More specifically, he explains that "the atemporal cinematic mode does not distort forward-moving time simply because of the demands of the story. . . . The distortion of time takes place in the filmic discourse . . . ; that is, it occurs in the way that the story is told, not in the story itself" (2011, 8). In this sense, the argument here differs because *Inception* is based on distortions of time in the story itself. Likewise, the various intersecting narrative strands of *Dunkirk* unfold along different timelines, although this is less visible than in *Inception*. What is distinct, however, about the trauma chronotope in Nolan's films is the way that it ties narrative strands together. As Martin Flanagan notes, with reference to Bakhtin, "chronotopes not only link disparate parts of narrative material together and play a part in the way in which we experience the text but provide the very 'ground essential for the showing-forth, the representability of events'" (2009, 58).

As well as reference to trauma, there is considerable scholarship on the intersection of space and time in Nolan's films (Cameron and Misek, 2014; Clarke, 2002; Furby, 2015; Kealey, 2015; Thorne, 2014), particularly as it informs his complex storytelling (Buckland, 2015). In addition, Margaret Toth identifies a potential noir chronotope in *Memento* through its time-space connections but does not link this directly to trauma, although she goes on to suggest that "Leonard's present is repeatedly, if fleetingly, punctuated by glimpses of his lost home, what I would describe not as a chronotope but as a mnemotope, or memory-place" (2015, 78). Robbie Goh too discusses

Memento in the context of a postmodern chronotope "that struggles to express the intensely dislocating experience of time-space encountered by the subject in the late capitalist, digital era" (2008, 63) and suggests that such dislocation finds cultural form in a range of productions. Therefore, while there is general recognition of the importance of time, space, and trauma to Nolan's canon, and limited discussion of a chronotope in *Memento*, to date, there is no suggestion of a trauma chronotope as it connects these three parameters.

THE CHRONOTOPE

Bakhtin restricted his concept of the chronotope to literary forms, but it is relevant to Nolan's films because of the way their filmic timelines and spaces are interdependent. Flanagan (2009) provides one of the few attempts to reframe Bakhtin's theory for cinema, suggesting, like Robert Stam (1992), that the concept is particularly suited to film. As Flanagan notes:

> The processes of transmission and reception of film are centred on the manipulation of time and space; at a particular place and a specific time, a visual representation of spatial reality unfolds at around 24 frames per second, projected onto a screen with definite spatial parameters. It is in its ability to show spatial changes through time, the capacity to represent motion figuratively, that film is set apart from other forms of expression, such as the novel or painting. (2009, 56)

And, as Stam furthers, this is "quite apart from the fictive time/space specific films might construct" (1992, 11). Flanagan clarifies the three main manifestations of the chronotope, namely, as that which "demarcates stable generic forms"; "a more local rendering of time and space" that includes chronotopic motifs; and lastly, where "the chronotope is drawn together with dialogism in postulating a chronotopic element in reading" (2009, 57). The chronotope in Nolan's films suggested here is not necessarily generically or historically motivated nor related to dialogism, but is, rather, thematically orientated through the motif of trauma whereby time and space are related to trauma and where time is rendered visible through specific representations of space. In this case, the spectator does not experience an actual shift in film (running) time but nevertheless may become disorientated through visual and narrative strategies. Moreover, tangible slowing up (through slow-motion editing) does occur in *Inception* while it is merely implied in *Dunkirk*. As Alexandra Ganser, Julia Pühringer, and Marcus Rheindorf explain, "the chronotope serves as a means of measuring how, in a particular age, genre, or text, real historical time and space as well as fictional time and space are articulated in relation to one another" (2006, 2).

TRAUMA, TIME, AND SPACE

If the precise relationship of time and space to trauma varies across Nolan's films, it is invariably implicated with trauma as a central organizing theme. This fictional connection reflects the temporal and spatial incoherence associated with real trauma which entails a range of symptoms including intrusive distressing memories of the traumatic event, disturbing dreams related to the traumatic event, dissociative reactions, avoidance, emotional numbing, hypervigilance, and an exaggerated startle response (American Psychological Association, 2022). Several of these symptoms are inherently linked to space and time; for example, nightmares and intrusive memories as well as flashbacks bridge the past and present both temporally and spatially. In this respect, Elsaesser notes that one of the features of trauma is the "difference between psychic temporality and linear chronological time" (2001, 197). For Elsaesser, "'[t]rauma' thus not only names the delay between an event and its (persistent, obsessive) return, but also a reversal of affect and meaning across this gap in time. . . . Besides involving repetition and iteration, the traumatic event links several temporalities" (2001, 197). Like Joy, Elsaesser also implicates space in this temporal bridging through reference to the Freudian concept of *Nachträglichkeit*, noting its significations of "shifts in temporality and space" (2001, 197).

Certain dissociative symptoms, such as depersonalization and derealization, have further temporal and spatial implications. As Richard McNally notes, derealization involves "a strange, dreamlike sense that one's surroundings are unreal; depersonalization, a sense of being disconnected from one's body; a sense of time slowing down or speeding up" (2003, 172). These elements are discernible in Nolan's films, and while the exact format that they take in real-world trauma may not translate exactly into cinematic form, nonetheless, time and space structure his narratives such that trauma is a persistent aspect.

THE TRAUMA CHRONOTOPE IN *DUNKIRK*

Dunkirk recounts the Second World War evacuation of Allied Forces from the titular town as enemy troops close in and thus reflects a significant historical trauma. Here, Nolan employs a distinctive cinematographic style and mise-en-scène to represent this moment. In this regard, one might argue that the film follows Stam's appraisal concerning the chronotope of the novel. As Stam states,

> The chronotope mediates between two orders of experience and discourse, the historical and the artistic, providing fictional environments where historically specific constellations of power are made visible. . . . These concrete spatio-temporal structures . . . are correlatable with the real historical world but not equitable with it because they are always mediated by art. (1992, 11)

At the same time as tracing events at Dunkirk, the film follows the air crews as they attack the enemy above the Channel to protect the men below while large numbers of small boats manned by both soldiers and civilians attempt a rescue mission. The relationship between space and time is paramount to the narrative structure, with Nolan, in an interview, revealing that the narrative is split into three sections told through differing points of view based on land, sea, and air (Stolworthy, 2017). As well as the desperate attempts to rescue 400,000 soldiers under fire from closing enemy ranks, the film also focuses on the experiences of individual shell-shocked soldiers. These various traumatic episodes are inherently linked to the space-time features of the film. The time aspect is explicitly conveyed in the opening scenes through the escalating sound of a ticking clock as the camera tracks behind a group of British soldiers who are ambushed by Germans in a French street and attempt to evade enemy gunfire. The repetitive ticking motif reverberates throughout the soundtrack, often accelerating in pace and growing louder at moments of extreme tension. Framing the soldiers in long shot from a rear-view perspective, the sequence reveals the empty street as a site of physical constriction, offering little shelter, with all but only one survivor, Tommy Jensen (Fionn Whitehead), a young British private. This sense of oppression—which intensifies as the film progresses—is accentuated as he escapes via back gardens and alleyways that are tightly framed, before suddenly his point of view opens onto the vast beaches of Dunkirk, providing a marked contrast to the previous sequence. Indeed, the screenplay describes the scene as "the longest, widest beach he's ever seen" (Nolan, 2017). This juxtaposition of spatial constriction and openness persists and escalates throughout the film as it continuously intercuts between the three perspectives of those fighting on land, air, and sea. The film is accordingly intertitled with these three locations and the timelines allocated to each location, "The Mole—One Week," "The Sea—One Day," and "The Air—One Hour," as described by Nolan in the aforementioned interview.

The mole refers to a breakwater that extends out to sea to enable larger vessels to rescue the soldiers. It becomes significant as a site of both hope and despair and forms the backdrop for the opening beach sequence. Here, the film follows Jensen as the scene opens out onto the beach, the camera sweeping round in a semicircle in extreme long shot from left to right as he surveys the lines of soldiers waiting to be rescued. He then encounters another soldier, who is burying a body in the sand and whom he befriends, although there is no dialogue between them. Subsequently, as Jensen watches the wounded being stretchered toward an awaiting hospital ship, his gaze settles on the mole where the ship is anchored. Immediately hereafter, the waiting soldiers come under Luftwaffe attack, the vulnerability afforded by the open stretches of sand being hinted at in the framing. For instance, just prior to the first overhead attack of the film, the beach is framed so that a series of vertical structures dissects the frame, with a slow zoom in to the beach between these vertical bars. As the men come under fire, Jensen throws himself to the ground, a ground-level static camera framing him in the foreground as the air-fire hits other soldiers in the background in quick succession, the line of fire progressively approaching Jensen. This ground-level shot is notable in that it integrates space, time, and trauma, emphasized through the sequence of firing that draws closer (via background to foreground action) to both Jensen, who is clutching his helmet, and the spectator.

A cut to an English seaside town signals the second key space of the film—the sea. Here, we learn that the Navy has requisitioned private leisure yachts and small boats in a bid to get closer to the shores of Dunkirk for the rescue mission. The film then introduces its third key space, the air, where a sense of urgency is quickly established as a squadron of three Spitfire pilots are instructed to check their fuel supplies before they set off on their mission and to "save enough fuel to get back." The spectator is subsequently reminded that time in the air is limited by frequent references to a broken fuel gauge in one of the aircraft and a sense that fuel is running out. Moreover, the expansiveness of the beach scenes, which renders the soldiers lined up waiting for evacuation vessels completely exposed, is echoed in the aircraft sequences. Here, vast stretches of sea and sky are likewise linked to vulnerability while equally tight composition of the three Allied aircraft provides equivalent moments of visual stricture. In short, expansive spaces are constantly reframed to suggest constriction.

This constriction is particularly evident as the narrative returns to Jensen and his newfound comrade, Gibson, when they attempt to deliver a soldier injured during the aforementioned overhead attack to the hospital ship, about to depart. In a protracted sequence, they run with the stretcher across the beach, camera panning alongside, toward the mole to reach the ship's ramp. However, their path is blocked by hundreds of soldiers and their route is constantly impeded, the time imperative here being the fact that the ship is leaving imminently—the viewer is cued numerous times to this fact by the various cut-off points signaled by the characters, including shouts of "about to leave!," "that's two minutes—you've missed it!," and "ready on the stern!" together with the sounds of horns blasting. In addition, the extra-diegetic soundtrack gathers pace as the camera rapidly intercuts between Jensen and Gibson (filmed with handheld camera variously in side-on long shot and close-up), the ship's officers, and the soldiers queued up on the mole as the two attempt to deliver the wounded soldier. The potency of the sequence is further enhanced by increasingly rapid editing and heightened character movements—for example, as Jensen and Gibson race toward the ship's ramp, the wounded soldier's head swings violently from side to side and is emphasized by the low camera position immediately adjacent to him. Finally, they succeed in their mission but are then ordered off the ship (narratively, because they themselves are not wounded). This scene (along with numerous others) evidences how, as Flanagan describes, "time and space, then, are the main constituents of film form, elevating the chronotope to an essential factor in any study of how cinematic texts create narrative effects" (2009, 57). At the same time as this frantic race across the beach, further crosscutting reveals that the hundreds of small boats on the English coast that have been requisitioned by the Navy have set off in a bid to facilitate the evacuation. The film thereafter intercuts between the soldiers at Dunkirk, those at sea, and those flying Spitfires above. In each scenario, time is made palpable while an emphasis on space persists, either through its cinematographic and narrative constriction or via attention to isolation and vulnerability in vast open expanses.

This vulnerability becomes apparent in the focus on one of the civilian boats requisitioned by the army and skippered by Mr. Dawson (Mark Rylance), his son, Peter (Tom Glynn-Carney), and their young hired hand, George (Barry Keoghan), whereby long shots and extreme long shots visualize the boat at sea to show its isolation. Concurrently, the camera crosscuts to frame the three Spitfires mid-air and then to each individual pilot—here, the camera cuts between their point of view of the control panels and rearview mirrors, and close-ups of their faces within the cockpit—again, attention is drawn to their spatial constriction which is exaggerated by tight framing. The time perspective becomes increasingly discernible in that their limited amount of fuel affords them an exact amount of flying time—as noted, this is repeatedly highlighted through attention to the fuel gauges, especially the fact that one of the pilots' gauges is broken. The first of the Spitfires is then downed as they come under aerial attack.

Crosscutting returns to the scene of the two friends, Jensen and Gibson, who had initially attempted to board the first-aid ship illicitly—however, this is bombed and sinks. The soldiers jump overboard while the wounded drown, and the survivors are transferred to another vessel. Here, they are directed below deck, although Gibson stays on deck, with Jensen telling another soldier that "he's looking for a quick way out in case we go down." Overall, there is a repeated reluctance to go below deck, signaling a potential connection between space and trauma. Below deck, imagery is tightly framed in close-ups and extreme close-ups, generating a sense of extreme claustrophobia. Gibson's anxiety proves well founded as the ship is torpedoed with those below deck becoming quickly submerged. He manages to open a hatch, and several escape while others drown. The screen cuts to black before underwater shots of the soldiers frantically struggling below deck intercut with imagery of them swimming underwater in the dark. Muffled screams and sounds of explosions add to the chaos. Subsequently, low-angle shots are directed toward the surface of the sea, the constricted spaces of the rescue vessel now a site of death and trauma.

Meanwhile, Dawson's boat rescues a man (Cillian Murphy) crouched on the hull of a partly submerged vessel. "He's shell-shocked George. He's not himself, he may never be himself again," Dawson tells George, using a term for trauma utilized by Freud in reference to World War One soldiers and the war neuroses ([1955] 2001, 217). When invited to go below deck, the shell-shocked soldier refuses, Dawson explaining to Peter that "he feels safer on deck, you would too if you'd been bombed," reiterating the fear of enclosed spaces displayed earlier by Gibson. Subsequently, the camera switches to the aircrew and again there is a verbal reminder of their remaining fuel—"40 gallons"—accompanied by a close-up of a watch, resonating with Nolan's preoccupation with time and echoing identical close-ups in *Inception*.[2] Here, the Spitfires come under further attack, the camera tilting through 90 degrees during their aerial maneuvers, creating disorientating spatial effects (again, akin to those in *Inception*) with one of the crew, Collins (Jack Lowden), ditching into the ocean. An extreme overhead shot from the perspective of the remaining Spitfire sees Dawson's boat, *Moonstone*, near the downed aircraft.

Aboard the civilian boat, the shell-shocked soldier becomes agitated when learning they are heading to Dunkirk and accidentally knocks George down the steps below deck. We later learn that George has sustained a brain injury and is unable to see, while in the air above, increasingly extreme close-ups of Farrier (Tom Hardy), the remaining Spitfire pilot, reveal his growing concern about the aircraft's smashed fuel gauge, magnifying the fact that fuel is running low. Overall, each of the sea, land, and air spaces are marked by traumatic events that are time limited.

Jensen and Gibson, along with another soldier Alex (Harry Styles), then join a group striding purposefully across the beach to board a grounded trawler (beyond the Allied perimeter) with the intention of waiting for the tide to come in to refloat the vessel. While they hide inside the trawler, the enemy begins to use the boat as target practice but machine gun it when they realize it is occupied. The rising tide causes the trawler to temporarily refloat before it begins to sink. In the meantime, Collins, the downed pilot, successfully lands on the ocean, although the cockpit is jammed, and he is unable to escape. Imagery inside the cockpit as it fills with water intercuts with that inside the damaged trawler, which is also becoming submerged, creating a spatial analogy alongside a sense of time running out for both. Once more, claustrophobic, tightly framed close-ups emphasize spatial constriction while time becomes a crucial variable in their survival. Throughout the film therefore temporality is rendered palpable in reference to trauma, through either diminishing fuel supplies or near-drowning experiences. As Bakhtin notes, "the chronotope, functioning as the primary means for materializing time in space, emerges as a center for concretizing representation" (1981, 250).

Once more, Jensen manages to escape the sinking trawler and attempts to climb onto another vessel which too is attacked from the air and finds himself swimming in oil, before Farrier shoots down an enemy fighter which crashes into the oil spill, igniting it. Again, Nolan employs underwater shots of bodies drowning beneath the burning oil to create a disorientating space where survival is measured in time. The closing scenes of the film witness the evacuation, first signaled by a medium close-up of Commander Bolton (Kenneth Branagh) as we see his eyes sweep across the horizon. The scene cuts to his perspective disclosing indistinct movement on the horizon before a point of view via his binoculars reveals hundreds of small boats approaching. These succeed in evacuating thousands of soldiers, who receive a heroes' welcome when they return home. Meanwhile, Farrier, the remaining airborne pilot, runs out of fuel and drifts down outside the Allied perimeter, the ticking sound again becoming prominent as he is captured by Germans and further reinforcing the film's space-time motif.

INCEPTION

Unlike *Dunkirk*, *Inception* is entirely fictionalized, and while it typifies the mind-game film, like *Dunkirk*, its narrative structure involves several plotlines with their associated spaces unfolding simultaneously, each liable to time constraints. It centers on the main character, Dom Cobb (Leonardo DiCaprio), a corporate spy who can infiltrate other characters' dreams and steal their ideas. In this case, he is commissioned to *implant* ideas (a process known as inception) in the business adversary, Robert Fischer (Cillian Murphy), of executive Saito (Ken Watanabe).[3] The intention is to devise a series of dreams within dreams, enabling Cobb's team to penetrate more deeply into Fischer's unconscious, narratively necessary to successfully implant the idea. As payment, Saito arranges Cobb's return to the United

States to live with his children from whom he has been separated because of allegations that he has murdered his wife. It transpires that she has in fact committed suicide and framed Cobb for her murder, which, together with Cobb's separation from his children, forms the film's traumatic core. This trauma is intimated in the opening scenes which witness an extreme close-up of Cobb washed up on a beach (in a dream space termed "limbo," described by Cobb as "raw, infinite subconscious") before a low-angle shot from his perspective looks up toward two children playing, their backs turned to him, and the scene unfolding in slow motion as if to suggest memory. A cut to an Asian-style interior, where Cobb now sits at a table opposite an old man, adds little clarification. "Are you here to kill me?" asks the old man, before the scene appears to flash-backward in time. Again, the viewer is cued minimally to the reasons for this but must assume that the events are unfolding in flashback since the two characters occupy the same location yet now appear more youthful. Their ensuing discussion of "idea extraction" in dreams begins the film's exposition.

The significance of the children in the opening scene becomes evident when Cobb later telephones them and they ask, "When are you coming home, Daddy?" Thereafter, Cobb's wife, Mal (Marion Cotillard), turns up in almost every sequence, infiltrating each dream layer related to the inception scenario as well as repeatedly materializing in flashbacks and intrusive memories. These images directly reflect Cobb's trauma—as Richard McNally explains, "There are several ways that people reexperience trauma in memory: intrusive recollections, nightmares, flashbacks, and psycho-physiologic reactivity to reminders of the event" (2003, 105). The death of his wife and the desire to see his children drive overall narrative causality, particularly with respect to time constraints, and bind the various dream layers to form a time-space imperative. This is first apparent during the inception sequence, which is orchestrated to occur during an airplane flight whose lengthy flight time is signaled as being crucial to the inception taking place. Here, both Fischer and Cobb's team are sedated in order to access multiple dream layers. These dream layers constitute the three key spaces of the film, the uppermost dream unfolding in a city, the second in a hotel, and the third in a hospital amid a snow-covered mountain landscape, the visual distinctions between their respective mise-en-scène serving to guide the viewer. At one point, Cobb and his new dream architect, Ariadne (Ellen Page), enter a fourth deeper state of consciousness, namely the aforementioned limbo, with each of these dream states requiring a synchronized "kick" (usually a physical jolt such as a fall) to return the dreamers to reality.

Akin to the time-space elements of *Dunkirk*, each dream narrative advances in linear fashion although here they unfold at different rates, so that the first dream state (the city, where Cobb's inception team is located in a vehicle that veers off a bridge into a river) often visually displays action in slow- or extreme slow-motion, whereas the deepest dream state progresses at a faster pace. This diegetic temporal incongruity is explained as resulting from acceleration in brain function to twenty times normal during each dream state. As a result, one week in the uppermost dream layer of the city equates to six months in the hotel and ten years in the mountain landscape. The ten-hour flight will therefore accommodate extensive activity in the various dream states, especially at the lowest level in order that the inception can take place and Cobb can be reunited with his children. The difference from *Dunkirk* is that this temporal stretching is made visible through editing techniques as well as the obvious aging of characters. Indeed, Cobb recounts to Ariadne that he and his wife spent fifty years in limbo, which equated to only five hours of real time, so that while they appeared to age, on return to reality, they had not.

Having been commissioned by Saito with the task of inception, Cobb flies to Paris to employ Ariadne, the film's causal-logic and spatio-temporal aspects at this stage appearing conventional. Even so, as Cobb questions her about how they came to be at their present location (they appear to be in a Parisian street café), the slow-motion collapse of the surrounding buildings indicates that they (and the spectator) are in a dream state, leading to viewer and character uncertainties about their spatial position.[4] Moreover, as Cobb and Ariadne awaken (from the Paris scene), she realizes they have been asleep for only five minutes, Cobb revealing that five minutes in reality equates to one hour in a dream state. Visually, extreme slow-motion effects convey the discrepancies in time, making time perceptible in line with Bakhtin's concept of the chronotope: "Time becomes, in effect, palpable and visible; the chronotope makes narrative events concrete, makes them take on flesh, causes blood to flow in their veins" (1981, 251). When Ariadne and Cobb subsequently return to the Paris dream, the physical architecture of the mise-en-scène is distorted so that the surrounding city streets seem to rise and fold over them while, at one point, the two appear to be walking along a street that is vertically rather than horizontally orientated. The film therefore manipulates not only time but also space itself. Moreover, as Ariadne and Cobb navigate Paris's dream spaces, its structure continues to shift, producing a perpetual state of spatial and temporal indeterminacy.

Crucially, the film at this point invokes images of Mal, although Cobb repeatedly visualizes Mal in the form of intrusive memories and traumatic flashbacks, including the scene of her suicide. In this scenario, Mal stabs Ariadne (death in a dream causes the dreamer to awaken), leading Ariadne to tell Arthur (Joseph Gordon-Levitt), who is managing the mission, that "Cobb has some serious problems that he's tried to bury down there," referring to Cobb's traumatized state. This becomes clear in a later sequence where Ariadne encounters Cobb alone, hooked up to the dreaming apparatus, and decides to join him. In the dream, Ariadne finds herself in an elevator and, when she descends to a lower floor, witnesses Cobb and Mal alone together. When Cobb and Ariadne ascend to the uppermost floor, they see Cobb's children and wife on a beach, Ariadne realizing that these are traumatic memories rather than dreams, with each floor of the elevator corresponding to different memories of his family. In fact, the image of his two children with their backs turned to him initially seen in the opening scenes recurs throughout the dream layers. In a cinematic flashback (as opposed to a traumatic flashback), Cobb explains to Ariadne that limbo became Mal's reality, and that she had become possessed by the idea that to get back to reality, they had to kill themselves.

In the ensuing inception sequence, Cobb encounters Mal in each dream layer, and notably, in a return to limbo where she begs him to stay. At this point, he confesses to Mal that he implanted the idea that her world was not real, but then tells her that he must let her go. In sum, he addresses his guilt and overcomes the trauma of her suicide. Here, he also locates Saito, returning to the opening scenes of the film.

Because the overall motivation of the film is to implant artificial thoughts into Fischer's mind during the ten-hour flight (and thus reunite Cobb with his children), there is continual tension created by the shortness of time available, replicating the urgency of the time-space relationship evident in *Dunkirk*. As a result, each dream state ultimately depends on the falling van in the topmost dream layer (everything must happen before the van hits the water—the vital kick—because the team must go back up each dream state before they can awaken in the reality of the flight). The film's complexity and obsession with time is ultimately concerned with inception of the idea in order that Cobb's trauma can be resolved.

Furthermore, as in the Paris scene, the spaces of the dream states are continuously liable to surreal effects. For example, in the uppermost dream state, the team is ambushed on the city streets when their vehicle collides unexpectedly with a freight train (this arising narratively because of Fischer's subconscious defenses), and when the van later veers and topples over a bridge into the river, tremors from the van as it comes under fire and crashes (seen in slow motion) cause analogous reverberations in the deeper dream states. For instance, the hotel spaces and its *mise-en-scène* are liable to disruption, with gravity appearing to shift (framed in close-up, the surfaces of drinks in glasses lie at canted angles rather than being horizontal) and glasses clinking at the bar as they slide in their racks, the second layer reflecting the chaos in the uppermost city dream state. As a result, the hotel corridors of the second dream layer appear to upturn owing to a "gravitational shift" triggered by the frantic city events, these spatial disturbances resulting in a disruption of narrative conventions (such as the 180-degree rule, and the eye-line match) that resemble the underwater and aerial scenes in *Dunkirk*. At the third dream level, an avalanche is triggered. In each dream state, rapid editing and constant changes in camera framing and angles accentuate the spatial instability. The same extremes of space that occur in *Dunkirk* are here articulated across the dream states with extreme long shots and long shots characterizing the broad expanses of the mountain complex, while close-ups and mid-shots dominate the hotel and van dream states. These contrasts are especially noticeable in relation to the falling van which is repeatedly seen in extreme long shots that cut to claustrophobic interior close-ups, especially when it hits the water and the dreaming passengers are submerged. Concurrently, time is mentioned specifically as a limiting factor, the implication of overrunning their time being that the inception will fail and Cobb will not be reunited with his children. This corresponds with Bakhtin's contention that "[i]t is precisely the chronotope that provides the ground essential for the showing forth, the representability of events. And this is so thanks precisely to the special increase in density and concreteness of time markers—the time of human life, of historical time—that occurs within well-delineated spatial areas" (1981, 250). Because the momentum of the film pivots around the crucial falling van, there is a tendency to forget the top layer of the real world aboard the airplane where Fischer and Cobb's team were first sedated. In fact, while the film repeatedly intercuts between the various dreams, it does not return to this top layer until the closing scenes. Effectively, though the characters' physical location remains in an airplane in mid-air throughout most of the film, the film focuses on their mental transition between dreams through time-space narratives united by the motif of Cobb's trauma. Moreover, the film's lack of resolution, instigated by the closing shot of the spinning totem, when it is unclear whether Cobb is in a dream or in the real world, leaves the spectator in an indeterminate place.

CONCLUSION

Overall, *Dunkirk* and *Inception* demonstrate a space-time association that is related to war trauma and guilt, grief and loss, respectively. This chronotopic motif extends across Nolan's films generally, signaling it as an auteurist trait, although the connections between the two parameters are not always identically represented. However, *Dunkirk* and *Inception* display a distinct similarity in the way that their three key narrative spaces have differing timelines. *Inception* makes this temporal differential more apparent in the use of extreme slow-motion editing and aging effects and is implicated in the story whereas *Dunkirk* signals the timelines of its narrative spaces through intertitles. Both films visually tie the various spaces together temporally by crosscutting throughout and narratively by trauma, enabling a Bakhtinian perspective of the chronotope to be applied.

NOTES

1. This phenomenon is explained by Sigmund Freud as "deferred action" over the course of his works, first postulating it in relation to his seduction theory and subsequently as underpinning the case of the Wolf-Man ([1955] 2001, 45).
2. Extreme close-ups of Cobb's wristwatch occur twice in the opening sequence, the second hand moving in slow motion and the sound of ticking amplified to draw attention to temporality.
3. As his main competitor, Saito wants Fischer to dissolve his recently deceased father's business empire.
4. The division between dream states and real spaces is a central trope of the film, although the use of a totem helps to establish this with Cobb's totem perpetually spinning in dreams and only toppling over in reality. Since the duration of the spinning totem differentiates real space from psychic space, it has an integral time-space element.

REFERENCES

American Psychological Association. 2022. www.apa.org/topics/trauma.
Bakhtin, Mikhail. 1981. *The Dialogic Imagination: Four Essays by M. M. Bakhtin*. Austin: University of Texas Press.
Buckland, Warren. 2015. "Inception's Video Game Logic." In *The Cinema of Christopher Nolan: Imagining the Impossible*, ed. Jacqueline Furby and Stuart Joy, 189–200. London: Wallflower Press.
Cameron, Allen and Richard Misek. 2014. "Modular Spacetime in the 'Intelligent' Blockbuster: *Inception* and *Source Code*." In *Hollywood Puzzle Films*, ed. Warren Buckland, 109–24. London and New York: Routledge.
Clarke, Melissa. 2002. "The Space-Time Image: The Case of Bergson, Deleuze, and Memento." *Journal of Speculative Philosophy* 16, no. 3: 167–81.
Elsaesser, Thomas. 2001. "Postmodernism as Mourning Work." *Screen* 42, no. 2: 193–201.
Elsaesser, Thomas. 2009. "The Mind-Game Film." In *Puzzle Films: Complex Storytelling in Contemporary Cinema*, ed. Warren Buckland, 13–41. Malden and Oxford: Wiley-Blackwell.
Flanagan, Martin. 2009. *Bakhtin and the Movies: New Ways of Understanding Hollywood Film*. London: Palgrave Macmillan.
Freud, Sigmund. 2001. *An Infantile Neurosis and Other Works: The Standard Edition of the Complete Psychological Works*. London: Vintage.

Furby, Jacqueline. 2015. "About Time Too, From *Interstellar* to *Following*, Christopher Nolan's Continuing Preoccupation with Time-Travel." In *The Cinema of Christopher Nolan: Imagining the Impossible*, ed. Jacqueline Furby and Stuart Joy, 247–67. London: Wallflower Press.

Ganser, Alexandra, Julia Pühringer, and Marcus Rheindorf. 2006. "Bakhtin's Chronotope on the Road: Space, Time and Place in Road Movies since the 1970s." *Facta Universitatis, Linguistics and Literature* 4, no.1: 1–17.

Goh, Robert. 2008. "Myths of Reversal, Backwards Narratives, Normative Schizophrenia and the Culture of Causal Agnosticism." *Social Semiotics* 18, no.1: 61–77.

Joy, Stuart. 2020. *The Traumatic Screen: The Films of Christopher Nolan*. London: Intellect.

Kealey, Erin. 2015. "No End in Sight: The Existential Temporality of *Following*." In *The Cinema of Christopher Nolan: Imagining the Impossible*, ed. Jacqueline Furby and Stuart Joy, 219–32. London: Wallflower Press.

McGowan, Todd. 2011. *Out of Time: Desire in Atemporal Cinema*. Minneapolis: University of Minnesota Press.

McNally, Richard. 2003. *Remembering Trauma*. Cambridge and London: Harvard University Press.

Nolan, Christopher. 2017. *Dunkirk—the Complete Screenplay with Selected Storyboards*. London: Faber and Faber.

Pheasant-Kelly, Frances. 2015. "Representing Trauma, Grief, Amnesia and Traumatic Memory in Nolan's New Millennial Films." In *The Cinema of Christopher Nolan: Imagining the Impossible*, ed. Jacqueline Furby and Stuart Joy, 99–199. London: Wallflower Press.

Russo, Paolo. 2014. "'Pain is in the Mind': Dream Narrative in *Inception* and *Shutter Island*." In *Hollywood Puzzle Films*, ed. Warren Buckland, 89–108. London and New York: Routledge.

Stam, Robert. 1992. *Subversive Pleasures: Bakhtin, Cultural Criticism, and Film*. Baltimore and London: Johns Hopkins University Press.

Stolworthy, Jacob. 2017. "Dunkirk, Christopher Nolan Reveals War Film Is Told through Three Perspectives, Has 'Little Dialogue.'" *Independent*, March 1, 2017. www.independent.co.uk/arts-entertainment/films/news/dunkirk-christopher-nolan-world-war-2-film-harry-styles-release-date-trailer-a7605241.html.

Stratton, Jon. 2019. "The Language of Leaving: Brexit, the Second World War and Cultural Trauma." *Journal for Cultural Research* 23, no. 3: 225–51.

Thorne, Kip. 2014. "Space-Time Visionary." *Nature* 515, no. 13: 196–97.

Toth, Margaret. 2015. "Memento's Postmodern Noir Fantasy: Place, Domesticity and Gender Identity." In *The Cinema of Christopher Nolan: Imagining the Impossible*, ed. Jacqueline Furby and Stuart Joy, 74–84. London: Wallflower Press.

Chapter 5

Back From the Future
Tenet *and the Politics of* Nachträglichkeit

Todd McGowan

A REVERSE TIME IMAGE

Politics errs when it focuses on the future. Although it seems as if the only possible point of political activity must be to create a better future, the key to creating a more egalitarian society lies in changing the past and turning our attention away from the future. The problem with focusing politics on the past appears self-evident: the past is over and done. What happened has happened. But the primary conceit dominating Christopher Nolan's films is that the past is never just over and done. From his first feature *Following* (1998) through *Tenet* (2020), Nolan stresses the malleability of the past. Through acts in the present, we reach back into the past and change its valence. Although Nolan literalizes the act of changing the past in *Tenet* through the reversal of entropy, the politics of this act does not require such impossible scientific feats. We can change the past through transforming our relationship to it, so that the past becomes the prologue to a different future.[1]

Interstellar (2014) marks a break in Nolan's preoccupation with time. Starting with *Interstellar*, Nolan contemplates how events in the future can actually reach back in time to alter the past, even though the past has already happened. This occurs through a singularity in *Interstellar* and through a scientific breakthrough in *Tenet*. By stressing the power of the future to change the past, Nolan points toward a new way of conceiving political activity that his earlier films only hint at. Such a reconception of politics bespeaks the convergence of Nolan's filmmaking with the implicit political project shared by Hegel and Freud.

One of the limitations of this political project is that it is only implicit, which is why Nolan's filmic engagement is so propitious. It appears in two thinkers who expressly disavow their political ambitions. For his part, Hegel insists that philosophy can offer no political counsel because, as he puts it in the preface to the *Philosophy of Right*, "the owl of Minerva takes flight only with the falling of dusk" (Hegel 1991, 23). Philosophy's insights come too late to have any practical effects. Similarly, in *Civilization and Its Discontents*, Freud refuses to give psychoanalysis any political bearing. He writes, "I have not the courage to rise up before my fellow-men as a prophet, and I bow to their reproach that I can offer them no consolation" (Freud 1961, 145). Instead of advising a politics of psychoanalysis, Freud contents himself to relieve the suffering of the few who come to an analyst. As he sees it, the destructiveness of the death drive cannot brook successful integration into the social order, which dooms us to a series of political failures. Like Hegel but for different reasons, he views theory as powerless against the mad rush of actual political events.

The explicit political pessimism of Hegel and Freud explains their obscurity as political thinkers. When one seeks a political program, one turns to thinkers devoted to a better future: Marx rather than Hegel, Reich rather than Freud. The problem with this decision is that it precludes a recognition that the past is the site of authentic political struggle. Hegel's claim that philosophy comes too late to offer political advice runs up against his philosophical recognition that the past is radically up for grabs according to how we interpret it. Freud's contention that he cannot act as a political prophet collides with his sense of the psychoanalytic cure as a way of reinterpreting one's past traumas and confronting rather than repressing them. In each case, an implicit political potential lies dormant. It falls to Christopher Nolan to unleash it.

Hegel is often thought of as the first thinker to bring history into philosophy. But Hegel does not relate to history as a historicist would. He does not accept that history unfolds narratively from beginning to end. This is why Hegel, despite his insistence on including history in philosophy, takes up a counterintuitive position on it. In his *Lectures on the Philosophy of World History*, Hegel articulates the oft-repeated lament about our failure to learn history's lessons. He states, "History and experience teach that peoples generally have not learned from history" (Hegel 2011, 138). Given his commitment to the importance of studying history, one would expect Hegel to join the chorus upbraiding humanity for this failure. But instead Hegel admits that people are entirely correct not to learn from history. He continues, "Peoples find themselves in such an individual circumstance that earlier conditions never wholly correspond to later ones because the situations are so different" (Hegel 2011, 138). Or, the lesson of history is that there is no lesson of history to learn and apply.

What history reveals to us is that events gain their significance retroactively through the act of interpreting them. Events have an implicit significance that the actors immersed in them cannot recognize. It is only when we consider events after the fact that their significance becomes evident. Hence, the act of interpretation becomes the primary theoretical act for Hegel. By interpreting, we recognize what is at stake in historical struggles. Hegel posits a fundamental blindness to significance for those caught up in historical events. He states, "the actions of human beings in world history produce an effect altogether different from what they intend and achieve, from what they immediately know and desire. They accomplish their interests; but at the same time they bring about something additional that indeed is implicit in their actions but was not present in their consciousness and intention" (Hegel 2011, 94). The inability to see the historical significance of an event is a political liability. One ends up acting against one's own political project—or on a completely different political terrain. Hegel sees this as an inevitable constraint of political action. Even though philosophy works in reverse chronology, politics cannot in Hegel's way of thinking, which is why he admits philosophy's political inutility.

Freud names what Hegel only conceptualizes. When he discovers that a subsequent event retroactively transforms an earlier occurrence into a trauma, Freud coins the term *Nachträglichkeit* or retroactivity to signify the process. He develops this concept most fully in reference to the brief case study of Emma that he includes in the unpublished (and unfinished) *Project for a Scientific Psychology* of 1895. Although this is not the first use of the term, it is the most edifying.

When Emma comes to Freud, she is unable to go into a shop by herself. Freud ties this to a traumatic scene in which she entered a shop and saw two clerks laughing together, which drove her to flee the store. Although Emma experiences this scene as traumatic, Freud can uncover no traumatic material here. Even the reasons that Emma gives for her trauma—they were laughing at her clothes—would not change if she were alone or with others, but the repression concerns only shopping alone. She is able to shop with others without difficulty. Freud's important discovery in Emma's case is an event in a shop that predates the two clerks laughing, which occurs when she was twelve years old. An earlier event in a shop occurs when she was only eight years old. Twice she goes into a shop to buy candy, and the shopkeeper sexually assaults her on both occasions. Emma discovers this memory through psychoanalytic therapy and does not link it to her experiences with the two clerks, but Freud does. He contends that this earlier memory becomes activated as a trauma through *Nachträglichkeit*, the retroactive causality that occurs with the later, nontraumatic event with the laughing clerks.

The trauma becomes a trauma in the future. Or, as Freud puts it in the *Project for a Scientific Psychology*, "We invariably find that a memory is repressed which has only become a trauma by *deferred action*" (Freud 1966, 356). *Nachträglichkeit* operates in the future anterior. An event will have become a trauma after a subsequent event. This idea—that the future can change the past—is central to Freud's project in psychoanalysis, even though the common conception of psychoanalysis sees it as a theory about the importance of the past (especially our childhood) influencing our future selves. Through the concept of *Nachträglichkeit*, Freud ponders how a future event might fundamentally shift the past by changing the valence attached to it.

In *Tenet*, the unnamed Protagonist (John David Washington) confronts a threat coming from the future that he must attempt to counteract by himself moving backward in time. Nolan shows this fight against the threat from the future by depicting movements in differing chronologies, which is why the film is so hard to follow on a first viewing. We see events occurring much earlier than other events in the film's running time, even though they actually take place simultaneously. For instance, the opera siege in Kyiv that opens the film takes place at the same time as the concluding attack on Stalsk-12, even though almost two hours of the film separate these two events. In this way, Nolan not only illustrates how *Nachträglichkeit* works but also provides a direction for orienting our political thinking around the possibility of changing the past.

The most obvious nod to *Nachträglichkeit* in *Tenet* occurs in the film's soundtrack. Much of the dialogue in the film becomes inaudible on a first viewing beneath the droning of the extradiegetical music. The score plays so loudly at key moments in the film that the spectator cannot clearly make out what the characters are saying. One might imagine that the music plays in this way to stress the unimportance of the dialogue in relation to the action, but in fact the dialogue is what allows us to understand the action. The conceptual complexity of the film demands that the spectator pay close attention to the dialogue despite the difficulty in making it out. Making sense of *Tenet* depends on hearing what people say, and yet the film's soundtrack presents a barrier to this.

The music obscures the dialogue in order to delay the spectator's comprehension of what is happening. It is only when the villain Andrei Sator (Kenneth Branagh) says his final words to the Protagonist that the reason for everything that happens in the film becomes clear. But these words occur amid a panoply of action on the screen and a constant throb of background music. Once one knows what to listen for, one can hear the words distinctly.

But when first seeing the film, it is not immediately evident that Sator's words to the Protagonist at this moment will contain an important explanation. Through this obscure revelation, the film forces the spectator to make sense of what is happening only after the fact. The difficulty of understanding the dialogue of *Tenet* demands that one approach the film retroactively. It places a formal demand for *Nachträglichkeit* on the spectator, a demand that echoes throughout the filmic structure.

THE VIRTUES OF DUPLICITY

Like all of Christopher Nolan's films, the fictional lie plays a central role in *Tenet*. It is a key component in the politics of *Nachträglichkeit* that the film embraces. The politics of *Nachträglichkeit* depends on recognizing the priority of the fiction because it is through the deceptive fiction that one ultimately arrives at a trauma through the retroactive process. The fiction is the starting point of all retroactivity. It establishes the structure through which one can return to the past and reinterpret it.

The fiction of *Tenet* itself exposes the total destruction of the earth's inhabitability wrought by climate change. The film uses a fictional structure to present climate change as so disastrous that it prompts a future generation to risk its own annihilation in a decision to destroy earth's past. Even though *Tenet* presents this political decision as that of the film's antagonist, it nonetheless reveals the inevitable logic that leads to it as a result of our current disregard for the state of emergency.

The entire narrative structure of *Tenet* turns on a deception perpetuated on Kat (Elizabeth Debicki), who incorrectly authenticates a Goya forgery made by Spanish painter Tomas Arepo (who is never seen in the film) for her husband, Sator. This deception leads to the control that Sator has over Kat—he threatens her with prosecution and depriving her of access to their son—and drives the Protagonist to attempt to steal the painting to end this control. Another Arepo forgery of a Goya painting initially provides the means for the Protagonist to introduce himself to Kat and eventually to meet Sator. The deception represents the entry point to the filmic narrative for the Protagonist.

In the same way, the spectator must accept the deception of reverse entropy and the paradoxes that it unleashes. Reverse entropy functions in *Tenet* like the process of inception operates in the eponymous film or like communication between future and present works in *Interstellar*. At any point during the filmic experience, the spectator could call the fiction into question and thereby break from the hold that the film has. But accepting this initial fiction is what makes possible the ultimate revelation about the politics of temporality in *Tenet*.

The sense of the film depends on submitting to the fiction without any way of initially making sense of it. Every film works in this way with the spectator, but *Tenet* makes the spectator's submission especially difficult by not providing the spectator with the usual clues about the direction of the narrative. One must accept the fiction well before one understands it because significance in the universe of *Tenet* always operates retroactively. The relentlessness of the film's obfuscation of what is going on makes it clear that significance only exists through the process of *Nachträglichkeit*.

The opening of *Tenet* is maddening in this regard. The film inserts the spectator in the Kyiv opera siege with no clues about who is conducting the siege, who the Protagonist is, who his allies are, or even whether the operation succeeds or not. One only learns these important details subsequently and in a piecemeal fashion as the narrative unfolds. Furthermore, *Tenet* keeps the spectator in ignorance about the significance of the events transpiring throughout most of its running time. Significance only becomes apparent retroactively. In this way, the spectator must accept the initial fiction and the misunderstanding that accompanies it in order to recognize the significance at the end.

We can see how this works within the filmic diegesis in the case of Kat and her experience aboard the yacht. She recounts the trauma of this experience on two occasions to the Protagonist. Both times, the film cuts to brief flashbacks of this time in which she quarrels with Andrei. The first reference occurs when she dines with the Protagonist just after meeting him. She tells him about the bargain that Sator offered her—abandoning her son in exchange for her freedom. Kat then recalls leaving the yacht for shopping on shore with her son and then seeing another woman dive off the boat as she was returning. The film cuts to the image of a woman diving from the yacht, creating the assumption that this was Sator's mistress, which Kat confirms. Kat tells the Protagonist, "I've never felt such envy." The Protagonist responds, "You don't seem the jealous type." She adds, "Of her freedom." What she does not recognize when she explains this experience is that she is the other woman and that she envies her future self in the past. She is only able to attain the freedom of the other woman when she adopts the position of retroactivity. It allows her to take a political stand that would otherwise be impossible.

The politics of *Nachträglichkeit* becomes clearest in the case of Kat. When she first tries to shoot Andrei, he recognizes that she will not be able to do it and grabs the gun from her hand. But after experiencing the trauma of him shooting her, she is able to shoot him. Even though the second act occurs earlier than the first, it comes later in Kat's own experience, thereby changing what she can do when confronting Andrei on the yacht. Rather than simply submitting to Andrei's violence, she is able to free herself from him by killing him. Without a recognition of the trauma through the *Nachträglichkeit* made possible by reverse entropy, this act would not have been possible, as we see when she is unable to shoot him earlier in the film (but later in chronological time).

The effect of *Nachträglichkeit* causes people to reinterpret the past and see the trauma that underlies every failed act. By bringing the trauma to the fore, the retroactive process pokes holes in the narrative structure that justifies the present. Recognizing trauma through a politics of *Nachträglichkeit* enables us to change the present by changing the past. But this is only possible when we first accept the fiction that structures events through a narrative that deceives us about their significance.

ACTION SCENES AS POLITICAL ACTS

Nolan's films bring together complex concepts—such as the physics of traveling through a wormhole or reversing entropy—with scenes of incredible spectacle. By the same token, his films create narrative puzzles for spectators to solve while bombarding the same spectators with visual and sonic excess.[2] This combination manages to take a popular form and reveal its otherwise hidden political potential. In *Tenet*, Nolan takes the form of a James Bond film and transforms it by highlighting the political possibilities of *Nachträglichkeit*. He does this by reformulating the structure of that most ideological of filmic structures—the action sequence.

When contrasting the action in *Tenet* with that of other action films, it is tempting to postulate that most action directors go awry because they have accepted the erroneous popular version of Hegel's philosophy. Nolan's film, in contrast, evinces a proper understanding of Hegel. If Nolan's other films take Hegel's claim that the false or the fiction is the necessary path to the truth (which I contend that they do), then *Tenet* hews even more closely to this philosophy. The way that Nolan structures the culminating action sequence in the film indicates this alignment with Hegel. The temporal pincer movement that concludes *Tenet* is a set piece with a unique structure: the attack on the antagonists takes place from both the present and the future, which makes it impossible to interpret the sequence according to a progressive narrative. The struggle takes place in both temporal directions—from the past toward the future and from the future toward the past—which shatters the image of a progressive unfolding of history.

Most action sequences, whatever their political content, operate according to the logic of a bad reading of Hegel. They are invested in the narrative of history as a narrative of progress. That is, they move from an initial position, a thesis, to a conflict with an antagonist or antithesis, and then conclude with the supersession of the antithesis and a change in the original position that produces a new synthesis. In the typical action film, the hero confronts the antagonist, defeats this figure, and then produces an improved situation, as is evident in a film like *Die Hard* (John McTiernan, 1988). This thesis-antithesis-synthesis structure appears nowhere in Hegel's philosophy, and yet it is the shorthand that most of his opponents—and, unfortunately, some of his proponents—use to describe his thinking. This model represents the key to viewing Hegel's understanding of history as progressive.

This progressive understanding of the action film does not apply to *Tenet*. Rather than moving from thesis to antithesis to synthesis, the action sequences in this film follow a logic that leads to contradiction, not to a resolution. Watching *Tenet* means confronting contradiction through a chronology that is at odds with itself, moving simultaneously forward and backward. It is impossible to arrive at a synthesis because temporality is not unidirectional. In this sense, *Tenet* is a Hegelian film, a film that uses reverse entropy to explode the association of the action sequences with the attainment of synthesis.

Tenet as a whole and the final action sequence in particular defy the logic of progress inherent in the model of thesis-antithesis-synthesis. The final action sequence is an assault on the closed city of Stalsk-12 in Russia. Like the earlier action sequences in the film, this one involves a failure. But in this case, unlike in the earlier ones, the Protagonist includes the failure in the plan, just as he includes action that commences in the future.

The assault on Stalsk-12 occurs through a temporal pincer movement. A pincer movement is a typical military strategy used to trap enemy forces between two different sections of an attacking force. In a temporal pincer movement, forces attack moving forward in time and moving backward in time. As one group of combatants arrives at the battle, the other group leaves. The battle occurs during the time of the overlap between movement toward the future and movement toward the past. The Tenet forces meet the opponent coming from two different temporal directions. The group moving forward in time is able to rely on knowledge gained from those moving backward, who will have already experienced the battle before the forward-moving forces begin to fight.

By assaulting Stalsk-12 from two temporal directions, the Tenet forces are able to fail to stop the detonation while at the same time removing the algorithm from the site, thereby derailing the possibility for the future generation to eliminate its own past, which includes the actually existing present. The advantage of the temporal pincer movement becomes clear when Neil (Robert Pattinson) sees that the Protagonist cannot penetrate the locked gate that blocks him from accessing the explosive device. By returning again from the future, Neil is able to unlock the gate and place himself in the path of a bullet that would have killed the Protagonist. It is only the *Nachträglichkeit* perspective that makes this intervention possible.

Since we lack the ability to reverse our own entropy in a temporal turnstile, it seems as if the political lessons of *Tenet* would be quite limited. But the type of political act that the film endorses does not require such a radical physical change. It demands a change in our political thinking. Rather than focusing our political efforts on constructing a different future, we should, the film suggests, turn our attention to the past. By changing the past, we change the coordinates of the present. Rather than rewriting the past to fit in with a narrative of the present, *Nachträglichkeit* interrupts the present's narrative by inserting a trauma into it, a trauma brought to light through failure. This is a point that sheds light on how we might approach *Tenet*, a film replete with nothing but failed actions.

THE PRIORITY OF FAILURE

Each of the major action sequences in *Tenet* ends in failure. Even more than its focus on reverse entropy, these failures cause the film to stand out. While there are heist films in particular that focus on failure—such as *Rififi* (Jules Dassin, 1955) and *The Killing* (Stanley Kubrick, 1956)—these films do not present failure as a form of success in the way that *Tenet* does. Instead, they depict failure as a genuine setback for characters trying to succeed. In these cases, the spectator experiences the failures as moments of devastation. The films show failure in the light of possible success.

From the perspective of the present, success appears as the only way to advance one's political project. To fail is to endanger the political struggle. It does not make any sense to embark on a political struggle with the hope of failing. But this is where *Tenet* proves politically helpful. The film reveals how failure can be recognized as a form of success through the process of *Nachträglichkeit*. The Protagonist is able to accomplish his aim not by succeeding but by arranging his failures through an interpretation that reveals the trauma that each of them activates. By linking each of these failed actions to a central trauma, which is the potential destruction of the world, the Protagonist is able to transform the failures into a political success.

The Protagonist's initial mission begins without any explanation of its aim. In the opening sequence of the film, he infiltrates the siege of the Kyiv opera disguised as a Ukrainian SWAT team member brought to thwart the siege, which is an attempt to steal plutonium 241 (which is really the last part of the algorithm for destroying the world) from a CIA operative known as the Well-Dressed Man (Jefferson Hall). The Protagonist saves the unconscious members of the audience at the opera from the explosives planted by the terrorists, but he is unable to escape himself. Sator's henchmen wipe out the CIA team, including the Protagonist, who appears to kill himself with a cyanide capsule, but the Ukrainian security forces escape with the plutonium that the Protagonist was trying to procure for Tenet. This failure leads to a second attempt to procure the plutonium 241 while it is being transported.

In between these attempted thefts, another failed heist occurs. The elaborate scheme at the Oslo Freeport is an attempt to steal the Arepo forgery and thereby break the hold that Sator has over Kat. The Tenet forces go so far as to crash a 747 full of gold into the airport in order to trigger the fire safety system that will allow the Protagonist and Neil to enter into the freeport storage area where they can steal the painting. The heist goes awry when the Protagonist's future self interrupts it (as part of a plan to return an injured Kat to a forward-moving temporality) and fights with his present self. But the real problem is that Sator has moved the painting, which means that the heist has no chance of success. It is designed to steal an object that is no longer there.

The next action sequence—the attempt to steal the plutonium 241 from the Ukrainian security forces—fails even more spectacularly, which results in the Protagonist handing this ultimate weapon, the algorithm, over to Sator. This sequence involves an elaborate heist that occurs while the convoy carrying the plutonium 241 travels through a crowded city. Four large trucks trap the convoy while the Protagonist crawls onto the roof of the armored vehicle carrying the object by using the ladder of a firetruck. All of this occurs so that the Protagonist can ultimately give the final piece of the algorithm to Sator, who plans to bury it where only the future generation can find it. This failure seems to have the most direct consequences, but it is a necessary one. It enables Sator to believe that he has succeeded, and thus it will deceive the people of the future about the location of the last part of the algorithm.

The final action sequence of the film fails as well. But in the sequence, the Protagonist and his team integrate the failure into the mission. The mission is designed to fail and can only succeed if it fails. The ostensible object of the mission is to stop the explosion at Stalsk-12, the closed city where Sator grew up, but this mission must fail in order to obscure the real mission, which is to remove the algorithm from the city unnoticed just prior to the explosion. If the Tenet forces are able to do this, then they will succeed in keeping the algorithm from the future generation that intends to use it to destroy the world.

Tenet stresses failure because of the role that it plays in the politics of *Nachträglichkeit*. Each failure in the film is a failure only from the perspective of the present in which the mission takes place. The Protagonist and the forces of Tenet fail to accomplish the aim that they set out for themselves, whether it be capturing the plutonium 241 on multiple occasions or stealing a painting on another. Put together, however, this series of failures is what enables the Protagonist to defeat Sator and defend the present from the attack launched by the future.

The politics of *Nachträglichkeit* is a politics of failure. It looks at past failed acts and recognizes the trauma that motivates them. To organize society around failure rather than around success is the implicit ideal of this vision of politics. But to do so would represent an end to repression, which is why it is impossible. We can nonetheless mark the significance of the traumatic disruption of the narratives that justify the present in order to make clear the persistence of a traumatic rupture. This is the political act that *Tenet* champions.

CONTRA GRETA THUNBERG

The narrative complexity of *Tenet* exists to obscure that the villain of the film is Greta Thunberg. Thunberg's activism stands out for her willingness to accuse political leaders and all adults of complicity in the approaching climate catastrophe. She sees climate change as an apocalyptic event that demands immediate radical action. Although she does not go so far as to call for a temporal strike on the present (which is what the future humans in *Tenet* do), she does chronicle the present age as criminal. This is what places her in the same position as the villains of *Tenet*.

Thunberg's interventions are plainspoken about the culpability of contemporary adults for the future. At the United Nations Climate Action Summit on September 23, 2019, she says, "How dare you? You have stolen my dreams and my childhood with your empty words" (Thunberg 2019). The present is guilty for stealing the future, which justifies extreme action on the part of the future. As Thunberg sees it, all older generations are complicit for their failure to recognize the ongoing catastrophe and their inability to take action to stop it. This is precisely the political position that leads the future generation in *Tenet* to attempt to destroy our present through the algorithm. By supplying the film's villain with this completely defensible and even logical motivation, *Tenet* displays a political complexity lacking in almost all action films, especially the superhero film. The contrast here is instructive.

One of the intractable faults of the superhero film as a genre is the motivation that drives the villain. In most cases, the villain simply wants destruction for the sake of destruction. Initially, *Tenet* seems to belong to the sad litany of superhero films that include Nolan's own earlier creations. Mention of the film's villain first occurs when the Protagonist visits arms dealer Priya Singh (Dimple Kapadia) for the first time in Mumbai. Priya discusses Andrei Sator as a Russian oligarch who serves as a broker between the present and the future. She leads the Protagonist to Michael Crosby (Michael Caine), and Michael links Sator to an explosion that occurred simultaneously with the

Kyiv opera siege that opens the film. It is only thirty minutes into the film that a picture of the villain Sator begins to develop.

When the Protagonist makes contact with Sator's spouse Kat, the spectator learns of Sator's treachery during the dinner that Kat and the Protagonist share. He holds his wife hostage in their marriage with knowledge that she wrongly authenticated a forged Goya painting that he purchased for $9 million. Sator also cripples the forger, Spanish painter Thomas Arepo, who bears partial responsibility for the deception. Sator's henchmen interrupt the dinner with the intent of maiming the Protagonist, perhaps in the way that they did Arepo. The Protagonist thwarts their assault and emerges intact from the restaurant, which surprises both Kat and her driver (who works for Sator).

The film creates an image of Sator as a despotic villain—a Russian oligarch, an arms dealer, an abusive husband—before even showing him to the spectator. When the Protagonist first meets Sator at another dinner aboard his yacht, he abruptly threatens the Protagonist without any extended preamble. Sator describes in graphic detail how he will kill the Protagonist, by cutting a hole in his throat and ramming his detached testicles into this opening. The medium shot of Sator as he articulates this threat shows him well lit against the dark background of the night sky and the out-of-focus yacht. He stands out starkly from this background. Sator calmly and authoritatively tells the Protagonist, "It is very gratifying to watch a man you don't like try to pull his own balls out of his throat before he chokes." This statement lets us know what to think of Sator. It is clear from the spectator's early acquaintance with such a character that he functions as a figure of pure evil bent on destruction because he enjoys destruction. It makes sense that William Goodman would claim, "it's essentially a fancy Bond movie, with Sator playing the over-the-top villain role" (Goodman 2021). If Sator is the film's villain, his analogy is certainly correct.

Later, we learn that Sator is dying and wants to kill everyone else in the world when he dies. If he cannot live, then he deems it appropriate that no one else lives. For a motivation to destroy every living being on earth, this appears to be even more threadbare than Rha's al Ghul's motivation for destroying Gotham. Sator does not even find the world depraved. He just wants to kill everything in order to have company in death. But despite the film's depiction of Sator's evil, he is not the film's villain. He is actually just a pawn in the struggle of the future against the present.

Over ninety minutes of *Tenet* pass before the spectator hears the term "algorithm." As the Protagonist and Neil take the injured Kat back through time while riding in a shipping container, the Protagonist hears a recording on his phone of Sator talking with his accomplices. In this recording, Sator says, "The material is not in the case. Get the other sections of the algorithm to the hypocenter." The Protagonist directly asks Neil about the algorithm, and Neil unveils the film's true villain. He explains that the future inhabitants of earth are using Sator to bring together the algorithm that will destroy their own past. When he offers this explanation, it seems as if the future inhabitants of earth share the senseless destructiveness of Sator. But Sator himself corrects this impression just before he dies in a phone conversation with the Protagonist. This conversation occurs at the climax of the film's final action sequence. This crucial exposition occurs on the audio track as the visuals show the Protagonist trying to thwart the burial and preservation of the algorithm. After Sator's revelation, the film's villain appears in an entirely different light. What seems like scarcely motivated villainy becomes apparent as a political act intended to save humanity from the devastation of a climate catastrophe caused by human actions.

When the Protagonist accuses Sator of being a fanatic out to destroy the world, Sator offers a compelling defense of his position. He states, "I'm not. I'm creating a new one. Somewhere, sometime, a man in a crystalline tower throws a switch, and Armageddon is both triggered and avoided. Now time itself switches direction. The same sunshine we basked in will warm the faces of our descendants for generations to come." The Protagonist is perplexed and asks, "How can they want to kill us?" Sator responds with a political explanation, saying, "Because their oceans rose, and their rivers ran dry. Don't you see? They had no choice but to turn back. We're responsible." At the climactic moment in the film, we see that Sator is actually helping future climate warriors who are trying to preserve the habitability of the planet from the devastation that their forerunners wrought. The figure who has hitherto appeared as a barbaric sociopath now comes into focus as a tool in the struggle against climate change.

After hearing Sator's explanation that places the Protagonist's own efforts in an entirely different light, Sator asks him if he wants to give up his attempt to stop the assembly of the algorithm. The Protagonist refuses and defends his position by claiming that every generation tries to ensure its own survival. Sator rightly points out that this is precisely what the future is doing as well. The apparent clarity of the moral struggle between the Protagonist and Sator disappears at this moment.

When the Protagonist argues that his fight against the future is purely a fight for survival, *Tenet* reveals a complete abandonment of the ethical terrain that he appears to occupy throughout the film. While Sator may indulge in barbaric acts and wants to destroy the world for egoistic reasons, he is nonetheless engaged in a political project more morally defensible than that of the Protagonist. The presence of his explanation at the end of the film complicates the heroism of the Protagonist by placing him on the opposite side of those fighting against climate change. Thanks to the Protagonist's actions, the environmental destruction of the earth is ensured. It is undoubtedly due to

Nolan's skill as a filmmaker that spectators find themselves cheering for this outcome at the end of the film. This outcome indicates the political limitation in Nolan's vision—his inability to take the politics of *Nachträglichkeit* as far as it needs to be taken.

Tenet reveals a political possibility that it fails to fully embrace. The future generation that attempts the political act of eliminating its own past appears as the film's villain. Despite embracing *Nachträglichkeit* as a political strategy, Nolan's film balks when confronted with its most radical possibility—not just resignifying the past but rendering it null and void, making it count for nothing. Subjectivity at its most radical has the ability to erase the past, to free itself from its own origins.

By eliminating its significance for the present, the subject can destroy the past's ability to persist as a cause for the present. This is what Jean-Paul Sartre grasps toward the end of *Being and Nothingness*. He writes, "It is I, it is the men of my generation who decide the meaning of the efforts and the enterprises of the preceding generation whether we resume and continue their political and social attempts, or whether we realize a decisive rupture and throw the dead back into inefficacy" (Sartre 1956, 694). Nolan is able to envision just such a "decisive rupture" that breaks with the past, but he can do so only as an act of evil that he structures *Tenet* to combat.[3] This marks the fundamental political limitation of the film. It advances the politics of *Nachträglichkeit* through its reenvisioning of the action sequence, but it identifies the ultimate version of this political act as an evil that must be extirpated. Nolan cannot go so far as to embrace the total break from the past that inheres in the act of *Nachträglichkeit*. But this does not completely take away the film's political achievement.

Nachträglichkeit implies that we must recognize that we are always at the end of history. In order to look forward, we must look backward to recognize the trauma in the events that constitute us. *Nachträglichkeit* is not just a psychic operation but also a political one, a way of conceiving politics that turns away from an emphasis on the future. It demands an abandonment of the narrative of progress that leftists as well as liberals accept. Thinking in terms of the politics of retroactivity requires us to think of emancipation without progress. This is the real challenge that *Tenet* lays out for the spectator (beyond just understanding the film's narrative!).

The ending of *Tenet* reveals this absence of progress in a stark manner. Even temporally, the Protagonist has gotten nowhere. He ends up on the same day as the Kyiv opera siege that opens the film. Rather than pointing to an open future in the way that most films do, *Tenet* points toward the past. This becomes clearest in an allusion that Neil makes just before he goes off to his imminent death. He tells the Protagonist, "For me, I think this is the end of a beautiful friendship." By inverting the famous line that concludes

Casablanca (Michael Curtiz, 1942), Neil suggests the different relationship to politics that *Tenet* advances. Rather than trying to change the future, Nolan's film locates political struggle in changing the way that we relate to the past. This offers the spectator a hard lesson: to embark on political activity when there is no hope for progress is to act without a future, to act for the sake of only the act itself. Conceived in this way, politics loses the end that would justify it. It becomes a struggle for a momentary emancipation. We act for the sake of who we were rather than what we will become.

NOTES

1. In "On the Concept of History," Walter Benjamin evinces an awareness that the real terrain of political contestation includes the past. The aim of political struggle, as he sees it, is to produce a different future by reawakening the revolutionary hopes of the past. This leads him to say, "The only historian capable of fanning the spark of hope in the past is the one who is firmly convinced that *even the dead* will not be safe from the enemy if he is victorious. And this enemy has never ceased to be victorious" (Benjamin 2003, 391). The political task for the leftist theorist, according to this logic, is to reignite the flames of hope that the forces of oppression have stifled in the past. This is the way to a better future.

2. Catherine Bernard appreciates the ability of the spectacular sequences in Nolan's film *Inception* (2010) to change spectator sensation. She writes, "the plot-driven sensationalism of Nolan's film may also produce a form of intelligent sensation" (Bernard 2017, 235).

3. The same structure manifests itself in *The Dark Knight Rises*. The latter film shows Bane leading a revolt of the underclass against the capitalist system, but it reduces him to the figure of a terrorist out to destroy Gotham in the guise of liberating it. The limitation of that film and of *Tenet* is that in each case Nolan imagines the radical act only in the form of an evil that his hero must combat. Perhaps this is the compromise that enables him to remain a popular Hollywood filmmaker, in which case it should be celebrated rather than lamented.

REFERENCES

Benjamin, Walter. 2003. "On the Concept of History." Trans. Harry Zohn. In *Selected Writings, Volume 4: 1938–1940*, ed. Howard Eiland and Michael W. Jennings, 389–400. Cambridge: Harvard University Press.

Bernard, Catherine. 2017. "Christopher Nolan's *Inception*: Spectacular Speculations." *Screen* 58, no. 2: 229–36.

Freud, Sigmund. 1961. *Civilization and Its Discontents*. Trans. James Strachey. In *The Standard Edition of the Complete Psychological Works of Sigmund Freud*, vol. 21, ed. James Strachey, 57–145. London: Hogarth.

———. 1966. *Project for a Scientific Psychology*. Trans. James Strachey. In *The Standard Edition of the Complete Psychological Works of Sigmund Freud*, vol. 1., ed. James Strachey, 243–397. London: Hogarth.

Goodman, William. 2021. "*Tenet* Really Explained, For Real This Time." *GQ* (7 January): www.gq.com/story/tenet-explained.

Hegel, G. W. F. 1991. *Elements of the Philosophy of Right*, ed. Allen W. Wood. Trans. H. B. Nisbet. Cambridge: Cambridge University Press.

———. 2011. *Lectures on the Philosophy of World History, Volume I: Manuscripts of the Introduction and Lectures of 1822–23*, ed. Robert F. Brown and Peter C. Hodgson. Trans. Robert F. Brown and Peter C. Hodgson. Oxford: Clarendon Press.

Sartre, Jean-Paul. 1956. *Being and Nothingness*. Trans. Hazel E. Barnes. New York: Washington Square Press.

Thunberg, Greta. 2019. Quoted in "Greta Thunberg's Speech at the U.N. Climate Action Summit." National Public Radio. www.npr.org/2019/09/23/763452863/transcript-greta-thunbergs-speech-at-the-u-n-climate-action-summit.

SECTION 2

COLLABORATIONS AND RELATIONSHIPS

Chapter 6

"There's a Point Where We Just Let the Music Take Over Everything"

The Collaboration of Christopher Nolan and Hans Zimmer

Bernadette Pace

Christopher Nolan is, perhaps, one of the most complex storytellers currently working in Hollywood. As a student of English Literature and an everyday cinephile, Nolan's oeuvre almost exclusively presents nonconventional methods of storytelling, resulting in all but three of his films subscribing to a nonlinear narrative construction. He works within the confines of the contemporary studio system, yet creates an auteur brand that allows audiences to assume that his films will be narratively and temporally complex. Thus, to situate the audience in such complex, distorted filmic worlds, Nolan places the role of narrative coherence on another cinematic element: the *music*. In the context of such complexity, director and composer discuss music during the script-writing process together. This is a task usually reserved for post-production, making Nolan's collaboration with composer Hans Zimmer a particularly notable one. Through a consideration of the ways Nolan and Zimmer collaborated on *Inception* (2010), *Interstellar* (2014), and *Dunkirk* (2017), this chapter suggests that they rely on music to help audiences navigate these complex films by presenting varying levels of tension in a film's soundscape.

Nolan's filmmaking centers on collaboration. Yet, his films carry unique traits consistent across his repertoire that tend to be recognized and celebrated as a Nolan hallmark.[1] This is made possible by his reliance on the same team of creative individuals across many of his films: Emma Thomas (producer),

Jonathan Nolan (co-writer), Hoyte Van Hoytema and Wally Pfister (cinematographers), Lee Smith (film editor), Richard King (sound designer), and David Julyan and Hans Zimmer (composers).[2] At this stage, it is worth noting that there are many arguments in scholarship that debate the concept of an auteur director in Hollywood: some view the auteur theory through the lens of authorship (Sellors 2007; Kawin 2008). Yet, for the purpose of this chapter, I will not debate if Nolan is, indeed, the sole author of his films. Instead, this chapter focuses on those directorial stamps that are associated with a particular auteur director: in Nolan's case, the director's continual return to creating such narratively and temporally complex films, and his reliance on music to help navigate the audience through such complexity. Thus, Nolan's return to the same team of individuals across his films fosters the director's auteurism and is, indeed, one of his most auteur traits.[3]

When Nolan began working with Zimmer, he was already a part of a long-standing collaboration with his previous composer, David Julyan. The two first became acquainted when they met at University College London (UCL) (Julyan and Oliver 2006). They collaborated on two of Nolan's short films—*Larceny* (1996) and *Doodlebug* (1997)—before working together on the director's early feature-length films—*Following* (1998), *Memento* (2000), *Insomnia* (2002), and *The Prestige* (2006). Little is known about the parting between the director and composer; however, Nolan's collaboration with Julyan came to an end with *Batman Begins* (2005).[4] As Vasco Hexel suggests, perhaps Warner Bros. wanted to hire "a more established composer," with Danny Elfman's iconic *Batman* (1989) sounds still in the memory of the contemporary audience (2016, 8–9).

HANS ZIMMER

Hans Zimmer took a relatively unconventional route into the Hollywood film industry. Surprisingly, the German-born composer had no formal higher education or musical training; in many interviews, Zimmer often expresses his childhood aversion to formal music lessons, growing up in a culture saturated with Western art music (Zimmer and Kermode 2019; Zimmer 2016). Once he graduated from school, Zimmer moved to London and pursued a range of projects, starting with work as a session musician (Hexel 2016, 1). In 1977, the composer joined a popular group—The Buggles—and they released a hit track titled "Video Killed the Radio Star." Zimmer eventually led the creation of the track's music video. According to the composer, he was interested in the growing potentials of the music video format and the relationship between the image and the sound (Zimmer 2016). In 1981, the music video was the first one ever to be broadcast on MTV (Zimmer 2016; Guerrasio 2015).

In 1980, Zimmer landed an internship with renowned English composer Stanley Myers. The composer hired Zimmer to deal with the influx of new musical technology because Zimmer had a vast knowledge of electronic instruments (Hexel 2016, 2). Zimmer observed how Myers worked with directors and was encouraged to join him for these meetings throughout his internship (Zimmer 2016). From 1984, he began composing for English films, collaborating with mentor Myers on the score for Steven Frears's *My Beautiful Laundrette* (1985), and composed for Chris Menges's *A World Apart* (1988) (Hexel 2016, 2). After the release of the latter, the director Barry Levinson approached Zimmer to join him on his next film. Late one evening, much to Zimmer's disbelief, Levinson visited his studio in London and asked if he would come to Los Angeles and watch a film he had already shot (Zimmer 2016; Zimmer and Pearson 2018).[5] So, in 1988, Zimmer went to Hollywood to score *Rain Man*.

Zimmer first collaborated with Nolan in 2005, when he scored *Batman Begins* with James Newton Howard. Little is known about how the collaboration between the director and composer began, although film critic Tim Greiving (2017) suggests that Nolan admired Zimmer's score for *The Thin Red Line* (1998). *Batman Begins* became Zimmer's eighty-third feature-length film score and the beginning of Nolan's thirteen-year collaboration with the composer. After the success of the film, Zimmer and Howard returned to compose the music for the final two installments of the trilogy—*The Dark Knight* (2008) and *The Dark Knight Rises* (2012)—and Zimmer continued his collaboration with Nolan for *Inception* (2010), *Interstellar* (2014), and *Dunkirk* (2017). Surprisingly, Nolan and Zimmer did not collaborate on *Tenet* (2020): the film score was written by another Oscar-winning film composer, Ludwig Göransson. According to Zimmer, this did not signal a departure from Nolan and Zimmer's partnership but was apparently due to scheduling conflicts: the composer had already committed to Denis Villeneuve's *Dune* (2021) (Chitwood 2019).

THE ROLE OF THE CONTEMPORARY COMPOSER

Every director works differently. The traditional Hollywood director and composer relationship usually begins once the image has been shot. When the director meets with the composer, they are usually joined by the sound designers, and the sound and film editors. It is common for a temp (or temporary) track to be used during this process; as Karlin and Wright explain in their scoring manual, this involves placing existing music alongside an edited film and is usually a task for the film and music editors (2004, 19). As Christian DesJardins notes, a temp track offers an accessible method for the filmmaking team to gain insight into what might work with the rhythm and emotion of the film or, ultimately, to gauge what the director is looking for (2006, xvi). This is useful because the other creators are often not from musical backgrounds, allowing a way of communicating that minimizes the use of technical language and, instead, shifts the conversation to center around the story. Then, the composer sets out to write the agreed-upon music. During this stage, the dialogue continues across the filmmaking team while adjustments are made to both the sound and image tracks during the editing and mixing stages of post-production.

Nolan and Zimmer intentionally avoid using temp music. The composer finds that writing a score after a director has experienced their images with temp music is an intimidating, and often lackluster, process.[6] Nolan, for related reasons, also finds limitations with temp music. He believes that when directors experience their images with the addition of temp music, they have difficulty deviating from any initial impressions because "you're moving away from what first inspired you" (Nolan 2018). Instead, Nolan and Zimmer do things differently:

> So, the way I've [Nolan] always worked with composers . . . is to say ok, let's look at the script, let's talk about the ideas and then sometimes before we're even shooting, or while we're shooting, start sending me ideas, musical ideas, demos based on the narrative concepts, based on just some visual images. (Nolan 2018)

This process, therefore, allows Nolan to have access to music that has been originally composed for his film, eliminating the need for temp music during post-production. Additionally, Zimmer writes most of a film's music before he sees any visual material of the film, either from the script or from conversations with Nolan. As Zimmer states, his collaboration with the director is built on trust (2016).[7] So, Nolan approached his collaboration with Zimmer differently from that of the traditional composer, influencing how the composer works.[8] Thus, the remainder of this chapter details how Zimmer worked on Nolan's more narratively complex films, *Inception*, *Interstellar*, and *Dunkirk*.

INCEPTION (2010)

Inception took Nolan more than ten years to write. After the release of each of his films, the director would return to the script to try and make more sense of the story (Thompson 2010). The most narratively complex of his films at the time of its release, *Inception* presents five layers of narrative that the characters travel between: reality, a dream, a dream within a dream, a dream within a dream within a dream (inception), and limbo.[9] Nolan discovered that he could not rely on the image alone to convey travel between these narratives because the characters were not always privileged to this information (Zimmer and Pearson 2018): they relied on personal totems (for example, a weighted die whose weight distribution was only understood by its owner) and sonic cues (Édith Piaf's version of "Non, je ne regrette rien") to situate themselves. The director needed to rely on varying moments of tension in the film's score to serve as sonic indicators that the layer of reality in the story is about to change. Thus, Zimmer had to be involved early in the script-writing process to ensure that the audience (and the characters) could navigate these narratively complex storylines.

The story follows a thief, Dom Cobb, trained to steal information from the subconscious mind of targets by entering their dreams. In the aftermath of a heist, he is framed for the murder of his wife, Mal, rendering him a fugitive unable to return home to his children. Cobb agrees on one last job in order to gain his freedom; however, this time around he is tasked with planting an idea inside a target's subconscious instead of stealing one. The job requires Cobb and his team to travel between different layers of the target's dreams to implant the intricate details of the idea. Time runs differently in each layer, where "five minutes in the real world gives you an hour in the dream."[10] When the characters travel further into the dream, the world above becomes more and more unstable, and so they require sedation; the sedation, however, also slows down time in each dream.[11] Hence, Nolan's main concern was that this temporally and narratively complex hierarchy could be too difficult for the audience to follow. The director could not finish writing the script until he was sure that music would fill the gaps that were lacking in the story (Zimmer and Pearson 2018). As Zimmer explains, the contribution of music was able to function as a guide:

> *Inception* was this sort of different problem whereby it was potentially a complicated story. . . . I thought if we just set this up right from the beginning that the music is interesting and a little provocative and a little different . . . and if you don't understand everything, that's okay too. At least it was an interesting journey. (Zimmer 2016)

Nolan's films are intended to be watched more than once, another hallmark of the director's auteurism. Upon first viewing *Inception*, the audience may miss these sonic cues, as Zimmer suggests above, that can help situate them within such complexity. After the first viewing, however, the audience can begin to recognize these sonic signifiers: the most significant one, of course, being *Inception*'s infamous "braaam" sound. Nolan writes "massive low-end musical tones" in his script to indicate instability in the narrative and prompt a shift to a different layer of dreaming (Nolan 2010). Thus, as Zimmer suggests, the "braaam" sound in *Inception* is used as a story point (Buchanan 2013). The sound is orchestrated by loud, dense, and repetitive French horns.

In one of the film's early examples of the "braaam" motif, Cobb is training the team's new architect, Ariadne (the architect constructs the dreamscapes that the team travels between). During Ariadne's training, Cobb takes her inside of his subconscious. He begins to share the general guidelines that she should follow when creating these worlds: one of these is that she must work subtly, otherwise the target's subconscious will recognize an intruder, and the world will become unstable. After Ariadne's line of dialogue, "my question is, what happens when you start messing with the physics of it all?" (0:28:32), she imagines the streetscapes in front of her folding on top of their current street level; at this stage, a variation of the "braaam" motif enters. When Cobb's subconscious becomes suspicious of her manipulations to the dream's design (0:29:41), the horns mimic the "braaam" sound in short pulses, adding a new layer of tension. The dream becomes more and more unstable as a result of Ariadne's actions, and the horns draw the audience's attention to this association.

The instability of the dream worlds is more frequent in the team's main job (1:01:25–2:11:40). When they enter the target's subconscious, they soon realize the task is not as straightforward as they anticipated: their target has been training to block out intruders, and the team encounters resistance. Therefore, the member of the team who occupies each layer (to help stabilize the dream and initiate the protocol to wake the team up at the right moment) must also defend the team: Yusuf (the chemist in charge of sedation) occupies the dream layer, while Arthur (the engineer) occupies the dream within a dream. Both layers become unstable (01:34:32–01:36:09) when Arthur and Yusuf are confronted by armed guards and engage in fight sequences: the horns enter abruptly, varying in volume throughout the sequence; the horns play the ascending notes of a scale, elevating tension as the fight continues; and, the horns increase in speed, presenting short musical pulses instead of the full-bodied, resonant sound of the original motif. Thus, these varying amounts of tension produced by the "braaam" sounds in these dreamscapes allow the audience to begin to navigate the film's temporally and narratively complex construction.

Similarly, the characters in *Inception* also rely on sonic cues to situate themselves within their layers of dreams and reality. The characters use a recording of Édith Piaf's version of "Non, je ne regrette rien" to warn them that they are about to be awakened from a layer of dreaming: this works similarly to how Zimmer and Nolan use the "braaam" sound to inform the audience that a narrative shift is about to occur. Zimmer tells us that Piaf's track is also incorporated into the score, providing an additional signal for the audience (Zimmer and Pearson 2018). Thus, as Engel and Wildfeuer suggest, a slowed-down arrangement of "Non, je ne regrette rien" in the score also helps situate the audience, since time runs more slowly in dreams than in reality (2015, 233–43).

While Nolan was filming *Inception*, Zimmer completed the score away from the image. When Nolan had finished shooting, he was reluctant to show the film to the composer because, up until that point, the music was achieving precisely what the director needed it to achieve (Zimmer and Pearson 2018). As with all of their projects, Nolan and Zimmer continued their collaboration throughout the post-production process, and these adjustments are made to the score when the soundtrack is edited to the image. These refinements do not dissipate the complexity of their collaboration but, instead, suggest that the collaboration between the director and composer is much more intricate than one may believe.

INTERSTELLAR (2014)

When Nolan approached Zimmer to collaborate on *Interstellar*, he decided to work a little differently. Instead of discussing the story with the composer or giving him access to the script, as with *Inception*, Nolan kept him in the dark: the director refrained from sharing any markers of the film's story, or its genre, with Zimmer. He did, however, give the composer a brief story written on a single piece of paper before he started composing the score:

> He [Nolan] was being very unspecific in his specificity by saying "hey, look. I'm just going to give you this page but I'm not going to tell you what the movie is about." And he gave me [Zimmer] this fable about what it means to be a father, and he cleverly steered it in a way that I thought that it automatically made me think about my relationship with my son. So, I wrote him this tiny, very personal theme. And then he told me this is a movie about the vastness of everything, the expanse of the universe, space and science fiction, and it's epic, and it's all these things. (Zimmer 2016)

As Nolan draws Zimmer's attention to above, the protagonist's actions in *Interstellar* are driven by his love for his daughter. The film is set on a decaying Earth whose resources are rapidly diminishing. Cooper, a former pilot and engineer, farms corn after the government deems space exploration nonessential and dissolves NASA. However, contrary to the public's knowledge, the space agency has continued to search for a way to ensure the survival of humanity. After Cooper and his daughter, Murph, stumble upon the concealed

NASA base, they recruit him to pilot the *Endurance* on a space expedition to another galaxy to search for a habitable planet for the preservation of humankind.

Since Nolan wanted to ensure that the relationship between father and daughter in *Interstellar* drove the narrative, the director wanted to produce a sound that could embody this feeling and was different from his previous collaborations with Zimmer (Nolan 2014). The director and composer decided to intentionally experiment with other instruments in this process: "we literally sat down and went 'okay, let's make a list of everything we have done and see what we are left with.' . . . We've done the big brass, we've done the big drums, we've done the synthesizer stuff. And Chris said, 'what about the church organ?'" (Zimmer 2018). Zimmer was wary that the sound of the organ carried existing audience associations in cinema: it could be too reminiscent of the gothic genre (Zimmer and Pearson 2018). Yet, regardless of his reservations, he was intrigued by the challenge. He found it poetic to use an instrument in such a complex space film that "by the 17th century, . . . was the most complex bit of technology ever built by man" (Zimmer and Pearson 2018).

The complexity of *Interstellar* stems further than its subject matter: the narrative is constructed around the real-life principle of relativity. When Cooper and his team travel to different planets within this alternate galaxy, time is manipulated: every hour spent on Miller's planet, for example, is equivalent to seven years passing on Earth. Thus, Nolan brought in the expertise of astrophysicist Kip Thorne (credited as a producer on the film) to help construct these narratively and temporally complex timelines. In the presence of such complexity, Zimmer asked to see the footage prior to composing because of its potential compositional demands (Zimmer and Pearson 2018). He needed to ensure that the pacing of the music presented time running faster on Miller's planet as compared to on Earth, for example. Zimmer states that he "had to hit this count and hit this count" in his scoring to align with the moments of extreme tension presented (Zimmer and Pearson 2018). The varying levels of tension in the score could, therefore, position the audience to understand that Cooper's presence on Miller's planet would have an irreversible impact on what was happening on Earth. Nolan, however, refused to share the footage. He insisted that Zimmer continue to write away from the image, and in the end, Nolan states that "it hit everything, [and they were] still in sync" (Zimmer and Pearson 2018).

The sound the audience hears during the Miller's planet sequence is densely layered: the tension caused by this density (in both the score and the sound effects) is used to remind the audience what is at stake. Cooper and two of his colleagues, Brand and Doyle, must enter and exit the planet as efficiently as possible to retrieve data that would determine if it could sustain human life (their other colleague, Romilly, stays behind to take advantage of the time dilation and work on his research). As they travel toward the planet at an extremely fast pace, alarms are sounding and rattling is heard. The unstable nature of these realistic sounds causes tension to rise before the Ranger breaks through the clouds to reveal Miller's planet; at 1:04:40, we are presented with a moment of sonic relief by the sound of an atmospheric pressure release. When the Ranger lands in the water, at 1:05:28, a deep, sustained drone is heard, shortly joined by a sound of water dripping and a clock ticking (simultaneously). This hybrid sound repeats every 1.25 seconds; fans have calculated that every time we hear this sound, a day passes on Earth ("*Interstellar*" 2018).

As Brand and Doyle make their way toward the mountains, we can faintly hear an organ. The instrument rises in volume when they discover that "the mountains" are, instead, enormous waves. Cooper soon realizes that they have landed in a swell, and at 1:07:10, a variation of the thematic motif titled "Cornfield Chase" is heard: this cue has already been heard in the film during sequences where the characters are racing against time. In the original theme, the cue consists of eight bars (that repeat with added embellishment), each with two notes, and the duration of the first note is half the length of the second note. However, the cue slightly changes during this sequence, with each bar consisting of two notes of the same duration. The same arrangement of notes is heard, with the second note of each bar remaining on the same pitch (E), while the first note of each bar belongs to the A minor scale (the key signature of the piece). Simply put, since we hear the notes of the A minor scale ascending, tension builds.

When Cooper discovers that the mountains are waves, the camera follows his gaze and pans from the base to the top of a catastrophic wave that is about to break. This revelation is mimicked in the score: the motif repeats and chanting is heard, while rapidly increasing in speed and volume before the camera reaches the summit (of the reveal and the wave) at 1:07:35–1:07:41. When the camera reaches the peak of the wave, the duration between the bars is elongated: the two notes are played in their original tempo; however, the second note is sustained with an oscillating downward instrumentation occurring simultaneously. This variation of the motif continues, becoming more pronounced as the scene continues. At 1:08:09, when Brand realizes that she will not make it back to the Ranger before the wave breaks, the score shifts and incorporates a more exaggerated extension of the original clock sound. From this point on, the motif continues without the second note of each bar: only the first note is heard as it makes its way up the scale before repeating. With each repetition of this variation, the tension builds as the characters race against time: horns are introduced on the beat; the organ and a range of wind instruments are layered, while simultaneously getting louder and louder; finally, chanting is introduced on each consecutive beat and reverbs, adding emphasis and a dramatic quality to the scene. At 1:08:58, the score is drowned out by the sound of the wave crashing on the Ranger. When they eventually leave Miller's planet and return to the *Endurance*, Romilly tells us that "twenty-three years, four months, [and] eight days" have passed on Earth. The varying degrees of tension produced by the soundscape in this sequence situates the audience within the narrative. The audience is reminded of the impacts that the crew's presence on Miller's planet will have on humankind: Earth is rapidly deteriorating with each passing second (and, thus, each passing day on Earth due to time's relativity), and the importance of this mission to sustain the very same human life on Earth.

Nolan and Zimmer used *Interstellar* to push the boundaries of their collaboration to achieve what they had not before. Their collaboration allowed them to experiment with layers of sounds, solely to challenge themselves and the limits of their creative partnership. As Frank Lehman argues, creating grand musical gestures from such minimal pieces of music is a Zimmer trademark: the composer uses an "obsessive reiteration" of these simple, minimal cues to have "an engrossing effect" on the audience (2016, 29). Thus, *Interstellar*'s soundscape presents different manipulations of tension in the score to place the audience within such temporal and narrative complexity.

DUNKIRK (2017)

Nolan and Zimmer's collaboration on *Dunkirk* was perhaps their most challenging film to date. While dealing with the sensitivity of real-life events, the director and composer attempted to achieve a unique cinematic experience: one where the audience can experience the impact on different groups of people in a war film. In order to achieve this, the film presents three intersecting storylines that each take place across a different length of time: the beach (one week), the sea (one day), and the sky (one hour). The film follows the story of the British, French, and Belgian soldiers stranded on the beach at Dunkirk during World War II (May 26 to June 4, 1940). Although surrounded by German forces, the exposed troops must rely on the air force to defend the beach from the sky as they await rescue: the Navy has enlisted civilians to chart their boats across the English Channel to France because military ships cannot dock on the beach. The points of intersection between these three storylines result in a complex relationship between the audience and a sense of time unfolding in each narrative. The soundscape, therefore, allows the audience to experience time in the same way that the soldiers, civilians, or pilots do in their respective narratives. Nolan and Zimmer achieve this by elevating or relieving tension in the film.

Zimmer originally composed an entire orchestral score before seeing the footage, but the composer believed that it did not work with the image (Zimmer and Burton 2018). In response to Nolan's suggestion, Zimmer composed this original score with an auditory effect in mind called "the Shepard tone": according to the director, this effect is an "audio illusion whereby you're going up the scale and by playing the incoming low notes louder than the outgoing high notes. Done correctly, you create this illusion of a continuing rise in pitch that never goes out of range" (Nolan and Collins 2017). In this way, the sound appears to have reached its apex with each consecutive note without ever actually doing so, creating the sensation of constantly increasing tension and a visceral experience for the audience. When Nolan and Zimmer reached post-production, editing the image to a completed score composed with the mechanisms of this sound illusion proved much more difficult than anticipated, however, as the composer explains:

> Before Chris went out to shoot the movie, we actually did a 100-minute framework of music. . . . Once the movie was done, one of the problems was, [with] a constantly rising sound, you can't cut into it. You can't edit it. It became enormously complicated, figuring out how to hide the edits. Plus, you as an audience figure out very quickly what is going on. So, it needs to shift and change and be like a chameleon. (Zimmer and Grobar 2018)

Nolan and Zimmer's typical working approach (creating the image and the sound independently) could not allow the Shepard tone to work subtly and, therefore, effectively when the image and the sound were edited together. This meant that the composer needed to start from the beginning and compose alongside the image if he intended to use the Shepard tone (Zimmer and Grobar 2018). Thus, Nolan and Zimmer worked more closely with each other and with other elements of the soundscape to achieve this. Since the main goal of the score was to build tension, as Zimmer reminds us, they used a combination of the Shepard tone, silence, and sound effects, and worked closely with sound designer, Richard King (Zimmer and Gorbar 2018; Zimmer and Burton 2018). Zimmer often blurs the boundaries between the conventional score and these cinematic sounds on Nolan's more narratively and temporally complex films; the composer suggests that he often takes on the role of the sound designer when conceptualizing his scores (Zimmer 2013). Indeed, sound effects appear on *Dunkirk*'s "Original Motion Picture Soundtrack," a somewhat unusual practice.

Nolan allows Zimmer's music to situate the audience within complex and intersecting timelines by relying on different levels of tension; the shifting levels of tension made possible by the Shepard tone allow the audience to experience time differently within each storyline. Indeed, as Eleonora Rapan argues, the Shepard tone can produce a psychological sense that "can project an eternity within a few minutes or seconds" (2018, 141). The sky timeline in *Dunkirk*, for example, takes place over one hour (the shortest time frame of the three). In the tightly confined space in the cockpit of the fighter jet, the sound effects are extremely realistic and loud: the minimal dialogue allows the deafening sounds of bullets hitting the exterior of the jets into the foreground. Time feels like an eternity for the audience, perhaps because the Shepard tone is at its loudest during this narrative (or, at the very least, the sound effects are at the same volume as the score). On the other hand, in the sea and the beach timelines, the soundscape during the moments of impact are usually isolated: the realistic sounds occur in the foreground of what the audience can hear. Instead, the Shepard tone is, more often than not, reserved for instances that anticipate moments of impact. This juxtaposition leads to varying amounts of tension, thus cementing the audience's unique and varying experiences during each narrative.

Achieving the desired levels of tension throughout these intersecting timelines forces the audience to experience these different manipulations of time at the same rate as the different groups of characters in the film. Moving away from the conventional war film, Nolan was quite adamant that the score needed to avoid emotion for much of the film. The director suggests that there were already so many emotions running through the storylines from the soldiers and civilians, and therefore the audience is already forced into the subject-position of these characters: *Dunkirk* embodies the experiences of being on the beach, on the boat, and in the fighter jet (Nolan and Collins 2017). Thus, rather than emotional or sentimental music that one might expect to hear in a war film, Nolan tells us that he opted for "ticking clocks and heartbeats, and the rustle of gear and breath and movement, and all of these tactile sounds" (Nolan and Collins 2017). Yet, as Zimmer suggests, the audience "earns emotion" after seventy minutes of wavering tension when we eventually hear the first of the composer's arrangements of Edward Elgar's "Nimrod Variations" (with the assistance from his colleague, Benjamin Wallfisch) (Nolan and Collins 2017). Commander Bolton (in charge of the evacuation on the beach) looks out toward the water, concerned, focusing his attention on something out of frame. At this point (1:10:13), the tension in the score has reached its height, with haunting strings playing scales, and is joined by sounds of a siren-like screech, a propeller, and a clock ticking. The final sound lingers on a high-pitched dissonant interval while Commander Bolton looks through binoculars. When he is asked what he sees, he simply replies "home" with a sign of relief on his face. At this moment, the score not only resolves but also transitions into Nimrod's familiar (and emotional) orchestral music (1:10:40): we hear enchanting and uplifting strings. This is a satisfying release from the tension, taking on one of film's music most traditional roles: that is, as "a signifier of emotion itself" (Gorbman 1987, 73).

A director and a composer can saturate an audience's film experience with varying levels of tension by integrating sound effects and grand, orchestral moments into a score. Nolan and Zimmer use this tension and release to situate the audience within such temporally complex narratives by placing the audience into the subject-position of the characters. As Darren Mooney suggests, "Nolan's films often feature a conflict between a character's subjective interpretation of events and the objective reality of this situation . . . manifest[ing] itself in terms of a fractured sense of time; time literally moving at a different pace for these characters than it does for the larger world" (2018, 143). This sound effect, however, is not unique to *Dunkirk*: Zimmer tells us that he has used the Shepard tone in almost every score he has composed for Nolan (Zimmer and Kermode 2019). However, there is an additional "secret ingredient" in *Dunkirk* that the director and composer refuse to share.[12] This "secret ingredient," and whether it actually does exist, adds to the pair's influence and position in the contemporary Hollywood film industry.

THE FUTURE OF THE DIRECTOR AND COMPOSER

It's my [Nolan's] job as a writer, director particularly, to try and be the audience for the film. . . . In that way my hope is that there are enough signifiers, there are enough familiarities to the rhythm of the piece I'm putting together that the audience can feel oriented, so even if they're confused by certain aspects, the feeling of the rhythm, you know, in almost a musical way is evolving. (Nolan and Cameron 2017).

Christopher Nolan's filmmaking trademarks distinguish him as one of the most notable auteur directors in the contemporary Hollywood film industry: in particular, his dedication to creating temporally and narratively complex films; his loyal fanbase that continues to seek out a particular "Nolan" cinematic experience; and his reliance on a filmmaking team that understands and fosters the director's style.[13] Nolan, therefore, places significant weight on music in his films, relying on the soundscape to help the audience navigate such complexity.

Nolan's continued collaboration with Hans Zimmer is beginning to become more normative in the contemporary film industry. The director and composer's influence among their peers is increasingly recognized through their impact on current Hollywood filmmaking practices (Zimmer and Pearson 2018). The use of the infamous "braaam" sound in *Inception*, for example, originated as a sonic device to prompt a narrative shift in the film, guiding the characters and the audience through a temporally and narratively complex hierarchy of dreams. Latterly, it has become "the blueprint for all action movies" (Buchanan 2013; Davis 2013). The practice of director and composer collaborating before images have been filmed allows music to take on these additional roles within the contemporary Hollywood film, compensating for the information deficit felt by the viewer. As a result, Nolan and Zimmer's complex approach to the soundscape of their films drives film sound further than it has ever been before. Thus, the collaboration between Nolan and Zimmer is paving the way for the future of director and composer relationships and the contemporary Hollywood film sound.

NOTES

1. In their study, Hill-Parks documents the reviews across Nolan's career, suggesting that Nolan's status an auteur director is celebrated (Hill-Parks 2015, 17–30).

2. Of course, it must be recognized that an ongoing relationship between an auteur director and a composer is not entirely unique to Nolan and Zimmer—other contemporary collaborations include Sam Mendes and Thomas Newman, and Tim Burton and Danny Elfman. Nolan and Zimmer's collaboration is, however, notable.

3. This, perhaps, might have something to do with the director's collaborators also inhibiting their own auteur qualities that they bring to Nolan's films. Hans Zimmer's compositions, for example, carry stamps that allow his compositions to be recognized as a Zimmer score (Lehman 2016, 27–55).

4. Surprisingly, Julyan returned to compose *The Prestige* after Nolan hired Zimmer to score *Batman Begins*. Julyan composed the score at Zimmer's production studio, Remote Control Productions, and Zimmer is also credited on *The Prestige* as an executive music producer (Julyan and Oliver 2006).

5. Zimmer often shares a personal anecdote about how Levinson's wife, Diana, had come across *A World Apart* and thought that her husband would really enjoy its score. So, she bought the CD for him (Zimmer and Pearson 2018; Zimmer 2016).

6. Zimmer tells the tale of having to compose music after an editor once used Samuel Barber's "Adagio for Strings," one of the most celebrated Western art compositions, as temp music: "everybody loved it and I was just going, 'what, are you trying to kill me?' Two weeks later, I'm still trying to write something as good as that. . . . The burden of that is just so impossible" (Zimmer 2016).

7. Directors return to collaborate with an existing composer for many reasons: their collaboration has proven successful in the past, a level of trust has been established between the two, or, perhaps, the studio might suggest a return to a specific composer or creator (Zimmer 2016).

8. Julyan's method of composing differs greatly from Zimmer's method. According to Julyan, his way of composing involved working very closely with the image, primarily composing music to scenes that had been shot. This is a practice that Nolan

rarely implements nowadays, as we eventually see in the director's continual collaboration with Zimmer in the following section (Julyan and Oliver 2006).

9. In the film's dialogue, the characters use the terms "levels" and "layers" interchangeably. In this chapter, I use the term "layers" to suggest that the characters can only access another layer of dreaming by travelling through the one they are currently inhabiting: they can only access a "dream within a dream" once they have traveled to "a dream," and so on. Using the term "level" implies that the characters can, perhaps, skip a level of dreaming, as if they were in an elevator (like Cobb and Ariadne do when navigating the memories in Cobb's subconscious).

10. According to the film's dialogue, ten hours in reality equates to one week in a dream, six months in a dream within a dream, ten years in a dream within a dream within a dream, and an infinite amount of time in limbo (Nolan 2010).

11. I use the term "above" here to suggest that when the characters travel to another layer of dream, they are traveling further down in the dream layer. Arthur (played by Joseph Gordon-Levitt) implies this in his dialogue: "my question is how we go down three layers with enough stability?" (Nolan 2010).

12. For further discussion on this, see Zimmer and Kermode 2019.

13. The use of the Shepard tone in *Dunkirk*, for example, was signaled not only in its soundscape but also in the script; Nolan wrote the three timelines using the same principle as the auditory illusion that guides the pacing of the film (Nolan and Howard 2017).

REFERENCES

Buchanan, Kyle. 2013. "Hans Zimmer Tells Juicy Stories about the Classic Films He's Scored." *Vulture*, November 5. www.vulture.com/2013/11/hans-zimmer-on-the-classic-films-hes-scored.html.

Chitwood, Adam. 2019. "Hans Zimmer Explains Why He Chose 'Dune' Over Christopher Nolan's 'Tenet.'" *Collider*, July 17. collider.com/why-hans-zimmer-isnt-scoring-christopher-nolan-new-movie-tenet/.

Davis, Edward. 2013. "BRAAAM! 10 Trailers That Use & Abuse The 'Inception' BRAAAM!" *IndieWire*, April 12. www.indiewire.com/2013/04/braaam-10-trailers-that-use-abuse-the-inception-braaam-99480/.

DesJardins, Christian. 2006. *Inside Film Music: Composers Speak*. Los Angeles, CA: Silman-James Press.

Dunkirk. 2017. Directed by Christopher Nolan. Burbank, CA: Warner Bros. Pictures.

Engel, Felix, and Janina Wildfeuer. 2015. "Hearing Music in Dreams: Towards the Semiotic Role of Music in Nolan's *Inception*." In *The Cinema of Christopher Nolan: Imagining the Impossible*, ed. Jacqueline Furby and Stuart Joy, 233–46. New York: Columbia University Press.

Gorbman, Claudia. 1987. *Unheard Melodies: Narrative Film Music*. Bloomington and Indianapolis: Indiana University Press; and London: BFI Publishing.

Greiving, Tim. 2017. "Hans Zimmer's Inescapable Shadow." *The Ringer*, July 20. Accessed August 10, 2021. www.theringer.com/2017/7/20/16078202/hans-zimmer-christopher-nolan-scores-dark-knight-inception-dunkirk-ff95a61d4038.

Guerrasio, Jason. 2015. "A Very Ironic Video Was the First One Ever Played on MTV 34 Years Ago." *Business Insider*, August 1. www.businessinsider.com/video-killed-the-radio-star-34th-anniversary-of-music-video-on-mtv-2015-7?r=US&IR=T.

Hexel, Vasco. 2016. *Hans Zimmer and James Newton Howard's* The Dark Knight: *A Film Score Guide*. Lanham, MD: Rowman & Littlefield.

Hill-Parks, Erin. 2015. "Developing an Auteur through Reviews: The Critical Surround of Christopher Nolan." In *The Cinema of Christopher Nolan: Imagining the Impossible*, ed. Jacqueline Furby and Stuart Joy, 17–30. New York: Columbia University Press.

Inception. 2010. Directed by Christopher Nolan. Burbank, CA: Warner Bros. Pictures.

Interstellar. 2014. Directed by Christopher Nolan. Burbank, CA: Warner Bros. Pictures.

"*Interstellar*." 2018. *Reddit*, July 21. www.reddit.com/r/MovieDetails/comments/9o1uwh/in_interstellar_on_the_water_planet_the/e2rf3v5/.

Julyan, David, and Glen Oliver. 2006. "Scorekeeper Chats with Composer David Julyan." *Ain't It Cool News*, December 19. legacy.aintitcool.com/node/31031.

Karlin, Fred, and Rayburn Wright. 2004. *On the Track: A Guide to Contemporary Film Scoring*, 2nd ed. New York: Routledge.

Kawin, Bruce. 2008. "Authorship, Design, and Execution." In *Auteurs and Authorship: A Film Reader*, ed. Barry Keith Grant, 190–99. Malden, MA: Blackwell Publishing.

Lehman, Frank. 2016. "Manufacturing the Epic Score: Hans Zimmer and the Sounds of Significance." In *Music in Epic Film: Listening to Spectacle*, ed. Stephen C. Meyer, 27–55. London: Taylor & Francis Group.

Mooney, Darren. 2018. *Christopher Nolan: A Critical Study of the Films*. Jefferson, NC: McFarland.

Nolan, Christopher. 2010. "INCEPTION by Christopher Nolan: Shooting Script." *Raindance*. Accessed July 5, 2021. www.raindance.co.uk/site/scripts/Inception.pdf.

———. 2014. "Director Christopher Nolan on *Interstellar*, Inspiration and Family." *YouTube*, December 16. www.youtube.com/watch?v=mddl8rrOyM4.

———. 2018. "'It's really about sticking to your guns': Christopher Nolan on Directing." *YouTube*, January 18. www.youtube.com/watch?v=0CaDZamA2ok.

Nolan, Christopher, and Bailey Cameron. 2017. "Christopher Nolan DUNKIRK Q&A: TIFF 2017." *YouTube*, September 15. www.youtube.com/watch?v=j0T2mMAfsx8.

Nolan, Christopher, and Andrew Collins. 2017. "'We fight like cats and dogs but in the best, the most productive way': Christopher Nolan Speaks Exclusively about His Extraordinary Partnership with Composer Hans Zimmer." *Classic FM*, July 18. Accessed on April 6, 2021. www.classicfm.com/composers/zimmer/music/christopher-nolan-interview/.

Nolan, Christopher, and Jack Howard. 2017. "I Love Christopher Nolan." *YouTube*, July 17. www.youtube.com/watch?v=0O2rRZmRVIo&feature=youtu.be&t=454.

Rapan, Eleonora. 2018. "Shepard Tones and Production of Meaning in Recent Films: Lucrecia Martel's *Zama* and Christopher Nolan's *Dunkirk*." *The New Soundtrack* 8, no. 2: 134–44.

Sellors, C. Paul. 2007. "Collective Authorship in Film." *The Journal of Aesthetics and Art Criticism* 65, no. 3: 263–71.

Thompson, Emma. 2010. "Special Features: The Inception of *Inception*," *Inception*. Directed by Christopher Nolan. Burbank, CA: Warner Bros. Pictures.

Zimmer, Hans. 2013. "Spitfire Interviews & Features: Hans Zimmer." *YouTube*, November 23. www.youtube.com/watch?v=me_8pWY2HpQ.

———. 2016. *MasterClass*. Accessed March 5, 2021. www.masterclass.com/classes/hans-zimmer-teaches-film-scoring.

———. 2018. "Hans Zimmer Breaks Down His Legendary Career, from *Gladiator* to *Interstellar*." *Vanity Fair*. *YouTube*, January 24. www.youtube.com/watch?v=GGs_NT4iL2c.

Zimmer, Hans, and Byron Burton. 2018. "Hans Zimmer on Capturing the Intensity of *Dunkirk* in a 90-Minute Score." *The Hollywood Reporter*, February 6. www.hollywoodreporter.com/movies/movie-news/hans-zimmer-capturing-intensity-dunkirk-a-90-minute-score-1080058/.

Zimmer, Hans and Matt Grobar. 2018. "Hans Zimmer Set Out after Complete Fusion of Sound and Image with *Dunkirk*." *Deadline*, February 22. deadline.com/2018/02/dunkirk-hans-zimmer-oscars-origina-score-interview-1202280792/.

Zimmer, Hans, and Mark Kermode. 2019. "Hans Zimmer with Kermode on Scala Radio." *YouTube*, July 20. www.youtube.com/watch?time_continue=5&v=mHm-KZbUZiIA&feature=emb_logo.

Zimmer, Hans, and Tommy Pearson. 2018. "Hans Zimmer on Scoring *Gladiator*, *Inception*, *Interstellar* & More." *YouTube*, July 25. www.youtube.com/watch?v=D1-eXPXQwzs.

Chapter 7

A "Virtual Carte Blanche"

Christopher Nolan, Warner Bros., and Authorial Power in Contemporary Hollywood

Kimberly A. Owczarski

After writing and directing the award-winning independent film *Memento* (2000), Christopher Nolan signed on to helm the studio-produced *Insomnia* (2002). Although his third feature, this would be his first distributed by a major Hollywood studio. Headlined by three Academy Award–winning actors, the thriller was well received critically, yet earned less than $70 million[1] in domestic theaters for distributor Warner Bros. In a year dominated by comic book adaptations like Sony's *Spider-Man* (which grossed nearly $404 million at domestic theaters), it is perhaps not surprising that Warner Bros. moved away from releasing adult thrillers like *Insomnia* to reinvigorate its key *Batman* franchise in order to compete more successfully at the box office. In that regard, Nolan's pitch for a new beginning to the *Batman* franchise came at the right moment for the studio. Nolan stressed a credible backstory for the superhero and incorporated the thriller elements he had honed on his previous features. After years of looking for the right approach to the property, Warner Bros. executives greenlit Nolan's film despite the tepid box office performance of *Insomnia*. Since this approval for what would become *Batman Begins* (2005), Nolan's relationship to Warner Bros. grew into a "virtual carte blanche," as writer Ben Fritz once described the studio's partnership with the director (Fritz 2014). Indeed, Nolan wrote, produced, and directed all of his next seven films with the studio.

To earn that carte blanche, Nolan's studio films were extremely successful. The three Nolan-helmed *Batman* films collectively grossed over $2.4 billion at the global box office and helped the studio's bottom line, too, through the sale of DVDs, merchandise, and comic books. This work was so fruitful that he also served as a producer on *Man of Steel* (2013) and as an executive producer on *Batman vs. Superman: Dawn of Justice* (2016) and *Justice League* (2017) as Warner Bros. attempted to relaunch multiple comic book–based franchises. While these properties have earned Warner Bros. billions in revenue, it is perhaps more impressive that Nolan's original films have also generated high rates of return. *Inception* (2010) grossed more than $825 million globally while *Interstellar* (2014) earned more than $675 million. The latter film is a case in point about the director's importance to the studio. With the project having been set up at Paramount initially, Warner Bros. traded its rights on multiple franchises to Paramount in order to participate in *Interstellar* and remain Nolan's chief studio base.

Perhaps no film shows the extent of Nolan's significance to Warner Bros. more than *Tenet* (2020). A big-budget original film with a complex narrative, *Tenet* was marketed primarily on the strength of Nolan's track record. However, like many films set to be released in 2020, *Tenet* became a victim to the global COVID-19 pandemic as theaters across the world shuttered in the spring and remained closed through the summer box-office season. *Tenet*'s original release date of July 17, 2020, was changed multiple times, eventually landing on a late August debut in certain international markets and on Labor Day weekend in the United States. Warner Bros. executives emphasized that *Tenet* deserved to be seen on the big screen and declined to offer it as a day-and-date release on digital platforms despite the raging pandemic. *Tenet*'s box office performance was lackluster, with Warner Bros. losing $50 to $100 million on the film, likely the only Nolan film to not generate any profits for the studio (Rubin 2020a).

Prior to its release, *Tenet* was heralded as the potential savior to the struggling movie business. While it may have underperformed given the circumstances, Nolan's vital role with the studio is key to understanding why *Tenet* had the release that it did. Nolan's partnership with Warner Bros. is unlike any other talent/studio relationship in contemporary Hollywood. This essay examines Nolan's unique relationship with Warner Bros. Indeed, the effect of that relationship reverberates throughout Hollywood, given the franchise mentality that currently grips the studios and the few big-budget original properties that filmmakers have the opportunity to create. Unreplicated in the film industry, the Nolan/Warner Bros. partnership demonstrates the power of authorship in the contemporary studio environment.

EVOLVING DIRECTOR/STUDIO RELATIONSHIPS

While the norm during the studio era, sustained director/studio relationships are not common in contemporary Hollywood. When the major studios released hundreds of films annually during the height of the studio era, directors functioned under house contracts in order to maintain the efficiency and profitability of the production system. Indeed, to remain under contract, directors "had to demonstrate their conformity and commitment to the studio's material concerns" which included the budget, stars, and genre allotted to the production according to scholar Ronny Regev (2018, 5). In this environment, directors served as "studio employees who worked under the command of an executive producer or head of production. But, unlike their colleagues [in other positions], directors enjoyed a certain degree of authoritative autonomy" (2018, 77). While often not involved in the writing or editing processes of a motion picture, directors were seen as the key creators on set. Regev thus describes the role of the studio-era director as a "contingent auteur" who exercised personal vision on set but whose power was limited in scope beyond that specific role (2018, 94).

When the studio era ended in the 1950s, the Hollywood production norm shifted from the factory-like model described by Regev to a focus on creating individual films. As a result, studios no longer contracted talent who worked continuously from one project to the next. With this shift, directors began to see more authorial power beyond the set in their new role as freelancers. In order to gain that power, however, the directors had to market themselves not only through their film work, but also in the paratexts that surround the filmmaking process. Aided by the auteur theory first popularized through the critics writing for *Cahiers du Cinéma*, the post-studio-era directors found an environment where each film needed to be promoted on its own merits and their names carried significant weight with critics and moviegoers. Timothy Corrigan argues that "[A]uteurism has [always] been bound up with changes in industrial desires, technological opportunities, and marketing strategies. . . . [T]he industrial utility of auteurism from the late 1960s to the early 1970s had much to do with the waning of the American studio system and the subsequent need to find new ways to mark a movie other than with a studio's signature" (1998, 40). It is within this environment that a new generation of filmmakers who attended film school and were steeped in not only Hollywood film history but also auteur theory emerged.

Directors like Steven Spielberg and George Lucas embodied the emerging business practices of this New Hollywood. For their collaboration on *Raiders of the Lost Ark* (1981), Lucas and Spielberg negotiated a deal with Paramount where revenues were evenly split with the filmmakers after the studio took its distribution fee, an unheard-of deal at the time (Schatz 2017, 29). Their ability to negotiate these terms was based on their box office track records and the name recognition audiences had for the filmmakers. The successful films that they directed and produced influenced Hollywood's blockbuster mentality, with the studios' revenue streams extending beyond the theatrical experience into video, merchandise, television, publishing, and video games, among others. In today's marketplace, the role of directors thus extends beyond the production itself. According to J. D. Connor, "Directorial labor is necessary not only to produce 'the text' but to generate value-added elements for aftermarkets" (2017, 138). From the marketing of sequels and extensions to DVD commentaries and alternative cuts, the director is an important consideration for the studios' bottom-line focus.

Many directors for franchise films in the last few decades have their roots in independent film. They bring with them not only critical cachet, but also distinct viewpoints and a keen understanding of filmmaking in difficult conditions. As Martin Flanagan notes, "[I]t has seemingly become standard practice to engage an art house or independent sector filmmaker to direct a substantially budgeted mainstream release" (2004, 20). Flanagan's essay investigates the marketing and critical positioning of Universal's comic book adaptation *Hulk* (2003) which largely centered on director Ang Lee's history, style, and thematic concerns. Flanagan argues: "The recurrent association of the film's creative essence with the mercurial talent of its auteur director, encouraged by Universal's promotional machine, was not necessarily the obvious strategy for an expensive movie whose mode of address needed to be broad and populist" (2004, 28). While the film itself was considered a box office failure, bringing in just $132 million from domestic theaters, Lee's involvement demonstrated the studios' "principle of product differentiation [which] creates a need for an ever-changing system of associations around event movies" (2004, 32). Because every film needs to be promoted individually in today's marketplace, the director's name is key to these associations, even with a known intellectual property like *Hulk*. For franchise films, thus, who directs is a landmark decision for the studio, a choice which has a lasting impact on the property's potential to be successful at the box office and in the aftermarkets. In that regard, Warner Bros. executives' decision to hire Christopher Nolan to direct an adult thriller helped set in motion the studio's franchise mentality for years to come.

A FRANCHISE MOVIE "UP FOR GRABS": ESTABLISHING NOLAN'S RELATIONSHIP WITH WARNER BROS.

Nolan's ability to move from *Following* (1998), a self-financed $6,000 film shot only on weekends over the course of a year, to the franchise film *Batman Begins* in just seven years is remarkable and is the result of his success as an independent filmmaker. While *Following* was playing at film festivals, Nolan was able to secure $4.5 million for his next project, *Memento*, from Newmarket Films, a film finance company with no record of distribution. Based on a short story his brother Jonathan wrote about a man suffering from anterograde amnesia, Nolan's script told the story primarily in reverse order. *Memento* played at many festivals and won several awards, including at Sundance and at the Independent Spirit Awards. While *Memento* did well on the film festival circuit, no distributor was interested in picking up the film despite its critical acclaim. According to Newmarket co-founder William Tyrer, the film's nontraditional narrative was a major obstacle: "If we had an offer for $8 million, we would have said 'fine'. . . . But the $8 million offer never came. . . . People thought it was too difficult, too obscure, and had no commercial potential" (Fierman 2001). With limited studio interest, Newmarket self-distributed the film and aggressively marketed *Memento* which helped it gross over $25 million domestically.

Despite its independent nature and nonlinear storytelling, Nolan believed that *Memento* had potential to cross over to mainstream audiences. Interviewed about the film prior to its theatrical release, Nolan made it clear that *Memento* was approachable: "I don't see *Memento* as an art movie, and I'll be very disappointed if it ends up being perceived that way. I think of myself as a pretty mainstream filmmaker, ultimately" ("Past Imperfect" 2001). And indeed, his next project would be for a major studio. In September 2000, before *Memento*'s theatrical release, Nolan secured his next directing position with Warner Bros. for a remake of the Norwegian film *Insomnia* (1997). This role was based on the critical acclaim he generated on *Memento* through festivals and initial screenings as well as the support he received from award-winning director Steven Soderbergh. In fact, Warner Bros. executives would not meet with Nolan despite his expressed interest in the project until Soderbergh agreed to serve as a producer (Kemp 2001). Once given the helm of the $45 million-budgeted film, Nolan built core relationships with Warner Bros. executives, particularly Warner Bros. Pictures president Jeff Robinov. According to Nolan, it was on *Insomnia* that he learned what making a studio picture entailed:

> I did a medium-sized studio film, where I certainly felt a lot of pressure, unquestionably, but I did not feel the pressure that you feel when you take on a beloved character in a huge franchise, you know? So I had agreeable timing and I was able to build my relationship with the studio [Warner Bros.] through that film and learn how to deal with the pressures of big-budget Hollywood filmmaking. (Feinberg 2015)

Released in May 2002, *Insomnia* performed well with critics and grossed more than $100 million worldwide, providing him a solid reputation with Warner Bros. executives.

Luckily for Nolan, these executives were at that moment searching for the right filmmaker to revamp their *Batman* franchise which had been dormant since the disastrous 1997 release of *Batman and Robin*. That film had fizzled at the box office and was loathed by critics and fans alike. Warner Bros. did not have any comic book films in the works, and the huge grosses amassed by Sony's *Spider-Man* franchise were too tempting to ignore. According to Nolan, it was the perfect time to pitch his take on the *Batman* franchise:

> When I was looking for what to do next, one of the things I heard about was that Warner Bros were looking to restart Batman. After the success of *Spider-Man*, they felt they ought to get their big guys off the bench. The great part was that they wanted to refresh and invigorate the franchise, but didn't have any specific concepts and were essentially looking for someone to come in and tell them what to do. It's pretty unusual to have this sort of movie up for grabs. (Pulver 2005)

Accounts differ about Nolan's pitch to Warner Bros. executives for *Batman Begins*, with some claiming it was a scant fifteen minutes, while others asserted it went ninety minutes (see Lewis-Kraus 2014; Fritz 2014). Regardless, Nolan had no script at the time but emerged with a pay-or-play deal from Robinov based on that pitch about Bruce Wayne's origins in becoming Batman (Bing and Dunkley 2003). Having given the reins to the studio's most valuable intellectual property to the young filmmaker, Robinov later claimed, "I don't think we ever made a leap like that with any other filmmaker" (Fritz 2014).

Robinov's decision to take a chance on Nolan with *Batman Begins* is all the more surprising given the stature of the company at the time. New media enterprise AOL had announced its purchase of parent company Time Warner in January 2000, which preceded over a year of regulatory approvals before the completion of the merger. In the midst of the government's review, the dot-com crash occurred where several new media companies, including AOL, lost significant revenue after being overvalued on the stock market. This put tremendous pressure on the entertainment assets held by Warner Bros. to perform well across divisions in order to help mitigate massive losses at the corporate level. The $150 million budget on *Batman Begins* was a huge risk, as Nolan had never directed a film on that scale before. Robinov's gamble proved correct; *Batman Begins* grossed over $200 million domestically and another $166 million internationally in theaters with an additional $170 million earned in DVD sales within a year of its release (Hughes 2015).

Nolan has maintained that the film was not pitched as part of a series, but its economic impact on Warner Bros. certainly indicated a new start to the superhero franchise. Less than a year after the theatrical release of *Batman Begins*, Nolan was confirmed for a $185 million sequel. With the surprise announcement in July 2006 of actor Heath Ledger in the role of the Joker, *The Dark Knight* (2008) faced intense scrutiny in the media and with fans. This changed when the film's Joker-focused marketing campaign kicked into gear in 2007. With the untimely death of Ledger in January 2008 months before the film's release, *The Dark Knight* shifted its marketing focus. Nolan, however, was not prominent in the studio's overall promotional efforts, with his name absent on the posters and in the initial teasers and trailers. Ultimately, the film broke several domestic box office records in its initial release, including earning the highest midnight screening grosses ever, the highest single-day record, and the opening weekend record on its way to grossing over $1 billion at movie theaters worldwide (Mendelson 2013).

In February 2010, Warner Bros. announced that a sequel to *The Dark Knight* would be written and directed by Nolan, and that he would also be developing and producing a new *Superman* film as well (Finke and Fleming Jr. 2010). Nolan's $250 million film featured more than an hour of footage shot with IMAX cameras and more than 11,000 extras for a specific action sequence, marking it as the grandest *Batman* film yet (Jolin 2012). *The Dark Knight Rises* (2012) grossed more than a billion worldwide, ending the trilogy in a spectacular fashion. Unlike the previous films, Nolan's name loomed large in most of the marketing materials for *The Dark Knight Rises*. According to Sue Kroll, president of Warner Bros. worldwide marketing, "Christopher Nolan as a brand is very powerful. . . . You can only say that about a handful of directors" (Fritz and Eller 2010). That status was earned, however, just as much from his successful *Batman* films as from the originals he created for the studio along the way.

A "PATH TO PROFITABILITY": NOLAN, WARNER BROS., AND ORIGINAL CONTENT

Nolan and his wife, Emma Thomas, a producer on all of his films, started their company Syncopy Films in 2001 as they moved from independent film into studio production. Employing just four people, Syncopy occupies real estate on the Warner Bros. lot but does not have an overall deal with the studio despite the fact that Nolan's next seven films after *Insomnia* involved them as producer, distributor, and/or financier. One of Syncopy's earliest projects was an adaptation of British novelist Christopher Priest's *The Prestige*, with the company acquiring the rights from Priest after sending him a VHS copy of Nolan's *Following* (Rahman 2014). Packaged by Newmarket Films, the company which produced and released *Memento*, Nolan signed on to direct, produce, and write the adaptation along with his brother, Jonathan, and Warner Bros. and Disney divided up the rights to the film's distribution. The deal was announced in April 2003, and *The Prestige* was intended to go into production prior to *Batman Begins*. The writing phase took longer than anticipated, so the project simmered while Nolan worked on the franchise film. Within months of the successful release of *Batman Begins*, casting decisions were announced, and *The Prestige* went into production in early 2006. Released later that year, the $40 million film was well regarded critically and earned more than $100 million worldwide at the box office.

Nolan's next film would be a sequel in the *Batman* film franchise, but he had an original project on the backburner: *Inception*. According to the director, he initially met with Warner Bros. executives about the project after he finished *Insomnia*, and they were ready then to hire him to write it, but he chose to work on *Batman Begins* and *The Prestige* instead (Fleming Jr. 2011). In February 2009, *Inception* was revealed as his next film after *The Dark Knight*'s exceptional box office run. Leonardo DiCaprio was announced as the film's lead weeks later. Due to *Inception*'s complex story, which involves a hired team entering into multiple levels of dreams in order to plant an idea into a man's subconscious, Nolan claimed that he could not have made *Inception* until he achieved the success of the first two *Batman* films:

> I wouldn't have been able to make this film until I had done the *Batman* films, because it's on such a massive scale, compared to anything else I've done. I had tried to write it smaller, on the assumption I might not be able to secure the budget I needed. What I found is, it's not possible to execute this concept in a small fashion. The reason is, as soon as you're talking about dreams, the potential of the human mind is infinite. And so the scale of the film has to feel infinite. (Itzkoff 2010)

Indeed, the $160 million budget, with another $100 million allocated for marketing, was uncommon for original concept films and considered to be a large risk. Given the film's complex storyline and its high budget, Robinov claimed in an interview: "I don't know if we would've made *Inception* without already having the relationship with Chris" (Goldstein 2010).

Nolan's completed script was presented to a room full of executives including Robinov and Kroll, among other representatives from the production, marketing, and distribution divisions of Warner Bros. and co-financier Legendary Pictures, before it was greenlit (Fleming Jr. 2011). From *Inception*'s start, Warner's marketing team was intricately involved to help the film achieve box office success. TV commercials announced that the film was "From the Director of *The Dark Knight*" before DiCaprio's name was even announced or he appeared onscreen, and the font in visual materials placed Nolan's name in a bigger size than DiCaprio's as well (Fritz and Eller 2010). Trailers gave very little information about the plot but emphasized the stunning visuals and key personnel, particularly Nolan. These measures were quite successful, as the film grossed more than $825 million globally in a year dominated by franchise films such as Paramount's *Iron Man 2*.

Of course, Nolan's follow-up to *Inception* as director, producer, and writer was *The Dark Knight Rises*, then the studio's leading franchise. He was clear in the press that this would be his last *Batman* film, despite agreeing to serve as a producer on a few of the upcoming DC Comics films. *The Dark Knight Rises*'s astounding box office of more than $1 billion worldwide secured Nolan a huge paycheck for his next film, *Interstellar*: 10 percent of the film's revenues, minus some studio deductions (Fritz 2014). Warner Bros. traded rights to the *Friday the 13th* franchise and the second *South Park* film to Paramount in order to participate in *Interstellar*, as Jonathan Nolan's original script had initially been acquired by Lynda Obst for Steven Spielberg to direct, and she was based at the rival studio (Kit and Masters 2013). Legendary Pictures also chose to help finance *Interstellar* rather than the upcoming DC Comics films, kicking in at least $25 million (Siegel and Galloway 2013). Legendary chose to stay with the filmmaker and an original concept film rather than with the guaranteed franchise.

With its $165 million budget, *Interstellar* featured big stars and huge effects given its premise about astronauts searching for hospitable places in the galaxy as Earth faces an impending climatic apocalypse. *Interstellar* was shot with multiple IMAX film cameras, and their use may have quadrupled the budget for the camera department as the cameras' use did for *The Dark Knight* (May 2018). *Interstellar* was released in select theaters in a film format, an expensive strategy as prints were about $30,000 each (Lang 2014). In early 2014, Paramount executives had announced the end of the use of film prints but provided an exception to *Interstellar* (McClintock 2014). The TCL Chinese Theater in Hollywood spent $600,000 in order to have a proper projector to show *Interstellar* during its premiere and theatrical run (Fritz 2014). These measures were likely due to Nolan's outspoken disdain for the digital format, as well as his stature in the industry at the time as a filmmaker who could deliver box office results, critical acclaim, and fan approval.

Interstellar grossed more than $675 million in theaters worldwide and earned five Academy Award nominations, winning one for Best Visual Effects.

Nolan's follow-up *Dunkirk* (2017) also earned multiple Academy Award nominations and won three. The film was a departure for Nolan as it was based on a battle and retreat that occurred during the early days of World War II. As such, the film faced challenges in appealing to American filmgoers. Nolan had wanted to direct a film about Dunkirk for years, but he knew he had to build a relationship with a studio before attempting such a project: "The road to getting this made was a lot of big movies for the same studio that made a lot of money and a lot of trust that developed between us" (de Souza 2017). While the film had a budget of $100 million, it was a significant decrease from his previous films. Producer Thomas explained:

> We knew we couldn't guarantee that this is going to be a massive box-office success even though we were opening it in summer and trying to position it very much as an entertainment. . . . So we asked for half the money that we'd had for Interstellar. We are not entirely reckless. We didn't want to make a film that was going to wreck our careers if it didn't work and if nobody went to see it. (Keegan 2018)

Still, the film did push the limits of its budget in Nolan's attempt to recreate what happened at Dunkirk. Massive expenditures included moving vintage ships from European museums, shipping antique planes from the United States, and reconstructing the famous Dunkirk pier which alone cost the production $900,000 (Lewis 2018). IMAX cameras were also used extensively and added to the film's sizable budget; indeed, the entire film was shot in a large film format now rarely used in the industry. Despite any worries whether a historical film lacking major Hollywood stars would perform well during the summer blockbuster season, *Dunkirk* grossed more than $525 million worldwide. Nolan's salary was rumored to be $20 million upfront plus 20 percent of the grosses ("Hollywood Salaries" 2016).

Nolan's *Dunkirk* follow-up was action oriented in the vein of *Inception*, an original concept film called *Tenet*. A January 2019 press release from Warner Bros. announced the film's release date as July 17, 2020. While complicated in its plot—time moves simultaneously forward and backward as an agent tries to stop the end of the world—*Tenet* featured rising star John David Washington, Nolan regular Michael Caine, and heartthrob Robert Pattinson in key roles. Like *Dunkirk*, *Tenet* would be entirely shot on IMAX and 70-mm film and had a rumored budget of $225 million. Warner Bros.' marketing division planned a massive push for the film centered on Nolan, including an IMAX-exclusive preview in December 2019 shown with Disney's *Star Wars: The Rise of Skywalker*.

Studio executives could not have foretold that a global pandemic would soon upend the entertainment industry and that these marketing measures would be for naught. Initially, Warner Bros. held steadfast to the July release date. As theaters closed and box office revenues dropped starting in March 2020, *Tenet* became poised as the film that could save both the summer box office and movie theaters. Stressed an unnamed marketing executive about the film's potential: "Chris Nolan believes in theaters so much that they will carve out this space. He'll have every single screen. Theaters are in tremendous trouble. They could stabilize stock prices and not have the whole summer slate collapse" (Thompson 2020). Yet with theaters in New York, California, and several other states closed or operating at limited capacity, in addition to valuable foreign markets likewise unavailable, the July release date looked increasingly untenable. After consulting with Nolan, Warner Bros. announced on June 12 a two-week delay for *Tenet*'s opening to July 31 (McClintock 2020a). Less than two weeks later, *Tenet*'s release was moved again to August 12. According to an unnamed Warner's spokesperson:

> Warner Bros. is committed to bringing Tenet to audiences in theaters, on the big screen, when exhibitors are ready and public health officials say it's time. In this moment what we need to be is flexible, and we are not treating this as a traditional movie release. . . . [W]e plan to play longer, over an extended play period far beyond the norm, to develop a very different yet successful release strategy. (McClintock 2020b)

While the spokesperson's statement emphasizes a "different" release strategy for *Tenet*, the film was still set to open in theaters simultaneously around the globe.

By July 20, however, the prospects still did not look good for a simultaneous international release of *Tenet*, and Warner Bros. announced yet another delay. *Tenet*'s new strategy was an international release for August 26 in seventy markets, with a limited release in the United States starting on Labor Day. Theaters had to guarantee a run of at least twelve weeks and agree to a 65 percent revenue split in favor of Warner Bros. in order to show the film (Jurgensen and Watson 2020). Despite being available in fewer theaters than is typical with blockbusters, the studio, Nolan, and theater chains were optimistic about the film's potential. Argued Nolan: "In the current industry in which we work, there's no path to profitability for a film like this that circumvents movie theaters" (Jurgensen and Watson 2020). Beyond the studio's fortunes, Richard Gelfond, the chief executive officer (CEO) of IMAX, suggested *Tenet*'s release was a lifeline to the theatrical business: "If this movie didn't follow this new release pattern, I didn't think the movies would be open until much later in the year or next year" (Jurgensen and Watson 2020).

Given the challenges of the pandemic, *Tenet* grossed just over $360 million worldwide. For the film that was supposed to save the industry, *Tenet* finished well short of expectations.

CONCLUSION

Warner Bros. executives' decision to release *Tenet* as many of the world's movie theaters remained closed or at limited capacity certainly led to the film's substantial losses and the perception of a poor box office performance. However, it placed as one of the highest grossing films internationally since the onset of the pandemic until finally surpassed in late 2021 by major franchise films such as Marvel's *Black Widow* and Universal's *F9: The Fast Saga*. Given *Tenet*'s original concept and complicated narrative, its box office likely would not have exceeded the performance of such established intellectual property, though likely it would have grossed significantly more in a normal year. In defense of its box office performance, Nolan stressed that the industry might be looking at *Tenet* through an inappropriate lens:

> I am worried that the studios are drawing the wrong conclusions from our release—that rather than looking at where the film has worked well and how that can provide them with much needed revenue, they're looking at where it hasn't lived up to pre-COVID expectations and will start using that as an excuse to make exhibition take all the losses from the pandemic instead of getting in the game and adapting—or rebuilding our business. (Rubin 2020a)

Nolan critiqued the lack of adaptation shown by the studios during the pandemic, especially in terms of the theatrical business.

A major change did come when Warner Bros. made the announcement in early December 2020 that all of its 2021 films would debut in theaters and on its newly launched streaming service HBO Max simultaneously as a result of the ongoing pandemic. The seventeen films affected included such major franchise films as *The Matrix 4* and *The Suicide Squad*. While WarnerMedia Studios CEO Ann Sarnoff claimed it was a "unique one-year plan," the fact that multiple studios like Universal and Disney had adopted similar models for some of their films suggested this might be the future business model (Rubin and Donnelly 2020). WarnerMedia CEO Jason Kilar claimed that this model would benefit not only the studio but the theaters as well: "Our content is extremely valuable, unless it's sitting on a shelf not being seen by anyone. We believe this approach serves our fans, supports exhibitors and filmmakers, and enhances the HBO Max experience, creating value for all" (Rubin and Donnelly 2020). However, the announcement caught talent associated with

Warner Bros. off-guard as they had not been consulted about the change. Days later, Nolan condemned the studio's plan, suggesting that "Some of our industry's biggest filmmakers and most important movie stars went to bed the night before thinking they were working for the greatest movie studio and woke up to find out they were working for the worst streaming service" (Masters 2020).

As the highest-profile talent associated with the studio, Nolan's words gained traction in the press as other filmmakers, such as *The Suicide Squad*'s James Gunn, began to look into potential lawsuits against Warner Bros. for breach of contract. In support of these filmmakers, Nolan noted that the studio's decision was significant: "It's very, very, very, very messy. A real bait and switch. Yeah, it's sort of not how you treat filmmakers and stars and people who . . . have given a lot for these projects. They deserved to be consulted and spoken to about what was going to happen to their work" (Boone 2020). Many in the industry surmised that the conglomerate's move would likely have the effect of severing ties with their most illustrious filmmaker. An unnamed veteran in the industry expressed disbelief at how WarnerMedia treated Nolan: "There are very few things in our business you can count on. . . . Chris Nolan's relationship with Warner Bros. would be toward the top of the list, which is what makes this so surprising and disappointing" (Rubin 2020b). With Nolan's follow-up to *Tenet* undetermined at that time, companies such as Sony and Apple were rumored to have approached him about securing his next project in the wake of the WarnerMedia decision.

In mid-September 2021, Nolan announced his next film would be about J. Robert Oppenheimer, the so-called father of the atomic bomb. Despite many studio and streaming suitors, he set up the project with Universal. He secured a $100 million budget for production and an equal amount for marketing, creative control, 20 percent of first-dollar grosses, a three-week blackout period before and after the film's release where no Universal properties would be in theaters, and a 100-day exclusive theatrical window (Kit 2021). While he experienced many of these same perks at Warner Bros., it was clear from its 2021 release slate that parent company WarnerMedia no longer viewed the theatrical exclusivity exercised on *Tenet* and Nolan's previous films as primary to its business model, and thus Nolan sought a new studio relationship. While his move to a new studio may be fortunate for the filmmaker in the short term, if the film fails at the box office, he will likely not find the freedoms and perks he experienced in his partnership with Warner Bros. as the studios refocus on their streaming platforms rather than the theatrical experience. Thus, the fallout from WarnerMedia's 2021 release plan is hard to deny. The new business model challenged the limits to this important studio/talent relationship, in an industry forever altered by the global pandemic. With the streaming wars rapidly waging among the Hollywood studios, the track record of Warner Bros.'s most important talent paled in comparison to the new opportunities presented in this newly evolving marketplace.

NOTE

1. All box office figures are taken from the website Box Office Mojo.

REFERENCES

Bing, Jonathan, and Cathy Dunkley. 2003. "Warners: Reloaded." *Variety*. September 21. variety.com/2003/film/news/warners-reloaded-1117892721/.

Boone, John. 2020. "Christopher Nolan Reflects on 'Tenet' Release, Reacts to Warner Bros./HBOMax Deal." *Entertainment Tonight*. December 7. www.etonline.com/christopher-nolan-reflects-on-tenet-release-reacts-to-warner-broshbo-max-deal-exclusive-157414.

Connor, J. D. 2017. "The Modern Entertainment Marketplace, 2000–Present: Revolutions at Every Scale." In *Directing*, ed. Victoria Wright Wexman, 137–53. New Brunswick: Rutgers University Press.

Corrigan, Timothy. 1998. "Auteurs and the New Hollywood." In *The New American Cinema*, ed. Jon Lewis, 38–63. Durham: Duke University Press.

De Souza, Alison. 2017. "Film-maker Christopher Nolan Had to Earn Studio's Trust to Make Dunkirk." *The Straits Times*, July 19. www.straitstimes.com/lifestyle/entertainment/going-to-dunkirk-on-his-own-terms.

Feinberg, Scott. 2015. "Christopher Nolan on 'Interstellar' Critics, Marking Original Films and Shunning Cellphones and Email." *Hollywood Reporter*, January 3. www.hollywoodreporter.com/news/general-news/christopher-nolan-interstellar-critics-making-760897/.

Fierman, Daniel. 2001. "'Memento' Takes Film Noir in a New Direction." *Entertainment Weekly*, March 30. ew.com/article/2001/03/30/memento-takes-film-noir-new-direction/.

Finke, Nikki, and Mike Fleming Jr. 2010. "It's a Bird! It's a Plane! It's Chris Nolan! He'll Mentor Superman 3.0 and Prep 3rd Batman." *Deadline Hollywood*, February 9. deadline.com/2010/02/its-a-bird-its-a-plane-its-chris-nolan-hell-mentor-superman-3-0-while-preparing-3rd-batman-24783/.

Flanagan, Martin. 2004. "'The Hulk, an Ang Lee Film': Notes on the Blockbuster Auteur." *New Review of Film and Television Studies* 2, no. 1: 19–35.

Fleming Jr., Mike. 2011. "Chris Nola Q&A about 'Inception.'" *Deadline*, January 7. deadline.com/2011/01/oscar-christopher-nolan-qa-inceptions-writer-director-is-a-hollywood-original-94704/.

Fritz, Ben. 2014. "Why Hollywood Loves 'Interstellar' Director Christopher Nolan." *Wall Street Journal*, October 30. www.wsj.com/articles/why-hollywood-loves-interstellar-director-christopher-nolan-1414677657.

Fritz, Ben, and Claudia Eller. 2010. "Warner Gambles on Unproven Commodity." *Los Angeles Times,* July 13. www.latimes.com/archives/la-xpm-2010-jul-13-la-fi-ct-inception-20100713-story.html.

Goldstein, Patrick. 2010. "Nolan Is a Studio's Dream." *Los Angeles Times*, July 20. latimesblogs.latimes.com/the_big_picture/2010/07/could-chris-nolan-have-convinced-anyone-but-warners-to-make-inception-.html.

"Hollywood Salaries 2016: Who Got Raises (and Who Didn't), from Movie Stars to Showrunners." 2016. *Hollywood Reporter*. September 29. www.hollywoodreporter.com/lists/hollywood-salaries-2016-who-got-933037/.

Hughes, Mark. 2015. "Christopher Nolan Talks 'Batman Begins' 10th Anniversary." *Forbes*, July 30. www.forbes.com/sites/markhughes/2015/07/30/exclusive-christopher-nolan-talks-batman-begins-10th-anniversary/?sh=3425dce5a8b5.

Itzkoff, Dave. 2010. "A Man and His Dream: Christopher Nolan and 'Inception.'" *New York Times*, June 30. artsbeat.blogs.nytimes.com/2010/06/30/a-man-and-his-dream-christopher-nolan-and-inception/.

Jolin, Dan. (2006) 2020. "The Prestige: Inside Christopher Nolan's Magic Movie Trick." *Empire*, August 17. Reprint. www.empireonline.com/movies/features/the-prestige-inside-christopher-nolan-movie-magic-trick/.

———. 2012. "The Dark Knight Trilogy: The Complete Story of Christopher Nolan's Batman Films." *Empire*, July. www.empireonline.com/movies/features/dark-knight-trilogy-complete-story-of-christopher-nolan-batman/.

Jurgensen, John, and R. T. Watson. 2020. "Christopher Nolan's 'Tenet' Makes a Global Bet on the Film Industry." *Wall Street Journal*, August 28. www.wsj.com/articles/christopher-nolans-tenet-makes-a-global-bet-on-the-film-industry-11598640209.

Keegan, Rebecca. 2018. "Meet the Woman behind Dunkirk." *Vanity Fair*, February 16. www.vanityfair.com/hollywood/2018/02/dunkirk-emma-thomas.

Kemp, Stuart. 2001. "Soderbergh: Expect Reduced Role for Studios." *Hollywood Reporter*, February 9. LexisNexis Academic.

Kit, Borys. 2021. "Inside the Studios' (and Apple's) Frenzy to Get Christopher Nolan's Next Film." *Hollywood Reporter*, September 15. www.hollywoodreporter.com/movies/movie-news/christopher-nolan-pitch-to-studios-including-apple-seeking-his-next-film-1235014132/.

Kit, Borys, and Kim Masters. 2013. "Warner Bros. Gave Up 'Friday the 13th' Rights to Board Christopher Nolan's 'Interstellar.'" *Hollywood Reporter*, June 5. www.hollywoodreporter.com/movies/movie-features/christopher-nolans-interstellar-warner-bros-562879/.

Lang, Brent. 2014. "With 'Interstellar,' IMAX Takes Aim at the Bigger Picture." *Hollywood Reporter,* October 29. variety.com/2014/film/features/with-interstellar-imax-hits-hollywoods-bigtime-1201341443/. Accessed July 22, 2021.

Lewis, Andy. 2018. "Making of *Dunkirk*: Christopher Nolan's Obsessive $100M Re-creation of the Pivotal WWII Battle." *Hollywood Reporter*, January 5. www.hollywoodreporter.com/movies/movie-features/making-dunkirk-christopher-nolans-obsessive-100m-creation-pivotal-wwii-battle-1070968/.

Lewis-Kraus, Gideon. 2014. "The Exacting, Expansive Mind of Christopher Nolan." *New York Times*, October 30. www.nytimes.com/2014/11/02/magazine/the-exacting-expansive-mind-of-christopher-nolan.html. Accessed July 20, 2021.

Masters, Kim. 2020. "Christopher Nolan Rips HBOMax as 'Worst Streaming Service,' Denounces Warner Bros.' Plan." *Hollywood Reporter*, December 7. www.hollywoodreporter.com/business/business-news/christopher-nolan-rips-hbo-max-as-worst-streaming-service-denounces-warner-bros-plan-4101408/. Accessed December 8, 2020.

May, Sam. 2018. "'The Dark Knight' Turns 10: How Christopher Nolan Launched an Epic Battle to Make Imax Blockbusters." *IndieWire*, July 18. www.indiewire.com/2018/07/the-dark-knight-imax-christopher-nolan-film-1201985173/. Accessed July 20, 2021.

McClintock, Pamela. 2014. "Christopher Nolan Talks 'Interstellar,' Plugs Film over Digital in Hollywood Reporter Q&A." *Hollywood Reporter*, March 26. www.hollywoodreporter.com/movies/movie-news/cinemacon-christopher-nolan-talks-interstellar-691456/. Accessed July 20, 2021.

———. 2020a. "Christopher Nolan's 'Tenet' Delays Release Two Weeks to End of July." *Hollywood Reporter*, June 12. www.hollywoodreporter.com/movies/movie-features/christopher-nolans-tenet-pushed-two-weeks-end-july-1285728/. Accessed September 5, 2021.

———. 2020b. "Christopher Nolan's 'Tenet' Delays Release to Mid-August Amid Spike in COVID-19 Cases." *Hollywood Reporter*, June 25. www.hollywoodreporter.com/movies/movie-features/christopher-nolans-tenet-delays-release-august-spike-covid-19-cases-1300382/. Accessed June 25, 2020.

Mendelson, Scott. 2013. "How 'The Dark Knight' Proved Irrelevance of Box Office Rank." *Forbes*, September 17. www.forbes.com/sites/scottmendelson/2013/09/17/how-the-dark-knight-proved-irrelevance-of-box-office-rank/?sh=36462d6617d2. Accessed June 21, 2021.

"Past Imperfect." 2001. *Filmmaker*. Winter 2001. filmmakermagazine.com/archives/issues/winter2001/features/past_imperfect.php. Accessed July 20, 2021.

Pulver, Andrew. 2005. "'He's Not a God—He's Human.'" *The Guardian*, June 15. www.theguardian.com/film/2005/jun/15/features.features11. Accessed May 25, 2021.

Rahman, Abid. 2014. "'Prestige' Author Slams Christopher Nolan's 'Dark Knight' Trilogy as 'Shallow' and 'Badly Written.'" *Hollywood Reporter*, November 28. www.hollywoodreporter.com/movies/movie-news/prestige-author-slams-christopher-nolans-752793/. Accessed July 9, 2021.

Regev, Ronny. 2018. *Working in Hollywood: How the Studio System Turned Creativity into Labor*. Chapel Hill: University of North Carolina Press.

Rubin, Rebecca. 2020a. "Christopher Nolan Defends 'Tenet' Box Office Results." *Variety*. November 3. variety.com/2020/film/news/christopher-nolan-tenet-release. Accessed May 20, 2021.

———. 2020b. "After Christopher Nolan's Explosive Remarks, Could Warner Bros. Lose Its Superstar Director?" *Variety*, December 10. variety.com/2020/film/new s/christopher-nolan-warner-bros-deal-hbo-max-1234849809/. Accessed May 13, 2021.

Rubin, Rebecca, and Matt Donnelly. 2020. "Warner Bros. to Debut 2021 Film Slate, Including 'Dune' and 'Matrix 4,' Both on HBOMax and in Theaters." *Variety*, December 3. variety.com/2020/film/news/warner-bros-hbo-max-theaters-dune-matrix-4-1234845342/. Accessed September 5, 2021.

Schatz, Thomas. 2017. "Spielberg as Director, Producer, and Movie Mogul." In *A Companion to Steven Spielberg,* ed. Nigel Morris, 27–44. Malden: John Wiley & Sons.

Siegel, Tatiana, and Stephen Galloway. 2013. "Legendary Scores Christopher Nolan's 'Interstellar' in Warner Bros. Divorce." *Hollywood Reporter*, August 14. www.hollywoodreporter.com/news/general-news/legendary-scores-christopher-nolans-interstellar-605010/. Accessed July 21, 2021.

Thompson, Anne. 2020. "Waiting for 'Tenet': As July 17 Looms, Hollywood Prays the Summer Can Be Saved." *IndieWire*, May 11. www.indiewire.com/2020/05/tenet-theaters-reopen-summer-movies-chistopher-nolan-box-office-1202230166/. Accessed September 5, 2021.

Chapter 8

Transnational Filmmaker, Fanboy-Auteur

Screening Nolan's Inception *in China*

Lara Herring

Since the release of *Batman Begins* (2005) in China, Christopher Nolan's films have performed increasingly well in the Chinese film market. As the world's fastest-growing film market, China has become the primary export destination for Hollywood films. Alongside the rapid development of the Chinese film exhibition industry, Chinese audiences have multiplied and diversified, and gaining access to this lucrative market has become imperative for Hollywood films. Hollywood has always been globally minded, and applying transnational filmmaking techniques is one of the ways that Hollywood films seek to ensure their products play internationally. This chapter focuses on *Inception* (2010) as an example of transnational cinema in the Chinese film market and in doing so explores the reasons for Nolan's success in China. In exploring the director's success in China this chapter examines how his role as a fanboy-auteur has helped to ingratiate him with Chinese audiences.

Within the field of cinema studies, the definition of transnationalism is a subject of debate.[1] Most notably, the term is often used as synonymous with concepts such as globalization, world cinema, and co-productions or collaborations between two (or more) countries (Higbee and Lim, 2010). Anna Tsing's (2000) work seeks to create a helpful distinction between the globalization ideology and the transnational as practice by suggesting that globalization refers to an overarching ideology whereas transnational refers to "transborder projects" which, while operating within the globalized ideology, do not necessarily promote it. I suggest that *Inception* is an example of this kind of transborder project. Ezra and Rowden explain that, in the most basic sense, the transnational can be understood as "global forces that link people or institutions across nations" (2006, 1). Dina Iordanova suggests that transnational cinema is "defined by a growing awareness of instability and change brought about by incessant journeying and border-crossing" (2007, 509). Iordanova continues that this mobility is:

> compounded by the foregrounding of locations that signify isolation and marginality, or presuppose a context that allows for reflection on fragile, mutating identities; where the meanings of "belonging" and "return" are questioned; where concepts of "centre" and "periphery" are challenged and gradually taken over by lively interactions between peripheries that put the centre in parentheses; and where diasporas-in-the-making, itinerants and travellers subtly problematise hierarchical notions of place.

As this chapter will show, *Inception*'s storytelling exemplifies these motifs, and Nolan's adoption of such themes and strategies positions him as a transnational filmmaker, which in turn helps to account for his success in the Chinese film market.

The dramatic rise, albeit not a steady trajectory, in Chinese box office for Nolan's films (see table 8.1) appears to indicate a growing popularity for his films.

However, it is important to evaluate these figures with respect to the context in which the Chinese film market was undergoing unprecedented change, and it is essential to view the performance of Nolan's films in China within the context of wider industrial developments. From the start of the 2010s, China underwent a so-called "multiplex boom" in which the number of cinema screens increased tenfold, overtaking the United States as the territory with the largest number of screens in 2016 (Schwankert, 2016). The multiplex boom led to a dramatic increase in access to cinemas and resulted in far larger attendance numbers. It is also important to remember that although China imposes a quota for all imported revenue-sharing foreign films, that quota increased over two decades, doubling from ten to twenty following China's

Table 8.1. Box Office Performance of Nolan Films. Created by Lara Herring.

Film	*China Box Office Total*	*% of Worldwide Film Gross*
Tenet (2020)	$66,600,000	18.3
Dunkirk (2017)	$50,970,494	9.7
Interstellar (2014)	$139,329,039	19.9
The Dark Knight Rises (2012)	$52,785,334	4.9
Inception (2010)	$71,345,823	8.5
Batman Begins (2005)	$1,049,000	0.3

entry to the World Trade Organization in 2001, and to thirty-four in 2012. Despite the relative opening of the Chinese market since 1994, foreign films that seek distribution in the Chinese market are still hampered by import restrictions, as well as obscure censorship practices and a lack of marketing opportunities.[2] Thus, Nolan's films have been able to enjoy a less hostile market, though not one without its complexities.

Of the eleven feature-length fiction films directed by Christopher Nolan, six have received a release in the mainland Chinese market, and since 2010 all Nolan's films have been released in China. Once a film is released in China it must, of course, prove popular with the market. However, for a foreign film to secure a release in mainland China it must first navigate a complex web of restrictions and censorship. It is incumbent on a foreign feature to seek to appease and appeal to the Chinese government to play to a Chinese audience, making it necessary for filmmakers and studios to consider both the Chinese Communist Party (CCP) as well as the Chinese audience in order to succeed in the Chinese film market. It is therefore the task of a foreign feature to woo not only the audience but the gatekeepers in the CCP also. As such, the fact that every one of Nolan's films since 2010 has secured a release in China speaks to his acceptance—both as a person and in terms of his film style—by Chinese officials.

Since reallowing foreign films into the Chinese market in 1994, those films released in China have been subject to regulation and censorship by the Chinese government. Censorship rules were first introduced in China in 1928 in response to the overwhelmingly negative portrayals of Chinese people and culture in foreign films. After reopening to foreign films in 1994, censorship was handled by the State Administration of Press and Publication, Radio, Film, and Television (SAPPRFT). Since 2018 censorship of films has been assigned to the China Film Administration, an arm of the Publicity Department of the Chinese Communist Party, which is also known as the Propaganda Department. Censorship of Chinese films has been directly linked to the promotion of political messages in the country's ongoing attempt to promote nation-building and, in the second half of the twentieth century, socialist ideology (Xiao, 2013). Censorship happens at two main levels: the censorship board (cutting scenes that are subject to the censorship rules) and self-censorship (i.e., preempting the censorship board). This includes ensuring that films do not negatively portray Chinese culture and society and do not promote Western models of society that feature individualism (Richeri, 2016). Censorship of films in China is multifaceted, acting as a way of controlling what cinemagoers see to incentivize nationalistic sentiment and discourage offensive anti-Chinese themes. The fact that so many of Nolan's films have received theatrical distribution in China reveals that the director's productions do not generally offend or contravene Chinese sensibilities and do not challenge the dominant political ideology in China. Perhaps the only overt example of a Nolan film that did not play in Chinese cinemas was 2008's *The Dark Knight* which not only did not receive a Chinese release but was not submitted for consideration. It was reported at the time that *The Dark Knight* did not seek theatrical distribution in China due to "pre-release conditions" and "cultural sensitivities" (Steinberg 2008). The cultural sensitivities in the film included scenes filmed in Hong Kong where a money launderer for organized criminals resides, and the brief appearance of Edison Chen, a Hong Kong singer who was embroiled in a scandal involving sexually explicit photographs posted on the internet earlier that year. Chen's scenes had already been reduced in the wake of the scandal, leaving only a brief cameo in the film that was inconsequential to the narrative. The details of these cultural sensitivities speak to the often-apparent contradiction between a film's aim to appease the Chinese censors and its aim to appeal to the Chinese audience.

Nolan's appeal with Chinese audiences can also be attributed to his characterization as a fanboy-auteur. Building on work about "fanboy-auteurs" and "promoted fans" by Suzanne Scott (2013) and Naja Later (2018), I suggest that the director's success can be attributed to his popularity with the lucrative fanboy audience demographic that characterizes the Chinese film market. Directors who work on popular Intellectual Properties (IP) can become considered what Suzanne Scott calls "fanboy auteurs" (2013, 441), and are able to create strong positive associations with a very lucrative demographic. This is even more so the case in China where there is a culture of obsessive fandom (Burton-Bradley 2021). Naja Later defines the "promoted fanboy" as "auteurs who are hired to create cinematic or televisual adaptations of beloved texts to which they themselves have professed fannish adoration; thus, they are fans who have been 'promoted' to official creator status" (2018, 536). Nolan's status as a fanboy-auteur in the traditional sense is derived from his association with the Batman franchise which acted as a gateway appeal for Chinese audiences. However, his popularity was made clear when *Inception* made more than seventy times the box office yield of *Batman Begins* (industrial developments notwithstanding). As a science fiction film that was particularly epic in scale and spectacle, *Inception* was able to gauge Nolan's appeal in China without the reliance on an existing IP. Nolan himself—his auteurist style and his association with the fanboy demographic—became the selling point, as proven by his later successes.

HOLLYWOOD IN CHINA: SCREENING *INCEPTION*

During China's so-called "multiplex boom" in the early 2010s, cinemas were being built across the country at an unprecedented rate, and with increased access, a growing middle class, and an influx of capital, China became the fastest-growing film market, increasing by more than 40 percent every year between 2010 and 2016 (Li 2016). The release of Nolan's films coincided with and benefitted from the increase in audience and from changing policies—such as China's increased foreign film quota—that came out of the dramatic developments in the Chinese film market. In 2010 *Inception* became the second of Nolan's films to be released in China. Not only was *Inception* granted a theatrical release in China, it was also reportedly released completely uncensored (China Daily 2010).

To understand *Inception*'s success in China it is important to start by acknowledging the role that *Avatar* (2009) played in developing the Chinese film exhibition industry, revealing the potential of the "new" market when it took over double the total box office revenue of any other film ever marketed in China (Rosen 2012). Prior to *Avatar*'s success the Chinese theatrical industry was underdeveloped, and box office figures were comparatively small, with most audience members preferring to watch films on the internet and the cinema being the least likely place they would watch a film (Zhang 2009; Zhou and Song 2008). *Avatar*'s success was unprecedented, but it can be attributed to a number of factors—including the film's use of transnational storytelling in its preference for action and spectacle as well as its innovative 3D technology and the fact that it was released on IMAX—that offered a persuasive motivation to watch the film at the cinema. *Avatar* also played well to Chinese audiences because of the inclusion of scenes filmed in Zhangjiajie National Park. *Avatar*'s runaway success, which has been discussed in academic work and in the trade press (see Tang 2011; LaFraniere 2010; Rosen, 2012), revealed the market for big budget "enhanced format" films, such as 3D and IMAX, in China. Under the revenue-sharing system for foreign imports, China stood to gain the most by screening enhanced format films, which can be charged at a premium cost per ticket. In 2012, when the quota was increased from twenty to thirty-four, there was a stipulation that the additional fourteen slots be allocated to enhanced format films. This helps to account for why all of Nolan's films since *Inception*, each of which was an enhanced format release, have made it into Chinese cinemas.

As news of the success of *Avatar* in China reverberated around the world, the emerging film market represented an enticing option for Hollywood imports. However, under the revenue-sharing rules of the foreign import quota whereby China receives the lion's share of a film's box office, it was also in the interest of the Chinese government to import and exploit Hollywood products. Since the reopening of the Chinese film market in 1994, Hollywood imports have been seen as a solution to the problem of underwhelming box office revenues, and when in 1994 the Film Bureau approved a plan to import ten revenue-sharing films per year, they specified they wanted to import "blockbusters that had already achieved good box office records overseas" (Su 2016, 15). In essence, China seeks to achieve the highest possible return on the fewest number of Hollywood imports. When *Avatar* smashed box office records it told the world that Chinese audiences wanted to see spectacle-oriented, enhanced-format action films. This became a blueprint for future imports, and *Inception* fit the bill.

Just as *Avatar*'s use of 3D persuaded Chinese audiences to see the film at the cinema instead of watching via the internet or a bootleg copy, *Inception* was similarly persuasive due to its appeal as an IMAX epic. The spectacular nature of the film was made clear in the film poster. Interestingly, *Inception* was not actually filmed on IMAX cameras but instead was filmed predominantly in anamorphic 35mm with "key sequences" in 65mm (Nolan in Weintraub 2010) and then reformatted for IMAX screens. Despite not being filmed with IMAX cameras *Inception* was promoted in China as a film to be experienced on IMAX screens.

Although *Inception* was not based on a preexisting IP, Nolan's popularity in China due to his moderate success with *Batman Begins* and the fact that the film had already done well at the global box office made it a potentially lucrative option for importation. That *Inception* was reportedly released uncensored was likely less to do with Nolan's popularity and more to do with the convoluted plot and the lack of any obvious taboos. The fact that the film remained "intact" provided another incentive to see it at the cinema, where the censoring of films often acts as a deterrent when uncensored versions are available in other forms. Although the film's reported uncensored release suggests an approval of Nolan and of the film, it was still subject to the Chinese protectionist tactics that are designed to safeguard the domestic market; *Inception* was released during a notoriously quiet period at the box office in China,[3] and there was a long piracy window as China was the last country to exhibit the film. Nevertheless, the film was a resounding success, achieving the fourth-biggest opening by a foreign film at that time, behind *Avatar* (2009), *Transformers: Revenge of the Fallen* (2009), and *Transformers* (2007) respectively (The Independent 2010)—all enhanced format films. In addition, these films also employ a transnational, spectacle-oriented storytelling style, which was a key to *Inception*'s—and more broadly, Nolan's—success in the Chinese market.

TRANSNATIONAL STORYTELLING IN *INCEPTION*

One of the reasons that Nolan's films have done so well in the Chinese market is due to his employment of universal themes and transnational spectacle-based storytelling. In their work on transnational cinema, Higbee and Lim suggest that the term "transnational" is taken "as shorthand for an international or supranational mode of film production whose impact and reach lies beyond the bounds of the national" (2010, 9). The authors argue that the term "transnational" is often used to describe international co-productions or global workforce collaborations irrespective of what "aesthetic, political or economic implications of such transnational collaboration might mean" (Higbee and Lim 2010, 10). As noted by Geoff King (2000, 9) it is necessary for films to consider the interests and concerns of potential audiences across the globe, especially in key markets, in order to achieve commercial success in the global marketplace. Moreover, King explains that "cultural resonances that might tap into the concerns of potential moviegoers are taken explicitly into account by market researchers" and feed directly into marketing and publicity campaigns (King, 2000, 9). Universality, then, is key to the global appeal of Hollywood films, and it is therefore the goal of Hollywood studios to make films that are not designed for any one market but instead navigate the cultural dimensions of globalization in order to produce products that are culturally malleable and appeal to a "universal audience." Part of this challenge lies in finding themes that are not culturally specific to any one market. One way of achieving this is to adhere to familiar narrative archetypes such as Joseph Campbell's (1968) "hero's journey" or Christopher Booker's (2004) seven basic plots and by avoiding ideological bias. Nolan's films are typically thematically existential, philosophical, and cerebral, and focus on concepts of time, identity, and consciousness, and *Inception* is no different. Each of these could be considered "universal themes" that one could say are part of every human experience. Nolan is a vocal advocate of filming on celluloid and is a passionate and adamant cinephile, actively promoting the cinematic experience. It is no surprise, then, that his films are so grand in scale and are designed to be seen on the big screen: his association with IMAX is testament to this. As a proponent of filming on IMAX, the director once stated, "I think IMAX is the best film format that was ever invented. It's the gold standard and what any other technology has to match up to, but none have, in my opinion" (Nolan quoted in Ressner 2012). In this way, Nolan's universal themes and his promotion of the cinematic experience lend themselves well to the market tastes of the Chinese audience.

Nolan's films are often nonlinear or feature embedded narratives, which are complex narrative forms that require a level of thinking and intelligence that is not traditionally expected from typical blockbuster viewing. Nolan has made a point of not "dumbing down" his films for audiences. In a preview for *The Dark Knight Rises* when audience members found the character Bane's voice to be unintelligible, Nolan begrudgingly agreed to make only minor changes, rather than completely remixing the sound, as requested by the studio (Martin 2011). The director's seeming indifference at times to bend to the whims or requests of the studio or even the audience serves to perpetuate his brand as a controversial and autonomous auteur. Since *Batman Begins*, all of Nolan's films have been heavily focused on action sequences and visual spectacles. Indeed, he has spoken about how his films are just as reliant on the visuals as the dialogue (Kit, 2011a), stating that it is "OK for a moviegoer not to understand what was said at times, as long as the overall idea was conveyed" (Kit 2011b). Thus, Nolan balances the narrative complexity of his films using the universal language of action and spectacle.

Unquestionably complex and cerebral, *Inception*'s plot was difficult to sell to prospective audiences. According to reports in China, Nolan assured Chinese audiences of *Inception*'s universal appeal in the lead up to the film's release, even suggesting they not try to follow the plot too closely, advising; "Do not feel you have to understand every aspect of it, it is intended as entertainment, and I hope you will enjoy the entertainment. . . . There is no test afterwards" (quoted in China Daily, 2010). According to the article by *China Daily* (2010) Nolan suggested that "Chinese audiences should just sit back and enjoy the ride, rather than get too involved in the complex plot." In fact, in recent years Chinese audiences responded favorably to Hollywood films that are accused of narrative incoherence, such as the *Transformers* films, suggesting that at times not understanding the dialogue may be of benefit to the overall experience. Thematically *Inception* delves into concepts of reality, of dreams, and of the subconscious itself, all of which are explored in apolitical ways that seek to question rather than to answer.

Inception employs several transnational cinema techniques that helped to appeal to Chinese audiences, including its international setting and its multinational casting. The film was shot in Japan, France, Morocco, and Canada as well as in the UK and the United States, meaning the shoot itself was an international undertaking. The action takes place across numerous national borders, as well as some imagined spaces (in dreams); there is no "homeland" in *Inception*; no specified country in which the film takes place. Dina Iordanova states in her work on transnational cinema that, in more recent years, "transnational cinema has yielded works that foreground questions of place and passage and explore diasporic life" (2007, 509). This is very much the case in *Inception* where the main characters live or work in countries that are not their native homes. Ezra and Rowden posit that in transnational cinema "identities are necessarily deconstructed and reconstructed along the lines of a powering dynamic based on mobility" (2006, 8). The goal of the lead protagonist, Dominick Cobb (Leonardo DiCaprio), is to find a way to return to his native country—the United States—where he has been wrongly accused of murdering his wife and is therefore exiled. In his fugitive state, Cobb is "stateless," traveling the globe in an attempt to ultimately find a way back home.

Cobb's attempts to make his way home exemplify the diasporic imagination of transnational cinema, where "a psychological investment in mobility is usually counteracted by the emotional construction of a homeland, which provides a foundational narrative of departure and a validating promise of return" (Ezra and Rowden 2006, 7). The underlying plot of *Inception* thus exemplifies the "new, culturally significant space" that is made possible through the endeavors of transnational cinema, a space that "allows the members of the growing community of global migrants to overcome the brand-mark ethos of lost homelands and experience a meaningful and coherent existence, one in which place is perpetually transformed by movement" (Iordanova 2007, 509).

By not centering the film in the United States, and by filming and locating it in numerous countries, *Inception* positions itself as a product of transnational cinema. The ensemble cast plays characters from numerous countries including Japan, France, Kenya, the UK, and the United States. The casting of Ken Watanabe was a particularly strong selling point for Eastern Asian audiences as was the casting of Leonardo DiCaprio. DiCaprio already had a sizable fanbase in China following the immense success of *Titanic* (1998). As such, *Inception* contained several elements that help to produce success in the Chinese film market. Indeed, so successful was it that it received a Douban rating of 9.3 (Douban 2021b) out of more than 1.7 million ratings and is the highest ranked of all Nolan's films on the Douban "top 250" list[4] (Douban 2021a). As China lacks a formal open system of professional film criticism (Wang 2011), opinions about films are restricted to online forums. Sites like Douban provide a platform for Chinese fans and intellectuals to talk about films, to offer critique, or to post a score on a review aggregator similar to IMDb and Rotten Tomatoes (Brzeski 2016).

Importantly, *Inception*'s transnational strategy was implicit, rather than explicit, and the film did not appear to overtly cater to Chinese audiences. Following the push within Hollywood to appeal to Chinese audiences in recent years, academics and the trade press have repeatedly accused Hollywood of "pandering" to Chinese audiences.[5] This type of transnational pandering is evidenced in three key areas: content, release dates, and marketing techniques. The techniques used to appeal to Chinese audiences and investors are exemplified by the inclusion of "special" references, techniques, and considerations that are specifically included (or excluded) to appeal to

Chinese audiences, censors, and financiers. Considerations of the Chinese film market influence Hollywood film content in three key ways: in the use of transnational storytelling, which simplifies cultural differences and blends cultures and nations, with emphasis on visual effects (VFX); in the incorporation of Chinese elements including casting, locations, brands, and culture; and in the avoidance of taboo subjects in efforts to pass the Chinese censorship process. Critics suggest that, in trying too hard to create content that will play in the Chinese film market, Hollywood has forfeited its identity (Robinson 2016). However, Hollywood has been operating on a transcultural "universal" storytelling model for as long as it has existed. The issue appears to lie with the very recent trend of including Chinese elements in films, as typified by the inclusion of Chinese locations and Chinese characters, as well as the drive toward films that are so focused on the "universal" language of spectacle that they lack complexity and narrative drive. *Inception*, however, does not forcibly include Chinese elements, and although spectacle oriented, it is very much driven by a substantive plot.

NOLAN AS TRANSNATIONAL FANBOY-AUTEUR

Inception's success in China is indicative of both Nolan's popularity and the wider relationship between China and Hollywood. Perhaps most resoundingly, it is evidence of the successful branding of Nolan himself. The director's success in the Chinese market demonstrates his appeal with the most populous audience demographic in the territory: young males. Nolan's early success was made possible in large part because of his association with the *Batman* franchise. *Batman* is particularly popular with young males and so-called "fanboys." The term fanboy is used to describe a male fan who is obsessed with a particular IP. IP is a category of property that is made up of intangible, intellectual works that include literary and artistic works, as well as copyrights, patents, and trademarks. IP is intrinsically linked with film franchises which are usually built around pre-sold properties, or existing artworks that already have an audience. Films based on existing IP have been an integral part of the Chinese and Hollywood film industries for years (Chen 2016), and since the turn of the twenty-first century this is even more so the case. Ben Fritz suggests that audiences have now switched loyalty from stars to franchises, noting that "moviegoers looking for the consistent, predictable satisfaction they used to get from their favourite stars now turn to cinematic universes" (2018, 85). Fritz explains that studios began to focus on the types of films "that delivered the biggest and most consistent profits to their publicly traded parent corporations" (2018, 22), which increasingly meant films that appealed to audiences overseas, particularly China, and that can "guarantee"—as best as possible—an audience, such as in the case of films based on existing IP.

Cinema's fanboys are generally interested in films that are adaptations or part of a long-standing franchise. The fanboy demographic has a disposable income and represents a hugely lucrative sector of the market: a preexisting fan. According to market research, the Chinese film market is increasingly made up of younger audience members in the 19–24 and 25–29 age groups (Statista 2021) owing to the increasing population and the burgeoning middle class. Factoring in the ramifications of China's one-child policy and the country's gender imbalance it makes sense that for years films released in the Chinese market have been aimed at men. This is no longer the case as the gender imbalance has decreased and is now more evenly split (Maoyan Entertainment 2021). However, it remains the case that Chinese audiences consistently prefer the genres of action, comedy, and sci-fi and are especially interested in superhero films and—more generally—films that are based on an existing IP. With *Batman Begins* being Nolan's first theatrical release in the Chinese market, and likely many Chinese audience members' first interaction with one of his films, the director benefited from *Batman*'s built-in fan-base, and was able to reach a far wider audience.

Thanks largely to the internet, IPs are now able to reach audiences in the farthest reaches of the globe. Take for example the *Doctor Who* fiftieth-anniversary special which was simultaneously broadcast in ninety-four countries (Booth 2013). The global appeal of intellectual properties such as *Doctor Who*, *Sherlock Holmes*, *Batman*, *Superman*, *Star Trek*, *Harry Potter*, *Star Wars*, and many more is made possible by the technologies and media consumption habits of the digital age. Furthermore, the internet has enabled and extended the concept of "intermediality," that is, the interconnectedness or intersectionality between different media. As noted by Nicolle Lamerichs, "the Internet has increased the visibility of fan practices and the number of people who actively engage in them" (2018, 14). In this way, the internet enables the flow of transnational cinema by permeating and "dissolving" national borders. The internet allows fans across the globe to connect, creating a global community that is based on fandom rather than geographical bounds or social setting. Fans—and for our purposes, fanboys—are not restricted geographically, culturally, or socially from engaging in global intellectual properties. Thus, fanboys are an inherently transnational audience demographic.

Another theme of the fanboy-auteur is the notion of authenticity and autonomy. Nolan's auteurist style is synonymous with impressive visuals and soundscapes, his work is known for choosing practical effects over visual effects, and his films are extraordinary in their scale—from mathematical manipulations of space in *Inception* to the complex visualization of the space/

time continuum in *Interstellar*. In the lead-up to the release of *Inception*, Sue Kroll, the president of worldwide marketing for Warner Bros., noted the power of Nolan's brand and how important the director's reputation was in selling a film otherwise difficult to market due to its convoluted plot. If Nolan's brand is taken as his role as a fanboy-auteur and his association with universal themes, spectacle-oriented storytelling, and enhanced format big-screen epics, then the success of *Inception* in China is testament to the Chinese film market preferences. Authenticity has become an important topic for debate in recent years.[6] Nolan's presumed and promoted authenticity, such as is characteristic of the fanboy-auteur, helps to ensure his auteurist legitimacy. There are numerous rumors and reports of Nolan's purported freedom from studio control (*Interstellar*'s sound mix, *Tenet*'s untenable plot, *Dunkirk*'s distinct lack of dialogue, to name a few) which serves to brand Nolan as an unwavering creative. *Inception*'s success proves that the director's branding as an autonomous fanboy-auteur and a purveyor of big-screen epics had succeeded in persuading Chinese audiences that Nolan films are worth seeing and worth seeing on the big screen, which paved the way for his future success in the territory.

CONCLUSION

Inception presents an apt case study of a Nolan film that succeeded in China on multiple levels: success in achieving distribution in China, in passing censors unscathed, in achieving success at the box office, and in realizing success in popular opinion. Part of this success of course is down to the backdrop of the developing Chinese theatrical market and the increased access to cinemas afforded by the multiplex boom. Thus, *Inception*'s route to the Chinese market, and the way in which the film was received, exemplifies the complex relationship between Hollywood films and Chinese audiences. This chapter has argued that it was Nolan's use of transnational cinema techniques and his position as a fanboy-auteur that ensured the success of *Inception* and indeed his films that followed. Since *Inception*, every feature film directed by Nolan has received a Chinese release, which is a distinction afforded to very few foreign filmmakers. Nolan's success in getting his films into China and his financial triumphs at the Chinese box office suggest that he has successfully wooed the Chinese audience as well as its gatekeepers. The popularity of his films adds to our understanding of the Chinese film market as well as our understanding of transnational cinema and of the powerful and lucrative credentials of a fanboy-auteur. The director's use of spectacle-oriented storytelling; his preference for the action, superhero, and science fiction genres; and his affiliation with a beloved IP inform the Nolan brand which, whether by chance or design, is particularly well suited to Chinese market tastes.

Nolan's success in China offers insight into Chinese audience tastes, proving that spectacle-oriented "fanboy fare" is popular. All of Nolan's films—including those that did not have a theatrical release in China—have a rating on China's equivalent of IMDb, Douban (Douban, 2021a). This suggests that, despite not being released in China through official avenues, the films have been seen via other means. In fact, of the five Nolan films that did *not* receive distribution in China, three are ranked in Douban's "top 250" highest ranked films (as of the time of writing *The Dark Knight* is ranked 28th, *The Prestige* is 77th, and *Memento* is 173rd) (Douban 2021a), proving not only that Nolan's films are popular, but also that Chinese audiences have found ways of engaging with his work even when it is denied a theatrical release. Out of Nolan's films, *Inception* still holds the highest spot on Douban's "top 250" list (positioned 9th) demonstrating the transnational appeal of the film—and the director—with Chinese audiences.

NOTES

1. See for example, Higbee and Lim (2010), and Berry (2010).
2. Foreign film studios notoriously receive short notice of a theatrical release in China, or when that release will be. Traditional print and advertising marketing avenues historically have not existed in China where advertising is closely monitored and controlled by the CCP (Gao 2007).
3. The first weekend of September is known to be quiet due to students returning to school (The Independent, 2010).
4. *Inception* is ranked ninth at the time of writing.
5. See for example Song (2018), Swanson (2015), Rosen (2015), Zhu (2014), and Qin (2017).
6. Ibid.

REFERENCES

Berry, Chris. 2010. "What is Transnational Cinema? Thinking from the Chinese Situation." *Transnational Cinemas* 1, no. 2: 111–27.

Booker, Christopher. 2004. *The Seven Basic Plots: Why We Tell Stories*. London: Continuum.

Booth, Robert. 2013. "Doctor Who One of Biggest Shows in the World, Says BBC Following 'Simulcast.'" *The Guardian*, November 24. www.theguardian.com/tv-and-radio/2013/nov/24/doctor-who-biggest-show-world-bbc-simulcast.

Brzeski, Patrick. 2016. "Critics Blamed for Chinese Films' Disappointing Box Office—The Hollywood Reporter." *Hollywoodreporter.Com*, December 29. www.hollywoodreporter.com/news/critics-blamed-chinese-films-disappointingbox-office-959753.

Burton-Bradley, Robert. 2021. "Stalking, Illegal Tracking, Assault: Is China's Fan Culture off the Rails?" *Www.Scmp.Com*, August 31. www.scmp.com/news/people-culture/china-personalities/article/3146972/explainer-why-chinas-celebrity-obsessed-fan.

Campbell, Joseph. 1968. *The Hero with a Thousand Faces*. Princeton: Princeton University Press.

Chen, Changye. 2016. "The Rise and Fall of Chinese IP Film Adaptations." *China Film Insider*, September 13. chinafilminsider.com/rise-fall-chinese-ip-film-adaptations/.

China Daily. 2010. "Nolan Dreams up Box-Office Winner." China.Org.Cn, September 2. www.china.org.cn/arts/2010-09/02/content_20849663.htm.

Douban. 2021a. "Douban Movie Top 250." Accessed February 2, 2022. Douban.movie.douban.com/top250.

———. 2021b. "*Inception* (Douban)." Accessed February 2, 2022. Douban.movie.douban.com/subject/3541415/.

Ezra, Elizabeth, and Terry Rowden. 2006. *Transnational Cinema*. London: Routledge.

Fritz, Ben. 2018. *The Big Picture: The Fight for the Future of Movies*. New York: Houghton Mifflin Harcourt Publishing Company.

Gao, Zhihong. 2007. "An In-depth Examination of China's Advertising Regulation System." *Asia Pacific Journal of Marketing and Logistics* 19, no. 3: 307–23. www.emeraldinsight.com/doi/10.1108/13555850710772950.

Higbee, Will, and Song Hwee Lim. 2010. "Concepts of Transnational Cinema: Towards a Critical Transnationalism in Film Studies." *Transnational Cinemas* 1, no.1: 7–21.

The Independent. 2010. "'Inception' Surprises by Cleaning up in China." *The Independent*, September 18. www.independent.co.uk/arts-entertainment/films/inception-surprises-cleaning-china-2075494.html.

Iordanova, Dina. 2007. "Transnational Film Studies." In *The Cinema Book*, 3rd ed., ed. Pam Cook. London: BFI.

King, Geoff. 2000. *Spectacular Narrative: Hollywood in the Age of the Blockbuster Cinema and Society*. London: I. B. Tauris.

Kit, Borys. 2011a. "Christopher Nolan Debuts 8-Minute 'Dark Knight Rises' Preview." *The Hollywood Reporter*, December 8. www.hollywoodreporter.com/movies/movie-news/dark-knight-rises-preview-christopher-nolan-271610/.

———. 2011b. "'The Dark Knight Rises' Faces Big Problem: Audiences Can't Understand Villain." *The Hollywood Reporter*, December 20. www.hollywoodreporter.com/movies/movie-news/dark-knight-rises-christian-bale-batman-tom-hardy-bane-275489/.

LaFraniere, Sharon. 2010. "Despite State Meddling, 'Avatar' Beats 'Confucius' in China." *The New York Times*, January 30. www.nytimes.com/2010/01/30/business/global/30avatar.html.

Later, Naja. 2018. "Quality Television (TV) Eats Itself: The TV-Auteur and the Promoted Fanboy." *Quarterly Review of Film and Video* 35, no. 6: 531–51.

Lamerichs, Nicolle. 2018. *Productive Fandom: Intermediality and Affective Reception in Fan Cultures*. Amsterdam: Amsterdam University Press.

Li, Jane. 2016. "How Bubble Burst on China's Cinema Industry 'Boom.'" *South China Morning Post*, December 29. www.scmp.com/news/china/society/article/2057887/how-bubble-burst-chinas-cinema-industry-boom.

Maoyan Entertainment. 2021. "Maoyan: China's Box Office Revenue Surpassed RMB20 Billion in 2020 to Become World's Largest Movie Market amid Pandemic." *PR Newswire*, January 4. www.prnewswire.com/news-releases/maoyan-chinas-box-office-revenue-surpassed-rmb20-billion-in-2020-to-become-worlds-largest-movie-market-amid-pandemic-301200097.html.

Martin, Daniel. 2011. "'The Dark Knight Rises': Christopher Nolan Asked to Re-Edit Bane Voice." NME, December 21. www.nme.com/news/film/the-dark-knight-rises-christopher-nolan-asked-to-876608.

Qin, Amy. 2017. "Pander or Diversify? Hollywood Courts China with 'The Great Wall.'" *The New York Times*, January 19. www.nytimes.com/2017/01/19/movies/the-great-wall-matt-damon-chinese-box-office.html.

Ressner, Jeffrey. 2012. "The Traditionalist." *DGA Quarterly Magazine* (spring 2012). www.dga.org/Craft/DGAQ/All-Articles/1202-Spring-2012/DGA-Interview-Christopher-Nolan.aspx.

Richeri, Giuseppe. 2016. "Global Film Market, Regional Problems." *Global Media and China* 1, 312–30.

Robinson, Joanna. 2016. "Did You Catch All the Ways Hollywood Pandered to China This Year?" *Vanity Fair*, August 5. www.vanityfair.com/hollywood/2016/D8/did-you-catch-the-ways-hollywood-pandered-to-china-this-year.

Rosen, Stanley. 2012. "Film and Society in China." In *A Companion to Chinese Cinema*, ed. Yingjin Zhang, 197–217. Oxford: Blackwell.

———. 2015. "Hollywood in China: Selling Out or Cashing In?" *The Diplomat*, May 26. thediplomat.com/2015/05/hollywood-in-china-selling-out-or-cashing-in/.

Schwankert, Steven. 2016. "China Overtakes US with Almost 41,000 Movie Screens." *China Film Insider*, December 21. chinafilminsider.com/china-overtakes-us-almost-41000-movie-screens/.

Scott, Suzanne. 2013. "Dawn of the Undead Author Fanboy Auteurism and Zack Snyder's '"Vision." In *A Companion to Media Authorship*, ed. Jonathan Gray and Derek Johnson. Chichester: Wiley.

Song, Xu. 2018. "Hollywood Movies and China: Analysis of Hollywood Globalization and Relationship Management in China's Cinema Market." *Global Media and China* 3, no. 3: 177–94.

Statista. 2021. "China Cinema Audience Age Distribution." Statista. Accessed February 2, 2022. www.statista.com/statistics/1061081/china-cinema-audience-age-distribution/.

Steinberg, Jacques. 2008. "No 'Dark Knight' for China." *The New York Times*, December 25. www.nytimes.com/2008/12/26/movies/26arts-NODARKKNIGHT_BRF.html.

Su, Wendy. 2016. *China's Encounter with Global Hollywood: Cultural Policy and the Film Industry, 1994–2013*. Lexington: University of Kentucky.

Swanson, Ana. 2015. "Stephen Colbert's 'Pander Express' Is a Brilliant Takedown of How Hollywood Sucks up to China." *The Washington Post*, October 10. www.washingtonpost.com/news/wonk/wp/2015/10/10/stephen-colberts-pander-express-is-a-brilliant-takedown-of-how-hollywood-sucks-up-to-china/.

Tang, Yong. 2011. "Avatar: A Marxist Saga on the Far Distant Planet." *TripleC: Communication, Capitalism & Critique. Open Access Journal for a Global Sustainable Information Society* 9, no. 2: 657–67.

Tsing, Anna. 2000. "The Global Situation." *Cultural Anthropology* 15, no. 3: 327–60. about.jstor.org/terms.

Wang, Grace. 2011. "Chinese Film Criticism: The Rising of a New Wave." *Rogerebert.Com*. Accessed February 2, 2022. www.rogerebert.com/etheriel-musings/chinese-film-criticism-the-rising-of-a-new-wave.

Weintraub, Steven. 2010. "Christopher Nolan and Emma Thomas Interview INCEPTION—They Talk 3D, What Kind of Cameras They Used, Pre-Viz, WB, and a Lot More!" *Collider*, March 26. collider.com/director-christopher-nolan-and-producer-emma-thomas-interview-inception-they-talk-3d-what-kind-of-cameras-they-used-pre-viz-wb-and-a-lot-more/.

Xiao, Zhiwei. 2013. "Prohibition, Politics and Nation-Building: A History of Film Censorship in China." In *Silencing Cinema: Film Censorship around the World*, ed. Daniel Biltereyst and Roel Vande Winkel, 109–30. Basingstoke: Palgrave Macmillan.

Zhang, Wei. 2009. "Dazhong Guankan Dianying Qingkuang Wenjuan Diaocha Baogao 大众观看电影情况问卷调查报告 (Report of a Survey on Film Viewing by the Populace)." *Zhongguo Dianying Bao* 21.

Zhou, Xing, and Weicai Song. 2008. "Gaige Kaifang 30 Zhounian Zhongguo Yingshi Yu Daxuesheng de Hudong Diaocha Wenjuan Fenxi Baogao 改革开放 30 周年中国影视与大学生的互动调查问卷分析报告 (Analysis of a Survey of University Students with Regard to Chinese Film on the 30th Anniversary of Reform and Opening)." *Dangdai Dianying* 7: 120–25.

Zhu, Ying. 2014. "'Transformers 4' May Pander to China, but America Still Wins." *ChinaFile*, September 4. www.chinafile.com/reporting-opinion/culture/transformers-4-may-pander-china-america-still-wins.

Chapter 9

Fractured Men and Cockney Boy

Michael Caine as Star Persona in the Films of Christopher Nolan

Stella Hockenhull

In line with auteur theory,[1] Stuart Joy notes that the film director Christopher Nolan enjoys authorial control over his work and that "[m]astery and obsession runs as a continuous theme through Nolan's films" (2015, 3). For instance, the director is interested in psychological dramas and unconventional narrative form; in addition, he rejects classical storytelling, replacing it with multifaceted narratives known as "puzzle plots." These are identified by Warren Buckland as an "arrangement of events [which are] not just complex, but complicated and perplexing; the events are not simply interwoven, but *entangled*" [original italics] (2009, 3). As he suggests, "The puzzle film is made up of non-classical characters who perform non-classical actions and events" (Buckland 2009, 5). Nolan's authorial themes also include the use of doubles, with the narrative of films such as *The Prestige* (2006) constructed around twins and clones, and friends turned foes and antagonists. Dark and somber sets accompany these stories, which are confusing and deceptive. Furthermore, his endings are open and ambiguous, the spectators asked to provide their own meanings and interpretation. In addition, Nolan is enthralled with rules and systems. His films often question identity and notions of selfhood, and characters are confused by who they are. According to Peter Deakin, however, the most dominant theme in Nolan's work is masculinity in crisis. As he explains, his films "are loaded with desperate men and the moments that drive them to extremes; visceral representations of fractured male heroes and anti-heroes, dual identities and male identity complexes" (2015, 85). Deakin is drawing on the work of Slavoj Žižek, who argues that "the 'undesirability of truth' and within that space, the fragility of control, may appear as Nolan's most dominant theme" (2015, 85). Deakin suggests that Nolan's themes are about concealment and include heroes and anti-heroes who are "masked men," and "narratives that require the unravelling of perverse truths and lies, all aggravated by ruptures in chronology" (2015, 85).

Just as Nolan's oeuvre has a distinct style and recurring themes and patterns, so his authorial control extends to his cast and crew. He often writes with his brother, Jonathan, uses the cinematographer Wally Pfister, the editor Lee Smith, production designer Nathan Crowley, and visual effects supervisor, Paul Franklin. In addition, his wife, Emma Thomas, is on the production team. Also, Nolan repeatedly uses the same repertoire of actors including Christian Bale, Cillian Murphy, Ken Watanabe, Marion Cotillard, and Anne Hathaway, along with British actor Michael Caine. Caine has appeared as supporting actor in eight Nolan films to date, commencing in 2005 as Alfred Pennyworth in *Batman Begins*. He reprised this character in *The Dark Knight* (2008) and *The Dark Knight Rises* (2012), and played other parts in *The Prestige*, *Inception* (2010), and *Interstellar* (2014), along with a voice cameo in *Dunkirk* (2017). Finally, he appears in a short sequence in *Tenet* (2020) as an Englishman and British intelligence officer.

If Nolan is to be perceived as an auteur then, arguably, his stars pose a challenge to his methods by undermining directorial control. As Richard Dyer suggests, stars confront the auteur in cinema because actors are not controlled by directors but are the main determinants of narrative, iconography, and style (1979, 62). For Dyer, stars operate individually from the director by bringing their own idiosyncratic style of performance with an individual range of expressive technique, movement, and gesture to the films in which they appear. As noted, Nolan uses Michael Caine for various roles, and he is one such star who has distinctive performance traits. In the parts that he plays for Nolan he is always an Englishman, appearing as a considerate mentor who offers emotional support and guidance to other characters in the films. This is especially significant for Nolan's theme of the despairing male because he offers solace to the heroes and anti-heroes via problem solving and compassion. Arguably, therefore, despite Nolan's authorial control and detailed scripts, Caine's performance provides something more than a supporting role. Instead, his characters interpolate the narratives, and they are specifically significant in countering the crises experienced by the "fractured male heroes" and the "desperate men" which Deakin speaks of. This essay analyzes Caine's performance as more than a supporting role in Nolan's films, arguing that the actor's style and idiosyncrasies are significant in the narratives because they provide constancy and guidance for the heroes as well as the physical means for them to survive.

Caine has had a long and outstanding acting career in which he has become known for his trademark distinctive working-class south London accent. In his early films he played the antisocial male where he was launched as a decent yet unconventional character on the periphery of society. As Robert Sellers notes of this period: "For the first time in British history the young working class stood up for themselves and said, 'We are here, this is our society and we are not going away' . . . [they] brought a dynamism and gritty edge to their performances that was startlingly fresh and unparalleled" (2012, xi). Caine appeared in films such as *The Ipcress File* (Furie, 1965) as Harry Palmer, a British spy with a criminal past who must pay for this misdemeanor by serving his country. In *Alfie* (Gilbert, 1966), he is a likeable rogue, and in *The Italian Job* (Collinson, 1969) his character, Charlie Croker, is the quintessential English cockney criminal. *Get Carter* (Hodges) was released in 1971, and Caine as Jack Carter is a ruthless character whose persona, as Robert Shail remarks, "played heavily on his working-class credentials. . . . Caine offers us a southern masculinity rooted in the cultural landscape of working-class London" (2004, 68). Caine's performance in this film was at its most callous, unlike his previous roles where his characters at least evoked humor and vulnerability.

It was Caine's working-class ordinariness and natural acting style that enabled audience identification. As Philip Drake notes, "individual stars become associated with a repertoire of performance signs" (2006, 87), and Caine is one such star who acts as determinant of his own style, taking control of his speech by introducing a slow and deliberate voice as well as "spacing his words as his thoughts dictate" (Caine 1997, 75). This type of delivery is also significant for dialogue which contains intonations distinct to him alone, and he carefully and methodically works on his roles to perform through the eyes of the characters. In addition, Caine constructs a specific acting style which Shail lists as "playful, humorous [and] self-confident . . . a notion of masculinity in which rebellion against the constraints of more traditional versions of British male identity is articulated both through gender representation and through the mobilisation of a certain definition of class identity" (2004, 68). His performance also involves what Christopher Bray terms a stylized naturalism: "Indeed, so 'natural' have many of Caine's performances been that they have often been taken for non-performances" (2006, vii). Caine deliberately concocted this version of himself early on in his working career. As he indicates, "To be a movie star, you have to invent yourself. I was a Cockney boy and obviously didn't fit anybody's idea of what an actor was supposed to be, so I decided to put together elements that added up to a memorable package" (Caine 1997, 138). This included wearing heavy glasses, smoking a cigar, retaining his working-class roots, and being amenable and reliable.

On the surface, Caine's early work established him as a rebel, and Dyer identifies those stars who do not conform to dominant cultural standards and exist on the margin of society as revolutionary types (1979, 59–61). However, Caine's characters are consistent with a traditional representation of masculinity, and they are principled working-class men with class who shoulder their responsibility and have a sense of honor. From this self-invention, Caine played a variety of roles, and although his reputation was established in British cinema, he also achieved star status in Hollywood, building on his humble beginnings to establish his screen persona as "a crafty Cockney Lothario" (Caughie and Rockett 1996, 41).

Unlike some stars that fade into oblivion as they age, Caine's fame continues, the actor working well into his eighties. He confesses to enjoying his mature roles (Shoard 2015) and, in the less prominent parts he plays in Nolan's films, while retaining some of his early characteristics such as an unconcealed confidence and sophistication, he loses many traits, for instance outrageousness and his position as a sex symbol, transforming into a benign father figure of stature: indeed he becomes nicer.

In *Batman Begins*, the first film that Caine worked on with Nolan, he plays the butler, Alfred, to the wealthy American Wayne family of Gotham City. When the parents of the young Bruce Wayne (Gus Lewis) are murdered, it falls to Alfred to care for him. Early on in the film, a young Bruce falls into a mine shaft near an area where he has been playing with his friend, Rachel Dawes (Emma Lockhart). He is subsequently rescued, and his father, Thomas Wayne (Linus Roache), carries him into their grand house accompanied by Alfred. The latter walks solicitously alongside the boy, enquiring in a south London accent, "Will we be needing an ambulance Master Wayne?" He is kindly and attentive toward the child: "Took quite a fall didn't we Master Bruce," he states in a calm voice, and when the father inquires, "why do we fall Bruce, so we can learn to pick ourselves up," the camera frames Alfred's compassionate steady gaze as he watches Thomas pass the boy to his mother. These are words he will later use and repeat to Bruce. In this instance, Caine introduces specific facial expressions and mannerisms: he emphasizes the use of his eyes for expressive effect, and seen in close-up, he deliberately turns toward the camera and his gaze remains steadfast when speaking or listening. Furthermore, he does not blink because, for him, "blinking makes your character seem weak" (Caine 1997, 61). Caine deploys calm, unhurried movements to emphasize his point, and, as he asserts, "a relaxed, centered walk creates a sense of strength. A centered walk can be very menacing" (1997, 84). It is this strength of character that Caine as Alfred retains to support Bruce throughout his life.

In the above sequence, the spectator encounters a domestic gathering, softly lit and framed by the doorway. Already it is clear that Alfred cares deeply for this family, a fact illustrated later when Bruce is orphaned and Alfred becomes the child's caregiver. Following the funeral, Alfred offers help and support by providing for the troubled child's basic domestic needs. In a muted voice he offers him supper. Seen in medium shot, he stands, his head to one side, a kind, caring expression on his face. The camera cuts to a shot of the boy; in rear view, he appears silhouetted against the window through which he stares, watching the departing mourners. A cut to Alfred's face reveals his somber expression in a soft light as the boy does not respond, and subsequently the older man's disappointment at Bruce's immobile figure. The camera frames Alfred in close-up and profile, his mouth turned down with sadness. He walks slowly toward the boy and places his hand under his chin, reassuring him that his parents' death was not his fault: "It was nothing you did. It was him and him alone." Seen in close-up, Alfred is composed; he gazes unblinkingly at the boy and speaks in a near whisper to comfort him. As Paul McDonald observes, it is "through attention to the micro meanings of the voice and body, [that] it becomes possible to find in the very smallest of details the most significant of moment" (2004, 40). This is one such noteworthy moment, and will be Alfred's position throughout the film. He is present as a key figure in the narrative and will always be available for the troubled Bruce, providing him with support and guidance, and preventing him from making mistakes throughout his life.

As the film progresses, Bruce becomes a desperate man, and while Alfred is initially represented as obsequious and submissive with his charge, he also becomes gently advising and goading. When the mature Bruce (Christian Bale) returns from university for his vacation, Alfred obediently carries the young man's bag through the giant hallway of his family home, thus re-establishing the old order. When Bruce announces that he is not returning to study, Alfred initially remains silent as though considering this predicament. However, Bruce then antagonizes him by criticizing Wayne Manor, describing it as a mausoleum. At this juncture Alfred hesitates and, despite his menial status in the household, turns sharply to face him; seen in close-up, he angrily reprimands him. Indeed, when Bruce talks about his terrible past, Alfred urges him to only look forward, thus enabling his development and progression. Whereas Bruce is afraid that Alfred will not support him, the latter reassures him; he adopts a cheeky grin reminiscent of his younger self in his earlier films and, smiling arrogantly, affirms "Never!" Alfred is establishing himself as the stronger of the two early on in the narrative, and it is this fortitude that enables Bruce to continue with his work and overcome obstacles.

Alfred appears during moments of calm, rather than the action sequences, and neutralizes the "moments that drive them [desperate men] to extremes" (Deakin 2015, 85). Furthermore, he not only offers solace to Bruce but is also a proficient aide, enabling him to complete his tasks. For example, later, when

Bruce begins to investigate the financial aspects of his father's company, he finds that Alfred is already extremely knowledgeable on the subject and also well versed in accounting. Furthermore, when the two are sorting out the specialist equipment for Bruce's transformation into Batman, Alfred continues to give advice on such aspects as the technical elements of the procedure. At one point, he is testing the Batman helmet, and bringing his hammer down on the newly designed headwear that Batman will wear, he drolly states, "May I suggest that you try to avoid landing on your head," just as the metal disintegrates. His timing creates an element of humor and breaks the seriousness of the moment, thus eliciting an appropriate reaction from Bruce, who nods his head smiling. Alfred retains this sardonic and ironic attitude throughout and reinforces Caine's trademark acting style: he rarely makes sudden movements and has a measured mode of delivery, frequently pausing to emphasize a point. This provides a foil for Bruce's volatile character traits and impulsive actions; Bruce may be a "fractured male hero," but to counteract this, Alfred is perceived as capable and dependable. Caine's aim is that his characters appear convincing, and Alfred's behavior appears natural and reasonable: as Caine concedes, the audience "must see a real person standing there, somebody just like them" (1997, 89).

Sometime later, Bruce is attacked by one of his adversaries. His dependence on Alfred is evident when he tries to summon the butler while having flashbacks of the attack on his parents some years earlier. Alfred's job is to rescue him, and the next shot shows him in close-up driving the car, tears of concern in his eyes. In an unconscious state, Bruce spends two days in bed before Alfred wakens him with a medicinal drink and to wish him felicitations on his birthday. Bruce is obviously in pain, and Alfred watches, seated motionless by the bed, thereby offering safety to his patient. The older man is humorous, courteous, and respectful in his approach, yet leads the way in proper behavior when Bruce informs him that he has to attend to a duty that his childhood friend Rachel (Katie Holmes) has alerted him to. Alfred reports that his guests will be arriving soon to celebrate his birthday and he will not be there to receive them, which would be indecorous. As Todd McGowan states, "When Bruce appears to stray from an ethical path, Alfred (Michael Caine) reminds him of the importance of his father's legacy" (2012, 91).

When, later, Bruce admits his failure to save Gotham City, Alfred repeats to him his father's wisdom, the camera framing the old man's face. "Why do we fall, sir?" he asks, recalling Thomas Wayne's earlier words, before he replies to his own question: "So that we can learn to pick ourselves up." Critic Peter Bradshaw notes the importance of Caine's performance in relation to Bruce: "Back home, the young corporate princeling works on his new persona, with the help of his butler and confidant Alfred, amiably played by Michael Caine" (2005), thus providing what Drake refers to as "external reframing signifiers." For Drake, it is important that

> Star performers [are] always recognizable as the products of stars, of individuals whose signifying function exceeds the diegesis (this is an economic imperative of stardom). It is by varying the ostensiveness of their performance, as well as external reframing signifiers (such as publicity and reviews) that they can manage this without disrupting the representational mode of the performance as a whole. (2006, 93)

Alfred operates as a salve once more to Bruce Wayne's (Christian Bale) struggle with alienation in the second film of his Batman trilogy, *The Dark Knight*. He appears early on in the film, smartly dressed in a dark three-piece suit and tie. As he marches purposefully forward, the camera cuts to a front perspective and shows him carrying a silver tray laid for breakfast. Alfred wears a stern look on his face, and a point-of-view shot reveals an empty bed. A cut back to Alfred shows his confusion as he pauses; his lips are pursed and he is clearly perturbed and displeased. He looks around the apartment shouting "Master Wayne," his voice echoing in the empty space. When he eventually finds him, it is in the cellar where the Batman operation is conducted. Alfred's appearance is in direct contrast to Bruce's. Whereas the butler is smartly attired and clean shaven, Bruce has a beard, his hair is unkempt, and he has not bothered to dress. Despite being a hero, his appearance is at odds with this status—he is lost. While Alfred retains his position as butler for Bruce, he also acts as his advisor. He explains to Bruce his mistakes when he "hung up his cape and cap . . . but you didn't move on, you never went to find a life, to find someone," suggesting that he return to some sense of normality. "There's nothing out there for me," states Bruce, his demeanor connoting what Deakin might describe as "'masculine malaise,' in which it will be understood that [Nolan] offers his male (anti-)heroes the fictional means and pathways to 'untruths' to transcend the limitations of their 'fractured' male existence" (2015, 85).

In a later scene Alfred physically mends Bruce. He helps to stitch his wounds which he acquired fighting during his nighttime activities in Gotham City, simultaneously teasing and bolstering him in his jovial south London voice: "Whenever you stitch yourself up, you do make a bloody mess." The camera shows Bruce's arm in close-up, before framing the two in shot as Alfred asks jokingly, "Did you get mauled by a tiger?" Alfred bestows Bruce with wisdom and knowledge to help him. He recounts stories from his own past, including an experience in Burma which is an allegory to guide and instruct the young man. In the script, Nolan suggests that, during this scene, Alfred's facial expression is solemn when he states that "some men aren't looking for anything logical, like money . . . they can't be bought, bullied, reasoned or negotiated with. (grave) Some men just want to watch the world burn" (Nolan and Nolan nd). Caine speaks this sentence quietly and in very close proximity to Bruce in order to convey the message, and Alfred's words appear to resonate.

Alfred remains a significant strong and reliable figure in the narrative of the last of the trilogy, *The Dark Knight Rises*, making his first appearance a few minutes into the film. Initially he appears "below stairs," issuing orders to the domestic staff of Wayne Manor. Speaking slowly and authoritatively, he is again smartly dressed, presenting order in chaos. Bruce, on the other hand, appears unkempt and unshaven, wearing a bathrobe and walking with a stick, thus demonstrating his weakness. He is residing in his bedroom in an unhappy and distressed state, and Alfred acts as his protector, preventing his employees from entering the room and helping Bruce to stay apart from the public. In this film, once more, Caine plays the conscientious employee who, on the surface, is subservient; he is caring, curt when he needs to be, and also, most of all, the jolly, ironic English southerner. While inserting quips into the conversation, he is also sagacious and offers words of wisdom and kindness. Throughout his life, it appears that the butler has had few personal relationships beyond that of serving his master, therefore leaving little time to travel. However, in *The Dark Knight Rises*, following a lecture to Bruce on why he should cease to be a hermit, he reminisces about the seven years when his young charge was away. Apparently, every year he visited Florence with the hope of seeing Bruce as a happily married man. In an emotional speech, his face half lit in the gloom of Wayne Manor, he tells Bruce that he never wanted him to return to Gotham City. He is unselfish, wanting a better life for Bruce, thus demonstrating his kindness. In Caine's trademark manner, his speech is delivered in a steady and measured mode, and his demeanor suggests that he is emotionally invested in this young man. The camera frames his serious face as he stands above Bruce, looking benignly down upon the troubled figure. When Bruce is retraining to resume his Batman activities, Alfred observes him, a solemn expression on his face, before pausing to give advice. "Yes, this city needs Bruce Wayne, your resources, your knowledge. It doesn't need your body or your life. That time's passed."

Despite the fast-paced action sequences in the film, periods with Alfred are calm and punctuate the narrative. When Alfred gives Bruce advice, and the conversation becomes impassioned, Nolan permits lengthy takes of Alfred's face and via the screenplay indicates the mode of delivery that Caine must adopt. Indeed, the script presents an important guide for Caine while not accounting for his own idiosyncratic style. When Bruce and Alfred part company at the end of the film, Nolan suggests that Alfred is "'QUIET' as he says, 'Goodbye Bruce' . . . Wayne mounts the stairs . . . Alfred watches him go. Turns. Alfred cries as he says these words" (Nolan and Nolan nd). When Alfred leaves Wayne Manor for the last time his face is stony, grave, and unblinking. Thus, while Nolan's instructions provide an indication of the figure expression required, Caine interprets them in his individual way to produce his own performance style.

At the end of the film, Alfred appears in the above-mentioned Florentine restaurant. He is casually dressed in a jacket and open-neck shirt and looks straight at the camera, his face shown in medium shot as he raises his eyes. A smile spreads over his face, and he nods his head as the camera frames Bruce and a woman seated at another table. The camera cuts back to Alfred, who rises and leaves the café. His protection of, and consideration for his friend's happiness and wellbeing, is thus demonstrated in these final sequences. In *The Dark Knight Rises*, Caine as actor and star presents a combination and arrangement of actions which work together to portray stability, kindliness, and strength—all traits which have aided Bruce's recovery.

In a similar vein to his previous roles for Nolan, Caine again operates as a fair and balanced figure in *The Prestige*. Set in the nineteenth century, John Cutter (Michael Caine) is an *ingénieur*, a stage engineer, in this instance for magic shows. Cutter opens the film giving evidence in court concerning a criminal case involving the supposed death of a fellow magician, Robert Angier (Hugh Jackman). He retains the same south London accent and measured manner as he explains the stages of his work. Cutter has spent the past few years arbitrating between two theatrical figures, Angier and another magician, Alfred Borden (Christian Bale). When the cross examiner asks him how the defendant, Borden, undertook a specific magic trick, Cutter replies sardonically, "He's a magician—ask him." Caine is drawing on his mannerisms and techniques using humor, an attribute made more amusing by his accent. Caine is again dressed in a dapper suit and retains his deliberate mode of delivery. Similar to his previous roles in *Batman Begins, The Dark Knight*, and *The Dark Knight Rises*, his actions are minimal to externalize his feelings, and he indicates with his forefinger when he wants to be direct. Like Alfred, Cutter is an authoritative figure in this film. At one juncture, when a magic trick goes awry, he lurches forwards to smash the side of a water tank in an attempt to release Angier's wife, Julia McCullough (Piper Perabo), who has become trapped inside. However, he is unable to save her, and after her death he takes the distressed Angier under his wing and becomes tutor, minder, and protector to him.

Cutter frequently plays the passive and immobile observer—a point noted by Anthony Scott, who also remarks on how Caine achieves narrative intervention: "The ever-reliable Michael Caine does not exert himself unduly . . . but then again, his job is to lull us with his wise, twinkly reassurance, so that we don't see the full dimensions of the story unfolding before us" (2006).

Indeed, it is Cutter's belief in Angier that prevents the spectator from fully understanding the deception taking place. Cutter constantly watches over him from the sidelines, and at one point when the magician is to perform a particularly difficult trick with a dove, his nerves almost get the better of him: "Fingers crossed" he states looking at Cutter, who replies encouragingly, a grin on his face and leaning toward his friend, "I'll have the champagne ready!" When all goes wrong and Angier is injured, Cutter is there to patch up his wounds, bending calmly over the maimed man. Again, he operates to physically as well as mentally aid the damaged individual.

Cutter has groomed a double, Gerald Root (Hugh Jackman), for Angier, the pair to perform a deception in a magic act. He watches from the sidelines as the two figures interact on stage. At one point Cutter becomes angry and intervenes in order to protect Angier; he physically pushes the drunken Root from the room before turning to grin at Angier and wish him congratulations. When Angier injures himself again following a trick performed by Borden, Cutter is there to help and counsel him: he bandages his leg while giving him a pep talk.

It is only later in the film that Cutter, an honorable man, realizes that Angier's behavior is obsessive and calculating, and he attempts to put a stop to it. The camera focuses in close-up on Cutter's unblinking eyes, a movement that Caine uses repeatedly, as he tilts his head to one side and declares that he is too old to join in his friend's mania. His voice becomes quieter as he slowly delivers the words, "I can't, I'm sorry," a kindly but sad look in his eyes. Angier is a man driven by his fixations and jealousy, and Cutter operates as an appeaser and cover for Angier's impairment.

At the end, Cutter is the upholder of high moral values when he realizes that he has been misled by Angier. He mentions Borden's child who is soon to be orphaned since her father has been found guilty of murder and will receive the death penalty. Cutter is distressed because he was deceived, and the camera frames him in close-up; his eyes are tearful as he realizes how he has been duped, not only by Angier but also by Borden. As Joy notes, "both men [Borden and Angier] are complicit in taking their craft more seriously than perhaps it is moral and healthy to. The rivalry . . . becomes a decidedly masculine search for superiority" (2015, 91). Cutter has acted as mediator and benefactor to these egotistical males, and *The Prestige* is based on misunderstandings and questions about individuality. Nevertheless, whereas Borden and Angier struggle with their own identities, Cutter has no doubt about his own moral self.

Caine's roles are less significant in Nolan's later films, yet his characters possess similar positions and traits to Alfred and Cutter. In *Inception*, Caine plays Professor Stephen Miles, the mild-mannered father-in-law of Dom Cobb (Leonardo DiCaprio). Miles is an academic and an intelligent and logical person. He has high morals and is angry at Cobb for being a neglectful father, believing that he should follow a more straightforward trajectory in life than his current position. The spectator first encounters Miles when Cobb surprises him on a visit to his workplace at a Paris university. Visible from a high-angle, point-of-view shot, his father-in-law is bent studiously over his desk writing, the camera subsequently cutting to a medium shot of Miles's head as he makes notes from an open textbook. Cobb's voice interrupts his thoughts, and Miles raises his head to see Cobb seated in an elevated position at the rear of a lecture theatre. His response at seeing his son-in-law is measured, expressing no surprise that Cobb has appeared: "No space to think in that broom cupboard," he replies to a derogatory comment Cobb has made about his office, his head to one side and a small smile on his face. There is little emotion between the two, and Miles remains seated and composed. Miles admonishes Cobb for being an absent father from his children, suggesting that "[i]t will take more than the occasional stuffed animal to convince those children they still have a father." When Cobb explains his reasons for being there, that he has found a way out of his mess, Miles sits back, his head cocked to one side, and stares steadily at him. In line with his previous characters in Nolan's films, Caine's delivery is minimalistic. Miles is situated in half light, his eyebrows raised and a half smile playing on his lips. Cobb is in turmoil, a damaged individual owing to the death of his wife, and Miles's role is to help Cobb's mental state of mind and return him to his children. He reminds him that his wife is no longer alive when Cobb makes reference to her as though she is. At this juncture, Miles leans forward, his mouth slightly open, and elbows placed on his desk in order to emphasize his point: "Come back to reality Dom," he requests. "Please," he entreats, nodding his head, an emotive and serious expression on his face. Miles's duty is to bring Cobb back to actuality, and he is relaxed in his demeanor, his aim to aid and heal this fractured individual.

When Cobb states that he has another task to complete before he can return to his children, Miles drops his head in concern. He is strong and decisive compared to Cobb, and eventually he agrees to help him, while simultaneously realizing the futility of his attempted interventions. As part of his positivity, a small smile lights up his face, and he decisively puts his glasses on. The next shot is of the two men standing in a hallway where Miles attracts the attention of a student, Ariadne (Ellen Page). Ultimately, Miles rationalizes that Ariadne will be a good influence on Cobb, a point made by McGowan who suggests that, "To help bring his son back to reality, Miles sends him to Ariadne.... The reason is that Miles wants a return to a patriarchal order for his son [*sic*] and knows that Ariadne will do so. She acts in the film as the stand-in for Miles and paternal authority" (2012, 157). Miles achieves this when, at the end of the film, he observes Cobb reunited with his children and smiles benignly before moving out of the frame. He has accomplished his goal, intervened in Cobb's mental state, and curtailed the younger man's extreme behavior.

Interstellar is the sixth Nolan film that Caine appears in. He is Professor Brand, a dependable old sage and father to Amelia (Anne Hathaway), and employed as a research scientist at the government agency NASA. Throughout the film his demeanor is measured, explaining his work and concerns to colleagues in exact and unhurried tones: "The last people to starve will be the first to suffocate," he states, as he half turns to the new recruit, Cooper (Matthew McConaughey), pointing his finger at him to reinforce his argument. Brand is honorable, kind, and considered in his approach, giving Cooper his word that he will solve any problems he may encounter on his forthcoming space expedition. The camera frames his face, leaving the spectator in no doubt that this is so. Brand's kindness extends to Cooper's children, Murph (Mackenzie Foy) and Tom (Timothée Chalamet), to whom he apologizes for sending their father away. In adulthood, Murph (Jessica Chastain) has gained a job at NASA, and the two have a serious discussion as he expresses his fears that his daughter and Cooper may never return, and if they do he may have failed to save the world from disaster. As he speaks he tilts his head to one side, and his expression is sad and pensive, Caine using his eyes for meaningful effect. Again, Caine's role as father figure continues in *Interstellar*, and, just as he functions as mentor to Bruce, Angier, Cobb, and Cooper, he also acts as guardian and protector of Cooper's children.

CONCLUSION

In an article in *The Independent*, Michael Caine branded Christopher Nolan "the new David Lean" and attributed him with being the one who "restarted [his] acting life" (Stolworthy, 2020) after casting him in *Batman Begins*. Clearly, the good working relationship was mutual, and Caine appeared in the director's films for nearly fifteen years with two further cameo roles of late. In *Dunkirk*, he is the voice on radio of a Royal Air Force flight leader at the outset of the film, giving orders to the fighter pilots, and in *Tenet* he plays Sir Michael Crosby from British Intelligence appearing for a few minutes at his club in London to give advice to Protagonist (John David Washington). However, these roles have become more transient, and in October 2021 Caine announced his retirement (Suri 2021). Nonetheless, Caine has brought his own distinctive style to Nolan's films, and during this period of his career with the director, he developed new distinguishing characteristics which can be discerned in line with his maturity. These carry significance for Nolan's narratives because the characters that Caine plays operate as steering figures who counter the difficulties that the director's troubled men must deal with. Indeed, at times he is a problem solver, and at others a compassionate patriarchal figure who has the ability to temper difficult situations and enable the heroes' recoveries. Previously, Caine was the star who existed on the margins of society and failed to conform, but this persona is replaced in Nolan's films by a kindly, amusing, and shrewd British gentleman.

NOTE

1. For further reading on auteur theory see Caughie (1981).

REFERENCES

Bradshaw, Peter. 2005. "Review: Batman Begins." *The Guardian*, June 17. www.theguardian.com/theguardian/2005/jun/17/1.

Bray, Christopher. 2006. *Michael Caine: A Class Act*. London: Faber and Faber.

Buckland, Warren (ed.). 2009. *Puzzle Films: Complex Storytelling in Contemporary Cinema*. Chichester, UK: Wiley-Blackwell.

Caine, Michael. 1997. *Acting in Film: An Actor's Take on Movie Making*. Lanham: Applause Theatre Book Publishers, Rowman and Littlefield.

Caughie, John (ed.). 1981. *Theories of Authorship*. London, Boston, and Henley: Routledge and Kegan Paul.

Caughie, John, and Kevin Rockett. 1996. *The Companion to British and Irish Cinema*. London: BFI.

Drake, Philip. 2006. "Reconceptualizing Screen Performance." *Journal of Film and Video* 58, no. 1–2: 71–88.

Dyer, Richard. 1979. *Stars*. London: BFI.

Joy, Stuart. 2015. "Introduction: Dreaming a Little Bigger Darling." In *The Cinema of Christopher Nolan: Imagining the Impossible*, ed. Jacqueline Furby and Stuart Joy, 1–16. New York and Chichester, UK: Columbia University Press.

McDonald, Paul. 2004. "Why Study Film Acting?: Some Opening Reflections." In *More Than a Method: Trends and Traditions in Contemporary Film Performance*, ed. Cynthia Baron, Diane Carson, and Frank P. Tomasulo, 23–41. Detroit: Wayne State University Press.

McDonald, Paul. 2011. *The Star System: Hollywood's Production of Popular Identities*. London and New York: Wallflower Press.

McGowan, Todd. 2012. *The Fictional Christopher Nolan*. Austin: University of Texas Press.

Nolan, Christopher, and Jonathan Nolan. nd. "Screenplay: *The Dark Knight*." www.nolanfans.com/library/pdf/thedarkknight-screenplay.pdf. Accessed September 29, 2021.

Scott, Anthony Oliver. 2006. "Two Rival Magicians, and Each Wants the Other to Go Poof." *New York Times*. October 20. www.nytimes.com/2006/10/20/movies/20pres.html.

Sellers, Robert. 2012. *Don't Let the Bastards Grind You Down: How One Generation of British Actors Changed the World*. London: Arrow Books.

Shail, Robert. 2004. "Masculinity and Class: Michael Caine as 'Working-Class Hero.'" In *The Trouble with Men: Masculinities in European and Hollywood Cinema*, ed. Phil Powrie, Ann Davies, and Bruce Babington, 66–76. London and New York: Wallflower Press.

Shoard, Catherine. 2015. "Michael Caine in Cannes: Playing the Elderly Is Better than Playing the Dead." *The Guardian*. May 20. www.theguardian.com/film/2015/may/20/michael-caine-in-cannes-playing-the-elderly-is-better-than-playing-the-dead.

Stolworthy, Jacob. 2020. "Inception 10thAnniversay: Michael Caine Reveals the Truth about Final Scene of Christopher Nolan Film." *Independent*, August 12. www.independent.co.uk/arts-entertainment/films/news/michael-caine-inception-christopher-nolan-ending-real-dream-leonardo-dicaprio-a8488286.html.

Suri, Sameer. 2021. "Michael Caine Announces Likely Retirement from Acting as He Notes 'There's Not Exactly Scripts Pouring out with a Leading Man That's 88.'" *Mail Online*. October 16. www.dailymail.co.uk/tvshowbiz/article-10098057/Michael-Caine-announces-likely-retirement-acting-88.html.

Chapter 10

Christopher Nolan and the Quays
Curation, Fandom, and the Filmmaker

Claire Parkinson

Following the release of *Interstellar* (2014) and long before filming for *Dunkirk* (2017) began, Christopher Nolan produced, directed, filmed, edited, and scored an eight-minute documentary film: *Quay* (2015). The film was screened as part of a touring program, curated by the director, alongside films by the Quays: identical twin brothers Stephen and Timothy, stop-motion animators from Pennsylvania. Nolan's short film documented his visit to the Quays' studio in London, where he interviewed the brothers and discussed their working practices. Unlike Nolan's feature films, the documentary short received relatively little press attention, and only a very small section of Nolan's fanbase sought out a screening. Despite Nolan's status as a major Hollywood auteur with a string of high-performing blockbuster hits behind him, the reception of *Quay* was muted, and the film divided fans. While the press and much of Nolan's fanbase had little interest in the film, scholarly engagement with it has been equally unenthusiastic. It is the case that Nolan's short films generally have been overlooked by scholars who have instead focused on his feature film releases. Indeed, discussion and analysis of the director's short films have, until now, been a major gap in Nolan scholarship, one which this chapter begins to rectify.[1] In this chapter I examine Nolan's collaboration with the Quay Brothers through the lens of fandom and argue that *Quay* and the touring program that Nolan curated are expressions of his fan behavior that are consistent with his identity as a "fanboy auteur."[2] I also propose that despite being relatively ignored or at best treated as an outlier in Nolan's career, *Quay* has a place within Nolan's body of work, sharing themes and aesthetic characteristics with his better-known feature films. To these ends, I examine paratexts and the context of the film's production and distribution to identify how the film and the accompanying touring program connect to key aspects of Nolan's identity as a "filmmaker" and "indie auteur," particularly his commitment to celluloid and links to arthouse cinema and the indie film sector.

THE "INDIE AUTEUR"

In February 2015 *Variety* carried an exclusive, albeit brief, piece of news about Nolan's next collaboration (McNary 2015). Far from the multimillion dollar deals with a major studio such as Warner Bros. and worlds away from high-profile collaborations with the usual roster of such Hollywood stars as Michael Caine, Tom Hardy, Christian Bale, or Cillian Murphy, the article explained that the production company Syncopy, owned by Christopher Nolan and Emma Thomas, would team with Zeitgeist Films for a series of Blu-ray releases. From the original Syncopy/Zeigeist deal, two Blu-ray releases were initially slated: the American release of *Elena* (2011), a Russian film directed by Andrey Zvyagintsev, and a compilation of fifteen short films by the Quay Brothers, with Nolan's film *Quay* included at the end of the Blu-ray running order. Other than the 2015 *Variety* article, there was little mention elsewhere of the deal or the Blu-ray releases. This situation was to change later in 2015 when press interest in the Quay Brothers' work and the release of the compilation *The Quay Brothers: Collected Short Films* (2015) was boosted with the announcement that Nolan had curated a touring exhibition of the animators' work. The focus of press articles was the news that the filmmaker would be premiering his new film and appearing in person with the animators on August 25, 2015, at Film Forum, an independent nonprofit cinema space in New York established in 1970 and best known for screening arthouse and independent films.

At first glance, the Zeitgeist/Syncopy deal may have seemed an odd pairing. In the first place Zeitgeist Films is a small company involved in the acquisition and distribution of what it describes as "quality foreign and independent feature films and documentaries to American screens" (Zeitgeist Films n.d). As a writer-director who made his breakthrough film, *Memento* (2000), in the American independent film sector before moving on to Hollywood features, forging a connection with a company that specializes in non-US arthouse films and documentaries may have seemed a puzzling move for Nolan. Coupled with the director's well-documented devotion to traditional film stock, the deal to distribute Blu-rays could also have been read as at odds with the director's zeal for photochemical film over other formats (see Molloy 2017, 383; Macnab 2017; Ressner 2012). However, Zeitgeist had a history with Nolan which stretched back to 1999 when the company acquired the North American distribution rights to the director's debut feature *Following*, an arthouse neo-noir described in a company press release as a "British psychological thriller" and an "international film" (Next Wave Films 1999).

Nolan's connection to the arthouse and indie sector has been core to his identity as an auteur working within the studio system. I have discussed previously that Nolan's movement from the independent to the studio sector was part of a wider trend led by the studios to bring indie filmmakers on to direct big-budget franchise films, leveraging their indie credentials and auteur sensibility within marketing strategies to appeal to both new audiences and existing fanbases (Molloy 2017, 375–80). From his early connection with Zeitgeist and after that with independent producer and distributor Newmarket, Nolan's career emerged from the arthouse and indie film sectors where *Memento* garnered the director a devoted fanbase and was established as a defining film in the Nolan "canon" (Molloy 2010, 5). The director has referred to himself as "an indie filmmaker working inside the studio system" (Kotler 2006). As well as bringing his own "indie sensibility" to studio films, part of Nolan's identity as an "indie filmmaker" is intrinsically tied up with his insistence on shooting with traditional photochemical film stock. As I argue elsewhere, the "film versus digital" debate has recurrent themes of artistry, artistic choice, and authenticity that, in part, function to reaffirm Nolan's status as a "filmmaker" rather than a "commercial director for hire" (Molloy 2017, 383). Indeed, Nolan's stance on using photochemical film stock places him firmly outside of usual industry practices, reinforcing his identity as a maverick artist-filmmaker fighting to maintain the authentic practices of his craft. It is therefore important to place Nolan's collaboration with both Zeitgeist and the Quay Brothers within this context.

In addition to Nolan's longstanding connection with the arthouse distributor Zeitgeist, the plan to release a Blu-ray, in the case of the Quays' films at least, was intended to follow a specially curated screening program of the animators' work on 35mm. As interviews and the post-screening conversations would reveal, for Nolan, the opportunity to tour the Quays' animations in their original 35mm format held greater importance for him than the later Blu-ray release. Speaking at an early screening, one of Nolan's first comments was to praise the quality of the screening: "What an amazing job they've done tonight presenting this film, so thank you very much. I'm staggered having just sat through the presentation of the only one of those films that I've been able to see a film print of previously—*The Comb*—at the ICA in London. To see *Street of Crocodiles* presented in the way it was originally made, it was a stunning experience" (Nolan 2015b). And in a second post-screening conversation, he went further saying: "how wonderful it is to see those films projected on 35mm. . . . it's such a thrill for me. I've admired the work for so long but to get to see it the way it was intended . . . incredible job" (Nolan 2015c). The comments were very much in keeping with arguments he has made in support of seeing films in movie theaters in their original format. According to Nolan, watching a film projected in the format intended by the filmmaker adds not only to the quality but also the authenticity of the experience for the audience (Russian 2021).

Nolan's enthusiasm for the Quays' work on 35mm is therefore unsurprising. The director has been vocal in the "film versus digital" debate, arguing to retain film as an option in the face of a widespread move within Hollywood away from shooting on 35mm film stock. By favoring photochemical film, Nolan's work process is often referred to as "traditional" in the sense that he retains a film-based workflow and expresses a preference for practical effects over digital.[3] But, in resisting the use of digital filmmaking, preferring to create his films "in-camera," and using photochemical film, Nolan's methods and format choices are atypical in the context of contemporary studio filmmaking. Arguing that film better suits his working practices, he claims that photochemical film is, in certain circumstances, cheaper than digital and "far better looking" (Nolan, quoted in Fischer 2012). Beyond the look of film though it is the tangible materiality of film and its existence as an object in the world that has value for Nolan who, in his address at the 2017 annual FIAF Congress, spoke of the "ongoing responsibility to maintain access to photochemical film prints, to see films the way in which they were intended to be shown, the way in which they were originally made, and to preserve them for future generations" (2017). The touring program of the Quays' work on 35mm, which was personally bankrolled by Nolan (Tafoya 2015), can therefore be understood as the filmmaker enacting this ideal of responsibility wherein the films were able to regain a particular notion of "authenticity" and, as material objects, resecure their place within the history of cinema.

Nolan has insisted that audiences are sensitive to the aesthetic qualities of film which in turn influences how they experience narrative affects: "Everyone's very sensitized to differences in imaging technology. . . . in terms of being sensitized to it and it having an effect on the way they perceive the story being shown; that's inarguable. That's a very powerful component of what cinema has always been" (Newsnight 2015). Highlighting the links between the aesthetic and affective, Nolan's argument for the "structure of feeling" (Williams 2015) of film connects it, as a medium, with films as texts in their material historical context. As a result, films do more than "tell stories"; they communicate their mode of production. As Luke Tredinnick suggests, "Films both speak the vernacular of their time and are constrained by the technologies of production" (2008, 84). Films, for Nolan, also have a material presence that is bound up with notions of authorial intent. As already mentioned above, in this sense, he insists that photochemical film has an authentic value and that where film stock has been used by the filmmaker, only by showing the film in its original format can that value be fully realized (Newsnight 2015). Authenticity is then conferred back onto the filmmaker by using a technology which is invested with years of film history with the photochemical print of a film being, Nolan has argued, "the authoritative version" (Newsnight 2015). Indeed, the director's stance on this matter would, five years later, see him part ways with Warner Bros. over its decision to release *Tenet* (2020) on the HBO Max streaming platform. His position on the subject was also expressed during a post-screening conversation with the Quays when Nolan pointed out that the opportunity to watch their 2000 film *In Absentia* as a 35mm print was a "unique experience" because, as the Quay Brothers explained, despite the film being shot on 35mm originally, it had only ever had one screening at the Barbican Centre in London. In addition, we can also assume that Nolan wanted audiences to experience his film *Quay*, shot on 35mm, in its original format.

For Nolan then, authenticity remains tied up with the original format of the film, a position that goes against Walter Benjamin's argument that mechanical reproduction replaces the unique material artwork with a generic copy (1970, 214). Instead, the technologies of analogue reproduction invest a film with specific aesthetic qualities, and each reel has its own "aura," retaining a connection to the original print of the film and to the purpose of the filmmaker while also having a life and history of its own as individual and unique objects in the world. As Darren Mooney explains, "Every film reel has actually existed in the world, and accrued some mark of that passage, sometimes denoted by imperfections that would not be present on a perfect copy of a perfect original. To proponents of celluloid over digital, these imperfections give celluloid texture, they make it feel substantial" (2018, 100). This distinction between digital and photochemical film has also fueled Nolan's concerns about the preservation of film for future generations. Although Nolan concedes that digital archiving has made films more accessible, digital formats are unstable, making film stock the only reliable method for "guarding these cultural treasures" (Newsnight 2015). Accordingly, Nolan's financing of the 35mm prints of the Quays' work and his curation of the touring program which aimed to introduce the Quays to new audiences fits with the director's wider position on and commitment to film preservation. And, while such an endeavor might initially suggest that the Nolan-Quay relationship is one of patronage, I argue that is inconsistent with Nolan's carefully crafted identity as a filmmaker. Instead, I propose that their collaboration is better considered through the lens of fandom.

THE FANBOY AUTEUR

Inasmuch as Nolan's commitment to film preservation can be seen to inform his desire to screen 35mm prints of the Quays' work for a new generation of audience, it is also the case that the touring program, of which his own film *Quay* was a part, can be understood as an act of fan curation. Derek Kompare defines fan curators as "more established fans . . . usually with deeper knowledge of, and access to, the fandom and its texts. . . . the key thing is *curators organize their expertise in service of bringing new people into the fandom*" (2018, 107, emphasis in original). Certainly, Nolan's intention for the touring program was that it would introduce the Quays' work to a wider audience (and to his own fans), and despite financing the endeavor, the way in which Nolan presented himself in relation to the Quays was not as a wealthy patron of their art, but primarily as a fan. Indeed, the director's admiration for the Quays' work was more than evident in interviews and post-screening conversations where he would tell of first discovering the Quays' work, its impact on him, and his continuing enthrallment with their films which he did not claim to understand but which captivated his imagination and influenced his own work. Nolan writes about watching the Quays' films: "I am right back where I started; open-mouthed in front of absorbing dream imagery that I cannot understand any more than I can forget" (2015a).

Autobiographical practices are important to fandom to establish an origin narrative that marks the beginning of an individual fan's commitment. As Matt Hills suggests, "affect, attachment and even passion" define fandom (2002, 37). In this regard Nolan clearly signaled his fan identity through these autobiographical practices of fandom, describing his first encounter with the Quays' work in affective terms. At the beginning of post-screening conversations with the Quays and in the liner notes for *The Quay Brothers: Collected Short Films*, Nolan offered his personal discovery narrative. He explained: "Twenty-five years ago, late one night, down in my parents' split level suburban basement, channel surfing the old fashioned way (instant anonymous imagery, no guide, no info), I hit my first taste of Quay—like an electric shock—like nothing I'd ever seen. The mystery of the Quay Brothers got its hooks into me. I spent two years (pre-internet) wondering what the hell I'd seen" (Nolan 2015a, 1). Fan narratives of initiation involve not only the first encounter but also accounts of seeking out further artifacts connected to their fandom (Kompare 2018). Nolan's introduction to the Quays followed just such a pattern and confirmed his status as an established fan while his language choices expressed the intensity of his instant attachment to the animators' work. By drawing attention to the length of time he had been a fan—twenty-five years—Nolan demonstrated the appropriate fan credentials that in turn validate his status as a "fan curator." To assert the level of his knowledge and understanding of the Quays' work, Nolan revealed not only that he had been intrigued by the brothers' animations since his teenage years, but also that he could identify where others had borrowed from their work, and that the Quays had influenced his own filmmaking, citing *The Prestige* (2006) as an example (2015a, 1; 2015b). Nolan admitted, "I see their work pillaged wholesale in music videos, commercials and even movies. I don't want to name names because one of the names is eventually my own. . . . Getting to meet the Quays, getting to see their studio was thrilling" (2015a, 1–2). His statements of course reveal his fannish enthusiasm but also reaffirm his connection to the arthouse filmmaking world. He asserts that he is a fan but also makes work that is "like" the Quays.³ Although Nolan never explains exactly how his films demonstrate the Quays' influence (and indeed the brothers admitted they did not see the references), Nolan nonetheless aligns himself and his work with filmmakers who are associated with complex, experimental narratives, arthouse practices, and dreamlike imagery. In this sense, by claiming to be influenced by the Quays, Nolan's statements discursively connect his fan behavior with his indie auteur identity.

Nolan selected three of the short films from the fifteen that appear on the Blu-ray for *The Quay Brothers—On 35mm* touring program in addition to his own documentary short. In the context of the touring program, Nolan's film acts as something of a guide to the Quays' work and processes. This amounts to what Kompare terms fan curation of the "suggested canon," an aggregating of materials "based on the *curator's perceptions*" which are proposed to form a set of key texts for other fans to "get into" (2018, 109). The screening program lasted 70 minutes, opening with *In Absentia* (Quays, 2000), followed by Nolan's 8-minute documentary short *Quay*, then *The Comb* (1990) and ending with *Street of Crocodiles* (1986). Nolan's curation of the program was questioned by some critics who felt that *In Absentia* was a challenging film to present to audiences who were unlikely to have encountered the Quay Brothers' work previously. *Street of Crocodiles*, perhaps their best-known work, was considered more accessible and an easier introduction to the animator's films.⁴ Nolan's rationale for his choice of films relied on his own perception of the value of a specific quality in the work—in this case the notion of "accident." Nolan explained, "What I love about all three of these films and the reason I chose these three in particular is, of all of your work, for me they have extremely organic qualities. . . . they don't feel accidental but they feel like they were informed by accident" (2015b).

Despite his deferential tone when speaking or writing about the Quays, Nolan is a particularly privileged type of fan. His curatorial fan behaviors are not constrained by lack of access to either the Quays or their films, he is financially able to create a canon that can be experienced in the form of expensive 35mm prints taken from the original films, and he utilizes his status and influence to expand the fandom. Nolan's enthusiasm for the Quay Brothers and their work offers an interesting dimension to his status as a "fanboy auteur." In their discussion of "fanboy auteurs," Anastasia Salter and Mel Stanfill explain that the "fan credentials" of directors are a key aspect of their marketing and branding which have come to signify "quality media-making" (2020, ix). Charting the rise of the "fanboy" as an ideal consumer, Salter and Stanfill contextualize it by pointing out that it has happened alongside the development of franchise media based on "geek culture," anchors for which have been the Marvel Cinematic Universe and DC Extended Universe (DCEU) (2020, xii). It is, of course, the latter of these media franchises with which Nolan is closely associated although not because of his Dark Knight series (which is not part of the official DCEU), but through co-writing and co-producing *Man of Steel* (2013) and being an executive producer on *Batman v Superman: Dawn of Justice* (2016), *Justice League* (2017), and *Zack Snyder's Justice League* (2021). Nolan's Dark Knight trilogy was always intended to be standalone, with narrative choices that precluded any continuation as part of the DCEU.[5] The details of Nolan's inclusion in the DCEU notwithstanding, however, it is the case that his fanboy auteur brand is intrinsically connected to the Batman films which paved the way for his later involvement in the DCEU, placing Nolan in the company of other fanboy auteurs such as Zach Snyder and Sam Raimi, who are trusted by comic-book fans to adapt the original texts for the screen (Salter and Stanfill 2020, 117). As Salter and Stanhill point out, fannishness on the part of the writer-director confers a certain type of creative authority that is appreciated by fans of the original source material (2020, 117). The fanboy auteur is therefore a particular identity with currency in the mainstream marketplace and is, in part, the product of a relationship between the filmmaker and his fans.

The director is well known for having devoted fans. Although the Dark Knight films certainly increased the number of Nolan fans, a hardcore fanbase was established earlier with the release of *Memento* (2000), a film which was able to take advantage of early film fan sites and forums where "a devoted online following of fans" were more than willing to discuss, debate, and analyze the filmmaker's work (Mooney 2018, 33). The intensity and devotion of Nolan fans has been widely discussed in the press, particularly following the decision in 2012 by the Rotten Tomatoes website to suspend comments after the film critic Marshall Fine received 900 threats within a few hours of posting a less-than-favorable review of *The Dark Knight Rises* (2012) (Sherwin 2012; Carlson 2012).[6] In an article titled "Why Are Christopher Nolan Fans So Intense?" one film critic opined, "It's a level of auteurist devotion so extreme it would make Andrew Sarris uncomfortable. It's extreme and extremely unusual. There's no modern director who earns this type of loyalty, at least not at this scale" (Singer 2014). Given the widespread loyalty to Nolan and his work by a fanbase renowned for their devotion, one would be forgiven for thinking that news of a new Christopher Nolan film in 2015 would have attracted high levels of fan interest. This was not the case however, and fan interest was noticeably subdued even with the news that Nolan would be appearing in person at the early screenings.

Beginning at Film Forum, "The Quay Brothers—On 35mm" toured to a further ten cities—Dallas, Los Angeles, Houston, Austin, Cleveland, Boston, Detroit, Seattle, Chicago, and ending in Toronto in October 2015—where it was screened at independent and arthouse cinemas. In reviews of the touring program the press commented on the incongruous pairing: the preeminent director of Hollywood blockbusters and the obscure experimental animators. Driving home a point about the differences between the filmmakers, one journalist noted "Most of Nolan's numerous fans have probably never heard of the Quay Brothers or seen their shorts" (Sharf 2015), while another more critical review opined: "Nolan is known for movies of 'depth,' overly serious films with puzzle-box plots that ultimately contain nothing, while the Quays actually operate on an extraordinarily deep and intuitive level" (Burgos 2015). The critical reception of the touring program highlighted the relative nature of film categorization and indeed of Nolan himself. Nolan's films are often referred to as having arthouse characteristics, being complex and requiring multiple viewings when set in contrast with other Hollywood fare and where Nolan's brand skillfully deploys the "indie auteur" identity. Yet, when considered in relation to the Quay Brothers, critics noted that Nolan is very clearly a mainstream director who signifies, at best, the Hollywood colonization of arthouse and indie filmmaking. In contrast with fan responses to previous negative or even ambivalent reviews about Nolan's work, the lack of fan reaction to the critical reception of *Quay* and the touring program bears some discussion.

Fan reaction to the touring program and news that Nolan was due to release a new short film was certainly muted. There was relatively little fan activity on social media with only two mentions of "The Quay Brothers—On 35mm" on the Nolan Fans Twitter account in the six months prior to the August premiere, and while comments in Nolan fan forums reflected some degree of interest in the upcoming event, the news that Nolan had made a documentary received mixed responses.[7] In the NolanFans.com forum, fans expressed a desire to go to the screening for three main reasons: to better understand Nolan's influences; to have an opportunity to ask Nolan questions about his other films; and to be one of the first fans to see *Quay*. But there was confusion over how Nolan could make a film in such secrecy, why he had made a documentary, and speculation about whether or not it would be feature length. Although there was general interest in sourcing the Blu-ray, if fans were unable to attend the screening there were also expressions of disinterest in the film and a widespread indifference toward the Quays' work. In this regard, some fans agreed that the obligation to Nolan as their favorite filmmaker overrode their lack of interest in the Quays. It was however the lack of discussion that was notable with only 124 replies about *Quay*, a mere fraction of the usual levels of discussion about a Nolan film on the fansite. There was even less discussion about Quay on Reditt, including in the Christopher Nolan Community (only three comments), while Rotten Tomatoes carried only one audience review in 2015 and Internet Movie Database (IMdB) had no user reviews on the film in its year of release. While it is the case that short films do not have the appeal of feature-length films for general audiences, the lack of fan engagement with *Quay* can be explained by recourse to Nolan's fanboy auteur identity. As Suzanne Scott explains, "the fanboy auteur's perceived ability to speak fans' 'language' and his liminal positioning (his ability to present him simultaneously as one of 'us' and one of 'them,' consumer and producer) is framed as his greatest asset, suggesting that he is an ideal interpreter between text and audience" (Scott 2012, 44). In the case of *Quay*, the relationship between fan and fanboy auteur broke down; Nolan and his fans were no longer speaking the same language. Despite the director's insistence that the Quays had influenced his own filmmaking, experimental arthouse animation and Nolan's foray into documentary was a step too far for many of even his most ardent fans.

QUAY

Quay begins with the title in lowercase white letters on a black screen. A ticking clock and the distant sound of what may be human voices form the soundscape to the opening shot of the film: a dimly lit doll's head and torso, almost silhouetted against out-of-focus spots of light. In the background of the shot someone turns on more lights, and the sequence cuts to two figures opening curtains and switching on strings of small lights in what appears to be a cramped room packed with old furniture and strange objects. A clock chimes eight times as more lights go on, and we return to the close-up of the strange figure from the first shot. Now fully illuminated we see that it is a Victorian doll, but the top of her head is missing and she has no eyes. To those who know the Quays' work, she is recognizable as one of the curiosities from their 1986 film *Street of Crocodiles*. On the last chime of the clock the shot cuts away from this strange figure. It is significant that Nolan's documentary begins in this way. The odd figurine from what is arguably the Quays' best-known and most celebrated work and the sound of a clock remind the viewer that this documentary about the animators is made by a filmmaker who is preoccupied with time. And, while Nolan is never visibly or audibly present in the documentary, this reference to the thematic concerns that shape each of his films continues to mark his auteur presence in *Quay*.

The chiming signals the beginning of the film, and from the opening up of the studio, we can assume the start of a day. But this is a Nolan film, and what follows may or may not be a single day condensed into eight minutes. Indeed, the end of the film is signaled by the same clock chiming nine times, but the image that accompanies it is at odds with the number of chimes. On the first chime of the closing sequence one of the brothers points away and says "that clock." The shot cuts to a clock face with a white dial, roman numerals, and the year 1806. The hands point to twelve, not to nine o'clock as we might expect from the number of chimes. As the chimes continue, the camera cuts from strange object to object and then finally to the Victorian doll which appeared in the opening sequence. The lights are switched off, and the brothers appear to exit the studio, leaving only the shadowy figure of the doll in the foreground of the shot. There is a visual balance to the film which begins and ends on the same figure, and the opening and closing chimes are clearly important sonic cues that signal the start and end of the film, but how much time has passed? Is this a day, is it an hour, or is the concept of time completely malleable as might be suggested by the incongruous clock image showing twelve when there are nine chimes? While the Quays play with time in their films—*In Absentia* from Nolan's curated program being an example of this—the director's use of these cues reminds us that irrespective of genre, his preoccupation with time in films remains. As Nolan has said, "Time is the most cinematic of subjects because before the movie camera came along, human beings had no way of seeing time backwards, slowed down, sped up" (NPR 2020).

Although modest in its length, I propose that *Quay* should be read as a documentary that draws on modernist strategies of experimentation that imaginatively reconstruct a world through the "open-ended, ambiguous play with time and space" (Nichols 2016, 22). This is achieved through Nolan's manipulation of the visual and sonic markers of time coupled with montage sequences and handheld tracking shots to describe the space of the Quays' studio. Using a handheld camera, Nolan follows the Quays through the narrow and cramped space of their studio. This sequence incorporates cutaways to close-up shots of strange objects, many of which are recognizable from the Quays' films. Although the camera follows the brothers as they move through studio space, the cutaways act visually to disrupt the viewer's discovery of the space, making it difficult to understand the layout of what appears to be a dark, chaotic, and claustrophobic space. As the brothers begin their day, one opens a case, and the sequence cuts to assorted books about French artist Marcel Duchamp, Spanish sculptor Juan Muñoz, Czech painter Jan Zrzavý, and Czech artist and architect Vlastislav Hofman, all of whom we might assume have influenced the twin animators from Pennsylvania. The sound of a ticking clock fades out to be replaced by the long, low, ominous sounds of a cello played with a bow. As the film progresses, the bowed cello is replaced by plucked strings that are then combined with the bowed cello to sonically and rhythmically echo the soundscape of the Quays' films *The Comb* and *Street of Crocodiles*.

The animators speak to one another quietly as they light a set that is occupied by a collection of strange puppet figures. One of the brothers then starts to recount how they came to use particular types of lights for their animations, and it is clear that this conversation is directed toward the camera and the audience. What is unclear is who is speaking. At no point in the documentary does Nolan tell the audience the names of the animators, nor give any sense of which of the identical twins is speaking. At times, the twins add to or complete each other's sentences, and Nolan overlays the brothers' voiceover with shots of them working and cutaways to close-ups of the objects in the studio. This pattern of shots further disrupts any possibility of identifying which twin is speaking. Moreover, when the twins discuss the importance of mirrors in their work—they often shoot into mirrors—the sequence includes shots of the animators' reflections. But the mirrors are old and the backings have eroded so that the reflections of the twins are partial, fragmentary, and strange, and the doubling effect adds to the visual confusion.

The visual and sonic confusion is such that the Quay twins seem to speak as one entity, drawing parallels with Nolan's 2006 film *The Prestige* in which a magic trick called "The Transported Man" is achieved by twins who play the same character on and off stage, a twist that is revealed to the audience at the end of the film. It is notable that Nolan states that the Quays influenced *The Prestige*, although he does not identify in what way, and the Quays have said that they have not noticed the references to their work in his film (Nolan 2015a). In paratexts, Nolan remarks that the Quays' work remains inscrutable and unknown, that their process is alchemic, almost magical. These connections, which can be traced through *Quay* and its paratexts, bear all the hallmarks of the type of recursive puzzle Nolan is well known for in his films: *Quay* makes visual and sonic references to the Quays' films and uses the same conceit as *The Prestige* in a narrative about the twin animators who influenced the 2006 film. There is thus a recursive aspect to *Quay* which borrows and returns the viewer each time to a reference point but remains ambiguous. At the end we do not know how the director was influenced by the Quays, and although the documentary appears to reveal the animators' process, as Nolan points out, at the end of it, the viewer, and even Nolan himself, is left feeling that they still do not fully understand how the Quays create their films. In this case, the twist is not revealed, and ambiguity remains.

Visually *Quay* references the brothers' animations, not only through the direct representation of the strange puppets and objects that have been used in their films but also through the lighting of the objects. A swinging light source illuminates some of the objects, creating the illusion of stop motion and emulating the aesthetic of the Quays' work. What is notable in *Quay* is Nolan's use of close-ups, even when the twins are speaking and particularly to draw the viewer's attention to the strange artifacts that seem to populate every surface and corner of the Quays' studio. Known for looser medium shots in his feature films, particularly when his characters are speaking, Nolan goes in close in *Quay*, cutting between close-ups and only rarely moving back for a wide shot. This echoes the Quays' style of filming which takes small details and odd objects and through close-ups makes them fascinating, unusual, and strange. Nolan echoes this shot choice and in doing so enhances the claustrophobic feel of the space. As in *The Prestige*, he favors natural light in *Quay*, the source of which is the few windows that illuminate only parts of the darkened studio. The result of this lighting choice is that most shots in *Quay* have rich shadows which add to the dark sometimes foreboding atmosphere of the space. Lighting in such a way that keeps details in shadow is part of Nolan's visual style in his feature films where, for example, he tends to use a keylight on the edge of the face so that three quarters of the face is in shadow. Thus, *Quay* presents an interesting combination of Nolan's signature style combined with references to the Quays' work.

Quay is a film that Nolan had complete control over and was shot with a minimal crew and with the director taking on the majority of key roles. Unusually, Nolan is credited as the producer, director, editor, and composer, but typically for him, many of the other crew on the film were people he had worked with previously. Roko Belic, with whom Nolan made his first short film *Tarentella*, receives a credit as does Andy Thompson, who is credited as a producer on *Dunkirk* and *Tenet* (as well as Nolan's assistant on *Batman v Superman* [2016], *Interstellar* [2014], *Man of Steel* [2013], and *The Dark Knight Rises* [2012]) and as sound recordist on *Quay*. On the face of it, Nolan's documentary short seems deceptively simple and gives an insight into the day-to-day work and processes of the Quay Brothers that he so admires. However, when considered in relation to other paratexts, I would argue that *Quay* not only fits thematically and stylistically quite comfortably within Nolan's wider body of work, but that it repays multiple viewings. *Quay* plays with time and space, it is preoccupied with doubling, mirrors, rich shadow, and ambiguity. There is no doubt that it is a Christopher Nolan film, made by a fan and an indie auteur.

NOTES

1. See also Stuart Joy's chapter on Nolan's short films in this volume.
2. See also Lara Herring's chapter in this volume.
3. Nolan also deviates from popular working methods, eschewing the use of shot lists and storyboards except for action scenes (Fischer 2012; Ressner 2012).
4. The later Blu-ray release in October 2015 took a somewhat different and more straightforward approach to the ordering of the Quays' films, presenting them in chronological order beginning with the 1984 14-minute film *The Cabinet of Jan Svankmajer* and ending with the 2013 film *Unmistaken Hands*.
5. For example, at the end of *The Dark Knight Rises*, Bruce Wayne (Christian Bale) retires. Any continuation of the narrative would have undermined Nolan's ending.
6. See also: Dobbins 2012; Associated Press 2012.
7. See: Nolanfans.com; twitter.com/NolanFans/; imdb.com; rottentomatoes.com.

REFERENCES

Associated Press. 2012. "'Dark Knight Rises' critics Draw Fire on RottenTomatoes.com." *Entertainment Weekly*, July 18. ew.com/article/2012/07/18/dark-knight-rises-rotten-tomatoes-suspends-comments/.

Benjamin, Walter. 1970. *Illuminations*. London: Jonathan Cape Ltd.

Burgos, Danielle. 2016. "The Quay Brothers—On 35mm." *ScreenSlate*, August 11. www.screenslate.com/articles/quay-brothers-35mm.

Carlson, Erin. 2012. "Rotten Tomatoes Shuts Down 'Dark Knight Rises' Comments." *The Hollywood Reporter*, July 18. www.hollywoodreporter.com/news/general-news/rotten-tomatoes-dark-knight-rises-351124/.

Dobbins, Amanda. 2012. "Christopher Nolan Understands Where Those Fanboys Were Coming From." *New York*, July 19. www.vulture.com/2012/07/christopher-nolan-understands-his-fanboys.html.

Fischer, Russ. 2012. "Christopher Nolan Explains His Love for Shooting on Film, and Disinterest in 3D." *SlashFilm*, April 13. www.slashfilm.com/520696/christopher-nolan-film-digital/.

Hills, Matt. 2002. *Fan Cultures*. London and New York: Routledge.

Kompare, Derek. 2018. "Fan Curators and the Gateways to Fandom." In *The Routledge Companion to Media Fandom*, ed. Melissa A. Click and Suzanne Scott, 107–13. New York and London: Routledge.

Kotler, Steven. 2006. "Mavericks to Mainstream: Indie's Rebel Helmers Have Morphed into Hollywood's Megapic Maestros." *Variety*, January 11. variety.com/2006/film/awards/mavericks-to-mainstreamers-1117935961/.

Macnab, Geoffrey. 2017. "Film vs Digital? In the Same Way that a New Generation of Music Lovers Are Rediscovering Vinyl, Cinema Enthusiasts Are Discovering, or Rediscovering Celluloid." *Independent*, August 31. www.independent.co.uk/arts-entertainment/films/features/dunkirk-film-digital-christopher-nolan-quentin-tarantino-paul-thomas-anderson-lawrence-of-arabia-a7918586.html.

McNary, Dave. 2015. "Christopher Nolan's Syncopy Teaming with Zeitgeist on Blu-ray Releases." *Variety*, February 19. variety.com/2015/film/news/christopher-nolans-syncopy-teaming-with-zeitgeist-on-blu-ray-releases-exclusive-1201437195.

Molloy, Claire. 2010. *Memento*. Edinburgh: Edinburgh University Press.

———. 2017. "Indie Cinema and the Neoliberal Commodification of Creative Labour." In *A Companion to American Indie Film*, ed. Geoff King, 368–88. Chichester: Wiley Blackwell.

Mooney, Darren. 2018. *Christopher Nolan: A Critical Study of the Films*. Jefferson, NC: McFarland.

Newsnight. 2015. "Christopher Nolan: The Full Interview." October 16. www.youtube.com/watch?v=VtH6kiPbMBw.

Next Wave Films. 1999. "Press Kit: Next Wave Films Sells North American Rights to *Following*." nextwavefilms.com/presskit/hiline.html. Accessed August 7, 2021.

Nichols, Bill. 2016. *Speaking Truths with Film: Evidence, Ethics, Politics in Documentary*. Oakland: University of California Press.

Nolan, Christopher. 2015a. "The Quay Enigma." In *The Quay Brothers: Collected Short Films*. Blu-ray liner notes. Syncopy 1–2.

———. 2015b. "Conversation with Chris Nolan/Stephen & Timothy Quay/Michael Atkinson." Recorded August 19, 2015, at 7pm. filmforum.org/film/quay-brothers-on-35mm-film.

———. 2015c. "Conversation with Chris Nolan/Stephen & Timothy Quay/Michael Atkinson." Recorded August 19, 2015, at 9.30pm. filmforum.org/film/quay-brothers-on-35mm-film.

Nolan, Christopher. 2017. "Moving beyond 'Film vs. Digital.'" The Academy of Motion Picture Arts and Sciences. May 10. medium.com/art-science/moving-beyond-film-vs-digital-bc1dac5d607f.

NPR 2020. "Christopher Nolan on Why Time Is a Recurring Theme in His Movies." December 14. www.npr.org/2020/12/14/946420812/christopher-nolan-on-why-time-is-a-recurring-theme-in-his-movies?t=1656236017533.

Ressner, Jeffrey. 2012. "The Traditionalist." Directors Guild of America. Accessed April 21, 2022. www.dga.org/Craft/DGAQ/All-Articles/1202-Spring-2012/DGA-Interview-Christopher-Nolan.aspx.

Russian, Ale. 2021. "Christopher Nolan Spotted at AMC Theatres as L.A. Reopens Movie Theatres for the First Time in a Year." *People*, March 17. people.com/movies/christopher-nolan-spotted-at-amc-theater-as-l-a-reopens-movie-theaters-for-first-time-in-a-year/.

Salter, Anastasia, and Mel Stanfill. 2020. *A Portrait of the Auteur as Fanboy: The Construction of Authorship in Transmedia Franchises*. Jackson: University Press of Mississippi.

Scott, Suzanne. 2012. "Who's Steering the Mothership?: The Role of the Fanboy Auteur in Transmedia Storytelling." In *The Participatory Cultures Handbook*, ed. Aaron Delwiche and Jennifer Jacobs Henderson, 43–52. New York and London: Routledge.

Sharf, Zack. 2015. "Why 'The Quay Brothers in 35mm' is One of Christopher Nolan's Greatest Accomplishments." *IndieWire*, August 20. www.indiewire.

com/2015/08/why-the-quay-brothers-in-35mm-is-one-of-christopher-nolans-greatest-accomplishments-59077/.

Sherwin, Adam. 2012. "Rotten Tomatoes Suspends Comments on *Dark Knight Rises* after Fans Send Death Threats to Film Critic." *The Independent*, July 18. www.independent.co.uk/arts-entertainment/films/news/rotten-tomatoes-suspends-comments-on-dark-knight-rises-after-fans-send-death-threats-to-film-critic-7956851.html.

Singer, Matt. 2014. "Why Are Christopher Nolan Fans So Intense?" *Screen Crush*, November 14. screencrush.com/christopher-nolan-fans/.

Tafoya, Scout. 2015. "Everything Is Twisted up and Strange: Stephen and Timothy Quay." *RogerEbert.com*. August 21. www.rogerebert.com/interviews/quays-nolan-ifc.

Tredinnick, Luke. 2008. *Digital Information Culture: The Individual and Society in the Digital Age*. Oxford: Chandos Publishing.

Williams, Raymond. 20215. "Structures of Feeling." In *Structures of Feeling*, ed. Devika Sharma and Frederik Tygstrup, 20–28. Berlin: De Gruyter.

Zeitgeist Films. N.d. "About Us." zeitgeistfilms.com/about. Accessed February 10, 2022.

All websites accessed February 2, 2022.

SECTION 3

POLITICS, IDEOLOGY, AND GENRE

Chapter 11

Situating Christopher Nolan's Ideological Use of Technology

Between Romanticism and Posthumanism

Ben Lamb

Nolan's blockbusters feature protagonists averting humanitarian disasters, be they global authoritarianism in *Inception* (2010); nuclear terrorism in *The Dark Knight Rises* (2012); global warming in *Interstellar* (2014); warfare in *Dunkirk* (2017); or World War III in *Tenet* (2020). To quell each crisis, protagonists ensure the human race survives by utilizing technology. I chart how Nolan's depiction of technology changes to propose that his authorial signature ideologically balances between a romantic sensibility, whereby humans unshackle themselves from technology to return to nature, and Haraway's definition of post-humanism, technological modification, and intervention whereby boundaries thought to exist between humans and machines have become "thoroughly breached" through an evolutionary process (Haraway 1991, 151).

McGowan (2012), Furby and Joy (2015), Eberl and Dunn (2017), Mooney (2018), and Joy (2020) characterize Nolan as a filmmaker who evokes trauma through facial close-ups, flashbacks, montage editing, slanted camera angles, and nonchronologically ordered narratives. Puzzle films emerge as audiences must reveal a truth hidden beneath regular misdirection, obfuscated knowledge, falsified history, and memories of unreliable protagonists. Joy in particular argues *Interstellar* is a key film that produces an ideological shift in Nolan's signature formula as it is an account of astronaut Cooper's (Matthew

McConaughey) ability to return to those he loves to achieve "post-traumatic growth" (Joy 2020, 113).

In Nolan's initial puzzle films characters are unable to achieve critical independence as a direct result of the way technology obscures their judgements and obfuscates their perceptions. As *Memento* (2000) concludes, it emerges that Leonard (Guy Pearce) is likely to have murdered a number of people he has been deceived into believing assaulted his wife. As the plot unravels through ten-minute scenes collectively sequenced out of chronological order, it has been argued that the film's narrative structure, in emulating the protagonist's anterograde amnesia, functions as "a unique posthumanist critique of the way we understand and explain ourselves through memory, subjectivity and consciousness" (Manea 2015, 295). The ways technologies are represented are also key to this reading as depictions of Leonard's interactions with technology sustain his delusions and enable others to exploit his amnesia. Leonard's carefully curated collection of notes and photographs, and tattoos across his body transform his outer self into a posthuman external memory device, but in so doing make his body "a contested public space vulnerable to manipulation and sabotage by others" (Krueger 2015, 179).

In contrast to existing Nolan scholarship, then, I propose that since the director's initial American feature he increasingly utilizes an ideological formula whereby a more optimistic posthuman outlook has emerged through the way in which his films have become increasingly colored by neo-romantic affect. Nolan's works utilize what Martin Lefebvre (2006) terms *"temps morts,"* whereby a director uses a shot of a landscape that "briefly becomes independent of the narrative but is based on existing knowledge of the principles of landscape painting traditions" (Hockenhull 2013, 12). As has been identified as regular practice within contemporary cinema, Nolan's works also utilize these *temps morts* to produce a neo-romantic affect that contemplates the spiritual qualities of landscape and nature, free from the film's narrative, and encourages the viewer to intuitively respond to the natural phenomena as being both beautiful and chaotic, as well as passive and aggressive (Rose 2007). As Nolan begins to embrace technology as a means of reconfiguring the human condition where posthuman evolution is conceived through "genetic engineering" or "mechanical or electronic enhancements to the human body" the extent to which this is realized is tempered by neo-romantic affect (Booker and Thomas 2009, 328).

INCEPTION AND THE NEO-ROMANTIC AFFECT

Inception is Nolan's first film to balance neo-romanticism with posthumanism. Dominick Cobb's (Leonardo DiCaprio) posthuman technology, which blurs the boundary between living organism and machine, enables people to engage in intersubjectivity. Human subjects can fully realize their imaginative potential by intravenously connecting to a suitcase device to share dreamscapes. Therefore, *Inception* has already been categorized by Philbeck (2015) as belonging to the latest stage of the posthumanism paradigm where science fiction cinema is increasingly obsessed with mind-uploading. This practice of transitioning consciousnesses to computer networks emerges in cyberpunk literature, notably William Gibson's *Neuromancer* (1984), and has since been depicted in films including *Existenz* (1999), *Avatar* (2009), and *Captain America: The Winter Soldier* (2014) (Philbeck 2015, 398). Unlike other mind-uploading films and Nolan's previous films, though, in *Inception* posthumanist capabilities provide the opportunity for spiritual transcendence synonymous with romantic texts.

After completing his mission at the very end of the film, Cobb returns home where he is reunited with his children in the family home, joining them in their back garden to appreciate the beauties of nature. As Cobb stands at the back door his point of view frames both children, backs to the camera, within a long shot of the garden doused in bright sunlight. This brightest shot of the film makes the grass shine a fluorescent green, and both children are filmed in slow motion as if frozen in time, the sounds of their laughter elongated to evoke a heavenly and idyllic atmosphere. In the final shot of the film Cobb embraces both children as they run toward him underneath the frame of his backdoor. Here, in capturing the familial embrace in the distance of a long shot, the camera remains firmly rooted to the dark wooden interior of Cobb's kitchen as it pans down to reveal Cobb's spinning top still whirling around to cast doubt on whether Cobb is still dreaming. Cobb's spinning top never collapses in his dreams. It matters not because Cobb, having harnessed the full potential of his imagination through the assistance of posthuman technology, has overcome trauma and found solace in his reconciliation with the natural world without obsessing over the degree to which his perceptions are objectively real.

The penultimate shot of Cobb's children basking in the warm glow offered by nature is part neo-romantic *temps morts* and part subplot that repeatedly interjects *Inception*'s narrative, presenting itself as Cobb's guiding vision for navigating the intersubjective mind-uploading networks. Toward the start of the film the audience first sees this same shot of Cobb's children playing in the garden three times as it interrupts the unfolding narrative. Having failed to unlock Saito's (Ken Watanabe) expansion plans for rival firm Cobol engineering, Cobb sits alone shrouded by darkness in a Hong Kong apartment where he drinks heavily and rests his gun against his forehead. Shrouded in darkness, Cobb occupies the foreground of a mid-shot silhouetted against the other skyscrapers outside the apartment window as if he himself is another hollow structure. He appears defeated and is contemplating suicide to escape being apprehended by the police or by Saito seeking retribution. The atmosphere of the scene is interrupted by a phone call. Cobb lifts the receiver to his face and hears the voices of his children greeting him. As both children say "hi" the camera cuts to the same penultimate long shot of his children at the end of the film sitting in their luminous green garden. With their backs to the camera both children are backlit to surround the shapes of their bodies with a warm orange glow and ethereal aura. When Cobb first hears his children's voices this stock image appears and interrupts the narrative for a couple of seconds before Cobb then sits back in relief at being able to hear their voices and then paces around the room with the receiver held firmly against his face. As he proceeds to ask whether his children are okay the camera then cuts back to the same shot of them both sitting in the garden, not moving and appearing frozen in time. Then after Cobb's children ask him when he is coming home, the protagonist retorts by inquiring which child asked that question as the scene cuts again to the same shot of both children. As we learn later in the film, this memory is the last time Cobb saw his children and is an image he frequently revisits by intravenously connecting to his posthuman technology when sleeping so as not to forget them.

The phone brings to life a neo-romantic affect that anchors Cobb and gives him purpose. He wants to achieve spiritual transcendence by reuniting with his children in their family garden. This is a far cry from how Nolan has previously depicted characters' interactions with telephony. In *Memento* the telephone is a key device used to manipulate Leonard as John "Teddy" Gammil (Joe Pantoliano) rings him in his hotel room posing as an anonymous detective to dispense misinformation that will lead Leonard to kill Teddy's rival drug dealer Jimmy Grantz. Similarly, in Nolan's second American feature *Insomnia* (2002), telephony plays a central role in fogging Detective Will Dormer's (Al Pacino) ability to make morally sound empathetic judgements. Late-night phone calls from Internal Investigations and murderer Walter Finch (Robin Williams) prevent Dormer from sleeping as both parties blackmail him through the night. These late-night phone calls worsen Dormer's insomnia as he more frequently slips in and out of consciousness, rendering him unable to determine whether he shot his partner Hap Eckhart (Martin Donovan) on purpose when pursuing Finch. In *Memento* and *Insomnia* telephony is utilized by antagonists to obscure the moral autonomy of protagonists and cloud their judgements.

In *Inception*, however, telephony summons neo-romantic affect that contemplates "the spiritual qualities of landscape and nature, free from the film's narrative, and encourages the viewer to intuitively respond to the natural phenomena" (Rose 2007). Protagonists in Nolan's films now interact with technology in a way that awakens a person's imagination as a gateway to a transcendent truth (Day 2012, 3). The telephone call enables Cobb to engage in a romanticist pursuit that reassesses his "relationship to others and to nature," privileges "the imagination as a faculty higher and more inclusive than reason," and seeks "solace in our reconciliation with the natural world" (Ferber 2010, 10). This vision is what drives Cobb's journey despite regularly being told his imaginative aspirations are scientifically implausible and unreasonable, be they a sedative that will keep somebody in a deep enough sleep to reach three perpetual layers of dreams or the ability to achieve inception. Undeterred, Cobb perseveres to achieve the impossible. In the final scenes Cobb manages to relocate Saito in the dream world and wake them both just in time to emerge through four layers of dreams where in each world their consciousness is facing imminent death. As Cobb wakes, his point of view reveals Arthur (Joseph Gordon-Levitt) and Ariadne (Ellen Page) affectionately smiling at him in slow motion, both in awe and astonishment at his ability to have effectively risen from the dead and the spiritual abilities that posthumanism has awoken within him. With minimal dialogue throughout Cobb's return home, diegetic sound is largely drowned out by Hans Zimmer's orchestral score that stirringly crescendoes to evoke Cobb's transcendental experience of waking up and leaving the airport. Having been able to privilege imagination over reason, Cobb then returns home to his children, reconciling with them and the natural world. Posthuman technology is an indexical device than can unlock the gateway to transcendent truth.

INTERSTELLAR AND THE SUBLIME

Following Nolan's balancing of posthumanism with romanticism, then, it could be assumed his next feature, *Interstellar*, a deliberate homage to Kubrick's *2001: A Space Odyssey*, would occupy a more outwardly posthuman ideology.[1] The critical consensus surrounding *2001* from Abrams (2007), Chion (2001), and Bukatman (1993) is that Kubrick's space opera endorses an advanced form of Haraway's posthumanism because humankind has successfully evolved into a new interplanetary species. The final shot of the "Star Child," a "planet-sized super intelligent foetus" (Abrams 2007, 248), is a new beyond-human form signifying a "positive" life-affirming beginning (Chion 2001, 148). This "triumphant rebirth from human to more-than-human" is "heralded by the . . . Richard Strauss theme" (Bukatman 1993, 283).

In a similar manner to *2001*, *Interstellar*'s final set piece sees Cooper enter a black hole to then find himself floating in a tesseract he himself defines as "a three-dimensional space inside a five-dimensional reality . . . built by a civilization that's evolved past the four dimensions of ours." Floating through this tesseract Cooper realizes a future race of posthuman species has been leaving clues through the course of the film to lead him here to send the coordinates of another planet, capable of sustaining life, to his daughter. Here, akin to the last act of *2001*, imagery is "drawn from religious conceptions of divine transcendence as a way of conveying the transcendence of humanity through technical change" (Roden 2015, 97). Once Cooper has successfully sent the message the tesseract self-destructs, and Cooper is swallowed by a blinding white light. As Zimmer's organ music and Cooper's breathing intensify in speed and volume, Cooper wakes up in a bright white bedroom, reborn to be reunited with his daughter. Murph (Ellen Burstyn) has now aged and is intravenously connected to various medical devices on a hospital bed that prolong her life. Now an elderly prophet figure, Murph instructs her father to travel to Edmunds' Planet, a rocky and mountainous planet, to accompany Brand and continue the survival of the human race. In essence the scene emulates 2001's concluding scene where an aged Bowman first sees and points at the Star Child. Both final sequences are cinematically potent because both directors abandon the "punctilious realism that characterises the greater part of the film in favour of a series of mythic, symbolic oppositions and substitutions" (Roden 2015, 95).

Compared to *2001*, though, *Interstellar* becomes increasingly wary of aligning the human species too closely with technology through neo-romantic sublime imagery of unsettling natural landscapes. Initially audiences are encouraged to share the spiritual awe Cooper's family hold toward advanced technology. Zimmer's organ music begins playing when a drone aircraft swoops above Cooper's unsuspecting family while they are trying to fix a flat tire by the side of a road. Abandoning the replacement of the tire, the family decides to chase the drone through crop fields to try and assume control of it. The camera assumes a low-angle view of the drone, approximating the family's point of view from inside the jeep, where they can just about see through the long glades of crops at the top of the frame. This is interspersed with a low angle shot looking down on the jeep, focusing on the wide-eyed wonderment expressed by Cooper's family in awe of this technology's mysticism. The drone-chase sequence concludes when Tom (Timothée Chalamet), having been instructed by Cooper to take over the driving while he assumes control of the drone from his laptop, has to emergency brake the jeep to stop it following the drone off a cliff edge into a reservoir. At this point the intensifying organ music ceases to play as the family walks out from the car to appreciate the reservoir in silence. Initially when the car and music stop, a long shot encourages awe of the landscape's grandeur.

At this point the frozen image appears to suggest that humans cannot solely invest their faith in technology, as blindly following the drone through cornfields and fences on a flat tire, narrowly avoiding tractors while resolutely affixing their gaze to a laptop or drone's flight path, disassociates the family members from the reality of their surroundings. The thrill of the scene is stopped dead in its tracks to pause on the landscape and evoke the sublime affect that romantic landscape painters sought to create. For philosophers Joseph Addison, Edmund Burke, Alexander Gerard, and John Ballie the sense of astonishment evoked by the sublime landscapes produce a "solemn sedateness" (Ballie 1996, 97). When such sedate moments are recreated in contemporary cinema, audiences are encouraged to experience Burke's dynamically sublime feeling of terror mixed with the pleasure of surviving that is "intensified by the threat of pain and death" (Carroll 2020, 152).

This sublime moment, though, is relatively short lived. Stopped dead in their tracks by a cliff face, Murph (Mackenzie Foy) proclaims "we lost it" to which Cooper playfully replies "no we didn't" as the camera then cuts to a long shot of the reservoir from behind Cooper and Murph's shoulders in the bottom left corner of the frame. As the drone emerges from the bottom right side of the screen, the camera readjusts on its axis in tandem with the drone as it elegantly glides and swoops over the reservoir from side to side. The organ music then resumes once it has been established that the drone is within Cooper's control. Cooper then kneels down alongside his daughter, and the camera reveals a close-up of him tenderly guiding her finger on the touchpad before they both set the drone down on the other side of the reservoir. This landscape shot is no longer free from narrative causality and brings both characters closer together. Once the drone lands, the film cuts to Murph and Cooper turning around to Tom while Cooper states "nicely done," and the camera pulls focus on them while blurring the landscape behind them. At this moment technology is a means of controlling the sublime grandeur of the landscape and bringing the family closer together. Through the course of the scene tall crops, a blinding sun, cliff edges, and unpredictable variances of surface could at any point derail their capturing the drone. Keeping focused on this technology, however, against the odds, is what offers them enlightenment and salvation. The sublime astonishment and accompanying solemn sedateness initially produced by the emergence of the reservoir's landscape is undercut by Cooper's masterful control of the drone technology. The scene concludes by reassuring audiences of technology's elegant ability to command such landscapes and the tenderness it encourages between family members.

Although the concept of the sublime has endured much transmutation throughout the decades, what all theorists who have written on it share is an interest in confrontations produced by the rages of the natural world such as the ocean (Burke) or the storm (Kant). Burkean sublimity in cinema is often the response to a visualized catastrophe in which an audience is "horrified at the atrocity but also awestruck at the manner in which it unfolds" (Warton 2013, 141). As *Interstellar* develops, the natural landscapes the astronauts come into contact with on different planets cannot be conquered by the technologies at their disposal. Thus, a deepened appreciation of the beauties of nature takes precedence over technology's ability to enhance the human condition.

When Cooper's Lazarus mission lands on its first planet, to explore whether other galaxies can sustain human life, Amelia Brand (Anne Hathaway) compromises the entire mission by placing too much faith in technology. Brand is resolute in her determination to find Miller's crew based on the signals they have received. Brand repeatedly asserts that the space shuttle "should be right here" despite waves the size of mountains hurtling toward them. Having spent too much time looking for Miller and attempting to extract his data, while narrowly escaping the waves, the astronauts compromise the mission by using too much fuel, leaving enough to visit only one of the two remaining planets. Here Brand learns her actions should be based on her instinctual decisions rather than favoring what the data have been telling them at the expense of her own perspective of the landscape.

When the crew first land on Miller's planet, astronauts Brand and Doyle (Wes Bentley) leave the landing craft (ranger) with their robot Case in a medium shot. Both characters keep their gaze focused to the ground and the shallow water they wade through looking for Miller's ship to appear. The camera then cuts to a bird's-eye view of their shuttle surrounded by an ocean of dark blue water, effectively rendering their technology to be a drop in a huge ocean that covers the planet's surface. This drawing attention to their insignificance is a repeated cinematic motif of neo-romanticism where a "lone vehicle in the landscape" evokes "isolation when confronted by nature" (Hockenhull 2013, 109). After Cooper proclaims that the mountains in the distance are actually waves, a very long shot looks to the horizon, free from the characters' perspectives, to add clarity to the previously blurred horizon and reveal that the mountains touching the sky in the distance are actually the same blue color as the water. As the waves move closer to the characters, a following camera shot of the wave pans upward as the nondiegetic music reaches a loud and terrifying crescendo of strings to reveal a wall of water that is beginning to block out the sunlight. This megawave moving toward the astronauts in this collection of shots framed outside the perspective of characters appears as if it is a static wall of water, not rolling as we would expect waves to do on Earth. As Brand, carried by Case, and Doyle get back to the ranger, Doyle is swept away by a wave before he has a chance to clamber inside after Brand. A shot of a seemingly still wall of water on its own, isolated from the character's perspective, fills the screen before cutting back to a shot of Doyle unable to get into the hatch, with the diegetic sounds of the water now halting Zimmer's music. As the ranger is carried by the wave, Cooper turns its engines off and so is at the mercy of the elements. The camera cuts between the chaos unfolding in the ship and bird's-eye views of the slowly moving waves where the ranger is minute in comparative size. Once the wave has passed, they are able to fly from the planet. The final shot of Miller's planet is a long shot of the next approaching wave. Doyle's body floats at the foot of the next wave in the foreground, surrounded by dark blue colors in morbid silence, concluding the scene with a chilling disquiet.

This use of the sublime in *Interstellar* utilizes shots of various landscapes in a similar manner to contemporary British horror films as analyzed by Hockenhull (2013). Here the landscape has more than a marginal presence; it acquires unsettling visual authority by drawing on specific codes and features evocative of a Burkean sublime. These visual qualities place a greater emphasis on their role as an "isolated setting" and by doing so become "a quietly antagonistic character in themselves" (Hockenhull 2013, 79). Thus the megawave sequence also unfolds along similar lines to a Turner painting. While his "illusions of mist are created through his rendering of uneven surfaces and indistinct hues, [which] forces the eye to constantly readjust," a similar sense of "uncertainty" is created here, as the use of color merges sky, sea, and land equally, diminishing the boat-like vehicle through weather conditions (Hockenhull 2013, 200).

As has been noted, "*Interstellar* argues love is a primal force like gravity" in what is "Nolan's most explicitly sentimental and emotional film" (Mooney 2018, 125). When the Lazarus mission has two final planets to choose from, Cooper ensures they will visit Mann's planet based purely on the data that Dr. Hugh Mann (Matt Damon) has transmitted, dismissing Brand's pleas to visit Edmunds' planet. Brand's reasoning is that she loves Edmunds, and "love is the one thing capable of transcending time and space" that they "should trust" even "if we can't understand it yet" and perhaps solving "this all with theory" is misguided. Cooper overrules Brand because his view is that love simply exists as a form of "social utility" created by humankind to rationalize events and is not an entity in its own right to be revered. It soon transpires, however, that Brand's decision would have led them to a habitable planet as Mann selfishly falsified his data so that he could be rescued from a planet incapable of sustaining life.

Interstellar is a film invested in romantic values in that, like Kant's and Burke's writings, depictions of sublime landscapes occupy a certain degree of superiority over flawed and relatively insignificant humankind who must succumb to, and reconcile with, nature's chaos. However, what makes something neo-neo-romantic is how the landscape is used to introspectively reflect on wider socio-political unease.

A key determinant that leads Brand to listen to reason over emotion and her senses over intellect, following her previous error on Miller's planet, is a video message of her father transmitted from Earth delivering Dylan

Thomas's poem *Do Not Go Gentle into That Good Night*, asserting she "rage against the dying of the light." Dylan's poetry is often likened to a "whirling romantic" given his emphasis on imagination, intense emotion, intuition, spontaneity, and organic form (Daiches 1966, 16). When Professor John Brand (Michael Caine) later recites the poem to Cooper's grown-up daughter Murph (Jessica Chastain) on Earth, she is able to solve the equation they have been laboring over her entire life. This particular poem, associated with romanticism, inspires both Brand and Murph not to accept death of humankind passively but opt instead to fight against extinction by creatively solving logical quandaries through a degree of emotional intelligence. After Brand's failure on Miller's planet, she takes heed of this advice and opts to follow "love" and her instincts over quantifiable data. Similarly, when Murph hears the professor repeating the same poem on his deathbed, after learning her father Cooper was never meant to return home, Murph uses this as instruction to return to her childhood home and demand that her brother Tom (Casey Affleck) move as the encroaching dust cloud is severely impacting the health of her nephew. In doing so, however, Murph finds the watch her father left her and understands that the second hand is providing her with coordinates that enable her to solve the equation she has spent her life trying to crack. Ultimately, as the characters becoming increasingly at the mercy of sublime landscapes on uninhabitable planets, black holes, and the dust sweeping through the Earth's atmosphere, their ability to survive becomes more dependent on the foundations of romanticism over posthuman capabilities. As Cooper explains, he is only able to send his findings back to Earth and into Murph's wristwatch through the "love" he and his daughter share. In essence, there is a shift from a high degree of reliance on technological rationalism to the reliance on emotion and connection to nature.

When Cooper is reunited with his daughter at the end of the film he maintains eye contact while holding her hand against his face. Previously, before leaving Earth, their contact was mediated by technology, when their hands lovingly touch on the laptop's trackpad controlling the drone or when they both keep their gazes fixed on the wristwatch Cooper gifts Murph while they embrace. Cooper and Murph's final exchange is now pure and unmediated by technology; the embodied and corporeal experience is now at relative odds with the posthuman focus on technological enhancement. Murph then instructs Cooper to join Amelia Brand, who is now alone on Edmunds' planet, so they can both repopulate a new home for humankind. Cooper walks backward, leaving the room his daughter is in without taking his eyes off her this time. Now Cooper appreciates and understands that a heightened sense of love unmediated by technology is key to the human race's survival. According to this penultimate scene *Interstellar* represents one of many cultural responses to the current political social and economic climate where the visual arts have favored neo-romanticism as an "appropriate reactionary response" to impending climate disaster (Hockenhull 2013, 211).

TENET

As a new decade of filmmaking unfolds, Nolan's endorsement of posthumanism has strengthened at the expense of his neo-romanticist outlook in the film *Tenet*. In Nolan's most difficult plot to decipher yet, scientists have developed the ability to "invert," a process of time traveling where the time traveler's actions and dialogue operate backward in reverse from the chronological ordering of time in the period they visit. Scientists of the future have hidden components of an algorithm that will invert the whole world, thus destroying our current present to preserve their existence in the future. Russian oligarch Andrei Sator's (Kenneth Branagh) attempt to bury the assembled algorithm through a controlled explosion for his employers to excavate in the future must be stopped by The Protagonist (John Washington), whose name we never learn, and his sidekick Neil (Robert Pattinson). A nod to romanticism occurs when The Protagonist must steal a Goya painting in order to establish contact with Sator's wife Kat (Elizabeth Debicki) to gain access to Sator's inner circle. Goya was a romantic painter renowned for reflecting contemporary historical upheavals. Goya produced four major print portfolios through his career: the *Caprichos*, *Proverbios*, *Tauromaquia*, and *The Disasters of War*. Across them all the Spanish painter captured the liberations of the Enlightenment, the suppressions of the Inquisition, and the horrors of war following the Napoleonic invasions. The Protagonist instructs Kat to look at the Goya painting without her specialist magnifying glass, asking "What does your heart tell you?" as to whether it is genuine or not. The Protagonist uses the painting as a means of instructing Kat to prioritize her emotional instinct over her professional expertise to deduce the truth. This stolen Goya artwork proves that the painting Sator and Kat currently own is a forgery, knowledge Sator uses to keep his wife Kat and their children hostage as it would destroy her credibility as an art dealer.

Despite nodding to the Romantics, *Tenet* provides a resolute endorsement of posthumanism by further blurring boundaries between living organism and technology. In order to invert oneself into the past people must remain attached to an oxygen mask so their inverted lungs can breathe air. These people also have the capacity to catch bullets and protect key individuals by traveling through time. At *Tenet*'s end it transpires that The Protagonist's sidekick Neil is Kat's child, who will be recruited as an adult in the future to protect The Protagonist through the past events just witnessed over the course of the film. *Tenet* concludes with The Protagonist saving Neil's life as a schoolboy when he receives a phone call from Kat stating the location and time she sees a mysterious-looking car following her outside her son's school. In the car, The Protagonist's former associate Priya Singh (Dimple Kapadia) is readying to execute Kat, but The Protagonist suddenly appears in the back seat, executing her and her henchman before they get the opportunity to dispatch Kat. Before The Protagonist shoots Priya in the back he states, "I told you you'd have to start looking differently at the world." In *Tenet* a new mode of perceiving time and space has been made possible through technological modifications to a person's body. Here The Protagonist has picked up a mobile phone message in the future and used telephony as a means of traveling backward in time to a specific location to change future events. Compared to *Memento* and *Insomnia*, where phones inhibit human potential, and *Interstellar* and *Inception*, where phone and video calls are devices used to trigger neo-romantic affect, now mobile phones are more synonymous with posthumanism and its ability to deliver the evolution of the human race.

NOLAN'S SILVER BULLET

In conclusion, Nolan's ideological development into being more closely aligned to romanticism through neo-romanticism as a means of mediating the excesses of posthumanism can be conceptualized by analyzing the way his protagonists' relationships with bullets has evolved. In the opening scene of *Memento*, before executing Teddy, Leonard finds a discarded collection of bullets in an abandoned car. The camera cuts to a close-up of Leonard's hand stroking the bullets and picking one up before his face turns to camera. Leonard's face contemplates, with a possible air of recognition, that he has already been to this location before and used the bullets to kill Jimmy Grantz. This close-up of Leonard's hands touching the bullets also makes the "remember Sammy Jankis" tattoo on his hand clearly visible. Visually, this opening scene appears to infer that Leonard has some ability to forge new memories as he is drawn to the bullets and knows something is likely to have happened here. This is underlined by the suggestion put forward at the end of the film by Teddy, just before his death, that Sammy Jankis could be an invented character used to delude Leonard into thinking he has no ability to forge new memories following his amnesia diagnosis. Leonard is blinded by, and drawn to, objects that cloud his thoughts with cathartic vengeance. Likewise, in *Insomnia* Ellie Burr (Hilary Swank), having been saved by Dormer from being another one of Finch's murder victims, attempts to throw away a bullet that implicates Dormer in Eckhart's murder. Dormer intervenes by grabbing her arm, stating "You'll lose your way" before dying of his gunshot wounds inflicted by Finch. In *The Prestige* Borden (Christian Bale) loses two fingers in persevering with his risky catching of a bullet magic trick in full view of a theater audience who is appalled when the trick goes wrong and severs Borden's fingers. Essentially, any attempt to diminish or conceal the boundary between human and machine in these three films (or in this case fusing the bullet mechanism with human) is not possible and directly results in trauma, death, or execution. Anybody who has used a bullet in contravention to the well-being of others will receive retribution as punishment.

When Nolan embarks on his romanticist/posthuman axis, then, his characters' relationship with bullets changes. *Inception* concludes with Cobb shooting himself and Saito after vowing to take "a leap of faith." Connecting with the bullet enables both characters to achieve transcendence in a vividly romantic world where fulfillment between humans, nature, and creativity is achieved. Then, following *Interstellar*'s recognition that technology has a part to play in producing a mode of posthumanism based on romantic values mediated by neo-romanticism, *Tenet* reveals that bullets can transform the human condition. When The Protagonist is exposed to a bullet inverted by nuclear fission he is able to summon it into his palm from some distance. The Protagonist can "catch a bullet" because, from the inverted "bullet's point of view," it believes it is being dropped forward in time. In Nolan's earlier films any attempt to breach the boundary between a bullet and living organism is a dangerous inhumane feat, guaranteed to traumatize a protagonist. For example, Leonard's frequent shooting of people in *Memento* has likened him to a "postmortal vampire" for "living off the deaths of others" (Hauskeller 2015, 212). From *Inception* onward, however, humankind's closer relationship with technology, and technology's capacity for occupying a degree of agency, permits a person to enter a fulfilling romantic existence and to continue the evolution into a posthuman species with beyond-human capabilities. Catching bullets is no longer associated with inhumane acts of revulsion; the act now signifies posthuman evolution that is ideologically grounded by neo-romanticism to varying degrees.

NOTE

1. "Nolan utilizes many of the iconic qualities of *2001* for his film, including themes of time travel that allude to *2001*'s Star Gate sequence, whilst Hans Zimmer's score for *Interstellar* is reminiscent of Strauss' 'Thus Spoke Zarathustra.' As in *2001* spinning wheels and circular imagery also occur throughout as a visual motif to provide further similarities. Nolan even goes so far as to reference the way light reflects

on the astronaut's helmet as a visual element, similar to that on Bowman's during the Star Gate sequence" (Peiler 2018, 160).

REFERENCES

Abrams, Jerold J. 2007. "Nietzsche's Overman as Posthuman Star Child in *2001: A Space Odyssey.*" In *The Philosophy of Stanley Kubrick*, ed. Jerold J. Abrams, 247–66. Lexington: University Press of Kentucky.

———. (ed.). 2007. *The Philosophy of Stanley Kubrick*. Lexington: University Press of Kentucky.

Ballie, John. [1747] 1996. "An Essay on the Sublime." In *The Sublime: A Reader in British Century Aesthetic Theory*, ed. Andrew Ashfield and Peter De Bolla, 81–100. Cambridge: Cambridge University Press.

Bukatman, Scott. 1993. *Terminal Identity: The Virtual Subject in Postmodern Science Fiction*. Durham: Duke University Press.

Burke, Edmund. [1757] 2008. *A Philosophical Enquiry into the Origin of Our Ideas of the Sublime and Beautiful*. Oxford: Oxford University Press.

Carroll, Nathan. 2020. "A Short History of the Long Take: Digital Cinema and the 'Infinite Cut.'" In *The Cinematic Sublime: Negative Pleasures, Structuring Absences*, ed. Nathan Carroll, 98–123. Bristol: Intellect.

Chion, Michel. 2001. *Kubrick's Cinema Odyssey*. Trans. Claudia Gorbman. London: Bloomsbury.

Daiches, David. 1966. "The Poetry of Dylan Thomas." In *Dylan Thomas: A Collection of Critical Essays*, ed. Charles Brian Scott, 14–24. Englewood Cliffs: Prentice-Hall.

Day, Aidan. 2012. *Romanticism*. London: Routledge.

Eberl, Jason T., and George A. Dunn (eds.). 2017. *The Philosophy of Christopher Nolan*. London: Lexington Books.

Ferber, Michael. 2010. *Romanticism*. Oxford: Oxford University Press.

Furby, Jacqueline, and Stuart Joy (eds.). 2015. *The Cinema of Christopher Nolan: Imagining the Impossible*. Chichester: Wallflower Press.

Haraway, Donna J. 1991. *Simians, Cyborgs, and Women: The Reinvention of Nature*. London: Routledge.

Hauskeller, Michael. 2015. "Life's a Bitch, and Then You *Don't* Die: Postmortality in Film and Television." In *The Palgrave Handbook of Posthumanism in Film and Television*, ed. Michael Hauskeller, Thomas D. Philbeck, and Curtis D. Carbonell, 205–13. London: Palgrave Macmillan.

Hauskeller, Michael, Thomas D. Philbeck, and Curtis D. Carbonell (eds.). 2015. *The Palgrave Handbook of Posthumanism in Film and Television*. London: Palgrave Macmillan.

Hockenhull, Stella. 2013. *Aesthetics and Neo-Romanticism in Film: Landscapes in Contemporary British Cinema*. London: I. B. Tauris.

Joy, Stuart. 2020. *Traumatic Screen: The Films of Christopher Nolan*. Bristol: Intellect Books.

Krueger, Joel. 2015. "At Home and beyond our Skin: Posthuman Embodiment in Film and Television." In *The Palgrave Handbook of Posthumanism in Film and Television*, ed. Michael Hauskeller, Thomas D. Philbeck, and Curtis D. Carbonell, 172–81. London: Palgrave Macmillan.

Manea, Tedora. 2015. "Our Posthuman Skin Condition." In *The Palgrave Handbook of Posthumanism in Film and Television*, ed. Michael Hauskeller, Thomas D. Philbeck, and Curtis D. Carbonell, 289–98. London: Palgrave Macmillan.

McGowan, Todd. 2012. *The Fictional Christopher Nolan*. Austin: University of Texas Press.

Mooney, Darren. 2018. *Christopher Nolan: A Critical Study of the Films*. Jefferson: McFarland.

Nolan, Christopher. 2019. "Christopher Nolan Introduces *2001: A Space Odyssey*." BBC2, 27 April 2019.

Peiler, Nils Daniel. 2018. "'But as to whether or not he has feelings is something I don't think anyone can truthfully answer': The Image of the Astronaut in *2001: A Space Odyssey* and Its Lasting Impact." In *Understanding Kubrick's* 2001: A Space Odyssey: *Representation and Interpretation*, ed. James Fenwick, 151–62. Bristol: Intellect Books.

Philbeck, Thomas D. 2015. "Onscreen Ontology: Stages in the Posthumanist Paradigm Shift." In *The Palgrave Handbook of Posthumanism in Film and Television*, ed. Michael Hauskeller, Thomas D. Philbeck, and Curtis D. Carbonell, 391–400. London: Palgrave Macmillan.

Roden, David. 2015. "Post- Singularity Entities in Film and Television." In *The Palgrave Handbook of Posthumanism in Film and Television*, ed. Michael Hauskeller, Thomas D. Philbeck, and Curtis D. Carbonell, 88–98. London: Palgrave Macmillan.

Rose, James. 2007. "There's Nothing out There: The Landscape in Greg Mclean's *Wolf Creek*." *Scope* 8 (June). www.scope.nottingham.ac.uk/filmreview.php?id=217 &issue=8.

Warton, John P. 2013. "Watching the World Burn: Intensity, Absurdity and Echoes of the Sublime in Contemporary Science Fiction Destruction." In *Terror and the Cinematic Sublime: Essays on Violence and the Unpresentable in Post-9/11 Films*, ed. Todd A. Comer and Lloyd Isaac Vayo, 134–49. Jefferson: McFarland.

Chapter 12

Dark Vision, Global Impact
Christopher Nolan, Box Office Hit Patterns, and Interstellar

Peter Krämer

In September 2021, Christopher Nolan closed what was up to this point by far the longest chapter in his illustrious career by announcing that he would *not* make his next film for Warner Bros., the major Hollywood studio he had been working with since *Insomnia* (2002).[1] His move was reported to be connected to disagreements he had had with Warner Bros. about the release of *Tenet* in 2020, and also to Warner Bros.' decision to release all its movies in 2021 simultaneously in cinemas and on the studio's new streaming service HBO Max. In the context of temporary movie theater closures all around the globe due to the Covid pandemic in 2020/21 and the long-term—and recently accelerated—rise of online services delivering movies on a subscription or pay-per-view basis into homes, Warner Bros.' new release strategy could be taken as an important step toward marginalizing cinemas altogether. As an avid supporter of the theatrical movie experience (Nolan 2020)—and also of the use of celluloid in filmmaking and film exhibition instead of their wholesale digitization (Foundas 2015)—Nolan protested and then moved on from Warner.

The deal he made with Universal assured him a $100 million budget and final cut for his next film and a share of its box office gross, three contractual stipulations not many filmmakers could hope to secure together. Trade press reports expressed a certain level of puzzlement about the fact that Nolan's dream deal was for a biopic of the nuclear physicist Robert J. Oppenheimer, not an obvious candidate for a global box office hit. It was noted, though, that Nolan had a long string of hits behind him, including somewhat unlikely contenders such as the World War II ensemble drama *Dunkirk* (2017), dealing not so much with *combat* than with the largely successful attempt to *retreat* from a military confrontation. If Nolan could turn *that* into a global hit, then surely anything was possible—although there was some agreement in the press that *Oppenheimer*, scheduled for release in July 2023, was unlikely to generate much, if any, profit for Universal, and that, more generally, there was simply not much of a future for this kind of filmmaking.

As will be discussed in more detail later, by 2021 the big-budget production sector and global box office charts had for some years been dominated by sequels, prequels, movies set in shared universes, reboots, remakes, adaptations (of novels, comics, television shows, computer games, Broadway shows, etc.), usually in the fantasy and science fiction genres. Indeed, Nolan had established himself as one of Hollywood's most commercially successful filmmakers precisely by making (as a writer, director, and/or producer) more or less futuristic or fantastic films featuring DC superheroes, starting with *Batman Begins* (2005). In addition to such (mostly rather loose) comic book adaptations, early on in his time with Warner Bros. Nolan had made two moderately successful films, one (*Insomnia*, 2002) a remake of a Norwegian thriller from 1997, the other (*The Prestige*, 2006) an adaptation of a 1995 steampunk novel.

Quite unusually, he also had a string of three science fiction hits—*Inception* (2010), *Interstellar* (2014), and *Tenet*—which, like *Dunkirk*, were based on his own original screenplays (one of them cowritten with his brother Jonathan). The distinction between original screenplays (that is, those not based on an already published source) and adapted screenplays can be somewhat difficult. For example, if Nolan bases his script for *Oppenheimer* on one biography (Kai Bird and Martin J. Sherwin's 2005 book *American Prometheus*), as has been reported (Kit 2021), it counts as an adapted screenplay. Should he however base it on several biographies, it counts as an original screenplay (VanDerWerff 2018). Hollywood's big movies very rarely fall into the latter category—but four of the hits Nolan has (co)written and directed since 2010 do, which makes him unique in contemporary Hollywood (to counter one objection straightaway: Quentin Tarantino might film his own original screenplays, but they are nowhere near as successful at the box office as Nolan's movies).[2]

In this essay, I take a closer look at the types of film Nolan has been making and at the level of their box office success, focusing on his Warner period but also briefly discussing his earlier work. I first establish Nolan's outstanding level of commercial success. I then relate his biggest commercial successes to hit patterns at the global box office with regard to the science fiction genre and the theme of major threats to humanity, showing that his work built on existing trends. Finally, I discuss *Interstellar* as being both an exemplary and an exceptional Nolan movie, dealing in a highly unusual fashion with a threat to humanity. I show that *Interstellar* stands out from the rest of Nolan's work, and also from Hollywood's biggest global hits in recent decades, by offering an uncritical celebration of science and technology and their deployment by powerful men and large organizations.

CHRISTOPHER NOLAN AT THE GLOBAL BOX OFFICE

In the voluminous literature on Nolan, the box office grosses of his films and their rankings in annual box office charts so far have not been the focus of much interest or research. But the figures for his films are certainly intriguing:[3]

1. *Following* (1998), production budget $6,000, global box office gross $48,000
2. *Memento* (2000), budget $9 million, gross $40 million, no. 86 in the global box office chart for 2001 (the film was released in the United States in 2001)
3. *Insomnia* (2002), budget $46 million, gross $114 million, no. 43 (all rankings here and below refer to the global box office chart in the year of release)
4. *Batman Begins* (2005), budget $150 million, gross $372 million [$374 million], no. 9[4]
5. *The Prestige* (2006), budget $40 million, gross $110 million, no. 54
6. *The Dark Knight* (2008), budget $185 million, gross $1,003 million [$1,006 million], no. 1
7. *Inception* (2010), budget $160 million, gross $826 million [$837 million], no. 4
8. *The Dark Knight Rises* (2012), budget $250 million, gross $1,081 million, no. 3
9. *Interstellar* (2014), budget $165 million, gross $678 million [$702 million], no. 10
10. *Dunkirk* (2017), budget $100 million, gross $525 million [$527 million], no. 19
11. *Tenet* (2020), budget $200 million,[5] gross $364 million, no. 5[6]

Following, which Nolan wrote, directed, edited, and produced when he was in his late twenties (after about a decade of making short films), is the kind of extremely low-budget 16mm production for which it is a great achievement to be shown in movie theaters at all. With regard to the other titles, one might say that, with thousands of films being released into theaters around the world every year, making it into the top 100 looks like a solid achievement. It is however perhaps more meaningful to focus on the number of films released globally by the major Hollywood studios—about 100 per year[7]—because most other films are not that widely distributed internationally in the first place. This suggests that *Memento*, which was not financed by a major studio and was distributed by a wide range of companies in various countries, nevertheless beat some of the studio competition; coming in at no. 86 is therefore quite remarkable. One could also factor in a film's budget and note that both *Following* and *Memento* generated box office revenues exceeding their budgets by a factor of five to eight—which does, however, not yet tell us much about profits for the distributor or the production company, due to the cost of marketing a film (advertising its release and delivering it to theaters) and the fact that about half of the box office gross stays with the cinemas.

The picture is much clearer for the Warner Bros. chapter of Nolan's career (whereby the studio was joined by Disney for *The Prestige* and by Paramount for *Interstellar*). *Insomnia* and *The Prestige* did *not* perform particularly well; their rankings are around the middle of the circa 100 studio releases, and the ratio of gross to budget strongly suggests that these films did not generate much, if any, profit from their theatrical release for Warner but most likely did so with regard to their video/DVD/Blu-ray releases and sales to television. With the exception of *The Prestige*, the box office performance of Nolan's films from 2005 to 2020 is, however, nothing short of astonishing. Six of the remaining seven titles made it into the annual top ten, and the seventh came in at no. 19, and for most of these films the gross/budget ratio was around 5:6, indicating that they were highly profitable even before revenues from video/DVD/Blu-ray and television came in. (Nolan's hit rate with other people's films—including three Superman/Justice League movies—for which he received a producer credit between 2013 and 2017—was similarly high.)[8]

Apart from *Insomnia* (scripted by Hillary Seitz), all of these films were (co)written by Christopher Nolan. Jonathan Nolan wrote the short story "Memento Mori" on which *Memento* was based,[9] and cowrote the scripts for *The Prestige*, *The Dark Knight*, *The Dark Knight Rises*, and *Interstellar*. David Goyer cowrote the script for *Batman Begins* and the (unpublished) stories which were then developed into the scripts for *The Dark Knight* and *The Dark Knight Rises*. Emma Thomas, Christopher Nolan's wife, (co)produced all of his films, and together with him has headed their production company Syncopy Inc. which they founded in 2001. In addition to collaborating with his brother and his wife (as well as superhero specialist David Goyer), Nolan worked frequently with the same crew and cast members. Nolan movies are thus made by a fairly stable team that has formed around the filmmaker, who also, presumably, did not get much studio interference once he had proven his commercial credentials, from 2005 to 2010, with the first two Batman films, which demonstrated that he could be trusted with a major franchise, and *Inception*, which showed that he could deliver major global hits from his own original scripts.

Some aspects of the above (own production company, a fairly stable team of collaborators, a string of global hit movies) also apply to other Hollywood hitmakers, but Nolan stands out for two reasons: he had six massive global hits in a row (from 2008 to 2020) and he (co)wrote the scripts for all of them. As far as I am aware, no other director in recent decades has had such a long, *uninterrupted* string of massive global hits, certainly not a string of such hits based on their own screenplays. What is more, four of the six films in this uninterrupted string of massive global hits were based on Nolan's *original* screenplays.[10]

GLOBAL HIT PATTERNS 1: ORIGINAL SCREENPLAYS AND SCIENCE FICTION

In recent years, global hits based on original screenplays have become exceedingly rare. For example, in 2010, the year that *Inception* was at no. 4 in the annual global chart, the rest of the top ten were made up of sequels and adaptations (in some cases a film was both a sequel and an adaptation), except for the animated *Despicable Me*. And in 2017, when *Dunkirk* was at no. 19, the rest of the top twenty consisted of sequels, adaptations, and remakes (including, for example, remakes of adaptations), except for the animated *Coco*.

Since 1977 US and global box office charts have been dominated by science fiction and fantasy (two genres which—with the exception of Disney animations—before then had largely been marginal in commercial terms; Krämer 2022 and forthcoming). This dominance became ever more pronounced from the late 1990s onward, with a particular focus on superhero comic book adaptations. These had previously been very successful with a series of four Superman (1978–1987) and four Batman films (1989–1997), but following *X-Men* (no. 9 in the global box office chart for 2000), they gradually took over the charts, with two titles in the top twenty in 2005, the year Nolan's first Batman movie was released; three in 2012, when Nolan's last Batman movie was released; four in 2013, the year of the Nolan-produced *Man of Steel*; and six in 2017, when *Justice League*, the last of the three Superman/Batman/Justice League films for which Nolan received a producer credit, came out. In 2018 superhero adaptations were at nos. 1, 2, 5, 7, 9, and 11 in the annual global box office chart, and in 2019 at nos. 1 and 4–6. This suggests that Nolan both contributed to, and profited from, the rise to dominance of superhero adaptations at the global box office.

Something similar applies to his non-superhero science fiction films. In the years before *Inception* came out, there had been numerous Transformers, Star Trek, and Terminator titles as well as more or less futuristic Bond and Mission: Impossible films in the annual global top 20, and such stand-alone hits (based on original screenplays) as *Avatar* and *2012* (nos. 1 and 5 in 2009). Between 2010 and 2020, the year of *Tenet*, there were more hits from these established franchises plus Planet of the Apes, Hunger Games, and Star Wars movies as well as stand-alone films (with original screenplays) such as *Gravity* (no. 8 in 2013). Nolan's three non-superhero science fiction hits thus also rode a wave.

By contrast, the success of *Dunkirk* had no precedent in the years before its release. *Dunkirk* is a historical epic, that is, a film dealing with events of great historical significance, whereby these events are staged in a spectacular fashion, thus echoing at the filmic level the impact these events had in the real world. Such films had been very prominent in (US and probably also global) box office charts from the 1910s to the 1960s, with a major revival in the 1990s. However, after the huge box office success of *Titanic* (no. 1 in 1997), *Saving Private Ryan* (no. 2 in 1998), and *Gladiator* (no. 2 in 2000), historical epics largely disappeared from the top ranks of the global box office charts, none making it into the top twenty from 2011 to 2019, except for *Dunkirk*.

It should be noted, however, that across the first two decades of the new millennium there were many hugely successful epic movies, but rather than looking back on the actual past, they concerned mythical, fantastic, or future turning points in history. These included two global hit epics that, while belonging in the science fiction/fantasy category, set their fantastic action against the backdrop of World War II and World War I: *Captain America: The First Avenger* (no. 17 in 2011) and *Wonder Woman* (no. 10 in 2017). It is also worth noting that the World War I movie *1917* was at no. 23 in 2019. So perhaps there is a chance for a revival of non-fantastic historical epics at the global box office, which *Oppenheimer*, a film centrally concerned with the development, and deployment, of nuclear weapons, could profit from. For now, though, the most important framework for situating Nolan's career is the success of epic fantasy and science fiction which his filmic output, after decidedly non-epic beginnings, increasingly participated in. At the same time, Nolan picked up on an established trend of hit movies dealing with global destruction or the threat of such destruction.

(THE THREAT OF) LARGE-SCALE DESTRUCTION IN CHRISTOPHER NOLAN'S OEUVRE

While the first feature films Nolan made were tightly focused—in terms of both location and time frame—crime thrillers, from *Batman Begins* onward his work has had a wider temporal and geographical range, and dealt with events of much greater import. These events affect not only a small group of protagonists/antagonists plus a few of the people they interact with, but are potentially, or actually, disruptive or transformative for the wider world, perhaps even all of humanity. *Dunkirk* depicts a critical moment in World War II. Had the evacuation of British troops not succeeded—in the words of the Imperial War Museum's website—it "would have meant the loss of Britain's only trained troops and the collapse of the Allied cause. The successful evacuation was a great boost to civilian morale, and created the 'Dunkirk spirit' which helped Britain to fight on in the summer of 1940" (IWM 2022). Failure to evacuate could well have changed the outcome of World War II.

The other films focus on scientific insights and technological innovations, mostly in conjunction with the depiction of powerful organizations operating largely in secret. *The Prestige* lacks this last element, but it does revolve around a revolutionary technology (to do with the exact duplication and instantaneous transportation of objects/beings) which here is only used by a magician, but surely has the potential to change the whole world were it to fall into the hands of corporations, governments, the military, or some international conspiracy. In *Inception* highly advanced military technology is employed to extract information from people's minds, and also to implant ideas in their minds so as to manipulate their decisions. Here this technology is used by corporations for the purposes of industrial espionage and the weakening of competing companies, but one has to wonder what uses secret services and the military can, and eventually will, put it to. In the three Batman films, in addition to conventional weapons and explosives, highly advanced methods (dispersion of a fear-inducing hallucinogen, a fusion reactor turned into a neutron bomb) are used to bring comprehensive destruction to Gotham City—while Batman deploys various nifty technologies to prevent this.

Finally, in *Man of Steel* (for which Nolan received a story credit), *Interstellar*, and *Tenet* humanity faces extinction. *Man of Steel* starts with a human-like species, which commands futuristic technologies on the planet Krypton, almost getting completely wiped out when excessive mining of the planet's core leads to its explosion. The infant Kal-El is sent to Earth both to take the genetic legacy of his species with him and perhaps to guide humanity so that it may avoid a similarly self-destructive path. Other survivors from Krypton arrive years later and set out to transform the Earth in such a way that humanity is destroyed and the planet can be colonized by Kryptonians, making use of the genetic legacy kept by Kal-El. Space ships and terraforming machines and technologies used to mine a planetary core, to store genetic information, and to breed a new population—all of this turns out to be maximally disruptive first for Kryptonians and then for humanity.

In *Tenet* the protagonist's search for stolen plutonium gives rise to revelations about a maximally sinister plot: the terminally ill antagonist intends to deploy a time-reversal device that will destroy humanity. He has gained access to this device by communicating with people in the future, who developed it precisely to save humanity which apparently is in very dire straits due perhaps to environmental destruction and nuclear war taking place in the time between the present and their time in the future. Their aim is to reverse—that is, to prevent—these negative developments so as to create a better future, but instead the antagonist wants to use the device to *extinguish* humanity in the present. Luckily, time-reversal technology can be used by the Protagonist to prevent this.

Interstellar deals with a global plant disease ("the blight") making food production in the near future ever more difficult, with half of the world's population already having died from starvation when the story begins, and the remainder expected to starve within a few decades. (It is not clear whether perhaps there has also been a global war; conceivably, the blight started out as a biological weapon.) NASA, working in secrecy, plans to colonize one (or more) of a selection of distant planets, which are newly reachable due to the mysterious appearance of a wormhole that allows travel to a distant part of the universe. As with the Kryptonians in *Man of Steel*, colonization (now carried out by what are presumed to be the good guys, rather than the villains) might have to proceed by breeding a new population from the species' genetic legacy (here kept in the form of 5,000 frozen embryos). Alternatively, it might be possible to transport much of humanity into space and eventually to inhabitable planets, but only if a scientific breakthrough can be made which will allow massive spacecraft to be lifted off the Earth. As in *Tenet* (but now with a positive outcome), future beings, who possibly are descendants of present-day humanity, reach back in time so as to create the wormhole and (by way of a message astronaut Joe Cooper sends to his daughter Murphy in the past) to enable humans to achieve that essential scientific breakthrough.

There is, then, an overall trend across Nolan's oeuvre away from geographically and temporally tightly focused stories involving only a few people toward more expansive stories about the populations of cities, countries, or whole planets, away from individualized (murderous and other) crime toward comprehensive attacks on, or threats to, a city or an army or all of humanity. Most disturbingly, there is the suggestion, which may occasionally be made explicit in dialogue, that people, communities, societies, and indeed humanity as a whole are on a self-destructive path from which they perhaps cannot, and do not even deserve to, be saved. (The antagonists in *Batman Begins* and *The Dark Knight Rises* speak of punishment for societal corruption.) Once again, Nolan has been participating in general trends at the global box office.

GLOBAL HIT PATTERNS 2: LARGE-SCALE DESTRUCTION

Truly large-scale destruction has been featured in Hollywood's top hits since the late 1970s, with planets exploding in *Star Wars* (1977) and *Superman* (1978) and the Earth's destruction being threatened in *Star Trek: The Motion Picture* (1979) (Krämer forthcoming). Following more hits about the threat of extinction-level events on Earth such as *Independence Day* (1996) and *Armageddon* (the top global hit of 1998), by the time *Batman Begins* was released in 2005, films about global or more localized but still very large-scale destruction were dominating global box office charts. They ranged from new versions of classic tales of death and destruction such as *Troy* (no. 8 in 2004), *War of the Worlds* (no. 4 in 2005), and *King Kong* (no. 5 in 2005), and very rare films about real global problems like the climate change movie *The Day after Tomorrow* (no. 6 in 2004) to the latest installments of science fiction and fantasy franchises such as *The Lord of the Rings: The Return of the King* (no. 1 in 2003), *The Matrix Reloaded* (no. 3 in 2003), and *Star Wars: Episode III: Revenge of the Sith* (no. 2 in 2005).

In the run-up to the release of *Tenet* in 2020, visions of ever more comprehensive destruction could be found near or at the top of the charts: in *Guardians of the Galaxy Vol. 2* (no. 8 in 2017) the whole universe is about to be transformed by the villain into an extension and reflection of himself; in *Avengers: Infinity War* (no. 1 in 2018) half of all life in the universe is extinguished; and in *Avengers: Endgame* (no. 1 in 2019) the villain aims (but fails) to erase the universe altogether. As in some of Nolan's films there is a sense of inevitability and perhaps even of just deserts in many of these global hits, most notably in *Infinity War* and *Endgame*: the villain's rationale is that if life cannot exist within the limits imposed by natural resources, then half of it has to be destroyed so as to establish a balance, or, failing that, a whole new universe has to be created to replace the existing one. Thus, Nolan's emphasis on (the threat) of large-scale destruction, with or without the claim that humanity deserves it, has been in tune with broader developments.

GLOBAL DESTRUCTION, SCIENTIFIC REDEMPTION, AND MALE FANTASY IN *INTERSTELLAR*

Perhaps Nolan's most provocative and controversial take on the kinds of global problems that are so prominent both in fiction and in real world debates is *Interstellar*. In the days after the film's initial theatrical release, I was not the only one quite surprised, even shocked, by what appeared to be its very dismissive stance toward, indeed its demonizing account of, people putting food supply and care for our earthly environment first, ahead of space exploration and colonization (Krämer 2014, Oatsvall 2014, and Gittell 2014).

Mainly due to the fact that the project was originally developed, from 2005 onward, by producer Lynda Obst together with theoretical physicist Kip Thorne (Shenoy 2017), science played a crucial role in story development and the production of the film as well as in its marketing and reception, arguably to a greater extent than for any other science fiction blockbuster of the last sixty years, with the possible exceptions of *Contact* (1997, produced by Obst and based on a novel by astronomer Carl Sagan, who in turn got advice from Thorne) and *2001: A Space Odyssey* (1968, directed by Stanley Kubrick from a script he wrote together with science fiction author and science popularizer Arthur C. Clarke).[11]

Partly due to this emphasis on science, the film was taken quite seriously by the press, audiences, and experts as a contribution to public debates about global crises and space exploration. Perhaps it is the way the film's (claims to) scientific accuracy and its resonance with public debates are combined with Nolan's typically complex storytelling and a highly emotional focus on foundational human relationships (notably between fathers and their children, especially daughters)[12] which turned it not only into a massive box office success but also one of the best loved and most admired films of recent times. The all-time "IMDb Top 250 Movies" chart, which is based on user ratings, has *Interstellar* at number 27, with only two films released during the last fifteen years above it (astonishingly both are Christopher Nolan movies: *Inception* at no. 13 and *The Dark Knight* at no. 4).[13]

In the extensive scholarly, journalistic, and popular discussions of the film, one question is rarely addressed in depth: why is there a need for humanity to leave the Earth? Because of the blight and also because it is human nature to go on exploring the world are the short answers. The blight has affected ever more food crops and caused widespread starvation. However, if the spread of the blight cannot be prevented on Earth, and there is no cure for it either, it will be difficult, if not impossible, to prevent it from being transported into space as well, eventually infecting and destroying all food crops grown on a space station or another planet. After all, the scheme that is eventually realized in the film (Plan A as outlined by Professor Brand) involves millions, perhaps billions of people and countless plants being moved in giant spacecraft off the Earth. In addition, enormous resources and efforts are needed to build these spacecraft. Even with the lift-off from Earth no longer a major issue (because Earth's gravity can be manipulated due to Murphy's scientific breakthrough) it surely takes many years, even decades, and *all* available material resources and labor—but only if it is possible to coordinate such a gigantic effort. And if such a gigantic global effort can be made, why not focus it on containing the blight or finding a cure for it, which just has to be so much easier to achieve?

The film offers an alternative to the evacuation of the Earth (Professor Brand's Plan B). It entails using a small spacecraft to bring the seeds of a human colony (in the shape of a few astronauts and plenty of frozen embryos) to another planet with no expectation that this colony would ever again have any contact with Earth. It would appear that, since there can be no expectation of finding edible vegetation on another planet, plants from Earth have to be taken along (also perhaps to provide food for the astronauts during their long journey).[14] What are the odds that the spacecraft and all its contents could be perfectly decontaminated? And even if they were, the film's ending is rather ominous: it is highly likely that the blight is present on the giant space station where Cooper finally sees his daughter again; while wandering around the station surely some of the bacteria or fungi causing the blight have attached themselves to his shoes or clothes or skin. Without any effort at decontamination, Cooper sets off to join Brand's daughter on a distant inhabitable planet, taking the blight with him.

There is a more general point to be made here: all those visions—promulgated in fiction and in public debates about humanity's future—of leaving the Earth behind after a catastrophe so as to live in space or on another planet seem to ignore the fact that unless our planet is physically ripped apart or vaporized (say, by an exploding sun), it will provide better resources for humanity's survival than empty space or another planet. No blight or nuclear war, no runaway climate change or supervolcano, not even an asteroid strike would make the Earth as uninhabitable as empty space. And if one wants to terraform a planet, that is, turn it into a near-duplicate of the life-sustaining Earth, then surely the best starting point is the Earth itself, even after a major catastrophe which has much reduced its life-sustaining qualities.

I am therefore inclined to conclude that the blight in *Interstellar*—as is the case with so many other speculations about the need to leave the Earth because of an imminent global catastrophe—is simply a pretext for, and a (actually rather absurd) rationalization of, a burning desire to leave the planet behind, to separate oneself from Mother Earth, to penetrate deep space (including black holes and wormholes), to inseminate other planets.[15] The bad puns are fully intended here, and indeed they rhyme with self-conscious puns in *Interstellar*, not least the naming of Dr. Mann, the most daring of wormhole explorers, the one who inspired and led the seminal first journey across the cosmos. He does, however, turn out to be a selfish megalomaniac, willing to lie and murder so as to become the father of a whole new population. On some level, then, Christopher and Jonathan Nolan acknowledge in their script that there is something problematic about their (very masculine) fantasy about scientific breakthroughs (here ascribed to a father-daughter team and future beings) and space technologies.

Indeed, in all the other films Nolan has made since *Batman Begins* science and technology are shown in a much more ambiguous or even straightforwardly negative light, especially when associated with powerful men and male-dominated organizations. What is more, none of Hollywood's other major global hits show the same level of contempt for Earth's natural environment and those who want to protect it, nor do other hits indulge the fantasy of (male) technological self-reinvention in space to the same extent.

CONCLUSION

Christopher Nolan's films will no doubt continue to attract a lot of attention, not least from film studies scholars and philosophers as well as from academics in other disciplines, including the sciences. This attention is, in my view, wholly justified because Nolan's films are characterized by enormous complexity and they grapple with fundamental questions about the human condition (both in the abstract and in the concrete historical circumstances of today). They have reached, and often intensely engaged (sensually, emotionally, intellectually, ethically), hundreds of millions of people around the world. His films and his cinema-related campaigning are of particular importance for anyone who remains attached to the experience of communally watching movies on a big theatrical screen.

Due to the pandemic and also perhaps to Warner Bros.' release strategy which Nolan was not happy with, *Tenet* did not perform as well at the box office as had been hoped, but it was one of only a few Hollywood releases that, one might say somewhat dramatically, kept movie theaters around the world alive in 2020 and 2021. Many of the top global hits of these two years were Chinese productions which made almost all of their money in their domestic market. Among the Hollywood releases that performed well almost everywhere the box office trends of recent years quickly reaffirmed themselves; the charts were filled with additions to long-running film series, adaptations, and remakes, with a particular emphasis on science fiction and fantasy and most especially on DC and Marvel superheroes, as well as on stories about large-scale destruction, global intrigues, and the possible end of the world (as we know it).

Nolan's original script for *Tenet* stands out, and while *Oppenheimer* may turn out to be an adaptation (rather than an original script), it is set apart from the rest of Hollywood's blockbuster output by virtue of being a historical epic. At the same time, it will fit in with certain box office trends, not least by showing how a world which had not known, nor been threatened by, nuclear weapons came to an end with the Manhattan Project, of which Oppenheimer, widely known as "the father of the atomic bomb," was the scientific director, and also, most likely, by staging the first-ever nuclear explosions in a most spectacular fashion. It remains to be seen what stance Nolan will take in this film on the (male-identified) pursuit of scientific knowledge and technological innovation which he seems to celebrate so vigorously, and rather deviously, in *Interstellar* but questions so comprehensively in *The Prestige*, the Dark Knight trilogy, *Inception*, and *Tenet* (as well as *Man of Steel*).

NOTES

1. This paragraph as well as the next is largely based on a number of press reports (Rubin and Lang 2021; Kit 2021; Rubin 2021).

2. See the box office grosses of Tarantino's films and their rankings in annual global charts on Box Office Mojo (www.boxofficemojo.com/); they are well below the grosses and rankings for Nolan's films which I discuss in the first section. All websites were last accessed on February 11, 2022.

3. See www.boxofficemojo.com/. Information on individual films can be found by searching for their titles. Annual global box office charts can be accessed here: www.boxofficemojo.com/year/world/?ref =bo_nb_hm_tab. On the top left one can select a year (before the late 1990s, these charts are not reliable due to missing figures for export income).

4. The figures in brackets include revenues from re-releases.

5. There is no budget figure given on Box Office Mojo. I have taken it from Rubin (2020).

6. Due to pandemic-related closures of cinemas in 2020/21, the global theatrical market shrunk to a fraction of its previous size, which is why the comparatively small gross for *Tenet* was enough for fifth place in 2020.

7. See "THEME Report 2019," Motion Picture Association, 2020, p. 20, www.motionpictures.org/wp-content/uploads/2020/03/MPA-THEME-2019.pdf.

8. Here is a listing of these films:
   1. *Man of Steel* (2013), production budget $225 million, box office gross $668 million, no. 9 in the global box office chart
   2. *Transcendence* (2014), budget $100 million, gross $103 million, no. 74
   3. *Batman v Superman: Dawn of Justice* (2016), budget $250 million, gross $874 million, no. 7

4. *Justice League* (2017), budget c. $300 million, gross $658 million, no. 14. Nolan was heavily involved in getting *Man of Steel* made. His role in making *Batman v Superman* is less defined, and writing credits went to David Goyer and Chris Terrio. Nolan's involvement with *Justice League* appears to have been rather marginal. *Transcendence* was the directorial debut of Nolan's cameraman Wally Pfister. It is the only of the above four films which was not a Warner Bros. production and release.

9. The story was unpublished at the time the film was made but later appeared in the March 2001 issue of *Esquire*; see classic.esquire.com/article/2001/3/1/memento-mori.

10. M. Night Shyamalan came closest to Nolan's achievement with four top 20 hits based on his own original screenplays from 1999 to 2004.

11. Nolan has long been a great fan of *2001*, and in 2018 it was he who restored film prints of the movie for a theatrical re-release marking the fiftieth anniversary of its original release (Tapley 2018).

12. Father-child relationships and/or relationships between paternal figures and younger men are also central to *Inception*, the Dark Knight trilogy, and *Man of Steel*, whereby the latter also centrally revolves around a mother-child relationship, motherhood to some extent being foregrounded in *The Prestige* and *Tenet* as well. More generally, familial relationships of this kind are central to many of the biggest box office hits since the late 1970s (Krämer 1998). With regard to Nolan's films, there is a lot more to be said about the absence and death of women in general and mothers in particular.

13. See www.imdb.com/chart/top/.

14. As BigBoiMaxy remarked in the "Food on the Endurance" thread on Reddit with regard to the food shortage caused by the blight: "If they could just grow food on space ships why didn't they make a bunch of space ships and send food to earth that way?" www.reddit.com/r/interstellar/comments/iv3aud/food_on_the_endurance/.

15. There is a sense that this fantasy concerns men using a barren planet to create a replica of Earth, thus, in a way, reversing the process by which Mother Earth originally provided the conditions for their creation. Rather than seeing themselves as creatures of Mother Earth, they can define themselves as the creators of a new Earth.

REFERENCES

Foundas, Scott. 2015. "Christopher Nolan Rallies the Troops to Save Celluloid." *Variety*, March 11. variety.com/2015/film/columns/christopher-nolan-rallies-the-troops-to-save-celluloid-film-1201450536/.

Gittell, Noah. 2014. "*Interstellar*: Good Space Film, Bad Climate-Change Parable." *The Atlantic*, November 15. www.theatlantic.com/entertainment/archive/2014/11/why-interstellar-ignores-climate-change/382788/.

IWM. 2022. "What You Need to Know about the Dunkirk Evacuations." Imperial War Museums. www.iwm.org.uk/history/what-you-need-to-know-about-the-dunkirk-evacuations.

Kit, Borys. 2021. "Cillian Murphy to Star in Christopher Nolan's *Oppenheimer*." *The Hollywood Reporter*, October 8. www.hollywoodreporter.com/movies/movie-news/cillian-murphy-christopher-nolan-oppenheimer-1235028622/.

Krämer, Peter. 1998. "Would You Take Your Child to See This Film? The Cultural and Social Work of the Family-Adventure Movie." In *Contemporary Hollywood Cinema*, ed. Steve Neale and Murray Smith, 294–311. London: Routledge.

———. 2014. "An Initial Response to *Interstellar*." *ThinkingFilmCollective*, November 17. thinkingfilmcollective.blogspot.de/2014/11/an-initial-response-to-interstellar.html.

———. 2022. "The Walt Disney Company, Family Entertainment, and Hollywood's Global Hits." In *The Oxford Handbook of Children's Films*, ed. Noel Brown, 569–90. Oxford: Oxford University Press.

———. Forthcoming. "The End of the World (As It Is Collectively Known at the Time): Hit Patterns in US and Global Box Office Charts." In *A Handbook of American Film History*, ed. Jon Lewis. Oxford: Oxford University Press.

Nolan, Christopher. 2020. "Movie Theaters Are a Vital Part of American Social Life, They Will Need Our Help." *Washington Post*, March 20. www.washingtonpost.com/opinions/2020/03/20/christopher-nolan-movie-theaters-are-vital-part-american-social-life-they-will-need-our-help/.

Oatsvall, Neil S. 2014. "*Interstellar* as Anti-Environmentalist Trope?" Neiloatsvall.com, November 10. www.neiloatsvall.com/blog/2014/11/10/interstellar-as-anti-environmentalist-trope.

Rubin, Rebecca. 2020. "Christopher Nolan Defends *Tenet* Box Office Results." *Variety*, November 3. variety.com/2020/film/news/christopher-nolan-tenet-release-1234822593/.

———. 2021. "Why Christopher $100 Million WWII Drama Oppenheimer Could be the Last of Its Kind." *Variety*, November 18. variety.com/2021/film/news/christopher-nolan-oppenheimer-ww2-movie-1235109373/#recipient_hashed=4570fe57833e1f5b393603068b4e17b9a8726a1bf2d69a89c0cb0e80a2fc1397.

Rubin, Rebecca, and Brent Lang. 2021. "How Universal Beat Other Studios to Land Christopher Nolan's New World War II Epic." *Variety*, September 14. variety.com/2021/film/news/christopher-nolan-universal-deal-1235064461/.

Shenoy, Gautham. 2017. "The Interstellar Contributions of Kip Thorne, the Man Carl Sagan Contacted for Physics Advice." *Factory Daily*, October 7. archive.factordaily.com/interstellar-kip-thorne-nobel-prize/.

Tapley, Kristopher. 2018. "Christopher Nolan Goes Analog Route to Restoring Celluloid Beauty of *2001: A Space Odyssey*." *Variety*, May 16. variety.com/2018/artisans/production/christopher-nolan-2001-a-space-odyssey-1202811669/.

VanDerWerff, Emily. 2018. "The Difference between the Oscars' Adapted and Original Screenplay Categories, Explained." *Vox*, March 2. www.vox.com/2017/2/25/14693400/oscars-original-adapted-screenplay-academy-awards.

Chapter 13

Mementos of the Afternoon

Christopher Nolan's Ambiguous Debt to Maya Deren

Will Brooker

BETWEEN *NOIR* AND THE *AVANT-GARDE*: LOCATING *MEMENTO*

Memento breaks Los Angeles into forgettable fragments. Margaret A. Toth describes its locations as "a series of temporary, interstitial spaces: motel rooms and lobbies, diners and restaurants, a shabby bar, a public bathroom, an abandoned construction site, a defunct oil refinery, a tattoo parlour, [Leonard's] car and a parking lot for mobile (rather than stationary) homes" (2015, 77; see also the very similar list in Knight and McKnight 2009, 152). The individual places are, she says, "generic," and add up to a "nonspecific" sense of the city, which was precisely the effect production designer Patti Podesta hoped for: "We wanted something anonymous. We were looking for a place you could not place. A no-place" (quoted in Mottram 2002, 154). Nolan added that the film's landscape was "not specifically LA . . . there's really nothing in the film that you could recognise as LA" (167).

And yet we can pin down these generic no-places to specific zip codes. The shabby bar, named Ferdy's in the movie, was The Blue Room, 916 South San Fernando Road at Alameda Avenue, Burbank (though the film hides it at a false address, 435 North Spruce). And *Memento*, for all its restless wandering, also has a core, a quiet central space, a temporary home to which it returns, reassuringly, in the black-and-white sequences. Leonard spends much of his time at the Discount Inn, which is in real life The Travel Inn, on 7254 Foothill Boulevard, Tujunga, California, 91042. And once that no-place is pinned on a map, we can see its relationship to the rest of Los Angeles, and its proximity to other places from other movies. Though the film refers to it as "out of town," the Travel Inn is just a casual drive—an easy trip for Leonard Shelby in his stolen Jaguar—south through Tujunga and Burbank, keeping Griffith Park on your left and then swinging right down Los Feliz—to another iconic cinematic location, nestled in the winding lanes of the Hollywood Hills. It is the Spanish-style mansion where Walter Neff visits Phyllis Dietrichson in Billy Wilder's *Double Indemnity* (1944).

That *Memento* sits within the territory of noir is one of the few points critics can agree on about Nolan's puzzle film. "Leonard appears to be a neo-*noir* character somehow transported back to and trapped in a classical *noir* chronotope," writes Toth (2015, 77); Todd McGowan connects him to the "hero in *film noir*" (2012, 47). Stuart Joy, comparing Nolan to Wilder, believes that "one of the most important features of Nolan's work is his similar engagement with *film noir*" (2015, 8), while Jason A. Ney describes *Memento* as one of Nolan's few "true," "pure" noirs (2013, 65). "*Memento* is a neo-*noir* psychological thriller," state Deborah Knight and George McKnight (2009, 147); James Mottram's book on the making of Nolan's movie calls it "a distillation of *film noir*, stripping down the parameters of the genre to their purest possible form, using its trappings to subvert" (2002, 39). Tom Shone's *The Nolan Variations* describes the movie as "a dizzyingly structured neo-*noir* with the eerie, sunlit clarity of a dream" (2020, 78). Finally, Claire Molloy's chapter "*Memento* as Noir" extensively explores the film's relationship to the elusive cycle of the 1940s and 1950s, and also offers a glimpse of the way *Memento* was promoted and received on its first release.

> Marketing materials referred to the film as *noir*, whilst in interviews Christopher Nolan spoke of being a fan of the "classic *noir*" *Double Indemnity* . . . and production notes for the film described *Memento* as "*film noir* pared down to its most visceral elements." . . . In critical reviews the film was variously described as . . . "a noirish thriller," "*noir*," "meta-*noir*," "neo-*noir*," "*nouveau noir*" and a "revenge thriller" that "uses a favourite plot device of postwar Freudian *film noir*." (Molloy 2010, 86)

Comparisons with *Double Indemnity* are frequent, not just because of Nolan's avowed fandom but also because both films share a nonlinear structure—though as Toth points out, *Double Indemnity*'s storytelling is "tamer" (2015, 75)—and because Leonard is a former insurance claims investigator, while Walter Neff sells insurance. Mottram sums up the similarities:

Like *Memento* . . . *Double Indemnity* begins at the end as Walter Neff staggers, seemingly shot, into the office of a colleague . . . like Leonard, Barton Keyes (Edward G. Robinson) is an insurance claims investigator, who shares many of Shelby's analytic skills. A film that influenced a generation of *noirs* with its retrospective narration, we always know what Neff's fate will be, whatever he says or does. *Memento*, of course, leaves us less certain, but Nolan's deliberate nod to the world of Wilder's film goes some way to show how he wishes to revitalize the "nostalgic image of guys in raincoats and fedoras coming down alleyways," as he puts it. (2002, 42)

But there is another house, another short drive away: south on Vine then west on Sunset Boulevard. Both *Double Indemnity* and *Memento* used exteriors, only shooting interiors on sound stages, so in that sense, they remain no-places. This house, 1466 North Kings Road, served as both the inside and outside for *Meshes of the Afternoon*, and was also the home of the writer and co-director (and main actor), Maya Deren.

Meshes of the Afternoon was shot, as its title card tells us, in "Hollywood 1943," a reference John David Rhodes describes as "sardonic" (2011, 111). Certainly, as Rhodes notes, "it would seem rather different from, say, Robert Stevenson's *Jane Eyre* or Alfred Hitchcock's *Shadow of a Doubt*, or any number of films made by the studio system in the same year" (2011, 8). It was completed, Deren joked, "for what Hollywood spends on lipstick" (2011, 12). It is fourteen minutes long. It is, unlike *Double Indemnity*, very rarely if ever mentioned in discussions of *Memento*.

On a map of Los Angeles, the Discount Inn forms the point of a triangle that links it with Maya Deren's house and the Dietrichson residence from *Double Indemnity*. *Memento*'s connection with noir has, as I have indicated, been thoroughly investigated. Its possible links with Deren's avant-garde experiment have not. In what follows, I will explore the influence of that other house; the echoes, in *Memento*, of *Meshes of the Afternoon*; and what they might mean.

MATCHING MOTIFS IN *MESHES* AND *MEMENTO*

Black-and-white stock was standard in 1943; by 2000 it was an artistic choice, and it provides the most obvious aesthetic link between *Memento*'s motel monochrome and the chiaroscuro of classic noir. But it also invites comparison between the hotel room in which Leonard finds himself, and the domestic space occupied by Maya—as Rhodes calls the otherwise-nameless character played by Maya Deren—at 1466 North Kings Road. In the simplest terms, selected stills from both films look remarkably alike. If we compare the images of Leonard in *Memento*'s first scene with those of Maya first entering and exploring her apartment, the patterns of contrasting light and darkness are equally stark, and the framing similarly fragmented: both films, for instance, include a close-up of the protagonist's blinking eye, on the threshold of sleep.

More broadly, both evoke an oneiric climate—"a trance film," said P. Adams Sitney of *Meshes* (quoted in Soussloff, 2001, 112); "a dream state," says Rhodes (2011, 68), "steeped in the logic of dreamscapes" (Keller 2015, 32), while Shone saw *Memento* as having the "eerie, sunlit clarity of a dream"—the experience of waking up and locating oneself. Leonard emerges from what feels like an afternoon nap, and she reclines in her armchair, then drifts into slumber. "It's like waking. It's like you just woke up," Leonard explains to Burt, trying to convey his condition.

The next step for our waking dreamers is to establish themselves in an unfamiliar space, and here both films use a roving camera to represent the protagonist's point of view, piecing together the environment from details. Nolan pans slowly from left to right across a cheap chest of drawers, taking in an edge of mirror and two glasses in sanitary packaging, then tilts up over a wardrobe cluttered with cheap wire hangers and a wall-mounted temperature control. Deren places her camera in the doorway—I use her name here for convenience as she was the writer, producer, and co-director, although it was technically Alexander Hammid's camera and for the most part his camerawork—and follows a hand-held arc from spread newspapers on the floor up to the wall, panning left to right across patterned curtains and candleholders, then moving to a kitchen nook. In both cases, the décor is banal—Nolan and his set designer faithfully recreate a generic, anonymous space, while Deren makes no attempt to dress up or disguise her living room—and most of the objects have no significance. But as in a video game, where interactive items are highlighted as distinct from mere background, key props seem to step forward from the mise-en-scene, loaded with further meaning.

Fittingly, the first, in both cases, is a key. "There's the key," muses Leonard, over an extreme close-up, while Maya takes one from her purse and fumbles, letting it tumble down the steps, then chases and scoops it up in a nine-shot rapid montage that demonstrates its importance. Leonard's next item is literally signposted by the instruction on his thigh—"Shave," directing him to a bag of disposable razors—while Maya sees a knife leap out of a loaf of bread, alive and animated like something from Jan Švankmajer's *Alice* (1988). And then the phone rings, and Leonard snatches it up with an urgent "Who is this?" and Deren's camera whip-pans to the left, discovering a telephone on the stairs with its receiver hanging off the hook.

A key, a blade, a telephone: these objects, recurring in the same order in two different dreams, are suggestive. The direct connections end there, as Maya focuses on a record player and an artificial flower, while Leonard puts his faith in Polaroids and tattoos. But the broader sense of an intense investment in objects—everyday items that seem to hold hidden significance—is central to both films. Turim notes that Deren cautioned against "a traditional psychoanalytical reading" of *Meshes*, "a static interpretation of symbols . . . a one-to-one deciphering" (Turim 2001, 85). Rhodes speculates in turn that Deren's "traffic in potentially vulgar symbols (flowers, mirrors, knives, the sea)" (2011, 92) is less about conveying actual meaning than a comment about symbolization; a knowing, slightly ironic performance of Freudian dream-work, rather than a genuine puzzle where each object stands for something (a key signifying freedom, for instance). "There is," adds Turim, "no single, simple key to Deren's image riddles" (2001, 85). *Meshes of the Afternoon* is, as such, a detached enactment of the ploddingly literal Freudian detection of 1940s Hollywood, such as Hitchcock's *Spellbound* (1945).

Similarly, when Leonard hires an escort to place the sad collection of his wife's "things" around his motel room—a plain white bra, a hairbrush, a battered paperback, and a teddy bear—she is wryly baffled ("Whatever gets you off") and the items lose their value for him. He burns them in the next scene. "Probably burned truckloads of your stuff," he muses. "Can't remember to forget you." Objects that seem invested with significance are in fact only empty symbols, meaningless souvenirs, shabby mementos.

"OK, so what am I doing?" Leonard asks himself, as he wakes up into a new color sequence and finds himself sprinting, panting, through a maze of mobile homes. "Oh, I'm chasing this guy." He catches up to Dodd, who pulls a gun and pursues Leonard. The dynamic is abruptly reversed, in one of the film's moments of pure comedy. "No . . . he's chasing me."

Who is chasing whom? The same question structures *Meshes of the Afternoon*, where Maya seems to be following the tall, hooded figure with a mirror for a face; but that figure also strides up the road and past her house while she watches from a window, and yet, uncannily, is inside the house too, advancing up the stairs to her bedroom. By the end of the film, Rhodes counts four Mayas, three of them seated in the kitchen area, and one asleep in the armchair.

Are there also multiple Leonards? In a sense. The screenplay distinguishes between them through their outfits and also by the extent of their injuries: "He wears a beige suit and blue shirt (no blood)" (Nolan 2001, 106); "He wears boxers and a plaid work shirt" (109). Most obviously, we learn as viewers to tell the difference between the casual, often shirtless Leonard of the black-and-white motel sequences and the suited Leonard of the color footage, but there are at least two other Leonards in play: the shorter-haired, clean-shaven

Leonard of the color flashbacks to his life with his wife, and the suave, slick Leonard of the black-and-white narrative about the Sammy Jankis case.

We might also note that Jimmy Grantz, the drug dealer, is a close enough match for Leonard that his shirt and suit fit perfectly, and that Jimmy's associate Dodd is described in Natalie's note as "White guy, 6'2, blonde," living in a motel, a description that could equally apply to Leonard. When they first meet, trading wisecracks through a car window, the two men almost precisely mirror each other, both with stubble, spiked hair, and wide grins. As such, Leonard faces off with his near-double more than once; it would not be such a stretch to suggest that, like Maya, he is caught up in a physical struggle to the death with versions of himself.

Other, more enigmatic incarnations of the protagonist trouble the narrative further: the Leonard of Teddy's Polaroid photo, pointing ecstatically at his chest; the Leonard who appears for a split second in Sammy's place, staring blankly at hospital staff; and the seemingly impossible Leonard in bed with his wife, a new tattoo confirming "I'VE DONE IT." They do not appear in the same physical location, but cuts connect them across time—as indeed eye-line matches and other conventions of continuity editing suture the multiple Mayas into a single space.

Meshes of the Afternoon is, then, an experimental film that explores the tropes and language of noir—a mysterious figure, a pursuit, clues to a crime, a murdered woman—as well as the avant-garde—jump cuts, unnerving transformations, nightmare logic. Aspects of its imagery and camera trickery recall *Un Chien Andalou* (Buñuel, 1929), but Deren's sensual performance also evokes the femme fatale, and her direction employs the techniques of mainstream suspense; the unnerving close-up on a knife leaping from a loaf of bread is closer to a shot in Hitchcock's thriller *Blackmail*, also from 1929, than anything in Buñuel. On one level, *Meshes of the Afternoon* is a murder mystery set in a Hollywood home; it concludes with a haunting shot of a dead woman, or more specifically, a dead wife, discovered by her husband (played by Deren's partner, Hammid). Seen from a certain angle, it looks a lot like *Memento*.

As a final intriguing comparison, we could run Deren's final sequence of discovery—the husband trying and pushing the door, crossing the threshold, and gazing down at the ghoulish sight of his wife slumped in a chair, surrounded by broken glass—alongside Memento's flashback of Leonard kicking open the bathroom door, stepping inside to see his wife's body shrouded in a shower curtain, and then having his own face smashed into a mirror.

Cinematographer Wally Pfister and set designer Patti Podesta hung the doorways with plastic sheeting, similar to that shower curtain, in the climactic sequence of Memento where Leonard kills Teddy (see Mottram 2002, 133). Leonard walks in from the bright afternoon, pushing ragged swags of draping to one side, and enters a dark passage. Cutting across time—a flashback to almost sixty years before—and across space, a drive south and west from Tujunga to the Hollywood Hills, we find an echo in Maya pushing her way through net curtains into her bedroom, navigating through veils of dream: the titular "meshes," perhaps, of that sunny afternoon in 1943.

READING *MEMENTO* THROUGH *MESHES*

Matching up motifs from the two films may seem a satisfying puzzle game, but apart from encouraging us to consider *Memento*'s echoes of experimental cinema, as well as its debt to noir, where does it get us? Can Nolan's feature-length millennial thriller about a man struggling with his memory have more than coincidental stylistic similarities with Maya Deren's 1943 short about a woman trapped within her daydreams? The key concepts explored in *Meshes of the Afternoon* certainly chime with those of *Memento*. Maureen Turim's list—"game structure, ritual, the divided and multiple self, the self in relationship to other, and the death drive and murderous impulses" (Turim 2001, 84)—refers to *Meshes* but could equally apply to Nolan's feature.

But Leonard Shelby is a man of his time—with the emphasis on both of those terms. He is, of course, male, and his narrative takes place at the end of the twentieth century, rather than at the end of the Second World War. The anonymity and fragmentation of his Los Angeles can be associated specifically with the late 1990s, as can his lack of memory; indeed, we might agree that the "condition" he frequently mentions is actually the postmodern condition (see Deakin 2015, 88). As Darren Mooney writes:

> In some ways, Leonard is expressing an anxiety about existing at "the end of history." If there is no more history, then there is no more time. If there is no more time, there is no more progress. To many observers, the nineties appeared like a time period trapped in amber. . . . Jean Baudrillard said that for "these generations which no longer expect anything from some future "coming," it was entirely possible that "the year 2000 will not perhaps take place." (Mooney 2018, 24–25)

As such, *Memento* is a Polaroid of its cultural moment, and Leonard's imposition of rules and rituals constitutes an attempt to restore, in Peter Deakin's phrase, "order and control in a perverse postmodern world" (2015, 88). But Leonard's condition is also seen by many commentators as specifically male, as well as typically late-1990s. Deakin's chapter is titled "Men in Crisis," a theme also identified by Claire Molloy, who reads *Memento*'s issues of memory and identity through contemporary discourses around the softer, more nurturing "New Man" and the previous individualistic and violent Rambo type, the "Retributive Man" (Molloy 2010, 95). She argues that Leonard is exploring these alternate masculine identities of the late 1990s—like trying on different suits for size and fit—and is unable to

> resolve them within one unified sense of self. As such the anterograde amnesia, the condition that stops Leonard from creating new memories, also inhibits the unification of his self-identity and in this sense a discourse of impairment is continually called on to rupture the desired coherence of masculinity. (2010, 96)

"I'm Leonard Shelby. I'm from San Francisco," he states twice, insisting on his identity in simple terms. "That's who you *were*, Lenny," Teddy interrupts on both occasions. "You don't know who you *are*." On a superficial level, Leonard has by this point "become" Jimmy Grantz, wearing another man's designer suit and driving his Jaguar, which bears Nevada plates. But his struggles are also internal: "You feel angry, you don't know why. You feel guilty, you have no idea why."

Molloy connects this tension between different discourses of masculinity—nurturing and vengeful, sensitive and aggressive—with Leonard's "impairment," which he also calls his "handicap." His search for a coherent sense of masculinity is disrupted by his "condition"—a condition that was broadly shared, if we take it as a metaphor for the postmodern and a cultural "loss of history," but which manifests itself in an extreme form for Leonard.

As such, Molloy finds a connection to noir through the trope of disability, and the figure of the "amnesiac" in such 1940s films as Hitchcock's *Spellbound* (2010, 94). This parallel with images of "impairment" in 1940s cinema is also identified by Toth but taken in an intriguingly different direction, and it is this angle that leads us back to *Meshes of the Afternoon*.

In a fascinating move, Toth compares Leonard not to the amnesiac men of noir but to

> another cinematic female type: the "medicalized" heroine of 1930s and 1940s "women's films," including Irving Rapper's paradigmatic *Now, Voyager* (1942). ... Leonard, whose medical condition and misguided revenge quest render him a cold-blooded murderer, evokes this "medicalized" heroine, a hysterical and pathological figure whose "symptom" threatens those with whom she comes into contact.. . . . *Memento* associates, in Leonard's fantasy, the restoration of psychic integrity with a realignment of traditional gender roles. (2015, 80–81)

If we accept that *Memento* contains traces of Maya Deren's "Hollywood, 1943" experiments, as well as the influences of mainstream 1940s Hollywood, we can use *Meshes of the Afternoon* as a lens through which to examine

Leonard's identity crisis in a new and different light. Deren's film also enacts a tension, suggests Rhodes, as it grapples with "'woman' as both object of (stereotypically male) desire *and* subject of thought and action, as the object *and* subject of thought and action" (2011, 94), a tension that would later be theorized by Laura Mulvey as the dichotomy between the woman as "bearer of meaning, not maker of meaning" (1992, 23) and "the man's role as the active one of forwarding the story, making things happen" (1992, 28). Laura Rabinovitz describes *Meshes* as "addressing a female subject who must contend with her own objectification" (2003, 56, quoted in Keller 2015, 4) and reassert her "power over the female image" (Keller 2015, 252).

Like classical noir and melodrama, *Meshes of the Afternoon* "had a specific historically-situated resonance and set of meanings" (Molloy 2010, 94)—Rhodes notes how unusual it must have been for a wife, Deren, to recruit her husband, Hammid, into a cinematic exploration of "the instability of the domestic sphere" (2011, 49)—but just as the tensions around wartime and postwar gender roles in noir find a revised form in 1990s neo-noir, so Maya's shifts between subject and objecthood can help us to understand Leonard's navigation of conflicting contemporary masculine discourses.

As Molloy notes, the film's framing of Leonard's body fits within those twin 1990s visual discourses of masculinity: the narcissistic, passive display associated with New Man personal grooming advertisements, and, through his tattoos, the self-inflicted pain and masochistic suffering of the Retributive Man, which can be traced from *First Blood* (1982) to *Fight Club* (1999). Yet as she also observes, "in *film noir*, it is traditionally the female body that is displayed as the erotic object, exposed to the male gaze" (2010, 96). *Memento* subverts and even reverses this convention through its fragmented close-ups of Leonard's chest and legs, especially in the scene where he is assertively undressed by Natalie, "inviting," as Molloy puts it, "careful and repeated contemplation." Her phrase perhaps unconsciously echoes Mulvey's account of the male gaze, whereby the female body freezes the narrative "in moments of erotic contemplation" (1992, 27), a perfect description of the moment when Natalie pulls Leonard's shirt open and positions him in front of her mirror.

Despite his repeated insistence, to himself and to others, that he is in control, the detective of the plot, moving the story forward—"I'm disciplined and organized," "I'm gonna kill him"—Leonard is a passive object, a beautiful tool manipulated by others, by Teddy, by Natalie, even by the hotel receptionist, Burt. His greatest achievement in terms of acquiring agency is choosing to manipulate himself. "Do I lie to myself to be happy? In your case Teddy, yes I will." We could see this as him wrangling between end-of-the-century masculine roles, trying to be the macho Rambo when he's really a sensitive New Man, but I want to push this interpretation a little further.

As Leonard might say, let's look at the facts. When Teddy mocks him for inspecting tire tracks, he calls Leonard "Pocahontas," the name of a Native American princess. When Leonard takes a blurry Polaroid of Natalie, Teddy sneers "nice shot, Leibovitz," referring to the female photographer. Natalie controls him during their scenes of intimacy, taking the role of the aggressive noir anti-hero with Leonard as the uncertain object of her desire and curiosity; in the morning, he pulls on her shirt and buttons it up, not realizing he is wearing a woman's garment. He is ambivalent compared to the more assertively sexual female characters; he shares a bed with Natalie but keeps his trousers on, and the escort mocks him for the charade with his wife's everyday items: "Was it good for you?" As Leonard explores the abandoned building, looking for Jimmy Grantz, the black-and-white footage is cut with color flashbacks to his wife that almost precisely match his movement and direction, linking the two of them across time, space, and memory. She runs to a window, right to left across the frame; he moves, similarly, into the light and peers out at Jimmy's car. She turns her head from right to left, in an exterior mid-shot; we cut back to the same action from Leonard, in tighter black and white. She walks through a doorway; Leonard emerges to face Jimmy. He is acting for her, we might suggest, pursuing revenge on her behalf; or we might take a cue from the flashback of their prone bodies lying on the tiled bathroom floor, face to face, and consider her as another of his doubles, another symbolic side of himself.

What does his wife represent to Leonard? She is called Catherine, but he never names her. He treats her instead as a sacred object. Natalie has to force him to go beyond the recitation of clichés—"She was beautiful. To me, she was perfect"—and really remember her as a person, but even so, his images of his wife are not just brief but shallow. She is coded as innocent, girlish, almost childlike: he treasures her old teddy bear. We see her in a pale top with a floral design, a soft cardigan, a pink flower-patterned dress, a short-sleeve shirt with a simple silver pendant, and what Molloy describes as "sensible, asexual white underwear" (2010, 92). Leonard keeps one of her plain bras, which contrasts both with the escort's low-cut, strappy top (teamed with a flashy, tacky necklace) and with Natalie's black bra, visible under her sheer black shirt.

The only hints that this remembered idyll may be incomplete are the glimpse of Catherine Shelby protesting "ow!" when Leonard pinches (or injects) her thigh, and her irritation when he interrupts her reading. One of her few lines, when he lectures her on the pleasures of the novel, is "Don't be a prick": a request that he drop his arrogant masculinity. (That the word is specifically gendered as "prick" rather than, for instance, the neutral "jerk," seems significant: note that Natalie refers contemptuously to Catherine as a "cunt.")

And that, I suggest, is what Leonard also wrestles in *Memento*: a tension, like Maya's in *Meshes of the Afternoon*, between the norms of assertive "masculine" agency and passive "feminine" objectification, between the traditional roles of the investigating detective who advances the plot and the Hollywood woman who serves primarily as visual spectacle. Like Maya, who both pursues her quarry aggressively and stands on display in a window, sensually sliding a key from between her painted lips, who runs a hand slowly and performatively over her body while reclining in an armchair, and who advances on her own sleeping form with a knife, Leonard is both furious avenger and victim, active and passive, subject and object, making things happen and to-be-looked-at; like Maya, he embodies both the traditionally "male" and "female" Hollywood roles identified by Mulvey, existing within "triangular structures of looking and desire" (Pramaggiore 2001, 245). The film's use of near-doubles as Leonard's targets enables this conflict to be physically enacted, as it is in *Meshes of the Afternoon*, when Leonard fights Dodd and Jimmy Grantz.

Leonard is fully nude when he grapples Dodd in a violent bedroom struggle, and he orders Jimmy to strip before they fight. That these physical struggles have such an intimate aspect—"What the hell were you guys doing down here?" asks Teddy—suggests an unsettling, violently sexual component to Leonard's revenge quest, which leads us in turn to a final, further proposal.

Clearly, Leonard invests the memory of his wife with ideas of innocence and victimhood. He was profoundly violated by the incident as he remembers it; his home was invaded, his wife murdered, his memory disrupted, his life stolen. Despite his attempt at heroic rescue, Leonard failed to protect his wife. Metaphorically, she represents a part of him, confirmed by the shots that link them as he waits for the man he believes is her killer. In his mind, Catherine Shelby has come to embody the side of Leonard that was made powerless and victimized. While he insists on his own aggressive agency and his control of the narrative, his claims to be a retributive avenger constantly ring hollow; they are undermined each time another member of the cast manipulates him, treating him as a patsy. On one level, the film therefore enacts his struggle to overcome the trauma of his own symbolic violation by performing traditional masculinity: in hunting his wife's killer, he is also seeking to conquer his weaker, "feminine" aspect.

In *Meshes of the Afternoon*, a menacingly aggressive incarnation of Maya, wearing reflective glasses and brandishing a knife, takes massive strides across dream country to stab her passively reclining double. "You have to come a long way," Deren explained, "to kill yourself." The tension between self and other in *Meshes*, says Sarah Keller, is ultimately expressed through "the film's murderous desire to . . . eliminate the other, which is also the self"

(2015, 53). Leonard's never-ending mission could, in turn, lead him through every town with a John G, on a symbolic serial-killing circuit that would never satisfy him, because he is only murdering doubles of his own violent side, rather than addressing his internal trauma from the assault. "You're not a killer, Lenny," Teddy smirks, pinching Leonard's cheeks. "That's why you're so good at it."

But we could take this reading even further. Popular debates around *Memento* commonly focus on whether Leonard's wife survived the criminal attack, and whether in fact he killed her with an overdose of insulin (see for instance Mottram 2002, 26–27). The question is rarely if ever raised as to whether Leonard really had a wife at all. We know that he doctored the police report, removing several pages according to Teddy; we hear from Teddy that Catherine Shelby survived the attack, but he is far from reliable himself. It is possible, within the terms of the film, that Leonard invented his wife, just as he seemingly invented Mrs. Jankis—who is portrayed in far more detail during his flashbacks, with much more dialogue—as an act of displacement, directing the attack he experienced onto the fictional Catherine Shelby and allowing himself the Hollywood role of heroic avenger. His memory of the incident has him kicking the door open and shooting her assailant neatly in the head: as Molloy notes, Leonard could not possibly have witnessed everything we are shown (2010, 93). Note that Deren's aim in *Meshes* was "to put on film the feeling which a human being experiences about an incident, rather than to accurately record the incident" (quoted in Keller 2015, 46); the film creates its own "impossible reality" (2015, 51).

If we accept that this is the case, what could Leonard be repressing and displacing through his insistence on a raped and murdered wife? Perhaps the deeply buried fact that he alone was (sexually?) assaulted that night, a memory that he has pushed onto an imagined female victim to make it more bearable for himself. Rather than simply battling his own violent side, then, he would also be trying to avenge his own violated body. His semi-naked struggles with Dodd and Jimmy would take on a newly disturbing energy in this light as brutal reenactments of the original crime, which Leonard has denied so completely that he can only experience it in a disguised form, seeking a catharsis that never comes.

READING NOLAN THROUGH *MESHES*

Nolan is notorious for his weak female characterization, with women commonly confined to a few limited roles—femme fatale (The Blonde in *Following* [1998]), eager innocent (Ellie Burr in *Insomnia* [2002]), idealized dead wife (Julia in *The Prestige* [2006]), or an uneasy hybrid of the above

(Mal in *Inception* [2010]). I have suggested, by reading *Memento* through the lens of *Meshes of the Afternoon*, that Leonard Shelby may project what he sees as his own "feminine" weakness, and the qualities of his life prior to a traumatic violation—perfect, beautiful, innocent—onto the half-remembered figure of a woman who might not ever have existed. If Catherine Shelby is a cipher, in this reading, it would be because she is an aspect of Leonard, rather than a fully formed individual.

Nolan is also well known for repeating motifs and themes throughout his oeuvre. Would it then be possible to apply a similar analysis to his other films, given that they return so clearly and consistently to the same patterns and concerns? Could such an interpretation reveal new dimensions? There are strong hints that they could also be influenced by *Meshes of the Afternoon* and its "non-ending forms of recursion, reflection, and circles" (Keller 2015, 33).

> All of Deren's ways of presenting modes of incompletion, noncausality, and unresolving arcs are in evidence in the film: themes, characters and objects *circulate* through the film rather than lead linearly towards a conclusion . . . preferring doubles and fragments, the film effects a strange math that adds up to an unexpected whole. (Keller 2015, 44)

That description could, with a simple switch of directors' names, surely apply equally to Christopher Nolan. His 1998 debut feature *Following*, like *Memento*, distinguishes between the same character (The Young Man) at different times through his clothes, hair, and injuries, and is structured around the question "who's chasing whom?" *Insomnia*'s detective, Dormer—his name a dream-reworking of "Sleep"—hallucinates in the endless white nights of Alaska, possibly imagining his antagonist and quarry (who might simply be "Dormer's conscience," suggested Nolan [see Shone 2020, 112]).

The Prestige is a nested puzzle of doubles and twins, framing flashbacks within recursive flashbacks; *Inception* takes the conceit even further, and closer to *Meshes of the Afternoon*, with its dreams within dreams. Coop, in *Interstellar* (2014), is revealed to be the ghost that haunts his earlier self. *Dunkirk* (2017) invites us to witness the same scenes multiple times from different perspectives, while *Tenet* (2020) includes the protagonist watching a second incarnation of himself, much like Maya observing her duplicate through a window, and fighting his inverted version in hand-to-hand combat. Even the *Dark Knight* movies, in which Nolan's personal approach is arguably diluted through its encounter with a franchise property, pit the vigilante against antagonists who represent twisted variants on his own psyche. "Mirror Face," the tall, robed figure from *Meshes of the Afternoon*, would make a plausible Batman villain.

Could we draw on *Meshes* to discover more complex readings of gender and identity in Nolan's troubled, fractured heroes—could Mal, for instance, represent an imaginary dream-aspect of Cobb, rather than a genuinely dead wife? Could the Protagonist of *Tenet* be physically fighting a side of himself, perhaps related to his bond with Neil that he regards as "inverted"? Could we reconsider Nolan's use of totems—the signs and symbols of *Batman Begins*, the spinning top of *Inception*—in the light of Deren's stubborn refusal of one-on-one correlations between objects and meanings? Could we even, more broadly, map Deren's model of "vertical" and "horizontal" film structure (Brannigan 2011, 104–5) onto Nolan's diagrams of his movies' complex narratives? Just as the rest of Leonard's story lies beyond the edges of *Memento*, so the length of this current chapter allows no time or space to pursue these speculations toward a fuller conclusion; but they offer a promising lead.

THE TWIST

The *Memento* and *Meshes of the Afternoon* case seems open and shut, with the potential to prize open Nolan's later films and reveal new meanings. But there is a final twist. Nolan has listed many influences on the making of *Memento*. They include Graham Swift's novel *Waterland* (1983) (Mottram 2002, 37), John Frankenheimer's film *Seconds* (1966) (Mottram 2002, 45), Lynch's *Lost Highway* (1997) (Shone 2020, 82), and Radiohead's album *OK Computer* (1997) (Shone 2020, 80). He was inspired by Terence Malick's *The Thin Red Line* (1999) and Tarkovsky's *Mirror* (1975) (Shone 2020, 88, 83). But nowhere—as far as I have seen—does he ever mention *Meshes of the Afternoon*.

There are clues, traces, ghosts of evidence. In 2010, at least one critic caught on to the parallel between Nolan and Deren, identifying *Inception* as a "*Meshes* of the Multiplex" (McCahill 2010). Then in 2015, Nolan curated 35mm screenings of experimental films by the twin brothers Stephen and Timothy Quay: the opening short, *In Absentia*—a nightmarish exploration of schizophrenia—evokes *Meshes of the Afternoon* (and indeed, *Un Chien Andalou*, and in turn the opening scenes of *Following*, *Memento*, and Nolan's 1997 short *Doodlebug* [Sharf 2015]). But nowhere in my research have I found a more solid link, or explicit acknowledgement.

Did Nolan ever watch *Meshes of the Afternoon*? Rhodes cites J. Hoberman's view that it is "probably the most widely seen avant-garde film ever made" (2011, 12). Nolan clearly has, and had, a keen interest in experimental cinema; is it likely that he knew *Mirror* and not *Meshes of the Afternoon*? Does it matter if we know? Rhodes states that we "have no record" of what

Deren's co-creator Hammid "was exposed to in Prague in the 1920s, of what he might have screened at his cinematheque. We can imagine: Eisenstein? Vertov? Germaine Dulac? Jean Epstein?" Like my own inquiry here—like *Memento*—Rhodes trails off into questions, but is content with uncertainty.

> Hammid was truly a man of the cinema, whereas . . . Deren makes only the scarcest and most desultory of references to cinema . . . Deren "knew nothing of the avant-garde films made in France–*Un Chien Andalou*, the films of Germaine Dulac, or Cocteau." . . . I don't think it's necessary to trace lines of actual influence from Dulac to Hammid's and Deren's film, even if, perhaps, the film were well known to one (or, less likely, the both) of them. (2011, 50)

Discussing the influence of *Meshes of the Afternoon*, Rhodes considers Peggy Ahwesh's *Nocturne* from 1998. "Here there is no direct reference to any scene, image, or editing pattern in *Meshes*, but one has the sense that, to paraphrase T. S. Eliot, *Meshes* is that which *Nocturne* knows" (2011, 110). And in turn, we can propose, *Un Chien Andalou* is that which *Meshes* knows. And *Meshes* is that which *Memento* knows.

Perhaps Nolan saw Deren's film and never explicitly named it as an influence; perhaps it became part of his unconscious landscape, informing his work without him realizing. Perhaps he absorbed its forms and patterns through some of the later work it shaped: Rhodes suggests Kenneth Anger's *Fireworks* (1947), Stan Brakhage's *Anticipation of the Night* (1958), and Sally Potter's *Thriller* (1979). Perhaps Nolan encountered *Meshes* through Kristin Hersh's music video for "Your Ghost" (1994) or indeed—and this is a surer bet, even if all the others fell through—through Lynch's *Lost Highway* (1997). We do not know. There is an ambiguity at the center of my argument, which threatens to undermine the story I have just told. But isn't that what *Memento* is all about? And isn't that what Nolan is all about?

REFERENCES

Brannigan, Erin. 2011. *DanceFilm: Choreography and the Moving Image*. Oxford: Oxford University Press.

Deakin, Peter. 2015. "Men in Crisis: Christopher Nolan, Un-truths and Fictionalising Masculinity." In *The Cinema of Christopher Nolan: Imagining the Impossible*, ed. Jacqueline Furby and Stuart Joy, 85–98. New York: Columbia University Press/Wallflower.

Joy, Stuart. 2015. "Introduction: Dreaming a Little Bigger, Darling." In *The Cinema of Christopher Nolan: Imagining the Impossible*, ed. Jacqueline Furby and Stuart Joy, 1–16. New York: Columbia University Press/Wallflower.

Keller, Sarah. 2015. *Maya Deren: Incomplete Control*. New York: Columbia University Press.
Knight, Deborah, and George McKnight. 2009. "Reconfiguring the Past: *Memento* and Neo-*Noir*." In *Memento*, ed. Andrew Kania, 147–66. Oxon: Routledge.
McCahill, Mike. 2010. "Meshes of the Multiplex: *Inception*." *Cinésthesia*, July 16. cinesthesiac.blogspot.com/2010/07/meshes-of-multiplex-inception.html.
McGowan, Todd. 2012. *The Fictional Christopher Nolan*. Austin: University of Texas Press.
Molloy, Claire. 2010. *Memento*. Edinburgh: Edinburgh University Press.
Mooney, Darren. 2018. *Christopher Nolan: A Critical Study of the Films*. Jefferson: McFarland.
Mottram, James. 2002. *The Making of Memento*. London: Faber and Faber.
Mulvey, Laura. 1992. "Visual Pleasure and Narrative Cinema." In *The Sexual Subject: Screen Reader in Sexuality*, ed. Mandy Merck, 22–34. London: Routledge.
Ney, Jason. 2013. "Dark Roots: Christopher Nolan and *Noir*." *Film Noir Foundation*, Summer. filmnoirfoundation.org/noircitymag/Dark-Roots.pdf.
Nolan, Christopher. 2001. *Memento and Following*. London: Faber and Faber.
Prammagiore, Maria. 2001. "Seeing Double(s)." In *Maya Deren and the American Avant-Garde*, ed. Bill Nichols, 237–60. Berkeley: University of California Press.
Rabinovitz, Laura. 2003. *Points of Resistance*. Urbana: University of Illinois Press.
Rhodes, John David. 2011. *Meshes of the Afternoon*. London: BFI/Palgrave Macmillan.
Sharf, Zack. 2015. "Why 'The Quay Brothers in 35mm' is One of Christopher Nolan's Greatest Achievements." *IndieWire*, August 20. www.indiewire.com/2015/08/why-the-quay-brothers-in-35mm-is-one-of-christopher-nolans-greatest-accomplishments-59077/.
Shone, Tom. 2020. *The Nolan Variations*. London: Faber and Faber.
Sousloff, Catherine M. 2001. "Maya Deren Herself." In *Maya Deren and the American Avant-Garde*, ed. Bill Nichols, 105–30. Berkeley: University of California Press.
Toth, Margaret A. 2015. "*Memento*'s Postmodern *Noir* Fantasy: Place, Domesticity and Gender Identity." In *The Cinema of Christopher Nolan: Imagining the Impossible*, ed. Jacqueline Furby and Stuart Joy, 74–84. New York: Columbia University Press/Wallflower.
Turim, Maureen. 2001. "The Ethics of Form." In *Maya Deren and the American Avant-Garde*, ed. Bill Nichols, 77–104. Berkeley: University of California Press.

Chapter 14

"Some Men Just Want to Watch the World Burn"

The Politics of Christopher Nolan's Dark Knight Trilogy

Gregory Frame

Christopher Nolan's The *Dark Knight* trilogy (2005, 2008, 2012) emerged at a moment of profound crisis in American society, between the threat of terrorism and the responses to the 9/11 attacks, followed by the near-collapse of the neoliberal economic order in 2008. Released across a seven-year period encompassing the Bush and Obama administrations, Nolan's films provoked varied political responses and became lightning rods for a host of reasons. This chapter will rehearse these arguments but take advantage of the critical distance afforded by the time that has passed since their initial releases to reassess the trilogy. It will consider the films in light of *Joker* (Todd Phillips, 2019), an origin story of Batman's archnemesis that posited his criminality as a consequence of his social marginalization due to his precarious employment and mental instability and prompted the argument that Arthur Fleck (Joaquin Phoenix) represents the kind of dispossessed, alienated white male who voted for Donald Trump. *Joker* emerged after the populist insurgency that caused profound political ructions around the world, a shift built in part on the dissatisfaction with conventional politicians' responses to the crisis of neoliberalism in 2008. This chapter will therefore consider *The Dark Knight* trilogy as part of the long interregnum between the near-collapse of the neoliberal order and the present moment. It will argue that the trilogy is indicative of the initial phase of neoliberalism's crisis, when politicians sought to preserve and rescue the system rather than fundamentally remake it, a failure that arguably led to the wave of populist anger that has characterized the period since 2012. In this, the chapter will suggest that the trilogy—but particularly *The Dark Knight* and *The Dark Knight Rises*—can be read as an exemplar of "capitalist realism" (Fisher 2009), an argument that the system we have (however problematic) is the only option, and any alternative will lead inevitably to chaos, violence, and disaster. In looking to rescue the decadent, corrupt, and violent Gotham City from the assailants who seek its destruction, Nolan's Batman can therefore be seen as a staunch defender of the neoliberal status quo.

The Dark Knight trilogy posits the rich, white, heterosexual male as society's bulwark against radical, existential threats. It did so at a time when this figure drew considerable popular ire as a consequence of the financial crisis of 2008. Nolan's films should therefore be read as conservative defenders of the neoliberal settlement, as "capitalist realist" (Fisher 2009) texts that seek rescue of the economic and political systems rather than fundamental reforms. In *Capitalist Realism*, Mark Fisher argues that following the collapse of the Soviet Union, we have arrived at a point where capitalism, whatever its imperfections and inadequacies, has become the only viable means of organizing our economy and society. In this he meant that any alternative to capitalism (or, indeed, any modest reform to capitalism as it currently existed) was considered unrealistic, or even unimaginable (2009, 1). One can certainly see his point in the policies that were adopted to address the collapse of the global financial system in 2008: the mobilization of state funds to bail out banks whose failure was considered so catastrophic that such a possibility could not be entertained is the essence of capitalist realism. The emphasis on incremental reform of our social, political, and economic systems after the seismic events of 2008 became the stated policy of most mainstream politicians. Organizations opposed to capitalism, like Occupy Wall Street and its desire for sweeping change of the system after the financial crisis, were caricatured as lunatic fringe movements in the popular press (Darling 2011), reinforcing Fisher's claim that anti-capitalist protest movements have become the "carnivalesque background noise to capitalist realism" (Fisher 2009, 14). As Fisher pointed out in a later work, "capitalist realism isn't the direct endorsement of neoliberal doctrine; it's the idea that, whether we like it or not, the world is governed by neoliberal ideas, and that won't change. There's no point fighting the inevitable" (2013, 90). Anyone who looked to seriously question the organization and operation of the financial markets, and the economic system more generally, was characterized as naïve, dangerous, or both.

This emphasis on "realism" was fundamental to Nolan's trilogy, which sought to depart from the ways in which Batman had been portrayed on screen, at least in comparison with the previous two installments *Batman Forever* (Joel Schumacher, 1995) and *Batman and Robin* (Joel Schumacher, 1997). These films, which followed Tim Burton's successful *Batman* (1989) and *Batman Returns* (1992), were detested by fans and met with critical derision.[1] *Batman and Robin*'s camp, cartoonish qualities—clearly influenced by the 1960s television series starring Adam West—were widely considered to have sounded the death-knell for the series (Winstead 2015, 573). By recruiting Nolan to direct *Batman Begins* (2005), Warner Brothers signaled that they were moving the character away from the "bright, colorful costumes, exaggerated set pieces, and cartoonish, one-dimensional villains" of Schumacher's films, and adopting the tone and style of the comics that had taken a turn toward "masculine brooding, violence, psychological complexity, and loneliness" (Winstead 2015, 575). As Todd McGowan notes, "The cartoonish villains of the Batman series (the Penguin, Poison Ivy, Mr. Freeze) disappear along with the outlandish gadgets that populate Batman's utility belt" (2015, 171). Nolan had by this point developed a reputation as a thoughtful, independent auteur following the critical successes of *Following* (1998), *Memento* (2000), and *Insomnia* (2002), adult-orientated thrillers that suggested he was a director capable of restoring the faith of Batman fans who had so vociferously rejected the apparent frivolity and camp of the previous two films. Dan Hassler-Forest contends that Nolan's *Batman* films should be understood as drawing upon "aspects of the franchise that fans had found the most 'authentic' at least from the 1980s onward—dark, violent, serious—and developed a campaign that maximized the film's legitimacy to these fans while also appealing directly to audiences that were only passingly familiar with this particular superhero" (2012, 89). Considerable emphasis was placed on Nolan's "vision" for *Batman Begins*, and how different it would be from the previous films, particularly in relation to the psychological depth of the central character, and the film's moral complexity (88). In essence, Nolan's involvement sought to infuse the series with the director's auteurist, arthouse prestige at the same time as problematically equating its heteromasculine tone and style with seriousness, and thereby distinguishing it significantly from the character's earlier cinematic incarnations. As Martin Fradley suggests, "this strategic devaluation of 'bad' Bat-pleasures (camp, homoeroticism, brightness, fun) in favour of darkness, violence and machismo are a series of transparently weighted value judgments about gender and sexuality" (2013, 26). The shift in tone and style is apparent from the very first moments of all three films, where the studio and production company logos are shown in black-and-white, blue, or cold gray, connoting seriousness and gritty realism.

This move toward seriousness was embraced by critics, many of whom read the films as reflective of the troubled political times in which they were produced. In addressing themes of terrorism, surveillance, and detention without trial, as well as featuring spectacular scenes of destruction and urban carnage, *The Dark Knight* trilogy can be understood through the prism of post-9/11 politics, and the ethical quandaries posed by the "war on terror." In Batman's willingness to bend (and break) the rules of a liberal society in order to restore order, *The Dark Knight* was read as a justification of George W. Bush's counterterrorism policies, legitimating its transgressions of international law and restrictions of civil liberties (McSweeney 2014, 118). There remains however some debate as to whether Nolan's films are critical of the status quo, or in fact reactionary reinforcements of it. Slavoj Žižek suggested that Bane (Tom Hardy) in *The Dark Knight Rises* represents the "dictatorship of the proletariat," Nolan's film envisioning the moment at which the working classes might seize political power and the means of production from the capitalist establishment (2012). Fisher (2012) considered this view problematic given Bane's ultimate intention to destroy Gotham City, suggesting Bane's stated "emancipatory project" was entirely undermined by the fascistic plan to cleanse the city by incinerating it. The film was understood as painting a revolutionary movement of the kind embodied by Occupy Wall Street around the time of its release as inherently dangerous, reinforcing the suggestion that the films were capitalist realist in approach. As Fradley argues, "As if to bear out Theodor Adorno's worst fears, the narrative arc of the *Dark Knight* franchise ideologically reaffirms the logics of the capitalist system from whence it sprang" (2013, 22).

The ways in which imagery from the trilogy, in particular Heath Ledger's astonishing performance as the anarchic, nihilistic Joker in *The Dark Knight*, found its way into our politics spoke profoundly to the febrile, anxious period after 9/11, and the maladies and morbid symptoms that emerged as a consequence of the 2008 financial crisis. The Tea Party, which drove right-wing populist opposition to President Barack Obama's reform of the US healthcare system in 2009–2010, used posters in its protests that made him up to look like *The Dark Knight*'s Joker, complete with greasepaint and bright red smile. Rachel Miszei-Ward explores the racial connotations of this, arguing that the poster puts forward the notion that Obama's reasonable, moderate, and inclusive approach (his "whiteness") is here constructed as a superficial veneer that disguised his radicalism beneath (his true "blackness") (2012, 183). Moreover, in branding Obama-Joker as "socialist," the poster continued the tendency after the collapse of the financial system in 2008 to equate any vaguely left-wing policy to alter the neoliberal status quo with potential anarchy and chaos, Obama viewed as posing a similar existential threat to the economic and political systems as The Joker himself. As Miszei-Ward argues of the Obama poster, "what is really feared is change as a disruption to American life, which can only lead to destruction and ultimately chaos" (2012, 184). Or, as Emanuelle Wessels and Mark Martinez put it, "The populist charge, that Obama is a masquerading trickster intent on redistributing white wealth to minorities through universal healthcare, is intertwined with the ways in which the popular culture villain has changed to become a reckless 'terrorist' who does not respect money, financial systems, and the 'established order' of medical care" (2015, 77).

In July 2012 James Holmes, having dyed his hair to look like Batman's archnemesis, opened fire at a midnight screening of *The Dark Knight Rises* in Aurora, Colorado, killing twelve and injuring seventy others. Fradley describes the incident as "a tragedy that doubled as something of a grim metaphor for the fate of a generation doomed to be lost in the long-term socio-economic aftermath of the global economic meltdown" (2013, 15). Mass shootings perpetrated by alienated white men proliferated in the years following, often motivated by racism and misogyny. There is certainly evidence in the films to support the view that Nolan's films should be read through the prism of 9/11 and the subsequent "war on terror": the Joker wears a suicide vest, and Batman exploits cutting-edge surveillance technology to spy on Gotham's population in the hope of catching him in *The Dark Knight*, and the beginning of *The Dark Knight Rises* demonstrates the ways in which The Dent Act (modelled on The Patriot Act, passed after 9/11) gives the city the power to imprison suspected criminals without recourse to due process. But the Obama-Joker poster and the mass shooting in Colorado suggest it is perhaps more instructive to consider what the films have to say about broader political developments. These phenomena can be interpreted as disturbing precursors to that which would come later: the backlash against the United States' first black president that would lead to the election of an openly racist authoritarian in Donald Trump, the popularity of whom was built in part on a reliable bedrock of angry white men driven by their feelings of economic disenfranchisement and social exclusion.

Considering *The Dark Knight* trilogy in light of *Joker* is potentially revealing in this regard, as the films emerge at either end of the long interregnum between the near-collapse of the neoliberal economic order and the political turn toward populism that has emerged as a response to it. As Adam Tooze contends, "the financial and economic crisis of 2007–2012 morphed between 2013 and 2017 into a comprehensive political and geopolitical crisis of the post-cold war order" (2018, 20). The absence of Batman in *Joker*, Todd Phillips's origin story of Batman's archnemesis, renders stark his status as defender of the neoliberal status quo in Nolan's films. Phillips's Joker, Arthur Fleck, is a mentally ill, impoverished loner, abused and discarded by a cruel, uncaring economic and political system, rather than a flamboyant trickster working with or alongside organized crime. Fleck responds to these circumstances by taking violent revenge against those he perceives to have wronged him, including a celebrity talk show host (Murray Franklin, played by Robert De Niro), and three suited financiers who taunt and beat him on Gotham's underground subway system. His violent actions inspire a popular movement against the rich elites of Gotham City, his supporters donning clown masks as they engage in violent protest and insurrection at the conclusion of the film. Jeffrey Brown argues that *Joker*, by removing Batman from the equation altogether, poses a challenge to the convention of the superhero film which posits the hero as the glorifier of the status quo. *With* Batman, the Joker becomes the embodiment of chaos, crime, and evil in opposition to the hero's order, justice, and good. *Without* him, "the Joker emerges as a counter-hegemonic embodiment of all the social failings that the status quo seeks to deny and dismiss. The film establishes the Joker as an icon of disaffected uprisings just as sympathetically as Batman is usually presented as a symbol of heroic social control" (2021, 13). In essence, in his absence, Batman's status as the defender of an indefensible system becomes obvious.

The contrast in characterization of Bruce Wayne's father, Thomas, between *The Dark Knight* trilogy and *Joker* renders this vivid: consistent with the comic books, Nolan's films portray Wayne Sr. sympathetically, as a doctor and wealthy philanthropist seeking to help Gotham's poor, and at least partially ameliorate the effects of a desperately unequal and unjust economic system. In *Batman Begins*, for example, Wayne Sr. (Linus Roache) explains how in response to the economic depression that has plagued the city, he helped to build a cheap public transportation system. In this regard, the Wayne Sr. of Nolan's trilogy can be read fairly clearly as a reinforcement of the neoliberal theory that wealth "trickles down" from the top through the largesse and generosity of the rich. Consistent with the establishment perspective of society's millionaires and billionaires in the aftermath of 2008, Wayne Sr. is characterized as a "wealth creator," the kind of supposedly benevolent figure mythologized and defended by the mainstream press. By marked contrast, *Joker* renders Wayne Sr. a rich businessman who speaks contemptuously of Gotham's poor, describing them as envious and blaming them for their own plight. He runs for the city's mayoralty in defense of the economic system that has created such stark inequalities. He is precisely the kind of individual at whom the violence and anger in the film is directed, and consistent with Batman mythology, he is murdered at the film's conclusion (though this time not in a mugging that goes awry, but by a violent protestor). The contrasting characterizations of Wayne Sr. demonstrate the extent to which Nolan's trilogy belongs firmly to the first phase of neoliberalism's crisis, at a point in which most mainstream rhetoric and significant financial resources were devoted to rescuing this system from collapse.

As Matthew Joseph Wolf-Meyer claims, "Batman's primary purpose is one of maintaining hegemonic stability and the position of the upper class, of which Bruce is a part," in order to preserve "the hegemonic order, and particularly one based upon class hierarchies and the privilege of power" (2006, 193). To reinforce this point, the narratives of all three of Nolan's films see

Batman/Bruce Wayne (Christian Bale) standing up against enemies that pose existential threats to Gotham. Batman defeats them all, often having to make significant ethical choices and compromises to save the city. In different ways, the Joker and Bane seek the destruction of the economic and political systems that undergird Gotham. Both could therefore be understood in Gramscian terms as "morbid symptoms" of the kind that emerge at moments of systemic crisis. As Milan Babic notes in relation to the current, ongoing crisis of the liberal international order,

> These symptoms are morbid because they show that the existing order suffers from existential problems that are unlikely to be solved within the limits of the old framework . . . a new, hegemonically stable order does not seem to be on the rise, ready to supplant the old one. This crisis period is thus shaped by morbidities that cannot be managed but at the same time do not represent a viable alternative for the future. (2020, 773)

The Joker, who has no respect for human systems, seeks to achieve social collapse by destroying faith in politics, whereas Bane attempts to foment an uprising against the city's social elite. Moreover, the narrative machinations of the latter film, which suggest Bane's populist revolution is nothing more than a front for The League of Shadows, a secret organization which considers Gotham a corrupt, decadent, and decaying city beyond redemption, is important in order to establish the worldview of the series (the League of Shadows also seeks Gotham's destruction in the first installment of the trilogy, *Batman Begins*). The Joker, Bane, and The League of Shadows have no "viable alternative" to the problems Gotham faces: the choice we are faced with is a status quo of economic inequality and political failure, or apocalypse. In this regard, the films have been read as reflective of the political philosophy of Thomas Hobbes, "who argued that human beings in their natural state are inclined to war and distrust. When the structures of social order are challenged by large-scale disasters, this 'natural state' rears its ugly head again, forcing representatives of that social order to step in and fight to reclaim the social construct" (Patterson 2008, 42). This may be true, but perhaps we should therefore consider the establishment's response to the crisis of neoliberalism as Hobbesian, inasmuch as it sought to rescue and further entrench the economic order by successfully inculcating widespread fear and mistrust of any alternative social, political, and economic formation: rather than engage meaningfully with their calls for economic, racial, and environmental justice, Occupy Wall Street, Black Lives Matter, and Extinction Rebellion have all been characterized by the neoliberal establishment as violent, criminal threats to law and order (Darling 2011; Adams 2020; Moir 2021).

The Dark Knight reinforces the tenets of capitalist realism through its construction and characterization of the Joker. Though the comic books offer competing origin stories for the character, the iterations of the story on which *The Dark Knight* was based see his malevolent anarchism as born of circumstances owing to his impoverished background. In Alan Moore's *The Killing Joke* (1988), The Joker is an unnamed, unemployed engineer working for a chemical company who aids and abets criminals looking to rob the playing-card company next door. Batman confronts him during the robbery, and he attempts to escape by jumping into the chemical plant's waste. His disfigurement, coupled with the fact that his wife and unborn child die as a result of a faulty baby bottle heater, drives him insane to the extent he cannot remember what made him this way. Seemingly playing on the competing versions of the story offered in the comic books, this uncertainty is true of Heath Ledger's Joker in *The Dark Knight*, who offers competing narratives of how he got his scars. The first suggests they were perpetrated by his abusive, alcoholic father, and the second that they were self-inflicted in solidarity with his wife whose face was slashed by gambling sharks to whom she was indebted. The Joker's origin stories suggest his anger stems from the cruel precarity foisted upon him by a broken, decaying society. As Richard D. Heldenfels suggests, "The existing social order—especially its demand for capital to ensure its survival—has given Bruce Wayne wealth and privilege but the Joker only poverty and despair . . . Batman/Bruce Wayne and their upper classes have caused the Joker's rage" (2015, 101). His aim, as he says to Harvey Dent (Aaron Eckhart), is to reveal to the gangsters and the police—ostensibly both sides of the social order the film constructs—"how pathetic their attempts to control things really are." His critique of a system that sees the lives of a soldier or a gangster as disposable because such deaths are expected, or "part of the plan," is a stark comment on the neoliberal system which has so convinced us that its injustices are natural and inevitable that we largely shrug our shoulders when confronted with them. As the Joker says, "Nobody panics when things go according to plan, even when the plan is horrifying," something that could easily be said of neoliberalism as a system of economic and political organization.

However, the inconsistencies in his story suggest he cannot be trusted. In some respects, it is tempting to read Nolan's Joker as precisely the kind of caricature of a dishonest welfare claimant demonized in the right-wing press in the years following the financial crisis, spinning melodramatic yarns as explanations for, or justifications of, his criminality. In this regard, *The Dark Knight* does its utmost to ensure that the Joker's anarchistic revolution should be viewed only with suspicion and fear. This requires a comprehensive "othering" of the Joker in comparison with Batman who, we have established, is the embodiment of heterosexual, masculine, capitalist power. This is reinforced by his appearance. In marked contrast to the earlier styling of Jack Nicholson in Burton's *Batman* as a smooth-talking, nattily dressed 1930s-style gangster, Ledger's Joker is dirty, with greasy, stringy hair, slapdash make-up, and disheveled purple suit, connoting poverty and social marginality. In contrast, every aspect of Batman's costuming and equipment is black, connoting his sober, clean, responsible, adult seriousness, whereas the Joker employs "drag, makeup, visual pageantry, and other elements of camp to prove that the citizens of Gotham can be pushed into depravity" (Winstead 2015, 582). Therefore, Batman's black costuming reflects not only his seriousness but also his heterosexual masculinity, whereas the Joker's style suggests the film asks us to view his anarchic nihilism as not only proletarian but also queer, and therefore even further outside the bounds of hegemonic acceptability as established by the film. This further undermines the Joker's critique of the status quo, for which he has no coherent alternative. The Joker admits to having no rules and no plans, and "wouldn't know what to do" if he caught the metaphorical car, viewing instead the world as inherently chaotic and determined by chance. As Alfred (Michael Caine) says, "Some men just want to watch the world burn." What renders the Joker particularly threatening in a film so invested in the idea of restoring the status quo is his lack of interest in money, which he displays in typically theatrical fashion by burning his half of the cash paid to kill Batman. In equating "the world" with money, the film reinforces the capitalist realist sense that our economic system has become as naturalized a part of the social fabric as the air we breathe, and therefore such disregard is, as J. Hoberman argues, "one of the scariest things about the Joker" (2013, 185). In reducing the Joker's opposition to Batman to the desire to bring about a wholesale collapse of social, economic, and political order in Gotham City, *The Dark Knight* reveals its capitalist realist credentials: as in the period during which the financial crisis took hold, any suggestion to reform or fundamentally alter the neoliberal settlement was caricatured as insane. Here, that insanity is characterized as proletarian queerness, in stark opposition to Batman's aristocratic, heterosexual masculinity.

The Dark Knight trilogy is somewhat confused by its attitude toward human nature, however. In perhaps the most famous example, the Joker orchestrates a moral test whereby he rigs two boats with explosives, one populated with ordinary citizens, and the other with convicted criminals. He gives the passengers on each boat the trigger for the other, assuming that it is inevitable one will blow up the other, as he believes people to be entirely self-interested. In the event both groups of people decline the opportunity, apparently restoring faith in humanity. However, despite this outcome, the masses are not to be trusted with the truth that Harvey Dent, previously viewed as the savior of Gotham City as a district attorney willing and able to stand up to crime and corruption, has turned into a violent criminal after the Joker murdered his girlfriend, Bruce Wayne's childhood friend, Rachel Dawes (Maggie Gyllenhaal). By bringing down Dent, The Joker has at least partially succeeded in proving "that beneath the superficial veneer of civilised society, man is little more than a brutal and savage animal" (McSweeney 2014, 120). It is for this reason that, after killing Dent, "Batman recognizes that if the citizens of Gotham learn about Dent's turn to the dark side, their faith in law and justice will be ruined forever, so he decides to take the blame for the murders that Harvey committed and offers up Batman as the villain that the people need in order to maintain their belief in the system" (McSweeney 2014, 122). Allowing Dent's image to remain unblemished suggests a deep suspicion of the masses, constructed as both infantile in their need to believe in a heroic figure, and potentially dangerous because of the concern as to how they might react if they knew the truth. *The Dark Knight* appears to arrive at the position that order—however it is restored and maintained, even if that means peddling untruths and undermining legal due process through the passage of The Dent Act—is preferable to the only alternative the film can imagine, which is the violent chaos embodied by the Joker. As Helena Bassil-Morozow argues, "The trickster film portrays the capitalist system as unstable, undermined by constant 'stirrings' from 'within'; ready to crumble, ready to be reduced to chaos" (2011, 93). The threat the Joker poses to the system articulates this vividly and clearly.

The Dark Knight is therefore very much a product of its moment, offering a moral compromise and restoration of a fragile social order more akin to a sigh of relief than an ideologically sound "happy ending." In this respect, rather than view it solely through the prism of the violations of constitutional and legal norms during the "war on terror," it is instructive to think of *The Dark Knight* as embodying the spirit of the interregnum period following the near-collapse of the neoliberal economic order. To save Gotham, Batman, in cahoots with his colleague Lucius Fox (Morgan Freeman), utilizes technology capable of spying on all the citizens of the city to find The Joker. While Fox objects to the wild (and unconstitutional) infringement of privacy, he acquiesces to Batman's demands on the basis that it is reasonable for men of benign intention to trample on constitutional norms in order to restore order. Many critics interpreted this as providing ideological support to the Patriot Act, legislation passed in the aftermath of 9/11 that radically expanded the surveillance abilities of law enforcement. This is no doubt a compelling reading, though it may be even more revealing to consider it in light of what was to come shortly thereafter. *The Dark Knight*'s rescue of Gotham's social, political, and economic order at the conclusion of the film reinforces the central tenet of capitalist realism: while the system may be far from perfect (indeed, it may be obviously corrupt, manifestly inadequate, and seemingly doomed to failure), our governing elites have so successfully convinced us that the only alternative is violent disorder that we passively accept what we are given for fear of something even worse.

This compromised conclusion of *The Dark Knight* and its restoration of a fragile order in Gotham City presages a more comprehensive engagement with the neoliberal crisis in its sequel, *The Dark Knight Rises*. The film attracted considerable critical attention for its apparently conservative politics. Telling the story of a proletarian revolution in Gotham that functions as cover for The League of Shadows' attempt to use Wayne Enterprises' fusion reactor to execute a genocidal destruction of the city, Fisher described it as "a reactionary vision which can only imagine radical social transformation as catastrophic" (Fisher and White 2012). Fradley suggests the film's political meanings are deliberately vague, so viewers of any persuasion would find something to support their worldview (20). However, it is difficult to see the film as ambivalent given the overwhelming evidence to the contrary. Bane is determined to show the people of Gotham the truth of their city, revealing the reality about Dent's crimes and attempting to destroy their faith in the system as a precursor to bringing it down. He attacks the Stock Exchange, bankrupts Gotham's rich, and sets up a kangaroo court to exile and kill them. The court is presided over by Jonathan Crane (Cillian Murphy), the malevolent psychiatrist who was the main villain in *Batman Begins*, suggesting we should not view these events with anything other than horror. Wealthy CEOs are hauled in front of him and sentenced to death or exile, with the latter effectively amounting to a death sentence. Žižek's claim that the film worries at themes of economic inequality and proletarian revolution without taking a definitive perspective seems wide of the mark. As McGowan suggests, while the film does highlight the injustice of Gotham's class system, "the primary voices of this indictment are those of the villains" (2012). The court scenes suggest that "the absence of the hetero-masculine power structure results in chaos, anarchy, and a world ruled by the lawless. It is the white male American dream that needs saving, and Batman shows up to deliver its salvation" (Winstead 2015, 583). Given that the revolution is prevented, Batman sacrifices himself to save Gotham from the explosion, and police officer John Blake (Joseph Gordon-Levitt) (whose real name is Robin) appears to have had Batman's mantle handed to him by the man himself at the conclusion, it seems the film is fairly definitive in its assessment that the restoration and maintenance of order, however imperfect, is contingent upon strong, male, vigilante action, and something to be celebrated.

The film's ideological standpoint can be further understood through the character of Selina Kyle (Anne Hathaway), the cat burglar who steals from the rich. She articulates her belief in a proletarian revolution at the beginning of the film, when she informs Wayne that he and his friends "better batten down the hatches, because when it hits, you're all going to wonder how you ever thought you could live so large and leave so little for the rest of us." She gives voice to the disenchantment with the persistence of the neoliberal settlement after 2008 that was embodied by the Occupy Wall Street protests, and consistently affirms her Robin Hood–like approach to theft where she claims to steal only from people with more than enough. However, the radical potential of the character as a counterhegemonic rebel is ultimately recuperated into a narrative which seeks the restoration of capitalist, patriarchal power and authority. By the conclusion of the film, Kyle seemingly abandons her radicalism, joins in the effort to defeat Bane, and stop Talia Al Ghul's (Marion Cotillard) attempt to destroy the city. An earlier clue that she is having second thoughts about a violent revolution against the super-rich comes when she surveys the wreckage of a wealthy family's apartment. She picks up a framed photograph of the family, the glass of which is shattered, and describes it sentimentally as "someone's home." She appears doubtful when her friend celebrates its violent confiscation. Through Kyle, the film determines that violent revolution and summary justice are unacceptable means to achieve political change. In humanizing the moneyed victims of this revolution, many of whom have built their wealth on the relentless exploitation of human labor and natural resources, the film takes a fairly clear stance: Bane's call for the ordinary people of Gotham to seize their city from the rich is something to be feared and rejected, not celebrated or supported. Kyle's reconsideration of her position and ultimate support of Batman is confirmation of this: rather than flee Gotham, which she beseeches Batman to do, she returns to play her part in restoring the hegemonic order.

With the benefit of hindsight, it is clear that the relationship between *The Dark Knight* trilogy and the politics of the time is worthy of reappraisal given the populist insurgencies in western democracies since the final installment was released in 2012. In this light, it becomes even more obvious that Batman/Bruce Wayne should be viewed as the defender and protector of capital and establishment interests at a time when such forces and institutions had come under considerable scrutiny after the near-collapse of the financial system in 2008. By positing the white, heterosexual billionaire as the hero and protector of a status quo that benefits his interests, Nolan's films should be interpreted as conservative responses to the crisis in its initial phase. Wayne personifies the benign capitalist that right-wing discourse sought to defend against populist anger after 2008, and to rehabilitate as an essential component in the recovery of the capitalist system after the recession. Following the billion-dollar success of *Joker* at the global box office in 2019 which posits Batman's archnemesis not as the nihilistic anarchist of Nolan's film, but as an (anti)hero for whom we are invited to have some empathy as an economically disenfranchised social outcast, it is difficult to view *The Dark Knight* trilogy as vocalizing anything other than a reinforcement of the neoliberal status quo. Indeed, *The Batman* (Matt Reeves, 2022) appears to take considerable inspiration from *Joker*. The film suggests The Riddler's (Paul Dano) hideous crimes are born of his political and economic marginality, and like Fleck, he inspires an army of the disaffected to rebel violently against the corrupt city establishment. Batman/Bruce Wayne (Robert Pattinson) is not the swaggering playboy of Nolan's trilogy but an addled recluse who comes to realize his vigilantism is an ineffective response to Gotham's social, political, and economic problems: he fails to prevent The Riddler's grand scheme from coming to fruition. Unlike Nolan's trilogy where Gotham City is worth saving because the alternatives are shown to be far worse, *The Batman* portrays it as entirely irredeemable: damp, decaying, and rotten to its core, it is more akin to the unnamed megalopolis in *Se7en* (David Fincher, 1995), and the film leaves us in no doubt that it is the rich, white men who slide easily between the worlds of politics, organized crime, and big business who are to blame. *Joker* and *The Batman* demonstrate that, in celebrating the rich white man as our great defender and protector rather than the cause of so many of the world's ills—social, political, economic, environmental—Nolan's vision of the caped crusader is no longer the hero we deserve, or need.

NOTE

1. See *Rotten Tomatoes* for a snapshot of the critical consensus on *Batman Forever* (www.rottentomatoes.com/m/batman_forever) and *Batman and Robin* (www.rottentomatoes.com/m/1077027-batman_and_robin).

REFERENCES

Adams, Guy. 2020. "Revealed: The British Arm of Black Lives Matter's Full Agenda—Abolish the Police, Smash Capitalism . . . and Close All Prisons." *Mail Online*, June 19. www.dailymail.co.uk/news/article-8441405/The-avowed-aims-British-arm-Black-Lives-Matter.html.
Babic, Milan. 2020. "Let's Talk about the Interregnum: Gramsci and the Crisis of the Liberal World Order." *International Affairs* 96, no. 3: 767–86.
Bassil-Morozow, Helena. 2011. *The Trickster in Contemporary Film*. London: Taylor and Francis.
Brown, Jeffrey. 2021. "A City without a Hero: *Joker* and Rethinking Hegemony." *New Review of Film and Television Studies* 19, no. 1: 7–18.
Darling, Brian. 2011. "Occupy Wall Street: A Movement Filled with Simple Minded Leftists Greedy for Publicity." *Mail Online*, November 8. www.dailymail.co.uk

/debate/article-2045040/Occupy-Wall-Street-A-movement-filled-simple-minded-leftists-greedy-publicity.html.

Fisher, Mark. 2009. *Capitalist Realism*. Winchester: Zero Books.

Fisher, Mark, and Jeremy Gilbert. 2013. "Capitalist Realism and Neoliberal Hegemony: A Dialogue." *New Formations*, 80–81: 89–101.

Fisher, Mark, and Rob White. 2012. "The Politics of *The Dark Knight Rises*: A Discussion." *Film Quarterly*, September 4. filmquarterly.org/2012/09/04/the-politics-of-the-dark-knight-rises-a-discussion/.

Fradley, Martin. 2013. "What Do You Believe In? Film Scholarship and the Cultural Politics of the *Dark Knight* Franchise." *Film Quarterly* 66, no. 3: 15–27.

Hassler-Forest, Dan. 2012. *Capitalist Superheroes: Caped Crusaders in the Neoliberal Age*. Winchester: Zero Books.

Heldenfels, Richard D. 2015. "More than the Hood was Red: The Joker as Marxist." In *The Joker: A Serious Study of the Clown Prince of Crime*, ed. Robert Moses Peaslee and Robert G. Weiner, 94–108. Jackson: University Press of Mississippi.

Hoberman, J. 2013. *Film after Film: Or, What Became of 21st Century Cinema?* London: Verso.

McGowan, Todd. 2012. "Should the Dark Knight Have Risen?" *Jump Cut* 54. www.ejumpcut.org/archive/jc54.2012/McGowanDarkKnight/index.html.

McGowan, Todd. 2015. "Stumbling Over the Superhero: Christopher Nolan's Victories and Compromises." In *The Cinema of Christopher Nolan: Imagining the Impossible*, eds. Jacqueline Furby and Stuart Joy, 164–74. London: Wallflower Press.

McSweeney, Terence. 2014. *The "War on Terror" and American Film: 9/11 Frames Per Second*. Edinburgh: Edinburgh University Press.

Miszei-Ward, Rachel. 2012. "Politics, Race, and Political Fly-Billing: Barack Obama as 'The Joker.'" *Comparative American Studies* 10, nos. 2–3: 177–87.

Moir, Jan. 2021. "Why I'm So Pleased to See XR's Wanton Vandalism . . . Each Stunt and Act of Sedition Is Another Nail in Your Coffin, not Ours." *Mail Online*, September 2. www.dailymail.co.uk/debate/article-9952847/JAN-MOIR-Im-pleased-XRs-wanton-vandalism-stunt-nail-coffin.html.

Patterson, Brett Chandler. 2008. "*No Man's Land*: Social Order in Gotham City and New Orleans." In *Batman and Philosophy: The Dark Knight of the Soul*, ed. Mark D. White and Robert Arp, 41–54. Hoboken: Wiley and Sons.

Tooze, Adam. 2018. *Crashed: How a Decade of Financial Crises Changed the World*. London: Penguin Books.

Wessels, Emanuelle, and Mark Martinez. 2015. "The Obama-Joker: Assembling a Populist Monster." In *The Joker: A Serious Study of the Clown Prince of Crime*, ed. Robert Moses Peaslee and Robert G. Weiner, 65–81. Jackson: University of Mississippi Press.

Winstead, Nick. 2015. "'As a Symbol I Can Be Incorruptible': How Christopher Nolan De-
Queered the Batman of Joel Schumacher." *Journal of Popular Culture* 48, no. 3: 572–85.

Wolf-Meyer, Matthew Joseph. 2006. "Batman and Robin in the Nude, or Class and Its Exceptions." *Extrapolation* 47, no. 2: 187–206.

Žižek, Slavoj. 2012. "The Politics of Batman." *New Statesman*. August 23. www.newstatesman.com/culture/culture/2012/08/slavoj-žižek-politics-batman.

Chapter 15

The Experimental Short Films of Christopher Nolan

Stuart Joy

Produced during his formative years as a student, Christopher Nolan's short films have attracted comparatively little critical attention when set against the backdrop of his feature filmmaking. Indeed, the existing discourse surrounding Nolan's work is overwhelmingly focused on the director's theatrical releases, Todd McGowan's *The Fictional Christopher Nolan* (2012), Jason T. Eberl's coedited collection with George A. Dunn titled *The Philosophy of Christopher Nolan* (2017), Darren Mooney's 2018 critical companion, Tom Shone's biographical account *The Nolan Variations* (2020), and even my own *The Cinema of Christopher Nolan* (2015) and *The Traumatic Screen* (2020) are guilty of avoiding an in-depth discussion of Nolan's short films. While these works each have something significant to offer readers, what is clearly missing from the current scholarship surrounding Nolan is a detailed analysis of his shorts.

There are practical reasons why these texts have been neglected thus far, partly because *Tarantella* (1989) and *Larceny* (1996) have not been made widely available; the former aired only once on public broadcast television, and the latter featured briefly at the Cambridge Film Festival.[1] But the reluctance of scholars to critically engage with Nolan's third short film *Doodlebug* (1997) is indicative of a broader disregard of the form (see Felando 2015, 2). With this in mind, this chapter attempts to address the assumptions surrounding the artistic and cultural value afforded to short films by offering an in-depth discussion of *Tarantella* and *Doodlebug*. Specifically, I argue that Nolan's well-documented preoccupation with the passing of time is heavily indebted to the structure and stylistic properties of the short film form.

SIZE MATTERS?

Christopher Nolan's career is often framed by critics in terms of scale and spectacle. Writing at the time of *Inception*'s release in 2010, for example, Dave Iztkoff argued that the film cemented Nolan's reputation as a "blockbuster auteur," one who had made "bigness his medium" (see Itzkoff 2010). Ten years later, following the release of *Tenet* (2020), Luke Holland went even further by labelling Nolan the only "mega-budget auteur" working in Hollywood today (2020). Nolan's widely celebrated status as one of the most financially successful filmmakers of the twenty-first century is perhaps unsurprising; the budgets of his films have increased steadily over the past two decades, and his films frequently earn in excess of $500 million while regularly receiving widespread acclaim. However, the critical and commercial emphasis on Nolan's blockbuster films highlights the need to focus our attention elsewhere on his lesser-known short films which, by comparison, only cost a few hundred dollars and barely last more than a few minutes. The significance of these films in cultivating Nolan's artistic identity should not be understated. From a practical perspective, he approached the production of his debut feature *Following* (1998) as a series of short films shot over numerous weekends (see Mooney 2018, 18). Elsewhere, the opening sequences of *Memento* (2000), *Insomnia* (2002), and *The Prestige* (2006) also bear the hallmarks of the short fiction film.[2] For example, these sequences engage rather than tell (see Riis 1998); whether it is the image of a bullet being sucked back into its barrel, a mysterious figure wiping away blood at the scene of a crime, or a vista of black top hats scattered among fallen branches in a glade, these openings arouse our curiosity. Such thinking about the function of the short film form is not new though; Tom Gunning (1986), for instance, has suggested that we see early short films as part of a "cinema of attractions" that directly solicits the spectator's attention, "inciting visual curiosity, and supplying pleasure through an exciting spectacle" (58). Thus, we can see how Nolan's feature filmmaking is indebted to the short film form especially when we consider the prologues of *The Dark Knight* (2008), *The Dark Knight Rises* (2012), and *Tenet*; these films contain, among other visual spectacles, a daring daylight bank heist, a mid-air extraction, and a time-defying hostage crisis. And so, contained within Nolan's short films are the antecedents of a thematic and formal schemata upon which he has built his subsequent career.

A BRIEF NOTE ON BREVITY

The French-Swiss filmmaker Jean-Luc Godard is among one of the most frequently cited film directors to have drawn a distinction between the feature film and the short film. He suggests that the latter, with its brevity and strict narrative economy, cannot offer sufficient depth or complexity of character. In comparison to the feature-length film, he says, "the short film does not have time to think" (1972, 110). Despite this and other similar claims, the brevity of the short film form is not an indicator of an inferior nor primitive kind of filmmaking, indeed quite the contrary. Anthony Julian Tamburri, for example, contends that the brevity and conciseness of the short film constitutes some of its most appealing characteristics (2002, 3). Similarly, Derrick Knight and Vincent Porter insist that equating the length of a film with narrative depth is a dramatic oversimplification of the pleasures that short films can offer (1967, 6). Elsewhere, the short film theorist Richard Raskin says, "More than any other form of cinematic narrative, the short fiction film heightens our sense of the preciousness and immediacy of the moment, both in the events portrayed and in the storytelling process" (2015, 173). In both respects, he argues, the short film demonstrates that "every second can be made to count far more than we might otherwise expect, and implicitly reminds us never to underestimate how much meaningful and enriching experience can be encompassed by the briefest span of time" (173). Film historian Tom Gunning acknowledges that while the short film form is principally defined by duration, short films are distinct from feature films in more ways than their running time (2015, 67). Instead of considering the length of a short film to be its defining quality, Gunning asks what other pleasures these films can offer when contrasted with their longer counterparts (2015, 67). He provides an answer by suggesting that there is something unique about the short film form that is rooted in the spectator's experience of time.

Drawing on the work of Viennese filmmaker Peter Kubelka, Gunning exposes the variety of temporal forms that short films can take by breaking up or ignoring conventional narrative patterns and seeking out precisely the defamiliarizing effects of noncontinuous time (67). He concludes that short films are not merely briefer than feature films but that their brevity can create an altogether different experience of time, one that is concentrated and intense (70). To argue, as Gunning implicitly does, that such intensity cannot be sustained throughout the duration of a feature film depends on the way that time is constructed and used. For instance, such intensity can be found in Nolan's own experiments with cinematic time across several of his feature films, notably through his use of cross-cutting: *Following*, for example, shuffles three different timelines, and *Memento* cuts back and forth between two, one running forward and the other backward. In *The Prestige*, Nolan shifts between four different time periods, and in *Inception* the spectator moves seamlessly between five. In *Interstellar*, time functions as a relative and physical construct that aligns a father's emotional struggle with the fate of humankind, whereas in *Dunkirk*, time is the enemy of the Allied soldiers awaiting rescue on the beaches of Northern France. *Tenet*, meanwhile, is constructed as if it were a narrative palindrome with time running in both directions so that cause and effect are blurred. The experience of time, then, is Nolan's greatest preoccupation visible throughout his feature-length films. But it is an obsession that is evident even in his earliest work, thereby foregrounding the significant role that short film plays in fostering the creativity of aspiring artists.

PICTURES OF THE PAST

Film's relationship to time has often been understood as central to its artistic and cultural significance. Walter Benjamin, for instance, was among the first to recognize the transcendent capabilities of the still image to capture the "Here and Now" (1931, 243). For Benjamin, the power of photography emerges from the way in which the past asserts itself in the present. Half a century later, Roland Barthes would also demonstrate an awareness of the temporal disjuncture inherent in the medium when noting, "The type of consciousness the photograph involves is indeed truly unprecedented, since it establishes not a consciousness of the *being-there* of the thing . . . but an awareness of its *having-been-there*" (1977, 44, emphasis in original). In film, however, he says, "the *having-been-there* gives way before a being-there of the thing" (1977, 45, emphasis in original). Here Barthes foregrounds what he perceives to be the fundamental distinction between a photograph's essential *pastness* and film's essential *presentness*, a quality also recognized by Nolan who says that "the camera literally sees time. Before the camera, before cinema, there was no way for human beings to visualize either a still frame instant or reverse chronology—visually seeing things backward" (quoted in Mottram 2020, 12). He goes on to note that "it's purely the product of the mechanism of the camera that allows us this great insight into reality. . . . It's a view of the world that can only exist cinematically" (Mottram 2020, 12). What Nolan appreciates is that the extraordinary nature of the moving image resides in its capacity not only to preserve the moment but also to give time a visible and real form by virtue of duration.

Cinema possesses a unique capability among the arts to represent duration. At the simplest level, a film's duration lies in its very nature; film unfolds in time. In her chapter "Timetravel and European Film," Wendy Everett calls attention to what she believes to be one of the defining features of film, that is, "[i]ts lack of tense system" (2005, 109). Now, one *might* argue that everything a film presents is already past tense. After all, the images shown were filmed and assembled in the weeks, months, and even years prior to exhibition; the only changes that occur during the screening of a film are the viewer's knowledge of what happened and when, and in what order. Accordingly, plot time is also in the past tense. However, Everett highlights how the viewer experiences the progression of filmic images (what is in actuality a continuous string of "and then" statements) as a series of continuous "now statements." She remarks, "It is the nature of the filmic image to be perceived by the spectator as actually taking place, as occurring in the continuous present" (2005, 109).[3] Film does more, however, than merely capture the duration of a moment; complex temporalities can be transmitted through the pattern of shot-to-shot editing. Writing in their book on fantasy film, Jacqueline Furby and Claire Hines note that "film can make time slow, stop, stretch, and reverse, leap ahead and back, shrink, speed up, be elided, or repeated; film is able to present time in any order, and reverse the future-directed flow of cause and effect" (2012, 150). Such complex manipulation of time is not commonly associated with the short fiction film form; Cynthia Felando, for example, suggests that a film's running time tends to correlate with its capacity for narrative complexity: "Thus, the 'shorter short,' of five minutes or less, favors rudimentary stories" (2015, 47). However, the experimental short film—while difficult to define—often seeks to explore a break from the linear experience of time by exposing the materiality and mechanical nature of the cinematic apparatus. I have argued elsewhere that such an embrace of modernist art techniques can be seen across Nolan's various feature films (see Joy 2020), but here I am suggesting that we can trace this interest to his formative experimentation in the short film form beginning with *Tarantella*.

TARANTELLA

Produced during a gap year between school and university, *Tarantella* was codirected with Nolan's childhood friend Roko Belic. Shot in color on Super 8mm, *Tarantella* presents four distinct vignettes, each separated by a fade to black. Described by Nolan as "just a surreal short, a string of images" (quoted in Shone 2020, 48), the film carries with it the torch of the avant-garde movement. It is beyond the scope of this chapter to present a history of the avant-garde,[4] and such a history does not even, as David E. James points out, "assert a single, restrictive formulation of the concept" (2005, 13). Nevertheless, in its simplest iteration, we might say that avant-garde filmmakers principally operate in opposition to their mainstream counterparts; these films are often low budget, deeply personal, and frequently disseminated outside of traditional distribution and exhibition channels (see Dulac 1987). It is also worthwhile noting that there has been a long-standing historical connection between the avant-garde and the short film form. Gunning, for instance, in his essay "An Unseen Energy Swallows Space" (1983), was among the first to identify the aesthetic and conceptual links between early cinema and the avant-garde. Central to his comparison of both types of cinemas is the temporal relationship between the spectator and the screen.

In what Gunning and André Gaudreault later go on to call the "cinema of attractions," the spectator is not positioned as an invisible voyeur deeply immersed in the film's fictional diegesis; instead, early short film relied on an exhibitionist mode of representation that knowingly aroused the spectator's visual curiosity through a direct and acknowledged act of display (see Gunning 1986). Writing a few years later, Gunning acknowledged that this unique spectatorial address amounted to an entirely different temporal relationship in so far as the "attractions" disrupted the traditional flow of time as a series of successive instants: "The potential shock of the cinema of attractions provided a popular form of an alternative temporality based not on the mimesis of memory or other psychological states," but rather "on an intense interaction between an astonished spectator and the cinematic smack of the instant, the flicker of presence and absence" (Gunning 1993, 10). For Gunning, the capacity of early film to create a break from the linear experience of time through moments of excess was akin to later displays of formal ingenuity, thematic content, and the stylistic inventiveness that defined the avant-garde (1993, 10). This is not to say that avant-garde cinema is incompatible with the sequential flow of narrative time that we associate with classical cinema. Elsewhere, Gunning notes that one could possibly "conceive of an avant-garde film that would make narrative strategies and their use of suspenseful time visible, making narrative form an avant-garde theme by defamiliarizing it" (2017, 22). This description brings to mind a film like *Dunkirk*, whose three separate narrative threads run at different speeds, repeat, and converge, leading to a formal identity crisis that neither Nolan nor his producing partner Emma Thomas can agree upon: "she thought it was an art film pretending to be a mainstream film, and I think it's a mainstream film pretending to be art film. The two things are very different . . . languages of filmmaking" (Nolan quoted in Shone 2020, 287–88). The filmmaker is right to point out a fundamental difference between the two forms, but it is here, at the intersection between mainstream and art cinema, that we can situate not only a film like *Dunkirk* but also most of Nolan's work beginning with his shorts.

Take, for example, *Tarantella*'s rich collection of disjointed scenes. The presentation of the images is in keeping with the experimental nature of the avant-garde which frequently undermines the traditional stabilities of storytelling. But, as with *Inception*, Nolan employs the framing device of a man's (Roko Belic) restless sleep which renders the film's loose narrative structure as one steeped within the logic of dreamscapes. This technique affords Nolan the legitimacy to embrace modernist filmmaking techniques that would otherwise have a distancing effect on the spectator. The first section, for example, contains multiple dislocations and discontinuities in space and time: fleeting shots of a ripple effect in water, the shadow of a ceiling fan cast against the backdrop of a grid, and the silhouette of a tarantula. Each of these moments represents, to use Gunning's words, a "temporal irruption rather than a temporal development" (1993, 7). However, by intercutting these images with an increasingly tight aerial zoom on the protagonist's strained facial expression, it becomes clear that these images are meant to be perceived as the mental projections of the dreamer, rather than abstraction for the sake of abstraction. In the film, a series of ensuing close-ups focusing on the young man's closed eyelids cement this oneiric association thereby neutralizing the "attraction" through a process of narrativization.

The next vignette begins with a point-of-view (POV) shot taken from the perspective of the protagonist as he walks down the hallway of a middle-class suburban home. He arrives at a well-lit living area containing, among other items, a large sofa, chairs, a bookcase, a piano, and a ceiling fan. The film then cuts to a low angle of a mysterious figure (Christopher Nolan) who abruptly appears in the room. Dressed entirely in black, the man raises an empty hand and "catches" a fallen wine glass; those familiar with the opening of *Memento* and the inverted scenes in *Tenet* will immediately recognize this technique of reversing the film stock to alter the spectator's perception of time. Here, even at this early stage of his career, Nolan's understanding of cinema's ability to make time visible is clear. The two men then sit at opposite ends of a dinner table; a right-to-left tracking shot of the man in black is momentarily interrupted by a close-up shot of a tarantula that adopts the same camera movement and direction. The shock of this unexpected shot comes from the unpredictability of the instant which has no grounding in conventional narrative logic. Instead, once again, it merely highlights the temporally disjunctive potential of the "attraction." The next shot also repeats the previous tracking motion, albeit on this occasion moving from left to right with a view of the protagonist. The next shot, a head-on composition of the man in black at the top of the dinner table, dollies forward as he moves a wine glass from his right hand to his left, thereby physically mirroring the protagonist. This shot is followed by a return to the imagery of the silhouetted tarantula, a close-up of a pair of human eyes, and then a fade to black. Such fractured imagery emphasizes the strange, dreamlike quality that makes the narrative trajectory of the film subservient to the cinematic form—that is, rather than serving the narrative, the form becomes the subject of the film itself.

The third vignette of *Tarantella* opens with a shot of the city streets taken from a moving vehicle. A quick cut to the protagonist sleeping again draws attention to our inability to distinguish between fantasy and reality, a recurring thematic trait of Nolan's subsequent feature films. The short film then cuts to several handheld shots of the young man running through a metropolitan area. A passing glimpse of the man in black staring directly into the camera is followed by a brief shot of the protagonist who is seen wandering through the hallway of the middle-class home once again, although on this occasion the interior is darkened. In his only documented discussion of *Tarantella*, Nolan's remarks are largely anecdotal. For example, he emphasizes the coincidental nature of using the same filming location where he would go on to shoot the chase scenes from *Batman Begins* and *The Dark Knight* (see Shone 2020, 48). However, within his comments exists a deeper reflection on the impact that his upbringing as a dual citizen of Britain and the United States had on his approach to filmmaking. He says:

> The interesting thing about my memory is I can still remember that impression, that feeling of how fragmented the city was. When you think about what your memories do, what your brain is doing, it's holding two contradictory ideas in the same physical space, sort of in opposition, with no problem. I'm the product of two cultures and I've grown up in two places, and I think that makes you think about the concept of home a little differently, because it's not as simple as geography necessarily. (Quoted in Shone 2020, 48)

The spatial and temporal defamiliarization that Nolan describes in this passage may offer a useful way of understanding the fractured narrative of *Tarantella* as well as the imagery contained within the short film. This is especially evident when combined with the knowledge that Belic was a first-generation immigrant also living *in* and *between* multiple cultures as the son of Czechoslovakian and Yugoslavian parents. In the film, for example, there exists a dramatic tension between interior and exterior spaces, the home and the city. In the scenes set in the middle-class suburban location, the protagonist looks unfamiliar with his surroundings, although at ease. In contrast, during the scenes set at night in downtown Chicago the young man seems afraid, running from something or someone. The erratic handheld camerawork and darkened visuals also emphasize the threat of the city, while the empty streets capture the loneliness and isolation of living in an urban environment.[5]

The concluding vignette of *Tarantella* starts with a shot of a static-filled television screen, but the pacing quickens due to a right-to-left whip pan around the setting that shows the protagonist asleep once again. A close-up of an eye with the superimposed footage from a moving vehicle is followed by a slow zoom on the tarantula. Unexpectedly, a bald statuesque figure appears on screen, his pained expression frozen in time. The camera zooms in on his gaping mouth before transitioning to a series of extreme close-ups (ECUs) of another face, its features distorted by the proximity of the camera. The film ends with an ECU of an eye, the camera slowly zooming in on the pupil before fading to black.

Ultimately, the film's conclusion refuses to satisfy the conventional narrative demands of cause and effect. Instead, the pleasure derived from watching *Tarantella* emerges from the enigmatic and repetitious imagery which enacts meaning through recursion rather than resolution. This is perhaps unsurprising given Nolan's preponderance for enigmatic endings in his feature films that frequently initiate a closed loop of desire among spectators whose desire remains unfulfilled, perpetually repeating itself in such a way that points toward the enjoyment of this failure (see Joy 2020, 35). In truth, I have glossed over many details of this complex film. Suffice to say that whatever else it may or may not mean, Nolan's first short film establishes a formal and thematic foundation upon which he would structure his next short, *Doodlebug*; once again, circularity, recursion, repetition, and open-endedness are at the center of this film, but what is remarkable is that these themes would go on to shape Nolan's understanding of film practice, film aesthetics, and filmic time throughout his subsequent career.

DOODLEBUG

The three-minute-long short fiction film, produced by Emma Thomas and Steven Street, was shot on 16mm during Nolan's time at University College London (UCL). The film features a lone character, a disheveled looking man (Jeremy Theobald) chasing what seems to be, at least initially, a bug. As it scurries around the dilapidated apartment setting, the man stalks his prey with a shoe in hand. He tries desperately to squash the eponymous "doodlebug" but fails on a number of occasions. Eventually, he corners his quarry only to discover that his victim is not a bug, but a miniature version of himself. Even more bizarrely, his diminutive doppelganger is chasing an even smaller man. In the short film's climactic moments, the man crushes his adversary with the shoe, only after we have witnessed his victim carry out the very same action. Suddenly, but not entirely unexpectedly, the giant likeness of the protagonist glides into view behind him, his eyes providing a hint of the same jubilant smile as he brings a larger shoe down on the protagonist. The film ends on a shot of the murder weapon which partially fills the frame; the credits roll and the screen fades to black, but the threat of an even bigger shoe exists, undoubtedly poised to drop in a never-ending cascade of cause and effect.

Despite this seeming closure, the meaning of *Doodlebug* is intentionally ambiguous, and the ending is left open to interpretation. This is an approach that has informed several of Nolan's subsequent feature films. Erin Hill-Parks, for example, remarks that "the endings of [his] films are left in an uneasy truce between characters and meanings, with the audience being offered only a partial resolution. The ambiguity frames possible resolutions, but forces the audience to examine their own understandings" (2010, 67–68). Instances such as whether Ellie (Hillary Swank) chooses to divulge Detective Dormer's (Al Pacino) indiscretions at the end of *Insomnia*; the proper meaning of Cutter's (Michael Caine) closing narration in *The Prestige*; and the fate of Cobb's (Leonardo DiCaprio) spinning top in the last moments of *Inception* are just a few examples of the unanswered questions that encourage viewers to repeatedly return to these films in search of meaning. In each case, the final reveal draws attention to how we are positioned as spectators and what, as a consequence, we may or may not understand.

Leading up to the conclusion of *Doodlebug*, a variety of camera setups are combined with a camera that is often in motion, leading the spectator to draw incorrect assumptions and to misunderstand actions and events. As Nolan explains on the audio commentary accompanying the DVD release of the film, this decision was primarily motivated by a desire to experiment with a more formal approach to filmmaking. He says, "The first film that we'd done [*Larceny*] was a short film that I did entirely handheld, black and white, 16mm. . . . But with this film I wanted to try a different technique and have every shot as a tracking shot."[6] However, the technical experiments of *Doodlebug* do not merely concern the practicalities of cinematic aesthetics. Instead, they have the effect of aligning the viewer with the protagonist as he stalks what we initially assume to be a bug. The positioning of the camera, for example, on several occasions as a POV shot encourages the audience to adopt a shared perspective with the character. Writing in *The Philosophy of Christopher Nolan*, George McKnight and Deborah Knight observe that:

> Whenever the protagonist looks at something, the camera position changes so we see what he's looking at, usually in closer detail. The scale of shots change with The Man's movements, frequently putting viewers in close proximity to his face and expressions. Camera position and movement along with editing create a sense of access and transparency. We seem to see and understand what is happening. But things are not as they seem. . . . What we were watching turns out to be something quite different from what we first thought. (2017, 104)

At the climax of *Doodlebug*, viewers are confronted with the realization that they have been misled through their epistemic alignment with the central character's subjective experience. The Man was not trying to kill a bug, but a smaller version of himself. Similarly, the protagonist of Nolan's debut feature was not following, but in fact being led; Leonard Shelby (Guy Pearce) was not on a quest to hunt down his wife's killer in *Memento* but repressing his own role in her death; it was not a criminal attempting to remove evidence in *Insomnia*, but Detective Dormer framing a suspect; and so on. In each ending, the revelation has the dramatic effect of causing a temporal reconfiguration as we rewrite our prior knowledge of the events that have transpired.

In an interview for the Associated Press, Nolan underscored the significance of film endings by contrasting them with the continuous nature of television serial dramas, saying: "The thing about cinema is it's a very different medium. Yes, it has photographic cameras, actors speaking, it has music and it's on a screen, but *it's the ending that defines the experience*" (Coyle 2018, emphasis added). Nolan's emphasis on the importance of film endings is shared by those who understand the intrinsic formal properties of the short film. Writing in *Discovering Short Films*, Cynthia Felando observes that in short film analyses endings tend to carry more narrative weight or intensity than their feature-length counterparts (2015, 57). She goes on to identify two distinct types of endings commonly found in the short film form: the "surprise" and the "twist" (2015, 58). The principal difference between the two can be measured by the degree to which a spectator is deceived; Felando tells us that "the surprise ending involves something that has not happened yet, so neither the viewer nor any of the characters can anticipate it with certainty" (2015, 58). In contrast, the twist ending "involves the climactic revelation of some key piece of story knowledge that has been withheld from the viewer and therefore produces a shift-or-twist in expectations about possible outcomes" (2015, 58). In either case, the significance afforded to the surprise or twist ending of the short film foregrounds the passage of time, and such endings are a frequent feature of Nolan's work. The twist ending of *Doodlebug*, for instance, calls for a complete retroactive revision of what has unfolded. The shape of time in *Doodlebug*, then, is not exactly linear, but cyclical. While the film possesses a forward-moving momentum—that is, it has a beginning and an end, the frames are presented sequentially, and the story follows a cause-and-effect logic—the film's diegesis extends outward beyond the boundaries of plot time. Nolan figuratively delays the film's resolution by positioning the protagonist at the center of an infinite time loop that elongates the temporal interstice between life and death; like Schrödinger's famous cat, The Man in *Doodlebug* is simultaneously dead and alive in what amounts to a stylistic homage to the recursive Droste Effect.[7] In doing so, the film offers a celebration of cinema's ability to perpetually defer the passage of time and even death.

THE TIME-TRAVELING SPECTATOR

Since the turn of the millennium, cinema's growing concern with time and time manipulation has become increasingly visible. This has come about, in large part, because the digital revolution (and the attendant immediacy associated with the production and consumption of on-demand data) has produced significant changes in human perceptions of time. The last few decades, for instance, have witnessed a dramatic transformation in how audiences consume film following the rapid development of new media technologies; from VHS to DVD to digital streaming platforms, we are now more than ever in control of cinematic time. Speaking to an audience at the Los Angeles County Museum of Art, Nolan highlighted the potential for new forms of storytelling and spectatorship permitted by the ability to rewind, pause, and stop the narrative flow of a film: "In an era where you can stop [a film], which we've all grown up in now, that changes what you can do with narrative and density of narrative and you don't need as linear a narrative anymore. You can have different layers, you can have different rhythms to it because people are, in a way, paying more attention" (quoted in Saito 2013). As a cultural artifact, then, film exists *outside* of time with the express ability of being able to communicate some value or message regardless of the context in which it is seen. However, more than this, the nature of film means that it can also be viewed and re-viewed again by the spectator. As such, it can be said that the stories, characters, settings, and actors transcend the boundaries of time through memory. In this regard, film is at once ephemeral and enduring.

In *Death 24x a Second*, Laura Mulvey acknowledges that the ability to repeatedly re-view a film has provided the spectator with unprecedented opportunities to discern new meanings. She says:

> The process of repetition and return involves stretching out the cinematic image to allow space and time for associative thought, reflection on resonance and connotation, the identification of visual clues, the interpretation of cinematic form and style, and, ultimately, personal reverie. Furthermore, by slowing down, freezing or repeating images, key moments and meanings become visible that could not have been perceived when hidden under the narrative flow and the movement of film. Although the alert spectator . . . may well have had the ability to read the cinematic language . . . at 24 frames a second, today's electronic or digital spectator can find these deferred meanings that have been waiting through the decades to be seen. (2006, 136)

While the sentiment of Mulvey's contention may appear obvious, what is being foregrounded here is a contemporary form of spectatorship that resists the linear flow of time in favor of appreciating the rich visual and semiotic depth of the moving image. Ric Beairsto suggests that short films are particularly suited to this type of spectator engagement due to their conciseness which in turn offers the potential for repeat viewings. He remarks, "By virtue of their brevity, short films can hope to be seen repeatedly, in a way that features can't . . . and with repeated viewing, a level of density can be infused within a short film" (2009, 90). Whether contextualized as the subject matter, the structure that shapes them, or measured by the briefest amount spent watching them, time is central to our experience of the short film. It is unsurprising, then, that Nolan's success can be partially understood by the way in which he tames time, a technique he has spent a career practicing.[8]

NOTES

1. *Tarantella* was distributed to the public via YouTube on April 22, 2021, due to the resourcefulness of Henry Adams, who was able to source the short film because of a lost media search. However, the video was removed on August 15, 2021, due to a copyright claim made by Christopher Nolan's production company Syncopy Inc.

2. Elsewhere, prior to the release of *Dunkirk*, Christopher Nolan attended the annual convention of the National Association of Theatre Owners (NATO), where he took the stage to introduce what he called a "short film version" of the film (see Tiranno, 2017).

3. A useful visual metaphor for this process can be found in Cobb's description of the way dreams function in *Inception*. He says: "We create and perceive our world simultaneously, and our mind does this so well that we don't even know it's happening. That allows us to get right in the middle of that process." In the film, he illustrates this paradoxical relationship by drawing two curved arrows, pointing at each other's non-pointed ends with a straight line separating the two. In this instance, the line represents the continuous present which is perpetually receding into the past.

4. See, for a good overview of the avant-garde in cinema, Robert Stam's (2000) *Film Theory: An Introduction*.

5. In light of Nolan's remarks, we might also understand the fragmented narrative of *Tarantella* within the context of migration and diaspora, that is, the voluntary or involuntary movement of individuals or groups from their country of origin—including their descendants and succeeding generations who reside in the new place. At its core, diasporic film and filmmaking are grounded in the experience of artists who have migrant backgrounds or have experienced displacement and migration (see Rueschmann 2003). These films raise complex questions about belonging, boundaries, borders, community, nostalgia, and "home," while functioning as a site to explore the many contradictions of cultural and personal identity (see Loshitzky 2010). Underpinning all diasporic films, however, is that they reflect the "double consciousness" of

their creators. In *Tarantella*, such double consciousness manifests itself in the literal form of the doppelgänger. This simple technique, one used frequently throughout literary and film history to denote a fractured identity, is amplified in the film by Nolan and Belic through repeated camera movements and shots, mirrored compositions, and a costume color binary—black and white—that sets the visual tone for interpreting an oppositional, yet interdependent relationship between the two characters.

6. Special thanks to Jeremy Theobald for clarifying the film alluded to in this statement.

7. The Droste effect refers to a picture within a picture within a picture that can in theory go on ad infinitum. The effect is rendered visibly in *Memento*'s poster artwork and features in a scene from *Inception* during which Cobb attempts to explain to Ariadne (Ellen Page) how to build dreams at the Pont de Bir-Hakeim in Paris, a bridge with a series of repeating iron arches reminiscent of a hall of mirrors.

8. Special thanks to Luciano Piazza, Terence McSweeney, Jacqueline Furby, and Kierren Darke for their support in writing this chapter.

REFERENCES

Barthes, Roland. 1977. *Image, Music, Text*. Ed. and trans. Stephen Heath. London: Fontana Paperbacks.

Beairsto, Ric. 2009. *The Tyranny of Story: Audience Expectations and the Short Screenplay*. 2nd ed. Raleigh, NC: Lulu.com.

Benjamin, Walter. 1931. "A Short History of Photography." Trans. Stanley Mitchell. *Screen* 13, no. 1 (1972): 5–26.

Cinema 16: British Short Films. Warp Films.

Countryman, Eli. 2020. "Directors, Theaters Express Worry over Warner Bros. HBO Max Deal." *Variety*. Last modified December 12. variety.com/2020/film/news/warner-bros-hbo-max-reacts-1234851888/.

Coyle, Jake. 2018. "Q&A: Christopher Nolan on the craft of 'Dunkirk.'" *Associated Press*. Last modified February 2. apnews.com/article/f6d116000c6b4f26ade6a09771dbfdac.

Dulac, Germaine. 1987. "The Essence of Cinema." In *The Avant-Garde Film: A Reader of Theory and Criticism*, ed. Catherine Gallagher and Thomas Laquers, 36–48. Berkeley: University of California Press.

Eberl, Jason T., and George A. Dunn. 2017. *The Philosophy of Christopher Nolan*. Lanham, MD: Lexington.

Everett, Wendy. 2005. "Timetravel in European Film." In *European Identity in Cinema*, ed. Wendy Everett, 2nd ed., 107–116. Bristol: Intellect.

Felando, Cynthia. 2015. *Discovering Short Films: The History and Style of Live-Action Fiction Shorts*. London: Palgrave.

Furby, Jacqueline, and Claire Hines. 2012. *Fantasy*. London: Routledge.

Furby, Jacqueline, and Stuart Joy. 2015. *The Cinema of Christopher Nolan: Imagining the Impossible*. London: Wallflower Press.

Godard, Jean-Luc. 1972. "Take Your Own Tours." In *Godard on Godard*, trans. and ed. Tom Milne, 107–15. New York and London: Da Capo Press.

Gunning, Tom. 1983. "An Unseen Energy Swallows Space: The Space in Early Film and Its Relation to American Avant-Garde Film." In *Film Before Griffith*, ed. John Fell, 355–66. Berkeley: University of California Press.

———. 1986. "The Cinema of Attraction: Early Cinema, Its Spectator, and the Avant-Garde." *Wide Angle* 8, nos. 3–4: 63–70.

———. 1993. "'Now You See It, Now You Don't': The Temporality of the Cinema of Attractions." *The Velvet Light Trap—A Critical Journal of Film and Television* 32: 3–10.

———. 2015. "Just Minutes to Go: The Short Film Experience." *Empedocles: European Journal for the Philosophy of Communication.* 5, nos. 1/2, 65–73.

———. 2017. "Countdown to Zero: Compressing Cinema Time." In *Compact Cinematics: The Moving Image in the Age of Bit-Sized Media*, ed. Pepita Hesselberth and Maria Poulaki, 19–27. New York: Bloomsbury.

Har-Even, Benny. 2020. "Tenet: The 70mm IMAX Experience Review." *Forbes*. Last modified September 7. www.forbes.com/sites/bennyhareven/2020/09/07/tenet-the-70mm-imax-experience-review/?sh=33436b4b1846.

Hill-Parks, Erin. 2010. "Discourses of Cinematic Culture and the Hollywood Director: The Development of Christopher Nolan's Auteur Persona." Ph.D. thesis, Newcastle University.

Holland, Luke. 2020. "PG Tips: How Christopher Nolan Became the King of the Family-friendly Action Film." *The Guardian.* Last modified August 24. www.theguardian.com/film/2020/aug/24/pg-tips-how-christopher-nolan-became-the-king-of-the-family-friendly-action-film.

Iztkoff, Dave. 2010. "The Man behind the Dreamscape." *New York Times*. Last modified June 30. www.nytimes.com/2010/07/04/movies/04inception.html.

James, David E. 2005. *The Most Typical Avant-Garde: History and Geography of Minor Cinema.* Berkeley and Los Angeles: University of California Press.

Jesser, Jody Duncan, and Janine Pourroy. 2012. *The Art and Making of The Dark Knight Trilogy*. New York: Abrams Books.

Joy, Stuart. 2020. *The Traumatic Screen: The Films of Christopher Nolan*. London: Intellect.

Knight, Derrick, and Vincent Porter. 1967. *A Long Look at Short Films: An A.C.T.T. Report on the Short Entertainment and Factual Film*. Association of Cinematograph, Television, and Allied Technicians in Association with Pergamon Press.

Lawson, Richard. 2014. "Interstellar Gets Lost in Space." *Variety*. Last modified October 28. www.vanityfair.com/hollywood/2014/10/interstellar-review.

Loshitzky, Yosefa. 2010. *Screening Strangers: Migration and Diaspora in Contemporary European Cinema*. Bloomington and Indianapolis: Indiana University Press.

McGowan, Todd. 2012. *The Fictional Christopher Nolan*. Austin: University of Texas Press.

McKnight, George, and Deborah Knight. 2017. "'Are you Watching Closely?': Narrative Comprehension in Nolan's Early Films." In *The Philosophy of Christopher Nolan*, ed. Jason T. Eberl and George A. Dunn, 101–14. Lanham, MD: Lexington.

Mooney, Darren. 2018. *Christopher Nolan: A Critical Study of the Films*. Jefferson, NC: McFarland.

Mottram, James. 2020. *The Secrets of* Tenet: *Inside Christopher Nolan's Quantum Cold War*. London: Titan Books.

Mulvey, Laura. 2006. *Death 24x a Second: Stillness and the Moving Image*. London: Reaktion.

Nochlin, L. 1967. "The Invention of the Avant-Garde: France, 1830–1880." In *Avant-Garde Art*, ed. Thomas B. Hess and John Ashbery, 1–24. New York: Collier Books.

Nolan, Christopher. 2005. "Christopher Nolan Interviewed by James Mottram." In *Batman Begins: The Screenplay*, xi–xxiii. London: Faber and Faber.

Paraag, Shukla. 2017. "Exclusive: Christopher Nolan on *Dunkirk*." HistoryNet. Last modified July 5. www.historynet.com/nolan-dunkirk.htm.

Raskin, Richard. 2015. *The Art of the Short Fiction Film: A Shot by Shot Study of Nine Modern Classics*. Jefferson, NC: McFarland.

Riis, Johannes. 1998. "Towards a Poetics of the Short Film." *P.O.V.—A Danish Journal of Film Studies*, no. 5: 133–50.

Ruddell, Caroline. 2013. *Besieged Ego Doppelgangers and Split Identity Onscreen*. Edinburgh: Edinburgh University Press.

Rueschmann, Eva. 2003. *Moving Pictures, Migrating Identities*. Jackson: University Press of Mississippi.

Saito, Stephen. 2013. "Christopher Nolan Toys with Time 15 Years after 'Following' and Talks of Being a Post-VHS Filmmaker." Last modified January 13. moveable-fest.com/christopher-nolan-post-vhs-following/.

Shone, Tom. 2020. *The Nolan Variations: The Movies, Marvels and Mysteries of Christopher Nolan*. London: Faber and Faber.

Stam, Robert. 2000. *Film Theory: An Introduction*. Oxford: Blackwell.

Tamburri, Anthony Julian. 2002. *Italian/American Short Films and Music Videos: A Semiotic Reading*. Indiana: Purdue University Press.

Tartaglione, Nancy. 2020. "CineEurope: Execs Express Optimism & Christopher Nolan Sends a 'Tenet' Update io Online Conference." *Deadline*. Last modified June 17. deadline.com/2020/06/cineeurope-christopher-nolan-tenet-cineworld-sony-disney-1202961508/.

Tiranno, Jacob. 2017. "CinemaCon 2017 Previews New Films, Excites but Falls Short Ooverall." *The Scarlet and Gray Free Press*. Last modified April 3. www.unlvfreepress.com/cinemacon-2017-previews-new-films-excites-falls-short-overall/.

Webber, Andrew J. 1996. *The Doppelgänger: Double Visions in German Literature*. Oxford: Claredon Press.

Zoller Seitz, Matt. 2014. "Reviews: *Interstellar*." *RogertEbert.com*. Last modified November 3. www.rogerebert.com/reviews/interstellar-2014.

Chapter 16

Catwoman in All but Name

Gender and Adaptation in Christopher Nolan's Selina Kyle

Miriam Kent

Catwoman is an elusive DC Comics antiheroine who has been adapted to myriad media. Emblematic of cultural issues relating to gender, race, sexuality, and power, she is "a significant, groundbreaking part of the historical lexicon of . . . the DC franchise" (Whaley 2011, 20). Otherwise known as Selina Kyle, the character returned to prominence in Christopher Nolan's final *Dark Knight* film. This chapter approaches *The Dark Knight Rises* (2012) as a hypertext sitting in complex relation to existing textual and cultural structures. Through ideological and discursively grounded textual and contextual analysis, as well as a critical reflection on paratextual sources, I examine how issues of adaptation, representation, and authorship manifest in this portrayal of Selina Kyle.

I discuss how Nolan's version of Selina negotiated highly gendered links with the figure of Catwoman, intersecting with issues of authorship and realism within the so-called Nolanverse of Batman films. Ultimately, Nolan's adaptation of Catwoman demonstrates the flexibility of a character who has been (re)defined throughout her publication history: a flirtatious foil to ward off homosexual implications between Batman and Robin; a sex worker occupying crime-ridden spaces in Gotham that Batman seeks to eliminate; a thief; and an antiheroic femme fatale (to name a few iterations).

Nolan's Selina, who is never referred to as "Catwoman,"[1] appeared within a distinctly postfeminist cultural moment characterized by the coexistence of popular culture's embrace of women's empowerment and a turn toward neoconservative practices that cast political feminisms as unneeded yet commercially appealing. Indeed, Selina is marginalized as a woman within the Nolanverse and occupies a story world overwhelmingly concerned with (white) masculinity. Her positionality aligned with Gotham's economically disenfranchised (in support of the film's villain, Bane) opposes the wealthy Bruce Wayne/Batman, whom she ultimately assists, and is likewise significant considering Catwoman's comic book history. The film results in what Angela McRobbie characterizes as postfeminist disarticulation (2009, 24) regarding Catwoman, denying the expression of a nuanced critique of social disparities through her eventual coalition with an ideological paradigm that ultimately reinforces the status quo while it simultaneously celebrates her heroism and puts forward seemingly radical notions of social reform. Her heroic femininity manifests as ironic masquerades that are attuned to postfeminist modes of women's subjectivity.

ADAPTATION IN LITERATURE AND COMICS: AUTHORSHIP AND GENDER

Superhero film adaptations have dominated the box office since the early 2000s. However, the Nolanverse films are unique for having been produced before the age of superhero franchises exemplified by Marvel's Cinematic Universe (MCU). While the DC Extended Universe (DCEU), like the MCU, incorporates serialized narratives across media texts, the Nolanverse, comprising *Batman Begins* (2005), *The Dark Knight* (2008), and *The Dark Knight Rises*, essentially forms its own continuity and arguably offered a filmmaker such as Nolan significant freedom emphasized by his status as an auteur.

To discern the significance of this iteration of Catwoman, it is worth considering the relationship between *The Dark Knight Rises* and the comics from which the character stems, as I do later. However, adaptation is a complex process, further burdened here by the combined pressures of auteurism and the source text. Further, a multimodal medium such as comics poses unique challenges and opportunities. As Dan Hassler-Forest notes, film adaptations of comic book characters, in this case Batman, "gave new form to a pop-cultural icon that had gone through diverse incarnations" including across media and throughout history (2017, 409). This complicates authorship and comics adaptation debates, which can be addressed through Dudley Andrew's conceptualization of "borrowing" (1984, 98), as demonstrated by Liam Burke:

> Traditionally, most comic book adaptations by Hollywood studios could be categorized as "borrowings." "Mythic" characters such as Batman and Superman have enjoyed non-stop publication since the late 1930s, undergoing a series

of tonal shifts and story additions that have become character mainstays. Consequently, the choice to borrow only the characters and setup, and not a particular story, allows for a more all-encompassing adaptation. (2015, 13)

Though it is not immediately clear what constitutes Burke's "all-encompassing adaptation"—characters and setup still vary widely across adaptational approaches—implicit here is the ongoing issue of fidelity. Many adaptation theorists reject the notion of fidelity as a marker of value. Moreover, as Shelley Cobb articulates, the discourses of fidelity criticism—including those that reject it—risk reproducing gendered hierarchies: "the language of fidelity constructs a gendered possession of authority and paternity for the source text within adaptation: the film as faithful wife to the novel as paternal husband" (2011, 30).

It is thus useful to consider adaptation "a form of intertextuality" (Hutcheon 2006, 8), generating meaning through the textual relations between iterations of media phenomena, including production, distribution, and consumption processes and paratextual discourses. Likewise, the act of adaptation itself is ideological, with Julie Sanders noting that "The theoretical and ideological forces that can be seen at play in many [adaptations] cannot be underestimated" (2006, 157). Robert Stam also argues that "many of the changes between novelistic sources have to do with ideology and social discourses" (2005, 42). Indeed, *The Dark Knight Rises*' story and themes reference sociopolitical shifts, including the 2007–2008 recession and "Occupy" protests. These were not necessarily present in the source texts. Thus, Francesco Casetti has characterized adaptations as "discursive formations which testify to the way in which society organizes its meanings and shapes its system of relations" (2004, 82).

While superhero comics attract diverse readers, they have classically been associated with men, presumably because of early comics' targeting of young boys. Women, queer people, and people of color are increasingly represented in comics, but it remains a male-dominated industry. The masculine and feminine embodiment of superhero characters have been worthy topics of discussion, the intricacies of which are beyond the scope of this chapter. Nevertheless, superheroes' gendered qualities are clear: most superhero films focus on male heroes with women as supporting characters—frequently as girlfriends placed within a position of peril, or even death, by a villain, spurring the hero into action in a narrative turn referred to as "women in refrigerators."[2]

All heroic bodies are exaggerated in their physicality within these media, leading to the fetishization of the superhero body. As Scott Bukatman notes, "Superhero comics present body narratives, bodily fantasies, that incorporate (incarnate) aggrandizement and anxiety, mastery, and trauma. Comics narrate the body in stories and envision the body in drawings. The body is obsessively centered upon" (2003, 49). Because of this aggrandizement (and anxiety), the superhero body is classically characterized as hypermasculine (for men) and hyperfeminine (for women), and sexualized accordingly through costuming and posing, reinforcing binary gender roles aligned with patriarchal ideals. Regardless, superhero representations remain complex and enmeshed with culture, including industrial contexts involving censorship and regulation,[3] and gain significance when considering factors including race. As summarized by Esther De Dauw, "the comics industry works to fold in any challenges to the dominant white heteropatriarchy in order to simultaneously cater to conservative and progressive audiences" (2021, 151).

Comics adaptations are therefore highly ideological since the texts they are based on are highly ideological. Mass-produced cultural phenomena, superhero blockbusters err on the side of dominant, hegemonic narratives, particularly regarding gender. However, the negotiation of those narratives accompanies this, resulting in a more complex process than a straightforward projection of messages.

These films exist as part of the palimpsestic interrelations (Hutcheon 2006, 8) surrounding Batman as a popular culture figure, as informed by poststructuralist adaptation approaches. However, the very existence of these films as being distinctly *of Nolan* exists in dissonant relation to poststructural approaches rejecting the paternalism of the source. Indeed, Cobb's critique of fidelity language parallels feminist approaches to auteur frameworks denoted as paternalistic and elitist. Yet, that these three films are described as forming a defined "Nolanverse" is significant, especially in a time when film authorship is arguably diffused by global multimedia brands, such as Marvel or DC (both of which are owned by billion-dollar corporations).

Supposedly it is precisely the idea of cinematic realism assigned to Nolan's authorship that has facilitated the emphasis on the films' ideological stance(s): "Due to the 'realist' aesthetics of Nolan's rebooted trilogy, much attention has been paid critically to the political leanings of the trilogy's narrative on terror, and the desire to interpret the symbolic and ideological meanings" (Fhlainn 2015, 158). This discursive realism, described by Darren Mooney as the "grounded aesthetic," is widely attached to Nolan's work (2018, 39). Nolan has adapted existing texts (including *Memento* [2000] and *The Prestige* [2006]), putting traditional auteurist designations at stake. Thomas Leitch notes the complexities surrounding auteurs who adapt, ranging from "the adapter-auteur as generic trademark" (such as Hitchcock) and "the adapter-auteur as solitary artist" (such as Kubrick) (2007, 245). Nolan's Batman auteurism falls within neither category, however, with accounts framing his artistic freedom as entitled by the failure of Warner Bros.' *Batman & Robin* (Joel Schumacher, 1997) (Mooney 2018, 39). Comics' questionable status as "literature" also problematizes this dynamic. Indeed, perhaps because of this, popular accounts suggested Nolan's engagement with Batman comics was minimal (it was cowriter David Goyer who dominated the discussion on this topic). However, paternalistic canonicity resurfaced in frequent references to "quality" superhero stories, including *The Dark Knight Returns* (Miller and Janson 1986), "Year One" (Miller and Mazzucchelli 1987) and *The Long Halloween* (Loeb and Sale 1999).

Mooney argues that "realism" became a "critical shorthand" for the *Dark Knight* films. He further highlights the flexibility of the term (and the loose ways it is applied), suggesting that "It is not that the films themselves are particularly realistic, it is that they impose their more outlandish and cartoonish elements upon a world that is recognizable to the audience" (Mooney 2018, 40). This is considered to be in contrast with Marvel superhero films, which follow a tonally lighter formula (Hassler-Forest 2017, 407–8). Indeed, the discourse of realism arguably clashes with perceptions of superheroes as fantastical.

Therefore, both auteurism and comics are useful contexts for these superhero adaptations. The Nolanverse films provide a representation of their source material but also a discursive Nolan-ness. Both reach into the cultural, social, and political contexts that circumnavigate these texts. The focus here is not necessarily on fidelity as a signifier of value, nor am I suggesting that the value of these films lies within Nolan's artistry. My emphasis is on the specific shape an adaptation (in this case a specific character—Catwoman) takes and understanding it within wider frameworks. Hence, I consider how *The Dark Knight Rises* functions culturally as an articulation of existing properties *and* a product stemming from a particular authorial vision, and, importantly, how these intersect with ongoing cultural practices relating to gender representation specifically. Therefore, I query exclusionary auteurist modes, highlighting the intertextual web of meaning-making resulting in gendered representations within adaptations.

WHO IS CATWOMAN?

Catwoman has a long history in DC print comics. However, the character's flexibility made her adaptation within the parameters of the Nolanverse feasible. This Selina represents an exercise in varied articulations of gender, race, and class that link interestingly to her comics history. Introduced as "The Cat" in Batman #1 in 1940 (Finger and Kane 1940), the character drew upon a cultural association between women and cats while engaging with the crime genre of the comics by designating her a cat burglar, a trait she also exhibits in *The Dark Knight Rises*.

Catwoman's propinquity to crime throughout her publication history cemented her status as an antiheroine and bears significance regarding class, to which I return later. Indeed, Tim Hanley argues that in earlier comics, "Catwoman was a classic femme fatale, a woman who used her sexual wiles for personal gain, and who was punished for violating the social order" (2014, 39). The character's approximation to crime therefore intersects with gender, sexuality, and indeed race. According to Deborah Whaley, Catwoman across time and media demonstrates "racial fluidity from ambiguously Chinese to white to Latina to Black" (2015, 23). Long before racial recasting became a topic of mainstream discussion, Catwoman was of a different race across various media.

Intersecting with issues of class and sexuality, the later "Catwoman" was presented as a working-class hairdresser and possible romantic/erotic interest for Batman—and was finally named Selina Kyle (Gibson, Kane, and Schwartz 1952). Arguably, Selina's presence was to offset possible homoerotic connotations inferred in the relationship between Batman and his boy-sidekick Robin, mostly spurred by a moral panic over comics and their effects on children led by the now-discredited psychiatrist Frederick Wertham. Whaley summarizes, "Catwoman created a narrative space of heteronormativity that strategically undercut the perceived homoeroticism between the characters Batman and Robin in the comic book and 1960s television series" (2015, 70).

Catwoman's crime roots were explored explicitly in later iterations. Notably, Miller and Mazzucchelli's "Year One" storyline (1987), a revisionist narrative exploring Batman's origins, reenvisaged the character as a sex worker who crosses paths with Bruce Wayne. Critical interpretations of Selina's reinvention as a sex worker were mixed. Hanley attributes this recasting to writer Frank Miller, whose work is associated with the Modern Age of Superheroes, roughly beginning in the 1980s, when superhero narratives became darker and self-reflexive. Frequently heralded as the era of "quality" superhero comics in paternalistic accounts of comics history, as noted earlier, critics credited such writers as Miller with giving cultural value to what was once regarded as children's entertainment. Selina's repositioning as a sex worker, to Hanley, was therefore facilitated by wider shifts in superhero comics narratives, with gendered implications:

> Miller could have taken Catwoman in any direction he wanted, but his penchant for dark, gritty tales and his noir sensibility made her a dominatrix. . . . As "Year One" began, [her] independence was gone. She had to answer to an abusive pimp, and also pay off the cops to keep them out of her hair. Her sexuality no longer belonged to her. (2017, 83)

Nonetheless, these elements of the character's origin were deemed more or less canon, and so the question that arises is not so much whether she should have been represented as a sex worker, but how that representation takes place. As A. Luxx Mishou argues, "Comics narratives exploring Selina Kyle's own history as a sex worker demonstrate contemporary cultural taboo and the narratives of victimization that continue to define sex work in majority culture" (2021, 44), contradictorily giving her a tragic past resting on respectability politics policing women's bodily autonomy in order to put forward a notion of women's empowerment. Selina's status as a sex worker was later extended, notably in Mindy Newell and J. J. Birch's "Her Sister's Keeper" (1991), which takes place within the same time frame and narrative universe as Miller and Mazzucchelli's story. "Her Sister's Keeper" presents the origin of Catwoman initially as a victimized sex worker abused by her pimp. Appropriating the cat-themed bondage suit she was expected to wear for clients, Selina uses it as a disguise while exacting revenge on her pimp. The refashioning of the suit does, to some extent, challenge the victim narrative, according to Mishou, but this conception of the Catwoman persona is also couched within patriarchal dynamics that she exists within and is motivated by (even the cat suit is employed ironically in relation to her pimp, who openly hates cats). Feminist activists face complex issues about sex work: Mishou defines debates and legislation targeting sex workers, eroding their safety and privacy, as symptomatic of cultural discourses that continuously vilify and police women's sexual autonomy. Catwoman's sexuality is thus a site of feminist struggle and, in turn, provides a point of negotiation regarding adaptation.

Despite—or because of—her narrative complexity, Catwoman has been adapted across media through the decades. Significantly, Catwoman in film and media has been played by actresses from a range of racial backgrounds— she was portrayed in the 1960s *Batman* television series (ABC, 1966–1968) by white actress Julie Newmar and mixed-race actress Eartha Kitt. Tim Burton's sequel to *Batman* (1989), *Batman Returns* (1992), featured white actress Michelle Pfeiffer; meanwhile box office failure *Catwoman* (Pitof, 2004) cast Halle Berry, who is biracial, in the central role. A version of Selina Kyle featured in *Gotham* (Fox, 2014–2019) is dubbed "Cat" and played by Camren Bicondova. Most recently, Zoë Kravitz, who is of mixed African American and Jewish heritage, plays the character in *The Batman* (Matt Reeves, 2022).

Wealth and class discourses have followed the character from text to text, intertwining with feminist goals of (financial) liberation: in the words of Genevieve Valentine, "She's been a sex worker, a socialite, and a CEO" (2018, 594). Catwoman's fluid modes of representation, while noteworthy, are not unique in the realm of superheroes, which undergo continuous revision as cultural phenomena enduring over decades. Revision remains integral to superhero texts throughout different media platforms (see Hyman 2017). Characters' histories are frequently erased and rebooted in comics, and screen media appearances can be equally diverse with different versions of the same character existing simultaneously. Catwoman is unique due to the specific way her racial, classed, and gendered subjectivity is constituted over time and in relation to wider theoretical frameworks. Selina in *The Dark Knight Rises* is thus adaptation as a process of revision—but, crucially, it is a process of revision of a character already under a process of revision; an intertext exposing further intertexts, ultimately coagulating with the sticky vocabularies of authorship and representation.

ADAPTING CATWOMAN FOR "NOLAN'S GOTHAM CITY"

The Dark Knight Rises implants Selina into a nigh-dystopian setting in which class struggles are foregrounded through terrorist Bane (Tom Hardy) in the wake of Bruce Wayne/Batman's (Christian Bale) disappearance following *The Dark Knight*. Gotham's power vacuum prompts Bane to incite an uprising against the wealthy ruling classes by targeting Gotham's economic center. Selina, a skilled thief, initially sides with Bane, seemingly for personal reasons. Following an attack on its football stadium, Bane forcefully rules Gotham and punishes the wealthy. Meanwhile, Wayne loses his wealth and, as Batman, is defeated by Bane, who breaks his back. Wayne is relegated to an underground prison in an undetermined region (presumably in the Far East), where he rehabilitates himself. On his return to Gotham, he unites with Selina to defeat Bane and avert a nuclear disaster.

As noted, *The Dark Knight Rises* is primarily concerned with masculinity: Bane's characterization is emblematic of the wounded, white working-class masculinity that was deemed "in crisis" following the economic recession after the near collapse of the global financial system in 2007 (Negra and Tasker 2014, 8). The potential to read Bane (and initially Selina) as a representative for the so-called "99 percent" during the subsequent Occupy movements against economic inequalities[4] has been noted (Baum 2016, 64). Nonetheless, the film maintains an ambiguous stance toward the political issues it evokes, including wealth disparity, policing, surveillance, nuclear power, and indeed, gender roles, again highlighting that a straightforward reading of superhero texts is neither desirable nor possible. The film concludes with order restored to Gotham—the revolutionary call to end corporate power and wealth inequality, characterized in the film as borderline-fascist, has seemingly dissipated.

Anne Hathaway's casting as Selina was announced in January 2011, alongside Tom Hardy as Bane (Fleming 2011). Nolan's penchant for realist aesthetics followed discussions of the character in media publications. The secrecy around the production of the film, assigned to Nolan's directorial authority, provided a vacuum in which commentators projected a dominant reading of discursive realism for the film. The alignment with realist aesthetics appears to coincide with the idea that Nolan specifically distanced the films from the comics: he was once quoted saying he "didn't want to treat [*Batman Begins*] as a comic book movie" (quoted in Shone 2020, 152). Moreover, allegedly, "his knowledge of the comic books was so slim that he sought out, as a screenwriting partner, David S. Goyer" (Shone 2020, 153). Investment in the superheroic qualities of the Nolanverse films was therefore thrust upon screenwriter Goyer, further distancing Nolan's authorial style from the perceived demands of the superhero genre.

The previous actresses who had played the character also appeared within these paratextual discussions, highlighting Catwoman's legacy. Interestingly, it was Hedy Lamarr whom Hathaway frequently referenced as having influenced her, and allusions to Lamarr being the initial inspiration for Bob Kane's Catwoman in the 1940s were made (Boucher 2011), recentering comics in the discussion, albeit in a roundabout way, given Lamarr's relative lack of actual involvement. Simultaneously, Hathaway's statement that "I probably should've felt more pressure playing Catwoman because of her history but I knew who was directing me so I focused on trusting Chris" (quoted in BANG Showbiz 2012) marks a break with the character and a reinscription of Nolan's authority.

Meanwhile, Selina's costuming clearly draws from the comics, especially Ed Brubaker and Darwyn Cooke's *Catwoman* series (2002). While some form of cat suit became synonymous with Catwoman relatively early in her publication history, *The Dark Knight Rises* notably drew inspiration from the goggles introduced during the Brubaker and Cooke run. Indeed, the goggles were a topic of discussion when images of Hathaway as Selina surfaced, as the goggles were interpreted as having the dual-function of representing cat ears when flipped up and not in use (Chaney 2011; Child 2011). The inclusion of "ears" cemented this version of Selina's status as Catwoman in these discourses.

Importantly, though, the discourses around Selina's appearance were rooted in the supposed practicalities of the costuming. This was noted by Hathaway in a statement that, again, marks Nolan as authority: "I love the costume because everything has a purpose, nothing is in place for fantasy's sake, and that's the case with everything in Christopher Nolan's Gotham City" (quoted in Boucher 2011). This idea (or ideal) of realism was also supported by the film's costume designer, Lindy Hemming:

> [Bane] is given some reality, as with all things Nolan, thus making him more interesting and believable. . . . When my research began, I had never heard of Bane. Catwoman of course I knew a little of, especially Michelle Pfeiffer's costume by the great Bob Ringwood (with Mary Vogt). However, as usual, we soon abandoned that path, and embarked on looking for real life parallels for both of them. (quoted in Laverty 2012)

While citing "real life parallels" seems redundant when considering the fantastical superhero genre, this statement has the discursive function of elevating Nolan's film to a more serious venue of realist art. Realism, coupled with references to the practicality of costumes within what Hathaway refers to as "Nolan's Gotham City" also takes on gendered qualities given that women's superhero costumes are often criticized for their impracticality.

Significantly, Nolan's realism filter reshaped some impractical elements of Selina's costume. The most obvious of these were the high-heeled boots which, considering the character's propensity for running, should presumably be deemed impractical and "unrealistic." Shown in a close-up in a scene in which she accosts villain John Daggett (Ben Mendelsohn), who works with Bane, Selina's boot has a metal heel, which she uses to pin Daggett to the wall. Subsequent close-ups reveal a blade in the silver heel, which she uses to exert pressure on Daggett's pinned-down hand. She subsequently slashes the leg of Daggett's associate Stryver after he ironically asks her, "those heels make it tough to walk?" Weapon of choice notwithstanding, Selina's heel-blades are justified through the film's broader discursive positioning within realism—the character has a practical reason for wearing high-heeled boots; her femininity is ironically weaponized. Thus, the reinscription of realism within this component of the costume also results in a reinscription of what might ordinarily be deemed limiting, hegemonic models of femininity within Selina. Positioning the character within postfeminist media can help illuminate how these feminized elements of costuming were embraced as "practical," as discussed below.

Women are relatively marginalized within Nolan's oeuvre, as are people of color. To add to this, women have been equally marginalized within superhero cinema, a trend stemming from the genre's relationship to action cinema, itself traditionally centered on action heroes. Nonetheless, Tosha Taylor suggests that the women of the Nolanverse are compelling in part due to Nolan's directorial stance. Selina in *The Dark Knight Rises* acts as a contemporary femme fatale, a noir character type combining dangerous femininity with sexual allure (2015, 65). Moreover, Selina's status as an antiheroine is cemented by her initial betrayal of Batman, which leads to Bane breaking his back. Building on this, it can be inferred that the crime elements of the Catwoman character lent themselves to Nolan's existing interest in film noir style, underscoring the character's flexibility to begin with. Further, Taylor links Selina's introduction during a masquerade ball to the masking of the femme fatale, who is never whom she appears to be (2015, 65). This masquerade motif has further contextualization, though, within the parameters of postfeminist masquerade.

While multiplex and shifting, postfeminist culture is largely seen as part of wider social developments in which feminist goals were mainstreamed, while political feminisms themselves were cast aside. The term is often associated with 1990s and 2000s media culture. According to Angela McRobbie, postfeminist culture is marked by "feminism taken into account" (2009, 8). In other words, Western media texts (as well as social institutions and legislation) discursively take account of (what are imagined to be) feminist criticisms of themselves "to suggest that equality is achieved, in order to install a whole repertoire of new meanings which emphasise that [feminism] is no longer needed" (McRobbie 2009, 12). Connected to individualist, neoliberal consumption and economic practices, the postfeminist "sensibility" (Gill 2007, 148) privileges an ideal postfeminist subject—an economically empowered woman who has benefited from (Western) women's liberation movements, whose goals have been more or less achieved. A desire for political activism and social reform in the name of feminism is therefore unreasonable.

Postfeminist masquerade, suggests McRobbie, arises when models of traditional womanhood are so heavily promoted that they inhabit an "unbearable proximity" to the postfeminist subject, who then enacts an "ironic, quasi-feminist inhabiting of femininity as excess, which is now openly acknowledged as fictive"—the postfeminist masquerade (2009, 64). Taking into account feminist and queer constructionist perspectives on gender as in-the-making (symptomatic of postmodern, fragmented identities), the postfeminist masquerade reframes femininity's artifice as an empowering means of self-creation while reinforcing the patriarchal-symbolic. In the superhero film genre, this results in an exchange of postfeminist masks taking place within individual characters (see Kent 2021, 93–118). Accordingly, *The Dark Knight Rises* highlights Selina's ironic, playful femininity, her talent for disguise, and, I argue, her ultimate alignment with the film's critiqued-but-recuperated capitalist hero. Thus, it follows that Selina is introduced in the film first as a maid, then a cat burglar, then, ironically, at a masquerade ball.

The postfeminist subject is self-sufficient, sexually liberated, professionally equal (to white men), self-monitoring (for instance in relation to her alignment with traditional femininity—a quality suggested to be unavailable to political feminists), heterosexual, white, and middle class; importantly, she has the freedom of so-called "choice" regarding the direction in which she takes her life. Regarding the media, Sarah Projansky summarizes: "With so many representations of successful women in the mainstream media—collectively forming a seductive and alluring image of success—logically, one might want to assume that historical, activist feminism had achieved sufficient social change to belay the need for further activism" (2001, 11). However, given the continued prevalence (including to this day) of harassment, sexual assault, and the institutional marginalization of women of color and queer, trans, and disabled women (including intersecting identities), these representations might be seen as (for want of a better term) unrealistic and, indeed, would not have aligned with many women's lived experiences.

Nonetheless, the focus here is not on the credibility of the depictions, but what relationship they have to wider cultural shifts. Falling well within the recession-era postfeminist femininities in which affluence is to be aspired toward through extreme resourcefulness (Negra and Tasker 2014, 7), Selina in *The Dark Knight Rises* foregrounds the gendered dynamics of what can be termed a simplistic prioritization of "realism" in Nolan's film. Thus, whereas an assumed feminist critique may condemn Selina being represented as fighting in heels, *The Dark Knight Rises* doubles down on her gendered costuming, justifying it through a gesture toward realism and constructing a character shown to indulge in the supposed frivolities of femininity.

A key component of Selina in *The Dark Knight Rises* is class, and in a discussion with Wayne, she is described by him as "Robin Hood"—she steals from the rich to give to the poor, or, in her words, "I take what I need to from those who have more than enough" (Wayne had previously caught her stealing from his house), clearly evoking the notion of the 1 percent. Indicating their class discrepancies, Wayne refers to Selina's living quarters in "Old Town," an apparently particularly crime-ridden area of Gotham. Indeed, this forms the remnants of an intertextual link between the film and comics as a scene in Selina's apartment building indicates. Donning a black dress and putting on Martha Wayne's stolen pearls, Selina contemplates herself in the mirror but is interrupted by a disturbance in the corridor: a young woman shouts, "I told you—money first!" Cutting to the scenario in the hall, a man threatens a blonde woman, whom he claims stole his wallet. While the exact dynamic between the man and blonde woman is unclear, the preceding dialogue indicates that a transaction took place. Indeed, the blonde woman, while credited as "Jen," bears resemblance to Selina's friend Holly Robinson, a sex worker who appears in both "Year One" and "Her Sister's Keeper." While both women's status as sex workers is ambiguous in the film, the presentation through the exchange with Jen, not to mention the Old Town setting, would seem to signal this.

Given the widespread distrust of the idea of mainstreaming sex work, the scenes' ambiguity is unsurprising, for while postfeminist culture entails a move toward the self-empowered, sexual liberation of women, this liberation remains heavily regulated. Nonetheless, this forms part of Selina's motivations in the film. Key here is Selina's pursuit of the "Clean Slate," a computer program that erases all traces of a person in every database, essentially allowing them to reconstruct their identity and start afresh. The postfeminist masquerade and the fragmented, reconstituted self that accommodates it, becomes even clearer here for Selina's character. Selina's conversation with Wayne suggests the nature of her past: "I started off doing what I had to. Once you've done what you had to they'll never let you do what you want to." Again, references to "doing what [she] had to" could be interpreted as sex work with relative ease, although within the more respectable umbrella of crime. Nonetheless, the possibility for Selina to erase the past is marked as a venue for self-empowerment, speaking to the feminist goal of agency and self-actualization.

Considering that by the film's ending Selina is united with Wayne, apparently living comfortably in Florence, *The Dark Knight Rises*' uses of postfeminist masquerade and self-invention presents a social fantasy in which Selina's aspirations to transcend class are realized. The character is shifted to a more individualist worldview than she had at the film's start. The emphasis, here, is not on addressing the structural inequalities that make life difficult for working-class people but rather on the aspirational forms of self-management undertaken by the disempowered to assimilate to the status quo. The casting of Hathaway is interesting to consider here, given the reliance on the narrative upon the privileges seemingly granted her by whiteness.

The postfeminist fantasy presented in *The Dark Knight Rises* significantly complicates the film's claims to realism. Indeed, the ongoing emphasis on realism results in what McRobbie refers to as disarticulation (2009, 24). Interestingly, this is also expressed through Selina's dialogue, especially through ironic quips, many of them gendered. For instance, after encountering Batman while fleeing from Daggett and his team of armed men, the Caped Crusader calls on her to get into his flying vehicle, at which she jokes, "My mother warned me about getting into cars with strange men," to which he responds, "This isn't a car." Ironic humor, here, emphasizes Selina's exceptionality as a superheroine by revising assumptions around gender, which become seemingly meaningless in this scenario, thereby eliminating the necessity for feminist intervention.

Feminist goals are implicitly present in the film, notably through the presence of a superheroine whose skills appear to be equal to the central hero. However, the film's lack of regard for the wider politics that might make feminism necessary marks a distinct disarticulation of feminism in its move to postfeminist sensibilities, which in many ways emerge through the film's claims to realism. It perhaps follows, then, that the character is not referred to as Catwoman at all—that Catwoman herself was disarticulated through the adaptation. While Catwoman is a complex character in comics today, this particular iteration of her, and her historicization within postfeminist media, is merely one component of what will remain a multiplicitous multimedia phenomenon.

NOTES

1. She is credited as "Selina" and referred to as "The Cat" in an on-screen newspaper headline.
2. Comics writer Gail Simone coined the phrase "women in refrigerators" after a Green Lantern storyline in which the villain murdered the hero's girlfriend and deposited her in a household fridge, prompting the hero to seek revenge (see Cocca 2016, 12; De Dauw 2021, 17; also, Kent 2021, 29–46).
3. Catwoman famously disappeared from comics for twelve years following the establishment of the Comics Code in 1954, which regulated comics content and deemed her inappropriate for young readers.
4. 2011's Occupy Wall Street protests became a global movement. Many events featured slogans referring to the "99 percent." This opposed the world's wealthiest "1 percent," who benefited from inequalities facilitated by the extreme models of neoliberal capitalism under which society operated. Further highlighting *The Dark Knight Rises*' adjacency to Occupy, reports suggested filming was conducted at these protests, again entrenching the film within realism discourses (Zeitchik 2011).

REFERENCES

Andrew, Dudley. 1984. *Concepts in Film Theory*. Oxford: Oxford University Press.
BANG Showbiz. 2012. "Anne Hathaway Loved Fight Scenes in New Batman Flick." *CTV News*, July 19. www.ctvnews.ca/entertainment/anne-hathaway-loved-fight-scenes-in-new-batman-flick-1.884974.
Baum, Bruce. 2016. *The Post-Liberal Imagination: Political Scenes from the American Cultural Landscape*. Basingstoke: Palgrave Macmillan.
Boucher, Geoff. 2011. "'Dark Knight Rises' Star Anne Hathaway: 'Gotham City Is Full of Grace.'" *Hero Complex* (*Los Angeles Times*), December 29. web.archive.org/web/20120103164918/http://herocomplex.latimes.com/2011/12/29/dark-knight-rises-star-anne-hathaway-gotham-city-is-full-of-grace/?utm_source=dlvr.it&utm_medium=twitter&dlvrit=63378.
Brubaker, Ed, and Darwyn Cooke, with Greg Rucka and Shawn Martinbrough. 2002. *Catwoman: The Dark End of the Street*. New York: DC Comics. [Collecting *Detective Comics* #759–762, August 2001–November 2002; *Catwoman* #1–4, January–April 2002].
Bukatman, Scott. 2003. *Matters of Gravity: Special Effects and Supermen in the 20th Century*. Durham: Duke University Press.

Burke, Liam. 2015. *The Comic Book Film Adaptation: Exploring Modern Hollywood's Leading Genre*. Jackson: University Press of Mississippi.

Casetti, Francesco. 2004. "Adaptation and Mis-Adaptations: Film, Literature, and Social Discourses." In *A Companion to Literature and Film*, ed. Robert Stam and Alessandra Raengo, 81–91. Oxford: Blackwell.

Chaney, Jen. 2011. "Anne Hathaway's Catwoman in 'Dark Knight Rises' Has Pointy Ears." *The Washington Post*, September 26. www.washingtonpost.com/blogs/celebritology/post/anne-hathaways-catwoman-in-dark-knight-rises-has-pointy-ears-the-internet-is-not-going-to-let-this-lie/2011/09/26/gIQAoqlhzK_blog.html.

Child, Ben. 2011. "Catwoman's Whiskers? Anne Hathaway's Costume Revealed." *The Guardian*, September 26. www.theguardian.com/film/filmblog/2011/sep/26/catwoman-anne-hathaway-costume-revealed.

Cobb, Shelley. 2011. "Adaptation, Fidelity, and Gendered Discourses." *Adaptation* 4, no. 1: 28–37. doi.org/10.1093/ADAPTATION/APQ011.

Cocca, Carolyn. 2016. *Superwomen: Gender, Power, and Representation*. London: Bloomsbury Academic.

De Dauw, Esther. 2021. *Hot Pants and Spandex Suits: Gender Representation in American Superhero Comic Books*. New Brunswick, NJ: Rutgers University Press.

Fhlainn, Sorcha Ní. 2015. "'You Keep Telling Yourself What You Know, but What Do You Believe?': Cultural Spin, Puzzle Films and Mind Games in the Cinema of Christopher Nolan." In *The Cinema of Christopher Nolan: Imagining the Impossible*, ed. Jacqueline Furby and Stuart Joy, 147–63. London: Wallflower.

Finger, Bill, and Bob Kane. 1940. "The Legend of the Batman." *Batman* #1. DC Comics, March.

Fleming, Mike. 2011. "Anne Hathaway Reviving Catwoman for 'The Dark Knight Rises'; Tom Hardy Is Bane." *Deadline*, January 19. deadline.com/2011/01/anne-hathaway-wins-selina-kyle-role-in-the-dark-knight-rises-98008/.

Gibson, Walter B., Bob Kane, and Lew Sayre Schwartz. 1952. "The King of the Cats!" *Batman* #69. DC Comics, February.

Gill, Rosalind. 2007. "Postfeminist Media Culture: Elements of a Sensibility." *European Journal of Cultural Studies* 10, no. 2: 147–66. doi.org/10.1177/1367549407075898.

Hanley, Tim. 2014. *Wonder Woman Unbound: The Curious History of the World's Most Famous Heroine*. Chicago: Chicago Review Press.

———. 2017. *The Many Lives of Catwoman: The Felonious History of a Feline Fatale*. Chicago: Chicago Review Press.

Hassler-Forest, Dan. 2017. "Roads Not Taken in Hollywood's Comic Book Movie Industry: Popeye, Dick Tracy, and Hulk." In *The Oxford Handbook of Adaptation Studies*, ed. Thomas Leitch, 407–23. New York: Oxford University Press.

Hutcheon, Linda. 2006. *A Theory of Adaptation*. New York: Routledge.

Hyman, David. 2017. *Revision and the Superhero Genre*. Cham, Switzerland: Palgrave Macmillan.

Kent, Miriam. 2021. *Women in Marvel Films*. Edinburgh: Edinburgh University Press.

Laverty, Christopher. 2012. "The Dark Knight Rises: Costume Q & A with Lindy." *Clothes on Film*, August 1. clothesonfilm.com/the-dark-knight-rises-costume-qa-with-lindy-hemming.

Leitch, Thomas. 2007. *Film Adaptation and Its Discontents: From* Gone with the Wind *to* The Passion of the Christ. Baltimore: Johns Hopkins University Press.

Loeb, Jeph, and Tim Sale. 1999. *Batman: The Long Halloween*. London: Titan. [Collecting *Batman: The Long Halloween* #1–13, December 1996–December 1997].

McRobbie, Angela. 2009. *The Aftermath of Feminism: Gender, Culture and Social Change*. London: SAGE.

Miller, Frank, and David Mazzucchelli. 1987. *Batman: Year One*. New York: DC Comics. [Collecting *Batman* #404–407, February–May 1987].

Miller, Frank, and Klaus Janson. 1986. *Batman: The Dark Knight Returns*. New York: DC Comics. [Collecting *Batman: The Dark Knight Returns* #1–4, June–December 1986].

Mishou, A. Luxx. 2021. "On the Fringes and Tassels of Respectability: Catwoman and Censoring the Femme Form." In *Intersectional Feminist Readings of Comics: Interpreting Gender in Graphic Narratives*, ed. Sandra Cox, 41–61. London: Routledge.

Mooney, Darren. 2018. *Christopher Nolan: A Critical Study of the Films*. Jefferson: McFarland.

Negra, Diane, and Yvonne Tasker. 2014. "Introduction." In *Gendering the Recession: Media and Culture in the Age of Austerity*, ed. Diane Negra and Yvonne Tasker, 1–30. Durham and London: Duke University Press.

Newell, Mindy, and J. J. Birch. 1991. *Catwoman: Her Sister's Keeper*. New York: DC Comics. [Collecting *Catwoman* #1–4, February–May 1989].

Projansky, Sarah. 2001. *Watching Rape: Film and Television in Postfeminist Culture*. New York: New York University Press.

Sanders, Julie. 2006. *Adaptation and Appropriation*. Oxon: Routledge.

Shone, Tom. 2020. *The Nolan Variations: The Movies, Mysteries, and Marvels of Christopher Nolan*. New York: Alfred A. Knopf.

Stam, Robert. 2005. "Introduction: The Theory and Practice of Adaptation." In *Literature and Film: A Guide to the Theory and Practice of Film Adaptation*, ed. Robert Stam and Alessandra Raengo, 1–51. Oxford: Blackwell.

Taylor, Tosha. 2015. "Saints, Sinners and Terrorists: The Women of Christopher Nolan's Gotham." In *The Cinema of Christopher Nolan: Imagining the Impossible*, ed. Jacqueline Furby and Stuart Joy, 62–73. New York: Columbia University Press.

Valentine, Genevieve. 2018. "Empire of a Wicked Woman: Catwoman, Royalty, and the Making of a Comics Icon." *Journal of Graphic Novels and Comics* 9, no. 6: 593–611. doi.org/10.1080/21504857.2018.1540139.

Whaley, Deborah Elizabeth. 2011. "Black Cat Got Your Tongue?: Catwoman, Blackness, and the Alchemy of Postracialism." *Journal of Graphic Novels and Comics* 2, no. 1: 3–23. doi.org/10.1080/21504857.2011.577280.

———. 2015. *Black Women in Sequence: Re-Inking Comics, Graphic Novels, and Anime*. Seattle and London: University of Washington Press.

Zeitchik, Steven. 2011. "Will Nolan's 'Dark Knight Rises' Occupy Wall Street?" *Los Angeles Times*, October 17. latimesblogs.latimes.com/movies/2011/10/christopher-nolan-dark-knight-rises-occupy-wall-street-christian-bale.html.

Index

Page references for figures are italicized.

35mm, 2, 138, 165–67, 169–70
3D technology, 137
70mm, 124

abduction, 37, 38, 43
acting, 33, 151, 154, 160
adaptation, 43, 47, 48–51, 122, 136, 198, 201, 208, 261–65, 268–74
amnesia, 17–18, 32, 63, 119, 182, 192, 220. *See also* memory loss
anachrony, 18–24
anagnorisis, 17–18, 24, 27, 35
analogue, 167. *See also* 35mm; 70mm
anamorphosis, 34, 36–40, 44n7
arthouse, 164–65, 171–72, 231
audience, 6, 7, 34, 48, 59, 97–98, 101–3, 105–10, 133, 135–45, 151, 166–69, 171–72, 174, 186–87, 254, 256; Chinese audiences, 135–45. *See also* fans
auteur/auteurism, 7–8, 97–98, 101, 109, 110, 117–18, 133, 136, 142–44, 149–50, 163–67, 168–72, 175, 231, 246, 262, 264–65. *See also* fanboy auteur; indie auteur
authenticity, 143–44, 165–67

authorship, 98, 116, 261, 262–65, 267–68
autonomy, 117, 143–44, 184, 267

Bakhtin, Mikhail, 63–66, 72, 74, 76–77
Bale, Christian, 3, 49, 150, 153, 155, 157, 164, 235, 268
Bane, 93, 140, 232, 235, 239–40, 268–70
Batman (character), 154, 155, 203, 232, 233–41, 262, 264, 266, 268
Batman (franchise), 1, 3, 115, 122, 231
Batman Begins, 59, 98–99, 119, 120–22, *134*, 136, 143, 150, 152, 199, 200, 204, 226, 231, 234, 239, 252
Batman v Superman: Dawn of Justice, 116, 170, 209
Belic, Roco, 2, 175, 249, 251, 252, 258
Benjamin, Walter, 93n1, 167, 248
Blockbuster, 1, 118, 138, 139–40, 181, 246, 264
Blu-ray, 164–65, 171–72, 176n4, 200
Bond, James (films), 85, 90, 202
Bordwell, David, 52
box office, 115–16, 118, 121, 122–23, 125–28, 136, 138, 197–202, 205,

208–9, 209n8, 262; Chinese box office, *134*, 137–38, 144
braaam, 6, 101–3, 109–10
bullets, 49, 52, 108, 192–93, 246

Caine, Michael, 7–8, 50, 124, 150–52, 154–61
capitalism, 66, 93n3, 230, 231–32, 237–41, 271, 274n4
capitalist realism, 230, 236, 238–39
Catwoman, 261–62, 265–74, 274n3
celluloid, 59, 139, 164, 167, 197
censorship, 135–36, 137–38, 141–42
CGI (computer-generated imagery), 3, 60
character-narrator, 17–18, 20–21, 25
China, 133–45
chronotope, 63–64, 65, 66–67, 68, 70, 72, 74, 76–77
cinema of attractions, 246, 250–51
cinephile, 97, 139
cockney, 50, 53, 149, 151–52
coherence, 35, 97, 220
Cotillard, Marion, 73, 150, 240
criticism, 141, 263, 271
Crowley, Nathan, 3, 150
Cutter, John, 50–54, 56, 58, 60, 157–58, 254

The Dark Knight, 121, 123, 136, 145, 155, 199, 200, 232, 236–37, 238–39, 246, 252, 261
The Dark Knight Rises, 93n3, 121, 123, *134*, 140, 156–57, 176n5, 181, 199, 200, 204, 206, 233, 246, 261, 262–63, 265, 268–73, 274n4
The Dark Knight trilogy, 3, 99, 150, 170, 209, 210n12, 225, 229–41, 262, 265
Dassin, Jules (Rififi), 87
Deren, Maya, 213, 215–27
dettaglio, 35, 36, 40
DiCaprio, Leonardo, 72, 122, 123, 141, 158, 254

digital, 3, 66, 116, 123, 165, 166–67, 256–57
Doodlebug, 2, 10, 98, 226, 243, 253–56
double, 33–34, 47, 49–50, 53–60, 149, 158, 223–26
dream, 64, 67, 72–77, 77n4, 100–3, 109–10, 111nn9–11, 122, 140, 183, 185, 216–17, 225–26, 251–52, 257n3
dream world, 102, 185
dreamscape, 102, 183, 216, 251
duality, 33, 38, 54
Dunkirk, 3, 51, 63, 64–65, 67–72, 73–74, 75–77, 106–9, 111n13, 124, *134*, 144, 150, 160, 175, 181, 197–98, 199, 201, 202–3, 225, 248, 250–51, 257n2
duplicity, 33, 35, 38, 83

Elsaesser, Thomas, 16, 28n1, 63, 67
enhanced format, 137, 138, 144

fanboy auteur, 133, 136, 142–45, 163, 168–72
fandom, 136, 143, 167, 168, 170
femme fatale, 15, 33, 218, 224, 261, 266, 270, 271
fiction, 31–35, 38, 40, 42, 43n3, 83–85
Fight Club, 16–17, 26, 221
film form, 70, 243–49, 255
film noir, 9, 21, 33–34, 65–66, 213–15, 218, 219–22, 270–71
flashback, 20, 22, 24, 25, 26, 47, 51, 52, 53, 64, 67, 73, 74, 75, 84, 154, 181, 218, 219, 222, 224, 225
focalizer, 17, 26
Following, 1–3, 4, 15–28, 79, 98, 119, 122, 164–65, 199, 199–200, 224, 225, 226, 247–48
Fox, Jorja, 9
fractured male, 149–50, 154
Freud, Sigmund, 5–6, 65, 67, 71, 77n1, 80–83, 217

gender, 143, 220–26, 231, 261–74
Genette, Gérard, 17

genre, 89–90, 103, 104, 143, 173, 198–99, 214, 269–71
Gotham, 1, 90, 93n3, 152, 154–56, 203, 230, 232, 233–41, 262, 268–74
gothic, 54–56, 104
Goyer, David, 200, 209n4, 265, 269
Gunning, Tom, 246–48, 250–51

Hardy, Tom, 3, 71, 164, 240, 269
Hathaway, Anne, 150, 160, 188, 269–70, 273
HBO, 3–4, 6, 126–27, 167, 197
Hegel, G. W. F., 6, 80–81, 85–87
hero, 86, 93n3, 139, 149–50, 154–55, 222, 234, 240–41, 271, 274n2. *See also* Superhero
heroism, 91, 223–24, 234, 262, 263–64
heterodiegetic narrator, 17, 20–24, 25–27, 28
history, 16, 80–81, 85–86, 92, 167, 181, 202, 219, 220
Hollywood, 1, 7, 60, 98, 99, 109–10, 115–18, 127–28, 133, 137–43, 166, 171, 198–201, 208–9, 220–21, 223, 246

identity, 9, 16, 31, 35, 53–54, 139, 149, 151, 165, 219–21, 226, 257n5
ideology, 4, 8, 133–36, 181–94, 238–40, 261–65
IMAX, 10, 121, 123, 124, 125, 137–38, 139
Inception, 51, 63–65, 71, 72–77, 93n2, 100–3, 109–10, 116, 122–23, 133–45, 158, 181, 182–85, 193, 199, 203, 210n12, 225, 226, 248, 254, 257n3, 258n7
indie auteur, 8, 164–67, 169, 171, 175
Insomnia, 1, 3, 48, 115, 119–20, 122, 184, 192–93, 199, 200, 224, 225, 246, 254, 255
intellectual property, 118, 120, 126, 142
Interstellar, 3, 41, 44n15, 79–80, 83, 99, 103–6, 116, 123–24, *134*, 143–44, 150, 160, 175, 181–82, 185–91, 192, 193n1, 198–200, 203, 204, 205–8, 225, 248

Joker (character), 121, 232–39
Joker (film), 229, 233–34, 240–41
Julyan, David, 3, 20, 98, 110n4, 110n8

kick, 73, 75
The Killing, 87
Kozloff, Sarah, 21
Kubrick, Stanley, 87, 185, 206, 264

language, 140, 142, 168–69, 172, 218, 263–64
Larry Mahoney, 2
Larceny, 2, 98, 243, 254
Ledger, Heath, 121, 232, 236, 237
limbo, 73–75, 100–1, 111n10
linearity, 16, 34, 51
Los Angeles, 59, 99, 171, 213–15, 219
Lost Highway, 15–18, 226, 227

magic, 47–49, 50, 51, 57, 59, 157, 158, 174, 193
male identity, 149–51, 239
manipulation, 4, 5, 6, 34, 35, 47, 48, 50–51, 66, 102, 106, 108, 143, 173, 182, 249, 256
Man of Steel, 116, 170, 175, 203, 204, 209, 210n12
Marx, Karl, 88
masculinity, 151, 219–23, 231, 236–37, 261–62, 268
McConaughey, Matthew, 160, 181–82
Memento, 1, 2–3, 17–18, 31–43, 51, 65–66, 98, 119, 145, 164, 165, 170, 182, 184, 192, 193, 199, 200, 213–27, 246, 247–48, 251, 255, 258n7
"Memento Mori," 200
memory loss, 26, 31
Meshes of the Afternoon, 215–27
mind-game film, 16–18, 26–27, 63, 72
mirror, 4–5, 31–39, 44n7, 44n9, 70, 172, 217, 218
modernism, 173, 249–53

Moss, Carrie-Anne, 32
motif, 4–5, 31–32, 33–34, 49–50, 54–56, 57, 66–67, 68, 76–77, 102, 105–6, 134, 188, 215–25, 270–71
multiverse, 5, 42, 43
Murphy, Cillian, 71, 72, 150, 164, 239

Nachträglichkeit, 5–6, 65, 67, 79–93
narrative, 5, 6, 15–28, 31–32, 34–35, 41, 43, 47–53, 59–60, 63–77, 83–87, 92, 97–98, 100–3, 104, 106–10, 119, 139–42, 149–50, 156–57, 168–70, 181–82, 183–85, 217–18, 235, 247–48, 250–52, 256–57, 263–64, 266–68
neoliberalism, 9–10, 229–41, 274n4
neo-romantic affect, 182, 184–85, 192
neo-romanticism, 182–85, 186, 188, 191–93
Newmarket, 3, 5, 48, 119, 122, 165
Nolan, Jonathan, 3, 5, 43n3, 97–98, 119, 122, 123, 150, 198, 200, 207–8
"Non, je ne regrette rien" (song), 101, 102–3

obsession, 20, 21, 47, 75, 149, 248
Occupy, 230, 232, 235–36, 240, 263, 268, 274n4
Oppenheimer (film), 10–11, 127, 197–98, 202, 208–9
Oppenheimer, Robert J., 10–11, 127, 197

Pacino, Al, 1, 184, 254
Pantoliano, Joe, 32, 184
Paramount, 116, 117–18, 123, 200
particolare, 35, 36, 40, 42
Pearce, Guy, 31, 182, 255
performance, 7–8, 150–51, 154–57, 218, 232
Piaf, Édith, 101, 102–3
Polaroid, 32, 36, 41, 42, 217, 218, 219–20, 222
posthumanism, 181–93
power, 117, 234–35, 237, 239, 240, 261, 268

The Prestige, 3, 5, 47–60, 98, 110n4, 122, 145, 150, 157–58, 169, 174–75, 193, 198, 199, 200, 203, 209, 210n12, 225–26, 246, 248, 254, 264
Priest, Christopher, 3, 48–49, 54–56, 122
primacy effect, 4, 27–28
puzzle film, 4, 16–18, 26, 27–28, 34–35, 63–64, 149–50, 171, 174, 181–82, 214

Quay (film), 3, 8, 163–75
Quay Brothers, 3, 8, 163–75, 226

realism, 10, 41–43, 59, 186, 230–31, 264–65, 269–74. *See also* Capitalist realism
Reich, Wilhelm, 80
representations of trauma, 5–6, 63–77, 81–89, 181–82, 183, 193, 223–24
retroactivity. *See* Nachträglichkeit
revenge, 47, 53, 54, 222, 223, 267
romanticism, 181, 183, 184–85, 187, 189–93. *See also* neo-romanticism

science, 42, 47–48, 60, 206–8
science fiction, 47, 136, 183, 198–99, 201–2, 206–8
Sci-fi. *See* science fiction
Selina Kyle, 239–40, 261–62, 265–74
short film, 2, 8, 10, 98, 163–64, 169, 172, 175, 243–55
sonic cues, 6, 101–3, 173–74
soundtrack, 20, 68, 69–70, 82, 103
spectacle, 136, 137–40, 142, 223, 246
star theory, 149–61
sublime, 185–91
superhero: characters, 263–65, 267–68, 273–74; films, 89–90, 143, 201, 208, 234, 262, 263–65, 271
Syncopy, 121–22, 164, 200, 257n1

tattoo, 32, 35, 36, 37, 38, 44, 182, 192, 213, 217, 218, 221

Tarantella, 2, 10, 175, 245, 249–53, 257n1, 257n1, 257n5
technology, 8, 60, 137, 139, 143, 166–67, 181–93, 203–4, 207–9
Tenet, 3–4, 41, 51, 79, 82–93, 99, 116, 124–28, 134, 144, 150, 160, 167, 175, 181, 191–92, 193, 199, 202, 203, 204, 208–9, 225–26, 246, 251
Tesla, Nikola, 47–48, 49–51, 53, 54, 56, 58, 61n4
Theobald, Jeremy, 253
Thomas, Emma, 2, 97–98, 121–22, 124, 150, 164, 200, 250, 253
Thunberg, Greta, 89–93
time-space, 65–66, 73–74, 75–76, 77n4
time-travel, 191, 193n1, 256–57
totem, 76, 77n4, 101, 226

transnational cinema, 133–34, 137, 139–45
Transported Man, 49–50, 50–51, 56, 59–60, 174
trauma, 81–82. *See also* representations of trauma

variability, 35, 38

Warner Bros., 3–4, 48, 98, 115–16, 119–28, 144, 167, 197, 200, 208, 231, 264
Watanabe, Ken, 72, 141, 150, 183
working class, 151–52, 234–35, 239, 267–68, 272

Zeitgeist Films, 2–3, 164–66
Zimmer, Hans, 3, 6, 97–110, 110nn1–7

About the Editors

Isabelle Labrouillère is a lecturer in Performing Arts and Film Aesthetics at the ENSAV (Ecole Nationale Supérieure d'AudioVisuel), Université Toulouse Jean Jaurès. She is in charge of the research master's programme, where she runs a seminar on Christopher Nolan. She is coeditor of three international conference proceedings and has written various articles on fantasy and the cinema, inter- and transmediality ("Intermediality as a Way to Debunk Tradition: New Perspectives on Terence Fisher's *The Curse of Frankenstein* [1957], Peter Lang Publishing) and postmodernism ("The New Conditions of Post-classical Entertainment: Duplication, Repetition and the Loss of Authenticity in Cronenberg's *Maps to the Stars*," Mimesis International). She is also the author of an article on *Memento* which will be published in September 2022: "L'écriture de la peau dans *Memento* (Christopher Nolan, 2000): du mutisme du corps tatoué à son devenir image." In *Imaginaires cinématographiques de la peau*, ed. Diane Bracco. Amsterdam and New York: Brill Rodopi.

Claire Parkinson is Professor of Culture, Communication, and Screen Studies at Edge Hill University, where she is also founding director of the Centre for Human Animal Studies. Her research interests include media, film, critical animal studies, and cultural history. Her publications include the monographs *Memento* (2010), *Popular Media and Animals* (2011), and *Animals, Anthropomorphism and Mediated Encounters* (2019) and the coedited collections *The Routledge Companion to Cinema and Politics* (2016), *American Independent Cinema: Indie, Indiewood and Beyond* (2012), *Beyond Human: From Animality to Transhumanism* (2010), and the forthcoming *Animal Activism On and Off Screen* (2023).

ABOUT THE CONTRIBUTORS

Will Brooker is Professor of Film and Cultural Studies at Kingston University, London. He is the author of several books and articles on popular culture and its audiences, including *Batman Unmasked, Using the Force, Alice's Adventures, The Blade Runner Experience, Hunting the Dark Knight, Forever Stardust,* and *Why Bowie Matters*. His most recent work is *The Truth about Lisa Jewell*.

Warren Buckland is Reader in Film Studies at Oxford Brookes University. His research interests include film theory, narratology, stylometry, and contemporary American cinema. He is the author and editor of several books, including *Narrative and Narration: Analyzing Cinematic Storytelling* (2020), *Wes Anderson's Symbolic Storyworld* (2019), *Hollywood Puzzle Films* (ed., 2014), *Film Theory: Rational Reconstructions* (2012), and *Puzzle Films: Complex Storytelling in Contemporary Cinema* (ed., 2009).

Gregory Frame is Associate Researcher in Film Studies at Bangor University. His work focuses primarily on the politics of contemporary American film and television. He has published in *Journal of American Studies, New Review of Film and Television Studies, Film & History,* and *Journal of Popular Film and Television,* as well as several edited collections. His first book, *The American President in Film and Television: Myth, Politics and Representation*, which was runner-up in the British Association of Film, Television and Screen Studies' Best Monograph Award in 2016, is still available in paperback through Peter Lang Oxford. He is currently working on a monograph exploring discourses of American decline in mainstream film and television, entitled *Twilight's Last Gleaming: American Film and Television since 2008*, which will be published by Bloomsbury Academic in 2024.

Lara Herring holds a doctorate in the field of media and communication from Edge Hill University. In 2021 Lara joined the School of Arts and Media at the University of Salford, where she is a lecturer. She is a former videographer and video editor. Herring researches in the fields of political economics, cultural studies, critical media industry studies, adaptation studies, critical animal studies, and transnational cinema. She has conducted empirical studies that include ethnographic research, archival research, discourse analysis, industrial analysis, content analysis, production analysis, and narrative analysis. In 2020 she completed her doctoral thesis on the contemporary relationship between China and Hollywood, conducting interviews with high-ranking Hollywood industry personnel. Previously, she has published work on how social media shapes the Chinese film industry. In 2019 she worked as a research assistant on projects funded by The Vegan Society to produce reports on non-vegan attitudes towards veganism.

Stella Hockenhull, previously a Reader in Film and Television Studies, is now an Honorary Research Fellow at the University of Wolverhampton. She has built up a strong research profile in British cinema and landscape with expertise in the correlation between film and painting. Publishing extensively in this area, she has produced a large body of work which includes three monographs, a number of articles, and chapters in various edited collections. Her interest in British cinema extends to women in the British film industry, in particular the division of labor and the gender politics within contemporary British cinema, resulting in her publication entitled *British Women Film Directors in the New Millennium* (2017). Extending into star theory, her research branches out into the field of animal studies, specifically animal stardom. "Celebrity Creatures: The 'Starification' of the Cinematic Animal" was published in the edited collection *Revisiting Star Studies* in 2017.

Stuart Joy is the course leader for film and television at Solent University. He is the author of *The Traumatic Screen: The Films of Christopher Nolan* (2020) and coeditor of *The Cinema of Christopher Nolan: Imagining the Impossible* (2015), *Through the Black Mirror: Reflections on the Digital Age* (2019), and *Contemporary American Science Fiction Film* (2022). Stuart's research interests include contemporary film theory and practice, media and cultural theory, film history, and gender representation.

Miriam Kent is Lecturer in Film and Media at the University of Leeds. Her interdisciplinary research centers on representational issues in contemporary superhero narratives, especially focusing on Marvel superheroes and comic book adaptation and drawing from feminist, queer, and critical race theories, as well as comics studies. Her monograph, *Women in Marvel Films* (2021, Edinburgh University Press) shows how the Marvel superhero film taps into political complexities regarding gender and related identity issues and provides an insight into gendered power dynamics in contemporary American popular culture. She has published widely on gender and superheroes, and her forthcoming research explores Marvel in the Disney+ era.

Peter Krämer is a Senior Research Fellow in Cinema and TV in the Leicester Media School at De Montfort University (Leicester, UK). He also is a Senior Fellow in the School of Art, Media and American Studies at the University of East Anglia (Norwich, UK) as well as a regular guest lecturer at the University of Television and Film Munich (Germany), Masaryk University (Brno, Czech Republic), and Palacky University Olomouc (Czech Republic).

He is the author or editor of eleven academic books, including the BFI Film Classic on *2001: A Space Odyssey* (2nd edition, 2020) and *"Grease is the Word": Exploring a Cultural Phenomenon* (coedited with Oliver Gruner, Anthem Press, 2020). He has published more than eighty essays in academic journals and edited collections.

Ben Lamb is the world's leading expert on British television crime drama, having published the definitive academic work *You're Nicked: Investigating British Television Police Series*. He is the English Studies and Creative Writing course leader at Teesside University. As a cultural theorist specializing in television studies, he examines in his published research modes of realism within different television production systems, genre theory, ideology, gender politics, feminism, and representations of social class. He is the producer of the film *Rewinding the Welfare State: A Social History of the North East on Film* supported by the National Lottery Heritage Fund and North East Film Archive.

Todd McGowan teaches theory and film at the University of Vermont. He is the author of *The Racist Fantasy*, *Universality and Identity Politics*, *Emancipation after Hegel*, and other works. He is the coeditor (with Adrian Johnston and Slavoj Žižek) of the Diaeresis series at Northwestern Univerisity Press and the editor of the Film Theory in Practice series at Bloomsbury. He cohosts the *Why Theory* podcast with Ryan Engley.

Gilles Menegaldo is an emeritus professor of American literature and film studies at the University of Poitiers. Founder and former head of the Film Studies Department, he has published many articles on gothic literature and cinema, horror films, film noir, and other film genres. He is author of *Dracula, la noirceur et la grâce* (2006, with A-M Paquet-Deyris) and editor or coeditor of thirty-five collections of essays, including *Film and History* (2008), *European and Hollywood Cinema: Cultural Exchanges* (2012), *Lovecraft au prisme de l'image* (2017, with C. Gelly), *Tim Burton, a Cinema of Transformations* (2018), *Spectres de Poe* (2020, with J. Dupont), *Le Goût du noir* (2020, with M. Petit), *Dark Recesses in the House of Hammer* (2022, with M. Boissonneau and A-M Paquet-Deyris).

Kimberly A. Owczarski is an Associate Professor in the Department of Film, Television, and Digital Media at Texas Christian University. She has published essays in Spectator, Journal of Film and Video, Quarterly Review of Film and Television, Journal of Popular Culture, Jump Cut, *Media Fields Journal*, and several academic anthologies.

Bernadette Pace is a postgraduate researcher at the University of Edinburgh. Her research interests lie in the cross-disciplinary space between music and film studies, with a particular interest in twenty-first-century Hollywood film music. Her current dissertation focuses on the collaboration between Christopher Nolan and Hans Zimmer, and their exploration of the concept of "time" through soundscapes.

Fran Pheasant-Kelly is a Reader in Film and Screen at Wolverhampton University, UK. Her research interests center on abject spaces, fantasy, and the medical humanities. She has written more than seventy publications including two monographs, *Abject Spaces in American Cinema* (2013) and *Fantasy Film Post 9/11* (2013), and is the coeditor of *Spaces of the Cinematic Home: Behind the Screen Door* (2015) and *Tim Burton's Bodies* (2021). She is currently working on several monographs including *A History of HIV/AIDS in Film, Television and the Media* (2022) and *The Revenant: Towards a Sensory Cinema* (2022).

www.ingramcontent.com/pod-product-compliance
Lightning Source LLC
Chambersburg PA
CBHW061433300426
44114CB00014B/1671